You Shall Not Kill

You Shall Not Kill

JOHANNES UDE

Translated by Ingrid M. Leder
Foreword by Hanns Kobinger

CASCADE *Books* • Eugene, Oregon

YOU SHALL NOT KILL

Cascade Books
An Imprint of Wipf and Stock Publishers
199 W. 8th Ave., Suite 3
Eugene, OR 97401

www.wipfandstock.com

PAPERBACK ISBN: 978-1-62564-763-4
HARDCOVER ISBN: 978-1-4982-8876-7
EBOOK ISBN: 978-1-4982-3588-4

Cataloguing-in-Publication data:

Names: Ude, Johannes, 1874–1965 | Leder, Ingrid M., translator | Kobiner, Hanns, foreword

Title: You shall not kill / Johannes Ude ; translated by Ingrid M. Leder; foreword by Hanns Kobinger ; foreword to English edition by Ulrich L. Lehner.

Description: Eugene, OR : Cascade Books, 2016 | Includes bibliographical references.

Identifiers: ISBN 978-1-62564-763-4 (paperback) | ISBN 978-1-4982-8876-7 (hardcover) | ISBN 978-1-4982-3588-4 (ebook)

Subjects: LCSH: Peace—Religious aspects. | Life and death, Power over.

Classification: JX1952 .U19 2016 (print) | JX1952 .U19 (ebook)

Manufactured in the U.S.A. NOVEMBER 8, 2016

Contents

PART II

Our position regarding the teachings and views of exponents of moral philosophy based on natural law and reason and Catholic (Christian) teachings of faith and morals about the commandment "You shall not kill" as presented in Part I

Foreword to the English Edition
Johannes Ude (1874–1965)—Maverick and Visionary

Ulrich L. Lehner

Clothed in a shabby cassock, barefoot, his coarsely chiseled face and pointy chin carrying gravitas and determination, an elderly, yet energetic priest climbed up to the speaker's desk. He did not intend to deliver a homily but to give an address on animal rights, pacifism, and the evils of unrestrained capitalism.[1] For some this charismatic priest with his loud, earth-shattering voice was a prophet; for others, he was a theological rebel or a dangerous radical. Johannes Ude (1874–1965) challenged his contemporaries, just as his readers today struggle to interpret him.

There was probably not a more educated Catholic theologian in the twentieth century than Ude. Although this seems to be an outrageous claim given the genius of Hans Urs von Balthasar or Karl Rahner, neither of these theologians can compete with Ude's five doctorates. Born in 1874 in St. Kanizan, Austria, as one of nine children of a village teacher, he soon felt a call to the priesthood. After his high school graduation in 1894 he was able to study and then graduate from the Pontifical University Gregoriana in Rome. There he received his first two doctorates in philosophy and theology. At the time, Rome was a center for Catholic philosophy, and Ude received a thorough training in the works of St. Thomas Aquinas as well as modern philosophy. In 1900 he was ordained a priest for the diocese of Graz, and began in 1902 to study botany and zoology in Graz. In 1905 he completed his habilitation, a third doctoral degree, in dogmatic theology. Ude became

1. See for example Johannes Ude, *Nieder mit dem Kapitalismus: Zins ist Diebstahl* (Graz: Österreichs Völkerwacht, 1925); and, *Christliche Moraltheologen als Helfershelfer des Kapitalismus* (Brüggen: 1957).

instantaneously famous when he was scheduled to celebrate the defense of his zoological doctorate because he wanted his student confraternity to show up at the defense. At the time, a strong anti-Catholic sentiment existed at the University of Graz, which was fueled by Ude's criticism of Darwinism. On the way to the defense, liberal students involved Ude and his comrades in a street fight while the professors watched without interfering. Christian-Social politicians protested against the University's apathy toward this harassment. Following these events, Ude's dissertation defense became one of the greatest university scandals of the Habsburg monarchy. In 1924 he received his fifth doctorate in economics. In order to be up-to-date for his publications on social issues he also studied four years of medicine, and art history as a balance. Teaching since 1905 at the University of Graz, he became a full professor there in 1917.[2]

When he celebrated his 90th birthday, Ude looked back on his life and confessed that the guiding principle for his work had been that morally right actions presupposed right knowledge. In order to be moral, he was convinced, a person had to consult reason *and* revelation, and consequently all areas of knowledge, be it medicine, economics or the natural sciences. A Thomist at heart, Ude defended the idea that we can arrive at a knowledge of God from reason; yet based on his biological, sociological and medical studies, Ude wondered how unhealthy life choices impede reason from arriving at this knowledge. How could the supernatural speak to a sick human body, which has become numb and ailing, unable to live according to God's order? Ude understood that moral theology should not be a "bandage" on society but had to radically change it. He became a proponent of the "life reform movement":

> Humanity today . . . is sick due to its unnatural ways of life; sick in their souls, but also their bodies. . . . Healthy is a human person, if she judges like God would judge, and does what God wants, if she arranges her whole life according to the demands

2. Among his more voluminous academic works until 1945 are *Monistische, oder teleologische Weltanschauung?* (Graz: Styria, 1907); *Der Unglaube: Dogmatik und Psychologie des Unglaubens* (Graz: Styria, 1921); *Das Wirtschaftsideal des Volks- und Staatshaushaltes: mit Anhang: Der österreichische Volks- und Staatshaushalt: eine Monographie des Volks- und Staatshaushaltes vom nationalökonomisch-ethischen Standpunkt aus auf der Grundlage chrislicher Lebensreform* (Graz: Styria, 1924); *Kann der Mensch vom Tiere abstammen?* (Graz: Styria, 1926); *Ist Maria die Mittlerin aller Gnaden?: Eine dogmatisch-kritische Untersuchung* (Bressanone: Weger, 1928); *Soziologie: Leitfaden der natürlich-vernünftigen Gesellschafts- und Wirtschaftslehre im Sinne der Lehre des hl. Thomas von Aquin* (Schaan i. Liechtenstein: Alpenland-Verl., 1931); *Die Autorität des hl. Thomas von Aquin als Kirchenlehrer und seine Summa theologica* (Salzburg: A. Pustet, 1932).

> of the Ten Commandments and the Gospel of Christ. Whoever leads a principled life like this, becomes a peacemaker.[3]

Thus, Ude's strict vegetarianism, abstinence from alcohol and nicotine, his pacifism, his fight against prostitution and for worker justice, flow from his creedal commitment to the Catholic faith and a profound prayer life, in which the mystics played an important role.[4] In the pre-1938 debates, when he used the vocabulary of the Eugenics movement, he made clear that his commitment was to *negative* eugenics, that is to educate future parents about the dangers of drugs, sexually transmitted diseases, and the effects on the human genome. He saw it as a Christian duty to avoid the birth of disabled children with such measures and institutional assistance; yet he never endorsed abortion or sterilization.[5]

His uncompromising, rigorist viewpoints brought him into conflict with all political parties in Austria, but also with the bishops. The struggle escalated in 1925, when Ude formed a political party and participated in elections, but his public ministry was only silenced in 1929. He had stated that priests and bishops received the holy Eucharist unworthily because they did not fight against the moral evils of the time; they ignored the exploitation of workers and farmers, and they endorsed the military as well as the "just war theory." It is not far fetched to call him a political and social visionary, but also a very imprudent man. His nickname "Savonarola of Graz" might therefore be partially justified.

It should not surprise us that Ude also clashed with the Austro-Fascist regime of Engelbert Dollfuss (1932–1934). He criticized state-sponsored terror and was suspended form his professorship in May 1934; only a year afterwards was he reinstated and his proscription from public speaking rescinded. Politically somewhat naïve, Ude still believed that fascism would bring the end of interest-driven market policies and achieve one of his central economic goals.[6] He even expressed sympathy for Hitler, who like Ude

3. Johannes Ude, *Wir wissen, um zu wollen* (Grundlsee: 1964), 3–4; on Ude as pacifist, see Reinhard Farkas, "Johannes Ude als christlicher Vorläufer der Friedensbewegung," *Wiener Blätter für Friedensforschung* (1997) 31–41.

4. Johannes Ude, *Die christliche Mystik* (Vienna: 1938).

5. Monika Löscher, ". . . *der gesunden Vernunft nicht zuwider . . . ?" Katholische Eugenik in Österreich vor 1938* (Innsbruck: Studienverlag, 2009) 59–70.

6. Ude was an ardent believer in the economic theories of Silvio Gesell (1862–1930). See Cordelius Ilgmann, "Silvio Gesell: 'A Strange, Unduly Neglected' Monetary Theorist," *Journal of Post-Keynesian Economics* 38 (2015) 532–64. On the fascist elements of the Catholic "Action Françoise" still, see Ernst Nolte, *Three Faces of Fascism: Action Française, Italian Fascism, National Socialism* (New York: Holt, Rinehart and Winston, 1966), ch. 1.

lived as a vegetarian and claimed to be a pacifist. In March 1938 he advocated for the annexation of Austria by Hitler-Germany, but his delusion with Nazism passed quickly. On the 8th and 9th of November 1938 he witnessed the brutality of the Nazi regime in the "Night of Broken Glass," in which Jewish shops and synagogues were either destroyed or looted. Like before, once he had realized something was wrong, he rigorously condemned it. With a courage that German and Austrian bishops and theology professors of both great confessions lacked, Ude wrote a condemnatory letter to the Nazi Governor and began a secret resistance network; he clandestinely distributed information letters with his ideas, in particular about the atrocities of the war and anti-Semitism. In his letter of 11 November 1938, Ude laments that the most rudimentary principles of humanity and justice had been betrayed, expressing his obligation to speak out in order to not become complicit in the events that are "suitable to soil the German name in front of the entire world and will us make appear as Barbarians."

> I condemn the bandit like, well-organized . . . attacks on Jewish synagogues all over Germany and Jewish ceremonial places and shops, which were set ablaze, destroyed or blasphemed. This is in my eyes a communist-bolshevist act that should never happen in . . . a state based on justice.
>
> I regret and condemn the mean assassination attempt on a Jew in Paris. Nobody has preached with more vehemence and more frankly than I about the moral obligation "Thou Shall not Kill" . . . I regret that German Nazis presumed to act "in the name of the German people" in a manner that reminds one of the lynching justice in the bush lands or the Wild West . . . It is inhumane and contradicts my most profound convictions . . . if members of the Jewish race are taken without difference at nights from their beds, are lashed like defenseless cattle, when families are torn apart and their members deported. . . . Whoever protects a criminal becomes a criminal.[7]

7. Maximilian Liebmann, "Die Reichskristallnacht—Johannes Ude war nicht zu feige," *Domus Austriae. Eine Festgabe für Hermann Wiesflecker*, ed. Walter Höflechner et al. (Graz: 1983), 263–72. Ude also mentions that he does not excuse the propaganda of "emigrant Jews," which can be read as an anti-semitic statement (Löscher, ibid., 68–70). I was unable to consult Johannes Ude, *Die Judenfrage* (Graz: Oesterreichs Völkerwacht, 1919) and idem, *Nationalismus, Sozialismus, Pazifismus* (Graz, 1936), which according to Löscher contain similar ant-semitic statements. For the context of Catholic theologians being trapped in anti-Jewish prejudices, anti-semitism and the use of "race", see the important book by John Connelly, *From Enemy to Brother: The Revolution in Catholic Teaching on the Jews, 1933–1965* (Cambridge: Harvard University Press, 2012).

He implored the governor to immediately obstruct the harassment of Jewish families and to stop the arbitrary violence inflicted upon them. Ude was not content with a private letter but knew that only a well publicized protest would be of help. He therefore sent a copy to emigrant newspapers, where it was translated into French and attracted international attention. As a consequence, the Gestapo charged him with treason and banned him from the county to a remote rural parish in Grundlsee, where he remained until the end of the war. Nevertheless, he used his secret newsletter to argue for an end of the war, defied the Nazis, and called for a world-government similar to the UN, which should prevent future wars. In 1944, he was charged with treason yet again, and almost starved to death in prison. This time only the approaching Allied troops saved his life.[8]

Far from retiring after 1945, he intensified his public ministry, fighting against economic injustice and for pacifism, and even ran as candidate for president of Austria in 1951. The priest was nominated thirteen times for the Nobel Peace prize, among others by Albert Schweitzer (1875–1965). He continued to be a thorn in the side of the Austrian bishops, who condoned post-war military service, since he believed a Christian must reject serving in arms. In 1963 he implored the Fathers of the Second Vatican Council to speak on the most pressing issue of the time, namely whether the Fifth Commandment, "Thou Shall not Kill", had to be understood universally and without exception, or not.[9] Two years later the Catholic maverick of pacifism died on 7 July 1965 in Grundlsee. Yet his theology—challenging Christians to rethink their connection with the world, the economic and monetary system, their stance on peace, and their relationship to animals—is yet to be rediscovered.

8. Reinhard Farkas, "Johannes Ude und die Amtskirche. Chronologie und Analyse eines Konflikts," *Mitteilungen des Steiermärkischen Landesarchivs* 47 (1997) 253–76.

9. Johannes Ude, *Staat-Kirche-Christentum-Einselmensch und deren Verhältnis zueinander* (Grundlsee: 1964).

Foreword

THIS BOOK, A GIFT from my longtime, dear, and revered friend Professor Dr. Johannes Ude, almost became the legacy of a warrior slain for championing human dignity and a Christianity of action.

It was written between 1941 and 1944, under constant fear of death during the dictatorship of Adolf Hitler, while my friend was exiled from his home province for having openly criticized the persecution of the Jews that occurred on November 8–12, 1938.[1] A few days before his second imprisonment, from August 1944 to April 1945, he entrusted me with this child of his heart as a personal gift to do with whatever I wished.

Because brave people safeguarded the manuscript by hiding it, it eluded the Gestapo. I now hand this book over to the public, to humanity, taking responsibility for neither its content nor its form, accompanied by the following wishes:

Because of this book, may many confessing Christians become Christians who will act.

May the people of all nations finally become citizens of one state.

May many unreflective persons start to think, even while living under the domination of political parties.

May women become mothers instead of breeding machines for cannon fodder.

The content of this work will be opposed and refuted, but God's word, "You shall not kill," remains God's word. Personally, I wish this book many enemies and long-lasting struggles so that it will not be silenced and die but will fulfill its mission and roar into deaf ears: "You may not kill—even though you are a Christian."

1. The night of November 9–10, 1938, is usually called *Kristallnacht* because of the glass of Jewish shop windows and synagogues that was shattered by the Nazis.

May God bless this book, which is dedicated to the untold victims of all nations and dictatorships of the Second World War, so that the millions killed were not murdered in vain.

Hanns Kobinger, graphic designer and painter
Grundlsee, Austria, on the Feast of All Souls, 1945

Preface: "The Eyes of the Eternal Brother"

Motto: Nothing is more urgent than to work against war, and every effort in this direction has to be regarded as laudable from a Christian viewpoint and best for the general welfare.

—POPE LEO XIII, ALLOCUTION TO THE CARDINALS, FEBRUARY 11, 1889

A FORTUNATE COINCIDENCE? NOT at all! There are no coincidences. It was the providence of God that placed Stefan Zweig's legend *The Eyes of the Eternal Brother*[1] into my hands at Christmastime of 1942. Actually, everyone should read this legend before reading our book; but since it is not available to everyone, I will begin with a summary.

Virata, the main character, or more accurately, the hero of this legend, returned home from a successful war as the victorious commander. However, during that war, in the dark of the night, he had slain a man without realizing that he was his brother. The following morning, to his horror, he saw what he had done. The dull eyes of his brother stared reproachfully at him and pursued him unrelentingly.

At the victory celebration the king presented his victorious commander with a sword as a reward, but Virata replied, "My king, let his sword remain in the arsenal because ever since slaying my brother, I vowed in my heart never again to touch a sword. He was my only brother, who grew in the same womb as I and who played with me at my mother's hands. Killing him made me realize that everyone who slays a human being is killing his brother. I can no longer be a commander in war because there is violence in a sword, and violence is the enemy of justice. Whoever takes part in the sin of killing is dead himself. I do not wish to create fear among others and

1. Zweig, *Die Augen des ewigen Bruders*.

would rather eat the beggar's bread than to act contrary to the omen that I have perceived."

So the king appointed Virata the highest judge in the land. Virata was severe but just, rendering judgment only after long and careful consideration. The legend continues: "Virata never pronounced a death sentence, not even over those guilty of the worst crimes, and he opposed anyone who urged him to do so, for he dreaded the shedding of blood. He either locked up the offenders in rock dungeons or sentenced them to a mountain, to break stones for garden walls, or to rice mills on a river where they had to turn the wheels with elephants. But he honored life."

It happened that Virata sentenced a young man—whose accusers had brought him from afar—after finding him guilty of several murders, to eleven years in the deepest dungeon and to be scourged eleven times a year. "His life, however," so Virata made clear, "is not to be taken because life emanates from the gods, and human beings may not touch that which is divine. May the sentence which I pronounced be just, but not the ultimate retaliation some would like." However, the condemned man did not deem the sentence just and said to Virata, "Why don't you just kill me? I killed—man against man. You, however, imprison me underground to rot as the years pass because when it comes to blood you have the heart of a coward and lack guts. Your law is arbitrary and your judgment reeks of torture. Kill me because I have killed."

Virata answered, "Your punishment is just."

"Just?" asked the convicted man. "Judge, which standard did you use? Who has scourged you so that you know how the whip feels? How can you playfully count the years on your fingers, as though the hours spent in the light are equal to the hours buried alive in darkness? Have you ever been imprisoned in a dungeon so that you know of how many springtimes you are robbing my life? You are an ignoramus and not a judge. Only he who feels it knows the whip, not he who wields it. Only he who has suffered may mete out suffering. You, the most guilty of all, is it your arrogance which keeps you from punishing yourself? I, overwhelmed by passion, took a life in anger. You, however, are taking my life in cold blood and are using a measuring weight on me which your hands have not balanced and whose full force you have not considered. Stay away from the steps of justice, you ignorant judge, and do not condemn living persons with the death knell of your word."

Deeply disturbed by these words, Virata began to reflect. He wanted to experience the dungeon for himself. He issued his orders skillfully, concealing what he was about to do. He descended into the terrifying darkness of the lowest dungeon to which he had condemned the young man, freed him, and had himself locked up instead so that he could feel the pain of scourging on his own body and experience the terrors of being abandoned. Virata found out what imprisonment was like by experiencing all its terrors. However, he had asked the young man to promise that after a month he would go to the king so that Virata would be freed.

"What if," Virata doubted suddenly, "he does not go to the king? Then I will have to spend eleven years down here." He became terribly agitated. However, the young man was dependable and kept his word. Virata was freed, and the king welcomed him.

Virata now addressed the king: "You, my king, called me a just man; however, I know now that everyone who dispenses justice causes injustice and commits sin." He continued to speak to the king, who did not want to get along without him: "Relieve me of my office. I can no longer speak the truth because I realize now that no one can be someone else's judge. It is up to God to punish, not to man. He who changes a man's destiny commits a sin, and I want to live my life without sin. Only he can be just who lives in solitude and has no part in anyone's destiny and deeds."

Consequently, the king dismissed Virata, who now lived alone in his house, praying and doing good works. Soon the reputation of his holiness spread, and people streamed to him to seek his counsel. One day, an argument ensued with his sons, who wanted to flog one of their slaves, but Virata refuted their right to do so. As a result of this heated argument, he realized he had no right to rob a human being of his freedom. He freed all of the slaves and said, "A just man may not turn human beings into animals. I will set all of my slaves free so that I do not sin against them in this world. I will do without them because might is seldom right, and I want to live without sin on the earth."

His sons, however, argued that Virata was interfering in their lives and forcing them to work by freeing their slaves. Their father replied, "I do not want to control you. Take the house and divide it as you wish. I no longer share either in the estate or in the sin. Whoever wants to live without sin may not participate in hate or in the destiny of others, may not eat from the toil of others, may not drink from their sweat, and may not cling to the pleasures of life or the sluggishness caused by a full stomach. Only he who lives in solitude lives for his God; only he who works is aware of Him, only he who is poor possesses Him completely. I want to be closer to the Invisible than to my own soil. I want to live without sinning. Take the house and divide it peacefully."

After Virata said this, he went far away and became a hermit. He worked and prayed, and called the animals of the forest his brothers and sisters. After a while, people, including the king, heard about his new way of life. The king hurried to visit Virata, was edified by his example, and asked if he could grant Virata a wish. Virata replied, "My king, nothing is mine, and yet, everything in this world is mine. I have forgotten that I once had a house in the midst of other houses and children in the company of other children. He who has no home owns the world; he who is detached, the fullness of life; he who is without sin, peace. I have no other wish than to continue to live on this earth without committing any sins." The king, who admired Virata, respected his wishes and returned home.

But soon Virata realized that he had been wrong again. His example was inspiring others to do likewise. Many followed, left everything, moved into the wilderness and, like him, lived only for God and for the salvation of their soul.

One day, as he was walking to town to get help to bury a hermit who had died, he passed a house. When the woman of this house saw him, she cursed him. Completely dismayed, Virata entered the house and asked the furious woman for an explanation. He learned that her husband, attracted by Virata's example, had abandoned house, wife, and children and had gone to live as a hermit. Since this left the family without a breadwinner, the children were starving. Virata replied that this was not his fault. Still raging, the woman asked, "How will you atone for the fact that you enticed a just man to leave the work which fed him and these innocent boys, with the foolish delusion that he would be closer to God living in solitude than an active life?"

Completely defeated, Virata realized his guilt and answered the woman, "Even he who does not act in this world commits a sin. The hermit lives also in all of his brothers. Forgive me, woman. I will return from the forest so that Paratika, your husband, will come back and awaken new life in your womb to make up for the past."

Virata returned to life in the world and went to see the king, who greeted him reverently and called him a wise man, but Virata replied, "Do not call me wise because my path was not the right one. For nonaction is also action. I was useless because I was concerned only about my own life and did not serve anyone else. Now I want to be of service again. I no longer want to be free of my will, for he who is free is not really free, and the inactive man is not without sin. Only he who serves is free, who surrenders his will to someone else, applies his strength to a task, and performs it without questioning. Only the process of a deed is our work; its beginning or its outcome is not. Its cause and its effect belong to the gods. Free me of my will, for all desire is confusion, and all service is wisdom." The king replied, "I do not understand you. I should free you, and yet, you are requesting a service. Does this mean that only he is free who serves another and not he who gives the orders? I do not understand this."

Virata answered the king, "My king, it is good that you do not understand this with your heart, because how could you be king and master if you understood it"? To the king's question of whether the master is greater than the servant and whether one service is greater or lesser before God and man, Virata replied, "No service is lesser and none is greater before God. Some services may appear greater to man, my king, but everything is a service before God."

Since the king now believed that the aged Virata had become childish, he asked him mockingly, "Would you like to be caretaker of the dogs in my palace"?

Virata bowed and became caretaker of the dogs. His sons, however, now were ashamed of him and no longer wanted to have anything to do with him; and soon Virata, at one time so well known and honored, was no longer remembered and died forgotten and alone.

This is the legend of Virata.

Deeply touched after reading this legend, I reached for the Bible and opened it to the words that Jesus, the wisest of the wise—he, God himself, he the Way, the Truth and the Life—had spoken: "In truth I tell you, in so far as you did this to one of the least of these brothers of mine, you did it to me . . . in so far as you neglected to do this to one of the least of these, you neglected to do it to me" (Matt 25:40, 45). And: "You, however, must not allow yourselves to be called Rabbi, since you have only one Master, and you are all brothers. You must call no one on earth your father, since you have only one Father, and he is in heaven. Nor must you allow yourselves to be called teachers, for you have only one Teacher, the Christ. The greatest among you must be your servant. Anyone who raises himself up will be humbled, and anyone who humbles himself will be raised up" (Matt 23:8–12). And: ". . . anyone who wants to become great among you must be your servant, and anyone who wants to be first among you must be a slave to all. For the Son of man himself came not to be served but to serve, and to give his life as a ransom for many" (Mark 10:43–45).

But only he can serve others and do good to them who has love, the true, all-embracing love that is always willing to sacrifice, the love that comes from God. For "love is always patient and kind; love is never jealous; love is not boastful or conceited, it is never rude and never seeks its own advantage, it does not take offense or store up grievances. Love does not rejoice at wrongdoing, but finds its joy in the truth. It is always ready to make allowances, to trust, to hope, and to endure whatever comes. Love never comes to an end . . ." (1 Cor 13:4–8); ". . . since the whole of the Law is summarized in the one command: '*You must love your neighbor as yourself*' (Gal 5:14); "All these: *You shall not commit adultery, You shall not kill, You shall not steal, You shall not covet,* and all the other commandments that there are, are summed up in this single phrase: *You must love your neighbor as yourself*" (Rom 13:9–10). We have to love, for "whoever does not love, remains in death" (1 John 3:14). Therefore, the purpose of your life should be to serve with love. Only when we have understood this will we be able to understand the important commandment "You shall not kill." Whoever kills has not understood the meaning of "*You must love your neighbor as yourself*" (Matt 22:39).

Introduction

Whoever has stood beside a deathbed (I have stood beside hundreds of them); whoever has been moved by inscriptions on headstones in our cemeteries; whoever has experienced the bloody harvest of death, in cities destroyed by bombs and on battlefields (I have seen dying and dead men on battlefields and, with thousands of other prisoners, was for many months at the mercy of hailstorms of bombs)—he knows what death is like and what it means to die. But only when we ourselves experience the unbending law of nature, that "every human being has to die," do we completely understand the mystery of death.

We know what life means, or, more correctly, we feel and experience it continually. And how much we human beings like to live! How we hang on to life with every fiber of our being, regardless of how wretched our life is. In fact, every sentient being, whether human or animal, resists the destruction of its life because each living being wants to be happy. But one can only be happy while one lives and as long as one lives. However, dying, the disintegration and destruction of the earthly, bodily, life is a deeply serious and bitter experience.

It is true that we human beings, especially faithful Christians, know that our life does not end with our earthly death but that we continue to live in eternity with God, who is life itself, and who has given us life. In fact, the first life could only come into being through the direct intervention of God because life can never spring from inanimate matter and its mechanical and chemical-physical properties. Experience tells us that each living being that exists is descended from another, already living being.

Dying, that is, the dissolution and destruction of the matter-bound body, occurs naturally from the essence of the matter that surrounds us. Change, transformation, and dissolution are characteristic of matter while at the same time converting it. Even though the natural dying process, that is, the natural dissolution of the life of the body, is bitter, nature resists all the more being killed, that is, resists the forcible destruction of life.

One could suggest that because of this natural survival instinct, human beings have a reverence for each life, so that, at least among humans, violent and intentional killing does not occur. However, murder and manslaughter are an everyday occurrence. The history of the human race consists of almost uninterrupted fighting and waging war. War, this craftily organized mass murder, commanded from above and according to a plan, has become a permanent institution of nations. The governments of nations claim for themselves the right to impose the death penalty on criminals and on those whose politics differ. What else than the intentional destruction of life is the wasting away and the slow dying of so many people in hideous dungeons, prisons, and concentration camps?

Every person who still has human feelings has to shudder when he considers that old, infirm, and sick men and women are forcibly exterminated like irksome vermin and that plans are being made to annihilate entire peoples and races. Some Christian textbooks even maintain that under certain circumstances one may kill.

The first humans were called into being by the Creator for the purpose of life, for everlasting happiness, so the Holy Scriptures inform us. However, through sin, through disobedience of God's holy command, our first parents lost life's happiness for themselves as well as for all of their descendants and were the cause of sickness, suffering, and death. For God in his goodness did not intend death.

After the first sin had been committed, God pronounced this judgment over our ancestors: "By the sweat of your face will you earn your food, until you return to the ground, as you were taken from it, for dust you are and to dust you shall return" (Gen 3:19). From the time Cain slew his brother, as chapter 4 of Genesis reports, until today, despite the existence of Christianity, human blood has been flowing without interruption on earth, the blood of human beings who have been killed violently. Some dictators literally play with human life and believe they have unlimited power over the life of their subjects, who should at all times, at the blink of an eye, be ready to take part in organized mass murder. Whoever is not willing to do so is shot on the spot.

In view of such hard facts, is it not fitting to write a book with the title *You Shall Not Kill*? Or perhaps we are generalizing when we say "you shall not kill." Should it not rather be titled "Except in certain circumstances, it is not permissible to kill"? But who dares to qualify God's commandment, which Christ has confirmed? God has commanded, "You shall not kill," without any qualification whatsoever—I cannot find a single modification in the entire Scriptures where this commandment is mentioned (Exod

20:13; Deut 5:17; Matt 5:21; Rom 13:9)—just as God has commanded, "You shall not bear false witness against your neighbor," "You shall not steal," etc.

However, the majority of Christian theologians and professors of moral philosophy teach that in certain instances it is permissible to kill. Therefore, we consider it a sacred duty of conscience to examine, from the viewpoint of Christian morality and theology, whether God's commandment "You shall not kill" is valid without qualifications or whether, in certain circumstances, one human being is permitted to kill another human being. To those who are convinced of the existence of God, we do not have to prove first that God is the absolute Lord of all life. God, indeed, is the Creator of all life. Because he has given it, he can also take it if he deems it good to do so. However, whenever God takes life, he is motivated by his wise intentions, his justice, and his love; for God is justice, and God is love. However, whether any human being has the right to take the life of a fellow human being has to be first proved. It is self-evident that I am never master over the life of my fellow beings. As humans we all have the same rights. Whenever someone claims for himself the right to kill another, he has to present irrefutable proof that God, the Lord of all life, has given him this right. Certainly, in this single instance, the commandment "You shall not kill" would be subject to a modification.

However, since the Catholic Church and other Christian churches, besides the great majority of national governments and political parties, permit exceptions to "You shall not kill," we want to examine this commandment from the viewpoint of moral law based on nature and reason and on Catholic theology. That is, as a moral philosopher and Catholic theologian, we want to find out whether the commandment "You shall not kill" has absolute validity or whether with God's explicit permission it can be modified so that in certain instances it is permissible to kill another human being.

We are convinced that our inquiry will be of general interest, especially in view of the dreadful war experiences of the last few years—that is, unless someone believes at the outset, without proof, that each war is a natural occurrence, that society cannot exist without the death penalty, and that self-defense is a self-evident natural law; and, therefore, the obligation of self-defense exists even if it involves killing the aggressor. We are not going to enter here into a discussion with those who already hold the above opinions because they agree with the familiar "*sic volo, sic jubeo, stat pro ratione voluntas*" (thus do I will, thus do I order, my will stands, not reason).

We will examine the divine commandment "You shall not kill," or stated more correctly, "you may not kill," or still shorter, "do not kill," in such a way that in Part I we are going to present the generally accepted teachings and opinions of Christian moral philosophers and theologians about whether it is ever permitted to kill. This analysis will demonstrate that, among others, moral philosophers and theologians of the Catholic Church defend killing in self-defense as justified, in fact, even make it a duty in certain cases. It is taught, for example, that the killing of the enemy in a so-called just defensive war is permissible and in special circumstances regarded as a duty and the will of God. Furthermore, governments and nations assume the right, under certain circumstances, to impose the death penalty on offenders. However, the precept of total war is rejected, and the duel is repudiated as sinful, as are murder and suicide. In a broad sense, the right to life of the individual, as well as the right of nations and races to their existence, is upheld. The right of abortion, that is, the killing of the child in the womb of the mother, which is defended by most physicians under certain circumstances, is rejected as a violation of natural law, as is the destruction of life at its beginning—in its seed—by means of sterilization, as well as the killing of the terminally ill, the disabled, the feeble, the aged, or those burdened with a hereditary disease.

In the second part of our discussion we will thoroughly examine all of these doctrines and opinions and, supported by valid reasons, will defend our point of view, which is opposed to some views or differs on many points. This analysis should offer proof that the Catholic theologian Franz Keller, professor at the University of Freiburg im Breisgau, was right when he stated in an address at the national convention of the Peace League of German Catholics in Munich, in September 1928,

> If, despite the official, international prohibition of war, preparations for war still play such an enormously important role in the life of the modern state, the root cause cannot be found only in the few fifteen or twenty puppeteers who wage war but also in the accepted mentality, the habitual thought patterns, and the hollow slogans which, without proof, are taken as Gospel truth. These established, even sacred, thought patterns are the most dangerous and disastrous instruments of war. This poisonous gas not only numbs the brains of the masses but even reduces to blind submissiveness scholars and theologians who are supposed to guide the people. Over the course of time, the poisonous gas of these soul-destroying thought patterns, unfortunately, has invaded the inner sanctum of the Christian proclamation of the Word and the scholarly explanation of the moral teachings of Christ our Lord.

However, if anyone believes that the views that we champion are not correct, let him enlighten us. We consider it a duty of conscience to be of assistance so that humanity, which seems often to have unlearned its independent thinking, especially about war and everything connected with it, is finally roused from its dazed condition.

The people of today, especially those who have lived during both world wars, or at least during the last catastrophic one, should at last answer whether they want to continue to claim the prevailing opinions about war and thus be implicated in the collapse of all culture and civilization. For no one—except for the defense industry, leaders of nations who are obsessed with the struggle for power, and other beneficiaries of war—will claim that the cunningly organized mass slaughter of both world wars (1914–18) and (1939–) was fortunate for the warring nations, advanced culture, or paved the way for world peace.

At last, someone has to have the courage, so our conscience appeals to us—even at the risk of giving offense—to shake up these thought patterns that tradition has rendered sacred. We take this chance because we seek truth and want to serve only the truth.

Whatever we advance here is the result of more than forty years of teaching, during which we have wrestled—among other issues—with all of the questions contained in this treatise.

Pentecost 1944

PART I

Teachings and views of exponents of moral philosophy based on natural law and reason and the Catholic (Christian) teachings of faith and morals regarding the commandment "You shall not kill"

1. The relationship between moral philosophy based on natural law and reason (ethics) and Christian teachings about faith and morals

Ethics based on natural law and reason is the moral philosophy that man perceives with the aid of his reason. This ethic is the result of the certain realization that man has free will, that mankind and the entire universe are God's creation, and that the personal Creator guides all beings to their final destination. This ethic is as old as humankind itself. It is one and the same in all ages and among all peoples and is unchanging in its demands.

Throughout history the universal and highest fundamental demands of this moral philosophy have been embodied in the Ten Commandments of God. By means of these commandments the relationship of human beings with their God-Creator and the relationships between human beings are regulated, taking into consideration the nature of everything God has created. Therefore, this philosophy always demands behavior that is in accordance with natural law, so that we can say that whatever agrees with natural law also is ethical. Whatever is not according to natural law is always unethical; and, conversely, whatever is unethical is never in accordance with natural law. Therefore, ethical behavior always agrees with God's natural order by which the universe and, as far as is possible, man with his free will are united into an integrated, vast, and harmoniously organized whole. Therefore the first rule of ethics is: Do what is good and avoid what is evil!

Ethical behavior is always behavior that observes the order that God has established in its entirety. Unethical behavior, on the contrary, is all behavior that violates the order established by God.

However, God, as history proves, has revealed his will to humans in a special way. A personal God's revelation, which we faithfully accept as self-evident, that is, we have to believe, started in the old covenant, first having been entrusted to the Jewish people. It was continued and completed in the new covenant by Jesus Christ, the Son of God. Taught by revelation, we know that God did not withdraw his grace from humanity, which had fallen away from him because of sin; but instead, through Christ's redemption, God enabled mankind to attain its supernatural destiny. This destiny is eternal contemplation and love of God in the life to come. Man is like a butterfly that does not know the light of the sun as long as it lives in its cocoon, but as soon as the cocoon bursts, the butterfly struggles toward the sunlight. For man, life on earth is similar to the cocoon stage. At the moment of death, the cocoon bursts open, and the light of eternity shines into the soul which has been freed from its earthly body.

Man should attain this supernatural destiny—the contemplation of God in the next world—in the Church founded by Christ, which, for this purpose, has been provided with special means of grace. The supernatural life, however, takes the natural life for granted and builds upon it. Consequently, there is no opposition or contradiction but complete agreement between the demands of the natural law and revealed Christian law. Therefore, no one can behave morally in the supernatural sphere if he pays no heed to the requirements of ethics derived from natural law and reason.

Therefore, man draws his knowledge from two sources—from reason and from revelation through faith. God, the author of reason and revelation, would contradict himself if knowledge gained by means of reason, that is, knowledge obtained from natural law, contradicted the realization of faith acquired through revelation. There is only one truth. It does not vary, and it is absolutely unchangeable. Of course, human reason can err; certainly, mankind has erred often, and, precisely for this reason, revelation is necessary. In order not to go astray, human reason can, and should, always use revelation as a means to realign itself because whatever God reveals is infallibly true.

Therefore, in the following analysis we are going to consult reason but will continually compare it with the appropriate precepts of revelation. In doing so, we will benefit especially from the fact that revelation has expressed itself clearly and unequivocally, particularly about the matters to be discussed here. However, where there are doubts about the content or meaning of a revealed precept, the infallible teaching authority of the Catholic Church will be decisive, as it has been commissioned by Christ to preserve and interpret revelation; and Catholics are bound to observe such decisions. For this saying applies: *Roma locuta, causas finita*, which means that whenever Rome, the infallible teaching authority of the Catholic Church,[1] has rendered a final decision, the matter is settled for Catholics, and the conflict of views has ended. It is noteworthy that this applies only to decisions about doctrines regarding faith and morals.

In matters where revelation does not express a viewpoint, or does not do so clearly, the infallible teaching authority has not rendered a final decision, and about which, therefore, differing views exist, each Catholic is free to follow the opinion that appears most reasonable to him. In order that no one doubts or even denies this truth, which is important for every scholarly discussion, the teaching authority of the Church has expressed itself unequivocally.

Instructed to do so by Pope Innocent XI, the Holy Office, on March 2, 1679, issued the following ordinance: "The Holy Father, by virtue of holy obedience, orders that all professors and others, in their printed or handwritten works, disputations, and leaflets guard against every condemnation and disparagement of opinions which are still being disputed, until the Holy See has rendered a decision."

Pope Benedict XIV said in *De synodo diocesana* VII, 4, 9, "In case of academic questions, the bishop does not have the authority to force upon members of his flock this or that opinion, even if it is only theoretical; *causae maiores* and the difficult questions regarding faith and church discipline belong before the Holy See, as long has been the custom."

Pope Benedict XV expressed himself thus in his letter *Ad beatissi*, on November 1, 1914: "Everyone is free to say and defend what seems right to him . . . everyone may defend his opinion freely, and no one may consider himself authorized to suspect his opponent of not being true to his faith and to church discipline because he considers the opposing view to be right."

Pope Pius XI declared in his encyclical *Studiorum ducem* of June 29, 1933, "No one may require of others more than the Church, the teacher and mother of all, requires; and in matters that are disputed in schools and by the most respected authors, and this or that opinion is held, no one may be prevented from accepting that opinion which appears to him to be more plausible."

1. This is usually the pope but can also be a decision by the world's bishops meeting in council.

If we stay within the boundaries of the above-mentioned rules of conduct of the teaching authority of the Church, and that is our wish, we may hope that our discussion about the great commandment "You shall not kill" will turn out to be quite stimulating and that explanations which are based on reason and revelation will at least gain some attention. For example, it may be noted here that Bishop Scheiwiler of St. Gallen in Switzerland made the following remarks in our *Sociology*, regarding our examination of the death penalty and the justice of war: "The author develops educational issues that today do not meet with general approval. Thus, the state is denied the right to institute the death penalty. Dr. Ude defends this viewpoint with keen arguments. Furthermore, he maintains that under today's conditions, a just war no longer exists; and, therefore, one has the right, indeed the duty, of conscientious objection. His position, strengthened by forceful arguments, will surprise some people but cannot be easily dismissed because of the newest military developments like air and gas war."[2]

Thus commented the bishop of St. Gallen, who with his point of view touches upon another significant principle that, in the free competition of opinions, is of extraordinary importance: Whoever cites an authority to support the truth of a disputed opinion should always remember that the opinion of an author (writer, professor) is worth only as much as are the reasons he offers for his opinion. For regardless of how much an influential person is considered an authority, this does not make him infallible.

2. Teachings about the Ten Commandments of God

As related in chapters 19 and 20 of the book of Exodus, God gave the people of Israel the Ten Commandments on the mountain of Sinai. On God's order, Moses delivered these commandments to his people. They were carved into two stone tablets. In chapter 5 of the book of Deuteronomy, the people are again reminded of these commandments, which are not something new in the history of mankind. Rather, this revelation on Sinai is a clear formulation and reinforcement of the moral requirements based on reason, well known since the beginning of man but with special consideration given to the uniqueness of the people of Israel.

2. Ude, *Soziologie*, 104–5.

By means of the naturally proper use of his reason, man, while observing his environment, easily recognizes the existence of God as the all-wise, all-gracious, almighty, and all-just Creator of heaven and earth. From this firm realization necessarily follows, first of all, the duty of religion, which can be summarized briefly in the sentence: You shall acknowledge and honor God. The first three of the Ten Commandments, engraved on the first tablet, regulate the relationship between man and God, while the other seven commandments of the second tablet guide the life of people with each other (Exod 20:1–17).

Through insight into human nature and the nature of our environment, the inquiring reason arrives at the knowledge of man's rights and duties by which the personal and social life of human beings should be regulated. If peace and good order are to reign among mankind, if each person is to have a dignified existence, and if everyone's human rights are to be guaranteed, a proper structure has to be provided in the life of the family and of the state.

The authority of parents and of the state has to be acknowledged. A reasoning unprejudiced person realizes without difficulty that since justice forms the basis of all human life, each human being has to be guaranteed his right to life and his right to property by his fellow human beings because every person wants to live a life of dignity and happiness. This insight is expressed in the two commandments "You shall not kill" and "You shall not steal." That sexual relations also have to be regulated has been expressed, one way or another, by all peoples, since the beginning of time, in the commandment "You shall not commit adultery." Furthermore, that the unreserved affirmation of truth is necessary for the existence of human order is expressed by "You shall not give false evidence against your neighbor." Completing the above commandments are these two: "You shall not covet your neighbor's wife. You shall not desire your neighbor's house or field, nor his male or female slave, nor his ox or ass, nor anything that belongs to him" (Deut 5:17–21 NAB).

However, the history of mankind tells us that, over the course of the millennia, the understanding derived from reason about the demands of the Ten Commandments has at times suffered a loss of clarity, has been combined with erroneous views, and, occasionally, has even been forgotten.

Even in times of most grievous error, however, a kernel of truth has remained alive; and in all ages men appeared and continued to speak out who, in the light of the commandments, urged moral conversion, so that we have to conclude: every nation has always accepted the Ten Commandments as guiding principles for how to live, even if often only in a very general and distorted form, and sometimes even mixed with grievous errors.

Nevertheless, the National Socialist reformer Alfred Rosenberg declared without reservation, "The laws given on Mount Sinai . . . may interest historians or tellers of legends but are not in the least relevant to religion. . . . They may be of interest to psychologists of peoples and races but do not have the least religious meaning for us. In this connection it is not blasphemous that I explain the insignificance of these matters; rather it is blasphemous that today one still dares to present these unimportant Jewish tales as religious documents."[3]

Wulf Sörensen, who may have been one of Alfred Rosenberg's students, writes,

> "Man should be noble, helpful and good." Does this not say far more than the Ten Commandments, which the Jew Moses had to give in the desert to the colored, down-and-out Hebrew riffraff in order to make understandable to this horde the rudiments of what it means to be human? Those commandments suited the Hebrew rabble, but for people of the North, these commandments constitute slander and an unforgiveable insult of the noblest blood. These precepts are the deadliest poison for our blood. . . . From the necessity for these commandments, which demand only the absolute minimum from a person to be called a "human being" one can readily see to what sort of scum with human-like faces they were given.[4]

Rosenberg, the National Socialist religious reformer of Germany, who was honored by his Führer Adolf Hitler for his literary achievements, and Rosenberg's students are convinced that the demands "You shall not lie," "You shall not steal," "You shall not commit adultery," "have nothing to do with religion," and that one can be considered a religious person even if one pays no attention to God's Ten Commandments. This means that a nation whose government approves and demands lying, killing, murder, stealing, and a lack of restraint in sexual relations can be an "Edelvolk"[5] and does all of this under the guiding principle mentioned by Sörensen: "Man should be noble, helpful and good."

Why then the Ten Commandments? ask Rosenberg, Sörensen, and those who parrot them. Why Christianity? Are not both allegedly alien concepts? Sörensen, for one, states, "This pure blood [meaning the Aryan blood of the National Socialists] cannot be experienced with the hate-filled eyes of Sinai or with the weak knees of Nazareth. It carries the divine—pure, clear

3. Rosenberg, *Die Dunkelmänner unserer Zeit*, 22.

4. Sörensen, *Die Stimme der Ahnen*, 33.

5. "Noble race."

and beautiful—in its red stream through the earthly eternity of the race. . . . God is too great, and we are too proud to beg. . . . And we do not regret that we cannot be cowardly. A man stands by his deed."[6]

What right do they have to talk about "the hate-filled eyes of Sinai"? Was it not National Socialism that systematically trained the entire nation to hatred and summoned it to revenge according to the familiar Jewish phrase "an eye for an eye and a tooth for a tooth"? According to the Graz *Tagespost* of November 29, 1943, the National Socialist Reich Minister for Propaganda, Dr. Joseph Goebbels, stated at a film program for youth in Berlin,

> The entire world has already rendered judgment about this cowardly and cynical way of fighting. The German people are responding with burning hate. There exists no more passionate demand than to pay back the criminals on the Thames in full measure for what they have done and are doing to us. The German people can be reassured: Day and night we are working with feverish diligence on the preparations for this retaliation. . . . We [the Germans] were once a sentimental people whose character was too kindhearted to bear a grudge and to hate, but that is in the past. The Britons have taught us how to hate. Every impulse of sentiment inside us has died.

So says Goebbels, who, however, keeps secret that it was Nazi Germany that, on the command of the Führer, blanketed Rotterdam, Warsaw, and Belgrade with bombs before even a single English bomb had been dropped on German territory. By saying this I do not wish to whitewash or in any way condone the air raids of the Britons and the Americans. On the contrary, murder remains murder, killing remains killing, and destruction remains destruction even if it is done in the spirit of retaliation—even the noblest end never justifies immoral means.

Nevertheless, despite Rosenberg, Sörensen, and National Socialism, we have to admit: even at the risk of being called "blasphemous," we declare that we regard the Ten Commandments of God a religious document of the highest importance for people of all times and regions of the earth, or, more correctly, as the religious document. In fact, by either accepting or rejecting this document, peoples and nations have determined their destiny, their fortune or misfortune, and are continuing to do so. Only there where God's Ten Commandments are observed without reservation is human society in good order. Only where they govern personal as well as public life can happiness and peace be found. Wherever these commandments are not observed and are considered to be insignificant, human society becomes

6. Sörensen, *Die Stimme der Ahnen*, 48, 50.

disordered and collapses, as history has always shown. There human happiness and peace cannot flourish. Nazi Germany has confirmed this truth by its unspeakable and disastrous downfall.

The merit of Christianity is and continues to be that it has always stood up for the observance of the Ten Commandments and has emphasized their fundamental importance for personal, social, national, and international life. Above all, the teachings of Christ point out that the Ten Commandments are summed up in one commandment of love: the love of God and of one's neighbor. For Christ commands, "*You must love the Lord your God with all your heart, with all your soul*, and with all your mind," and adds, "*You must love your neighbor as yourself.* On these two commandments hang the whole Law, and the Prophets too" (Matt 22:37–40; Mark 12:30–31; Luke 10:27). Christ teaches us that every person, whether friend or foe, is our neighbor.

Man's unbiased reason easily comprehends that the Apostle Paul was right when he wrote to the Galatians, "The whole Law is summarized in the one commandment: *You must love your neighbor as yourself*" (Gal 5:14), and in his letter to the Romans, "The only thing you should owe to anyone is love for one another, for to love the other person is to fulfill the law. All these: *You shall not commit adultery, You shall not kill, You shall not steal, You shall not covet,* and all the other commandments that there are, are summed up in this single phrase: *You must love your neighbor as yourself.* Love can cause no harm to your neighbor, and so love is the fulfillment of the Law" (Rom 13:8–10).

Unfortunately, there is not a single country in the entire world where all of God's Ten Commandments are observed without reservation. Therefore, it is no wonder that everywhere there is privation, misery, discontent, and hate, that the entire planet Earth has become a single vast arena of war, and that the nations and peoples scheme how best to slaughter and destroy one another. As if killing, murder, and destruction were the means to bring humanity happiness and peace!

3. Teachings about the original rights of human beings with emphasis on the right to life

ETHICS, BASED ON NATURAL law and reason and, therefore, also on Christian moral philosophy, grants every human being the right to life as the first and inviolable right without distinction of race, nationality, language, religion, or political affiliation. In addition, it grants the rights to work and to ownership and use of property, including mineral resources and raw materials. Further, it grants the right to self-determination, within the scope of moral law, especially self-determination of religion and affiliation with a specific religious denomination. Finally, it grants the right of cultural development and of language. All of these rights can be expressed in the personal right to a dignified existence, which each person possesses before the state and independent of it, according to the will of God, which no one can contest.

Likewise, each nationality, even if it is in the minority, has the right to existence, the right to its language and cultural characteristics, and the right to cultural development.

Every individual human being, as well as state and church, has to respect these rights granted directly by God and guaranteed by him and has to safeguard and guarantee them for one another by all ethically permitted means because these rights are purely personal natural rights. Because they are bestowed by God in accordance with the nature of man, they are inviolable. For God, the absolute Master of life, has given life to man, whereas the individual person is only a beneficiary so that he can use his God-given life span in the manner his Creator desires because life on earth is a preparation for the eternal life in the hereafter.

God is the Creator of life. Even the natural sciences, although often alienated from God, teach that anything living can only stem from another living organism. Matter, with its chemical and physical properties, can never create life. Each living cell is derived from another living cell, and each living nucleus can only originate from another living nucleus. A so-called *generatio aequivoca* (the creation of life from inanimate matter by means of its mechanical, physical, and chemical properties) is absurd and can only be contended by an amateur scientist or someone who subscribes to the theories of Darwin or Haeckel, the falsifier of science.

Because all human beings are identical in nature, racial attributes do not make them significantly different. Every person possesses the above-mentioned rights—first of all, the right to life from which all other rights are derived.

Since the universal personal human rights are part of the nature of human beings, that is, these rights were bestowed by God—for humans existed before state and church were founded—no individual or state has the authority to deny these rights. Each person may and must demand that no one deny his personal rights. Furthermore, no one may forego these rights, which are bestowed on him by natural law, for no one can fashion his life according to God's will without claiming these rights.

Because man has the duty to preserve his God-given life and to mold it as God desires, he has to have the right to the use of everything that is necessary to maintain and perfect his physical and spiritual life. Each person has to provide himself with proper nutrition, clothing, shelter, as well as education according to his mental abilities. All of these can be provided only by work.

Since every person has the duty to work, he also has the right to work because most of the things absolutely necessary for life are not merely lying around but can only be used and enjoyed if labor is applied. Through work man earns the right to own the objects he has worked on. Wherever unemployment exists, it is a sign that the right to property and the right to its use have been seriously violated.

We are justified in saying that the most serious cause of every disorder of society is the violation of the human rights conferred by moral law, which is based on natural law, reason, and Christian teachings. For the earth has more than sufficient land and raw materials for all people, so that everyone can exercise his right to their use—provided, however, that everyone unreservedly obeys the great commandments: "You shall not kill" and "You shall not steal."

The material, economic, and moral deterioration and collapse of the German nation during World War II demonstrates how low the German people have fallen because they disregarded all of these moral demands. However, the other peoples and nations of the world are in no better position. It is important to note this so that no nation, no government, and no individual should dare to make Germany alone responsible for all the troubles in the world.

Yet no one will refute that Germany is the most hated country in the world because of its National Socialist teachings, for nowhere else has human life been deemed cheaper and more worthless, and nowhere else have personal rights been less respected, than in the Nazi Reich.

Therefore, the German nation will only be able to get back on its feet—the same applies to all other states of the world—if it sincerely respects personal human rights; that is, if it unreservedly acknowledges the rights to life, to property, to use of material goods, to personal freedom, and to cultural development of all peoples and nations. Furthermore, Germany, in sincere cooperation with all other states of the world, has to regulate and promote the life of the family and the nation, respecting all of these personal human rights.

Without question, the demands of natural law also include the duty to eliminate capitalistic exploitation by means of interest, which, to a great degree, is the cause of the violation of human rights. The nature of the capitalistic economy is that some individuals and states misuse the goods they own—money, land, houses, machines, raw materials, food, etc.—in order to appropriate for themselves, without compensation, the fruits of the labor of others, which should belong to the latter. This constitutes unearned gain. Therefore, the capitalistic economy seriously violates the justice of the individual and of society. The facts prove that capitalism continually disputes these basic human rights and makes it impossible for millions of people to exercise their right to life, to property, and to the use of goods needed to support life. The same is true of communism.

However, in states ruled autocratically by fascism, communism, and National Socialism, a possibly even more grievous exploitative system has been added to customary capitalistic methods, which is the organization of the political party.

Such political systems, which use violence to suppress and deprive people of their human rights, can only end when the Ten Commandments become the foundation and guide for all of personal, social, national, and international life.

There is no improvement in sight, however, as long as a so-called Führer and high officials in the National Socialistic Reich are able to state in public meetings, without punishment or opposition, "that one can and should ruthlessly exploit Polish citizens and give them only barely enough to eat so they can work, because after the German victory, the Polish people are to be turned into fertilizer." These are the exact words a Nazi speaker used in a meeting in Oberdonau in 1942.

But before the other nations cast the first stone at the fascistic, communistic, and National Socialistic states, let them search their own conscience and contemplate whether they themselves have not transgressed God's Ten Commandments.

The view of human rights held by exponents of ethics based on natural law and reason and by believers in Christian revelation is limited by some reservations when it comes to the right to life. By far the largest percentage of Christian moral philosophers and theologians—I am thinking, first of all, of our Catholic ones—grant governments the right to inflict the death penalty in certain cases. Furthermore, they teach that in self-defense, and, accordingly, in a so-called just defensive war, it is permissible to kill the aggressor, that is, the "enemy." Thus, under certain circumstances, killing would not be a sin but a moral action. We are going to discuss these reservations more thoroughly in the second part of this work. However, we note here already that, supported by weighty arguments of reason and, above all, by the teachings of Christian revelation, we deny to every human being, including government officials, the right to take anyone's life, even that of the worst criminal, that is, to kill with "justification." Also, we deny not only the right to self-defense but especially the duty of self-defense; consequently, we must repudiate every war and therefore also compulsory military service and the just defensive war. In our opinion, the "just defensive war" is no longer possible in light of the modern methods of waging war.

Therefore, we believe firmly that the great commandment "You shall, you may not kill" is meant to be absolute, that is, it permits no exception. We would like to note also that whoever kills someone, or has him killed, has not only the life of that one person on his conscience but kills with him all of his potential descendants. No one knows what talented human beings would descend from this individual if he had not been killed. This thought occurs to me when contemplating the many young human beings, usually the strongest and healthiest, who are sacrificed in a war. This idea has to trouble the conscience of all those who are doing everything possible to preserve the most capable of every race. In every war, however, the opposite is true.

4. Teachings about suicide and murder and the obligation to preserve life

As has been mentioned above, man not only has the right to life but also the obligation to preserve it. Therefore, he has the right to all means necessary to maintain a healthy and energetic life and also the obligation to earn and use the necessary means to maintain and improve his life.

God has given life to man. The body of the first human being was indirectly formed by God from existing matter; the soul, however, was directly implanted by God, just as God implants a soul into every person at the time of conception so that he can serve God and, therefore, can attain everlasting life in the hereafter.

God could not disregard the fact, without renouncing himself, that he, as the Creator of human life, is also its destination. This is substantiated by the essence of God and by the essence of human nature which man has received from God. Therefore, man's entire earthly life should be devoted to the glorification of God, which is necessary for the attainment of man's eternal goal, provided that man follows God's will in every situation of life. For man is only a beneficiary and steward and not the absolute master of his life.

Of course, man has free will and can, if he so desires, take his own life. However, this is an unwarranted interference in God's sovereign and exclusive proprietary rights over man, who belongs to God in body and soul and is obligated to place his life entirely in the service of God, as long as it pleases God to keep him alive on earth.

A human being could only dispose of his own or someone else's life if God had expressly given him this right; but the delegation of such a right cannot be proved by reason and even less so by revelation. On the contrary, it is precisely revelation, in both the old and the new covenant, which provides irrefutable evidence that God alone is the Master of life and the span of life. We cite the following passages from the Holy Scriptures: "Since his days are measured out, since his tale of months depends on you, since you assign him bounds he cannot pass . . ." (Job 14:5); "You shall not kill"—either someone else or yourself (Exod 20:13; Deut 5:17; Matt 5:21; 19:18; Rom 13:9).

Nowhere in the Gospel can we find the slightest indication that God has given to a human being, or to any judicial position he may hold, the right to dispose freely over his own life span or the life of a fellow human being. Any plausible reasoning that alleges that in certain cases suicide is permissible is proven false by the Gospel. Suicide—the intentional destruction of one's own life—is a serious sin.

Of course, whoever considers human life to be strictly of this world, that is, whoever denies God as Creator and as the final destination of human life, could regard suicide valid in cases where life no longer seems worth living. This may include incurable illness, cases of severe affliction and pain, and when someone's honor is deeply offended or someone's love is rejected.

However, any proponent of ethics based on natural law, reason, and Christian revelation has to reject suicide as well as murder in all circumstances as an immoral act. For, to say it once again: Whoever is not the owner of something but only its beneficiary and steward may not destroy it without the express order or explicit or implicit agreement of its owner. No one can produce such an order or agreement from God regarding the life of human beings. However, should reason point to exceptions in which it is allegedly permissible to voluntarily take one's own life or have someone else do so, we have to reply: Neither a seriously ill person nor a suffering one—and even less so other people—may render an infallible judgment on the adequacy of the reasons put forth that would make a suicide permissible. Where are the boundaries between permissible and no longer permissible? Such a question is unnecessary; for everyone who advocates ethics based on natural law and Christian revelation is obliged to persevere under all circumstances and to accept death from the hand of the sovereign proprietor of all life, that is, from the hand of God. No life that has God as its final goal is worthless. Every person who is seriously ill, grieving, despairing, or depressed should remember this. Therefore, one should serve God until one's last breath. Thus every human being, regardless of how wretched his living condition, can be useful to others through his example of patience and resignation to God's will and at times even inspire imitation by his heroism. On the other hand, while one can feel sorry for the person who commits suicide, one can never honor him as a hero or emulate him, except if one is biased, materialistic, or only concerned about this world.

Regarding the use of the means necessary to maintain life, we believe that human beings have the obligation to live in accordance with natural law. For as we noted earlier, everything that agrees with natural law is ethical and, conversely, everything that is ethical also accords with natural law.

God created human beings in such a way that they are dependent on food, clothing, care of the body, education of the mind, and the acquisition of property and, therefore, on work, land, and raw materials. For God does not want man to live in misery but desires that every person live with dignity so that his entire life can develop harmoniously, and he can be strong and healthy in order to fulfill, completely and well, the mission assigned him by God. Therefore, man has to do everything possible to keep healthy and to avoid all that would damage his life and health.

Life is holy because it has God, the Creator and Sustainer of life, as its destination. The soul of each person, as we stated above, was created directly by God's hand. Therefore, parents and their children have the responsibility to see to it that a healthy soul lives in a healthy body; but unfortunately, this principle is often violated. We merely have to reflect on how people live contrary to nature and how already egg and sperm cells are damaged through use of alcohol, tobacco, and other unhealthy substances.

One of the most important tasks in educating young people, who especially need good examples, is to make them aware of these ideas because the more the individual is convinced of the sacredness of life, the more reverence he will have for his own life, the life of all of his fellow human beings, and even for the life of animals and plants. The more closely people conduct their lives according to this belief, the clearer will be their awareness of why God has given the great commandment "You shall not, you may not kill." If God had envisioned an exception to this command, he would already have stated so at the time he revealed it or on other occasions; but this did not happen.

The more reverence a person has for the sacredness of life—that is, for every human life, but also that of animals and plants—the more he will strive to protect and maintain life, the more he will dismiss every thought of destroying life and will condemn suicide, murder, and every other destruction of life as a serious sin.

Man is not the absolute master of his own life and even less so of the life of another human being. Therefore, each willful, intentional killing of a fellow human being is a transgression of God's rights as well as of the right of life that God has guaranteed to every person and protected with the commandment "You shall, you may not kill."

Even though human life, animal life, and, even more so, plant life are not on an equal footing, the reverence and respect for life extends to animals and plants; and the efforts of human beings who protect animals and plants increase in importance and meaning the more senselessly and cruelly man treats these creations.

5. Teachings about self-defense

THE TEACHINGS ABOUT SELF-DEFENSE and its justifications, as presented by Christian moral philosophers and theologians, who are generally in agreement, can be summed up in the following sentence: Self-defense is resistance with physical force to an unjust attack on one's life, body, or property at the moment of the attack. Theologians and moral philosophers teach that every person has the right to defend himself by force and even by killing, if there is no other way, at the moment of such an unjust attack.

According to this teaching, a person may resort to self-defense if the attack is an unjust one that cannot be evaded. Only in such a case and only at the moment of the attack is self-defense permitted. It is emphasized that only the amount of force absolutely necessary to repel the aggressor is permitted. This means that whoever wants to render the aggressor harmless by wounding him may never kill him. It is taught, however, that if circumstances make it necessary to kill the aggressor, this does not constitute a violation of justice or of the command to love one's neighbor because the aggressor has placed himself in danger of being killed. But it is not permitted to use force if one fears a future attack. However, a few older theologians are of the opinion that it is permissible to prevent a certain unjust attack by the use of force.

It is taught that in a case of self-defense, the assaulted person may not satisfy his desire for vengeance but may only fend off the aggressor and may not continue to use force after the attack has ended because self-defense should always only be a preventative measure.

Self-defense, which in the most extreme instance can lead to the killing of the aggressor, is justified with the statement that it is an appropriate and necessary means of self-preservation that does not violate the obligation to do justice, the duty to love, or the promotion of public safety.

Self-defense, so one tries to prove, does not violate justice because in self-defense, where the right to life of the victim is set against the right to life of the aggressor, the right of the victim has precedence.

It is maintained that self-defense does not violate the obligation to love one's neighbor because, as result of the unjust assault, the attacked person has a choice of whether he or the aggressor should suffer. The supporters of self-defense argue further that the virtue of love obliges no one to prefer the other person when both are in the same predicament. Love obligates only that we help our neighbor by sacrificing our life, limb, or property if the neighbor is in great need, cannot help himself, and would perish without our sacrifice. But this only applies when the person who is attacked defends himself and, in doing so, possibly endangers the aggressor's life. For the aggressor can save himself. He merely has to desist from the attack. Neither does self-defense violate public order and safety; on the contrary, the public welfare even demands that everyone has the right to defend himself when attacked; for if this were not the case, all aggressors would have free rein to endanger the life, limb, and property of others and thus create such public insecurity that people would continually expect to be attacked. The right to self-defense, one reasons, contributes to public safety, which would be constantly endangered if murderers, robbers, and thieves could not be stopped forcibly.

Furthermore, it is generally taught that it is permissible—precisely because of the command to love one's neighbor—to protect and defend the life of another person from an aggressor. One maintains that under certain circumstances self-defense is an obligation. For example, a husband and father is obligated to defend the life and honor of his wife and children against an aggressor. Likewise, it is a duty to defend the unjustly attacked fatherland with weapons. Therefore, in the case of a so-called just defensive war one speaks of general compulsory military service and the right to kill the enemy. In the second part of our examination we are going to discuss self-defense more extensively since, for good reasons, we hold a different opinion and deny that there is a right to self-defense and even less so a duty of self-defense. It is strange that Christian theologians, in supporting self-defense and its obligation, accept only the reasons given by moral philosophers but intentionally omit revelation, while we are able to prove our opposing view directly by revelation.

6. Teachings about abortion, sterilization, and the killing of frail children, the terminally ill, those with hereditary diseases, the mentally impaired, and the mentally ill

In regard to the above teachings, two sizable groups stand in opposition to one another. The first one makes the completion of a pregnancy mandatory, while the other repudiates this demand. Some advocates of abortion want to win acceptance for the absolute right to kill an unborn child during the first three months of pregnancy; others permit it only under certain circumstances. However, the opposing group unconditionally repudiates killing a child in the womb and absolutely and consequently requires the completion of a pregnancy. The last group includes Christian moral philosophers and theologians.

Those who would permit abortion under certain conditions list the following circumstances. It is argued that a mother finds herself in a situation of self-defense if the prognosis is that her life will be severely endangered by the birth of the child. However, a physician has to make such a prognosis or has to find that the mother has tuberculosis. In addition to justifying abortion on medical grounds, eugenic, social, and economic reasons are advanced. This means that the birth of "racially inferior" children is to be prevented, and it is argued that it would be immoral to bring children into the world who are destined to live in misery and economic deprivation. Therefore, impoverished parents should be able to kill the child in the womb without being punished. The motto in this case is "Fewer children, happier children"! According to this viewpoint, parents who cannot support more children would actually have the right to limit the number of offspring through abortion or to prevent being blessed with children. The fact that many physicians believe that abortion is not a dangerous intervention strengthens the views of abortion advocates.

The Christian ethical and moral viewpoint regarding artificial and intentional abortion can be summarized like this: The artificially initiated and intentional aborting of a fetus is a grave sin, a breaking of the fifth commandment: "You shall not kill." Therefore, abortion is absolutely forbidden under all circumstances. Hence, no government law may give a mother the right to decide as she wishes over the fate of the child in her womb, even during the first three months of pregnancy. Therefore, no physician, actually no one, may perform an abortion, even if the life of the mother is in great danger. This does not constitute a case of self-defense because the child growing in the womb is not an "unjust aggressor." The fetus has a right to life, just as does the mother, because the fetus already has a soul. Therefore, the intentional killing of this developing life falls under the commandment "You shall not kill."

If even in the most serious case, that is, when the life of the mother is endangered by the child she is carrying, an intentional abortion is not permitted, it is even less permissible for eugenic or social and economic reasons. Holding this viewpoint, moral philosophers and Christian authorities, rightly so, cite the statements of leading medical authorities who absolutely condemn abortion as child murder and point out that there are sufficient modern surgical and gynecological methods by which to save both mother and child in even the most difficult delivery.

Popes and bishops of the Catholic Church who—for whatever reason—consider every abortion reprehensible have imposed church penalties on those who intend to perform an abortion and on those who aid in the process (e.g., Pope Sixtus in 1588, Pope Gregory XIV in 1591, and in modern times, Pope Pius IX). The *Corpus juris canonici* (the book of church law) summarizes these penalties in Canon 2350, Paragraph 1: "*Procurantes abortum, matre non excepta, inccurrunt, effectu secuto, in excommunicationem latae sententiae Ordinario reservatam; et si sint clerici, praeterea deponantur.*" (If the abortion succeeds, whoever carried it out, the mother not excepted, will be excluded from the community of the Church. Only the local bishop can lift this penalty of excommunication. If Church officials have been involved in an abortion, they are removed from their position.)

Again and again, the Roman Curia, in agreement with the respective pope, has decided appeals according to the above stated viewpoint. We refer, among others, to the decisions and answers of the *S. Congregatio Officii* of May 28, 1885, of July 24, 1895, and of May 4, 1898; furthermore, to the decision of the *Congregatio de Propaganda Fide* of March 20, 1908, and several others.

We are going to explain more fully the Christian position on the sterilization of men and women as well as on the killing of persons considered to be mentally impaired, the frail elderly, those with inherited illnesses, and the mentally ill. The sterilization of the above groups was especially advocated by the National Socialist government, which legally controlled and carried it out extensively.

The Nazi government, appropriating Friedrich Nietzsche's ideas, considered itself justified, "in the name of the German people, for the protection of the German-Aryan race and the general welfare," to eliminate and mercilessly annihilate, like irksome vermin, all those it judged to be "inferior." For according to the National Socialist book of ethics, only those persons are entitled to live and procreate who are healthy, strong, productive, and racially sound. Those who can no longer work are a burden to society, unwanted mouths to feed, and parasites; therefore, they have to be annihilated or at least kept from reproducing. The inhabitants of institutions for the mentally ill or retarded, hospitals for the incurably ill, homeless shelters, and homes for the aged were to be eliminated as rapidly as possible in the National Socialist German Reich. Many thousands were gassed or poisoned.

We are going to explain from a Christian viewpoint the position a faithful Christian has to take regarding the sterilization of those considered to be mentally impaired and those belonging to "inferior" races. A Christian has to judge these actions of the Nazi state according to natural law and the precepts of Christian morality. National Socialism distinguished between a "master race"—to which belonged foremost all German "Aryans," and of those, above all Nazi Party members—and other races that were regarded as inferior, to a greater or lesser extent, and existed only to serve the "master race."

We are going to advance the relevant principles of the Catholic Church's point of view. Since, however, the supernatural builds on and presupposes what is natural, the Christian demands coincide completely with the requirements of ethics based on natural law. Therefore, it is sufficient to explain how sterilization is to be judged from the perspective of natural law. This question is relevant to the commandment "You shall not kill" because the reproductive cells of men and women have only one natural purpose, which is to call forth new life, and these cells, at the moment of their union, are given a soul by God.

The question that we have to consider is this: May any human being or any state authority, by forcible intervention, interfere in the path of these reproductive cells and thus prevent new life, either to improve the race or for economic reasons?

The fact is that because among Germans, as well as among other peoples, the number of mentally impaired people is growing rapidly, society has the greatest interest to prevent these persons from reproducing. Rightly so, the idea "*mens sana in corpore sano*" (a healthy mind in a healthy body) is emphasized. However, in view of the desirability of physical and mental fitness and the improvement and ennobling of the race, it is demanded to slow down as much as possible the growth of the impaired population. Above all, the mentally impaired, sociopaths, and persons without inhibitions continue to produce descendants who are mentally impaired, chronically ill, or have criminal tendencies; and because all of these are largely a burden on society, public costs to care for them are rising.

Here are a few examples. Ida Jurke, an alcoholic, died in 1740. She had 709 descendants. Of these, 106 were born out of wedlock, 181 became prostitutes, 142 were beggars, 46 lived in shelters for the impoverished, and 76 were criminals, of whom 7 were murderers. These congenitally afflicted men and women were imprisoned a total of 116 years. Ida Jurke's descendants were supported from public funds for 734 years.

Another research project concerned the fate of 814 descendants of 215 alcoholic families. Of their 814 children, only 739 (78.6 percent) survived. Of these, 372 (50.3 percent) were feeble-minded, 301 (40.8 percent) were alcoholics, 167 (22.7 percent) were mentally ill, 151 (20.4 percent) suffered from epilepsy and hysteria, and 71 (9.7 percent) became criminals. The remainder were physically weak, consumptive, and suffered from encephalitis or convulsions.

It goes without saying that something has to be done about the increase of mentally impaired persons. Indeed, it is a matter of conscience for each individual, for society, and especially for the state to reduce mental impairment, especially among the new generation, to take preventive measures against it, that is, to eliminate its causes.

Two methods are seen to be useful to accomplish this: to lock up all mentally impaired persons or to subject them to compulsory sterilization. The first method, however, is said to be a costly burden on the government budget, especially during economically hard times. The second method, said to be much less expensive, appears safe and ensures against unwanted children, which is not the case with the first method.

Since it is the tendency today to increase the powers of the state as opposed to the rights of its citizens, one is inclined to grant the state the right to protect itself against the unwanted offspring of mentally impaired persons by compulsory sterilization and by permitting only citizens with healthy genes to reproduce. Yes, the National Socialist state (and also the fascist and communist states) is totalitarian, that is, it claims unlimited power to act in all areas, including the question posed here, according to the opinion of the Führer, whose will alone is decisive.

Therefore, those persons whose thinking is ruled by eugenics and economic considerations and who acknowledge the totalitarian power of the state do not question sterilization but take it for granted. For them compulsory sterilization of impaired persons is the lesser evil in view of the health of the state and the protection of the race, which they believe would be seriously damaged by these individuals.

Opposing such compulsory sterilization, advocated by race theorists and carried out by state authorities, is the Christian teaching, supported by natural law, which says that no state may protect itself against the unwanted offspring of mentally impaired persons by compulsory sterilization. In support of this position we have to say that sterilization is not permissible. No one, including the government, may do something that is morally impermissible, even if such an act could bring about much good, for even the noblest purpose does not sanctify immoral means. The commandment "You shall not kill" is binding, always and in all circumstances. Even the noblest good cannot be justified when the moral order is violated. Therefore, we must do everything to make sterilization illegal. Man is created in God's image and as such may not be reduced to a mere means.

The absolute preservation of God's image in man demands that human beings always and everywhere should judge as God judges and desire what God desires. Therefore, one may never choose a so-called lesser evil, which in itself represents an immoral act, in order to prevent even the greatest evil or to attain the greatest good, even if the prevention of the greater evil is ever so necessary or the attainment of the good is ever so desirable and urgent. Whatever is immoral, that is, forbidden by God under all circumstances, may not be done and can never be permitted by God because he is holy and just.

The most basic human right is the right to life, and all other rights and duties are derived from it. Life, as we have explained above, is sacred. Man is only the beneficiary of this right. Only God has exclusive and unconditional discretion over life. Therefore, man may and should make use of his life in complete dependence on God.

Life has been given to man as a means to prepare himself for the eternal goal the Creator has intended for him, namely, his union with God. Human life is precious because of man's final goal. Therefore, as we have proved above, suicide is morally impermissible under any circumstance. We, and others who share our view, go so far as to deny the state the right to impose the death penalty. As we shall explain later in more detail, we also defend the view that from the Christian standpoint war is absolutely unacceptable because there is no such thing as a "just defensive war" among civilized countries. Every war is irreconcilable with the Sermon on the Mount.

Since every human being has a God-given right to life, no other person, nor humanity as a whole, may violate this right. The right to life of every person is protected by the commandment "You shall not kill," just as the right to property in order to be able to establish a dignified existence is protected by God by the commandment "You shall not steal." Therefore, the rights of the community, that is, of the family and the state, are limited in relation to the inalienable rights of individuals and their eternal goal. The community, like its individual members, is obligated to observe unreservedly the ethical requirements, whatever the consequences.

In addition to the right to life, every individual has the right to the inviolability of all parts of his body because man can realize and exercise his right to life only by proper use of all these parts. Through the harmonious function of all life-serving parts—no part is given to man without a purpose—health and well-being are realized. Insofar as man uses his body to maintain his health and well-being, no other person, nor the community, has the right to prevent this or to intervene in the functions of this God-given body. This includes the sexual organs, which God has given to every person in light of the commandment he issued in paradise: "Be fruitful and multiply, fill the earth . . ." (Gen 1:28).

An intervention in his right to the inviolability of the body and its parts, to which man is entitled regardless of the state and its rights, is in itself immoral and, therefore, not permissible to an individual or a state authority.

Therefore, the position that as a measure of self-defense the state may prevent the reproduction of impaired offspring is completely wrong because even if it were supposed that the right to self-defense existed—and we do not believe it does—the producing of impaired offspring by mentally impaired persons can in no instance be called an unjust attack on a state's right to life or property.

Surely, the reproduction of impaired offspring is a misfortune that the community should prevent as far as possible. However, this should not be accomplished by sterilization, which is a morally impermissible intervention into the right to life of the individual, but instead by isolating and locking up mentally impaired persons and, especially, by appropriate preventative measures to remove the causes of mental impairment, such as alcohol, nicotine, prostitution, and unnatural ways of living.

The personal right of human beings to the use of all parts of their body and the right to its inviolability are unchangeable and unassailable rights that a state may not take away even when they are misused. However, the curtailment of freedom—for example, locking up mentally impaired persons or criminals—is a morally acceptable method to keep such individuals from harming others or endangering the general welfare. Each right and each law, in some way, limits personal freedom but does so in a morally acceptable manner.

The government has the responsibility to secure, protect, and promote the general welfare in an ethical manner. Since government authorities cannot possibly punish every violation of the public welfare, they cannot prevent all abuses that occur in a society. However, the idea that the state, in the interest of the general welfare, may do everything it wishes, that is, exercise absolute power, is a serious, Machiavellian error. State authority also has to respect each individual's right to life and thus the inviolability of his organs.

The right of the state to intervene in the function of the parts of the body essential to life constitutes despotism, for it is impossible to draw with certainty the line between those mentally impaired and those not impaired. Therefore, what right does the state have to perform sterilizations? Even though pertinent reasons are advanced for compulsory sterilization, these are not able to refute, beyond a reasonable doubt, the weighty reasons against it. Therefore, the moral permissibility of compulsory sterilization is doubtful in every case; and wherever there is doubt whether an action is moral, that action should not be carried out. However, curtailing the freedom of mentally impaired persons is morally permissible. Therefore, from a moral standpoint, we can consent only to the latter method and have to flatly refute the right of the state to compulsory sterilization.

However, if morality is ignored in judging our question—that is, if it is regarded purely from the point of view of a veterinarian, to use a provocative expression—then, as a more effective method, the state could also be permitted to kill mentally impaired persons. It is a fact that the Nazi state, to an unheard of extent, killed what it called *Minderwertige*, which means "inferior people." Unfortunately, the German people, with very few exceptions, remained silent about this. However, one person who spoke up was Cardinal von Galen.[7]

It is clear where the idolatry of the state's authority leads if its bearers are granted unlimited powers. Since government authority is exercised by fallible persons, subject to error and passions, it cannot claim omnipotence and do whatever seems right according to the *Führerprinzip*. The absolute

7. Galen, *Das Recht auf Leben*.

moral law ranks above the power of the state, and the Führer and every political party are bound by it. This includes physicians who have to render judgment about whether someone is impaired, and they certainly are not infallible in their diagnosis.

When alleging that the state has the right to sterilize mentally impaired persons, two values have to be compared: (1) the right to the inviolability of the body, which no unbiased person can deny; and (2) the public welfare, which is the responsibility of the state.

By whatever means sterilization is accomplished, it is an unnatural intervention into the personal right of the individual to the inviolability of his body. However, the elimination of adverse social and economic conditions does not represent a greater or more valuable good to which this right should be sacrificed, especially since the reproduction of impaired persons can easily be prevented by the morally permissible means of curtailing their freedom by isolating them.

Considering that all social and economic harm can never be completely avoided among human beings because they are damaged by original sin, it is not right to sacrifice, to a misunderstood and exaggerated concept of the general welfare, the individual's self-evident right to life, to health, and to the inviolability of his body. Everyone's personal rights, granted by natural law, are independent of every society and outrank it.

It would only be right and more beneficial if government officials would endeavor to eradicate the stimulants that damage society and would provide a natural way of life, because it is well known that alcohol, tobacco, eating much meat, unhealthy living conditions, and malnutrition cause much physical and mental impairment to the reproductive cells. On the basis of his extensive and thorough research, the director of the mental hospital in Salzburg, Dr. Schweighofer, has drawn the following conclusion: "Alcoholism of the parents clearly is damaging to their offspring and manifests itself in the physical and mental impairment of the viable children and, in its more serious stages, already destroys the child in the womb."

The well-known Professor Forel comments, "Strong persons who begin to drink produce weaker children. . . . A brief review of various human races and their interrelation demonstrates that alcohol has degenerated and annihilated entire tribes, while, on the other hand, even races with a low level of development practicing abstinence are tremendously tough and viable."

In addition, in an economy solely concerned with profits (a capitalistic-interest economy), resulting in a housing shortage, squalor, and unemployment, the genes of the race and nation are continually damaged. In the interest of promoting the general welfare and preventing severely damaging abuses, the state and its citizens have available numerous preventative and curative measures. It is a matter of conscience that both the government and the individual citizen employ these measures before considering a damaging intrusion into the personal right of all people to the inviolability of their body and its parts. Therefore, to protect the reproductive cells against being poisoned and weakened, the fight against the most damaging agents, alcohol and nicotine, has to be conducted with all seriousness.

If, from the standpoint of natural law, we have to deny the state's right to sterilization, we must deny it doubly so to a government that does nothing effective to eliminate alcoholism and nicotine addiction but only takes half-baked measures. Government officials, physicians, judges, teachers, and others have even less of a right to get worked up over sterilization the more they themselves are slaves of alcohol, tobacco, and an unwholesome or unnatural lifestyle. Only those state and church officials have pure and honest intentions who by their own example demonstrate to humanity how to live naturally, in such a way that one's nation and race are not damaged but ennobled and improved!

We consider the struggle against narcotic substances, an unnatural lifestyle, and the capitalistic economy to be the prerequisite to preventing the degeneration of the race. If we continue our habitual ways, the individual, and thereby the race, will deteriorate further and further. Many who are healthy today will be dragged into the whirlpool of degeneration until the entire race is ready for sterilization. Such a protection of the race is laughable and self-condemning. Prevention must come first!

In 1930, the teaching authority of the Church, Pope Pius XI, in his encyclical *Casti connubii*, clearly advocated the view delineated above regarding the impermissibility of sterilization. This encyclical includes the following statements:

> Finally, that pernicious practice must be condemned which closely touches upon the natural right of man to enter matrimony but affects also in a real way the welfare of the offspring. For there are some who over solicitous for the cause of eugenics, not only give salutary counsel for more certainly procuring the strength and health of the future child—which, indeed, is not contrary to right reason—but put eugenics before aims of a higher order, and by public authority wish to prevent from marrying all those whom, even though naturally fit for marriage, they consider, according to the norms and conjectures of their investigations, would, through hereditary transmission, bring forth defective offspring. And more, they wish to legislate to deprive these of that natural faculty by medical action despite

> their unwillingness; and this they do not propose as an infliction of grave punishment under the authority of the state for a crime committed, not to prevent future crimes by guilty persons, but against every right and good they wish the civil authority to arrogate to itself a power over a faculty which it never had and can never legitimately possess.
>
> Those who act in this way are at fault in losing sight of the fact that the family is more sacred than the State and that men are begotten not for the earth and for time, but for Heaven and eternity. Although often these individuals are to be dissuaded from entering into matrimony, certainly it is wrong to brand men with the stigma of crime because they contract marriage, on the ground that, despite the fact that they are in every respect capable of matrimony, they will give birth only to defective children, even though they use all care and diligence.
>
> Public magistrates have no direct power over the bodies of their subjects; therefore, where no crime has taken place and there is no cause present for grave punishment, they can never directly harm, or tamper with the integrity of the body, either for the reasons of eugenics or for any other reason. St. Thomas teaches this when inquiring whether human judges for the sake of preventing future evils can inflict punishment, he admits that the power indeed exists as regards certain other forms of evil, but justly and properly denies it as regards the maiming of the body. "No one who is guiltless may be punished by a human tribunal either by flogging to death, or mutilation, or by beating."[8]

Certainly, the state may not kill or mutilate a convicted criminal.

The position of the Catholic Church about sterilization is clear. It rejects it completely from a Christian moral view. Therefore, no state has the right to prevent the reproduction of mentally impaired persons by sterilization. Even more so, from a Christian standpoint, sterilization of healthy persons at their request has to be rejected as a grave moral offense. By being sterilized such persons wish to enjoy sexual relations but rule out children as an unwanted consequence.

The common welfare can only be realized satisfactorily if the personal rights of the members of society are not violated.

However, regarding the extensive killing by the Nazi state of the incurably ill, the mentally and physically impaired, the deformed, the frail elderly, and those unable to work, we have to say that from the National Socialist viewpoint, the killing of the above is obvious because in the totalitarian

8. Pope Pius XI, *Casti connubii*, paras. 68–70.

state—which is entirely secular and materialistic, whose philosopher is Nietzsche, and which is based on the principle that everything benefiting the state is permissible—the above "racially inferior" groups damage the economy and, therefore, have to be eliminated.

According to the Nazi perspective, only that person has the right to live whose work is useful to the state and whose blood is racially of first quality. Blood, race, and soil are the only criteria of the ethics of a National Socialist, and the will of the Führer is the final, infallible word. He, however, has decided with Nietzsche that everything that is sick, weak, or impaired has to be annihilated. In the eyes of a true Nazi, mercy is an unmanly weakness.

In sharpest opposition to this purely materialistic appraisal of life stands Christianity with its view that only God and not the human being is the master of life and that even the life of the most wretched person is of inestimable value in time and eternity. It also teaches that the life of a mentally retarded, an incurably ill, or a so-called racially inferior person has social significance in that the afflicted person, by patiently bearing his suffering, is setting a good example. Moreover, others can lighten his burden by practicing the works of mercy toward him.

Furthermore, illness, impairment, frailty, and the failing of physical and mental powers are a constant warning that man is only a pilgrim on this earth and that his goal is eternity. At the same time, however, the numerous members of society who are unemployable, handicapped, or sick are a constant and serious indictment that society has failed. Much of this distress and misfortune has to be attributed to alcoholism, nicotine addiction, unrestrained sexual immorality, an unnatural lifestyle, malnutrition, as well as housing squalor and shortage.

By what right does a government simply annihilate those persons it considers impaired but whose conditions, in many respects, it caused itself, instead of being conscious of its own implication in the victims' faulty lifestyle, repairing whatever can still be repaired? Or, should children kill their own parents or have them killed when they become feeble and unable to work—when, according to the Nazi *Weltanschauung*, they become "parasites"?

Moreover, those who believe that in the interest of the race and the community all that is defective and weak should be mercilessly annihilated must consider that when they grow old they themselves could become burdens to society because of their frailty and inability to work—that is, they could suffer the same fate that they now cause others to endure.

The destruction of impaired life, so Christianity teaches, is nothing but murder, which is a sin. The killing of impaired human beings may not be excused as "self-defense," for these persons are not at all unjustly attacking the life or property of the public but, rather, are indebted to others for their life and existence.

A society that permits the killing of impaired individuals or is silent and lets it happen condemns itself and may not call itself Christian. National Socialism utterly rejects a Christian society and declares with its prophet, Nietzsche, "Christianity is a revolt by everything that crawls on the ground against everything lofty. The Gospel of the inferior creates inferiority."[9]

He also wrote, "Everything that is excellent, proud, high-spirited, and, especially, whatever is beautiful is hurtful to the ears and eyes of Christendom. . . . Up to now, Christianity is the greatest misfortune to humanity."[10]

Nietzsche continued, "The Christian movement, as a European development, from the beginning has consisted entirely of the refuse elements of every kind."[11]

National Socialism advanced its claim by appropriating Nietzsche's view: "The first precept of our love of neighbor is: The weak and misfit should perish, and they should be assisted in doing this. What is more harmful than any kind of depravity? It is compassionate action toward the misfit and weak practiced by Christianity."[12]

It is Christ against the Antichrist. These Antichrists, however, are fallible human beings, weighed down by all kinds of passions, vices, and weaknesses, who in their megalomania presume that they may infallibly judge everything and as representatives of the German "master race" do anything they wish without incurring punishment while using the most brutal methods of force at their disposal. The power of National Socialism extends only as far as the brutal means it has available.

It is always a matter of either-or. Either Christ or Antichrist, according to the words of Christ: "He who is not with me is against me; and he who does not gather with me scatters" (Luke 11:23).

7. Teachings about being trained and armed to fight the duel

THE TERMS SELF-PROTECTION AND self-defense have long played an important role in the life of humanity and of nations. The entire previous section,

9. Nietzsche, *Der Antichrist*, 415.
10. Ibid., 431
11. Ibid., 430.
12. Ibid., 360.

in which we explained the views generally held today on the subject, is a part of the larger chapter on "self-defense" and "self-protection."

First of all, self-defense serves to forcibly prevent or ward off an unjust attack on one's life, limb, or property at the moment of the attack. This self-protection often results in the death of the aggressor, but it can also fail so that the victim bears the brunt of it. We explained earlier the views on self-defense held by exponents of ethics based on natural law, reason, and Christian morality.

Some people claim that the duel is another form of permissible self-protection. However, Christian moral philosophers and theologians reject the duel as unethical and refute the reasons presented in support of it.

The duel is single combat in order to achieve satisfaction for an actual or imaginary insult to one's honor, with time, place, and the type of lethal weapon to be used agreed upon in advance.

Those who justify the duel demand and take for granted that the opponents know how to handle the weapons usually employed. Moreover, those who believe in the right to self-defense advocate that everyone be trained in the use of weapons and be armed, because anyone who wants to successfully repel a possible aggressor not only has to be able to use lethal weapons but also has to carry them with him at all times.

Those who favor the duel refer to history, pointing out that in Roman and German regions the courts at times ordered that a dispute be settled by the contenders fighting one another. In the course of time the view was developed in certain circles—in the military, among the nobility, and in student societies—that it is the duty of a trained and armed man to challenge to a duel the person who insulted his honor, or else he would be judged to be dishonorable and cowardly, expelled from his circle and treated with contempt. In order to maintain the respect of his peers the insulted person was forced to seek satisfaction of his honor by means of a duel. This view, handed down from generation to generation without being questioned, led slowly to the conviction that the duel is a suitable method by which to defend and restore one's injured honor. Hand in hand with this it was taught that it is a man's duty to be trained and armed to fight and that no one could be a real man without training. This ability would also serve to safeguard justice and to protect him, his family, and his homeland.

Whoever justifies the right and especially the duty of self-defense logically also has to support the right and, in certain situations, the duty of every person to bear arms and to be able to use them, as advocates of general conscription maintain. In the Nazi state even children were taught to use weapons, and boys were allowed to carry a sword.

The teaching of Christian theologians and moral philosophers about the duel is expressed in this statement: Dueling is forbidden by ethics based on natural law and reason and by Christian moral law. Yet some Christian theologians, despite the condemnation of the duel by several popes (Nicholas I, Stephen VI, Alexander II, Celestine III, Innocent III—all in the ninth century) and by the Council of Trent, defended the viewpoint that it cannot be proved purely by reason that the duel is not permissible in certain circumstances. In 1890 the Roman *S. Congregatio Concilii* ruled that dueling between students was subject to church penalties.

The following will prove that in every case dueling is a totally inappropriate method of redressing an actual or imagined insult to one's honor: Natural law prohibits every action that endangers one's own life or that of another because every human being is obligated to preserve his life, his health, and the inviolability of his body by appropriate means.

Furthermore, each person is obligated by natural law not to endanger in any way the body, life, or health of his fellow human being. As a beneficiary of his life, no person may expose it, intentionally or unintentionally, to mortal danger, nor may he endanger the life of another. Dueling is not justified self-defense; rather, both participants have agreed to intentionally endanger the life of the other. The death of the person who uttered the insult does not restore the honor of the insulted any more than does the death of the latter, for frequently one has to expect that the insulted person will die. The outcome of a duel is decided by technique, skill, and chance.

The contention that the duel constitutes self-defense is not valid, for neither one of the dueling parties is in a situation of having to defend himself because both intend to engage in single combat and thereby are putting life and limb in danger. Each of the parties intends to harm the opponent.

The insulted honor can only be restored effectively by a retraction, that is, when the person who issued the insult confers honor on the offended person. Whoever loses his life in a duel indirectly commits suicide because he voluntarily endangered his life without sufficient reason; and whoever slays his opponent is guilty of unjust killing. Therefore, governments and state authorities permitting duels are implicated in the offense and its resulting harm.

To conclude, the duel is unethical because it violates natural law. Therefore, one may not choose this means, regardless of how good are its intended ends, for the noblest ends never justify unethical means.

8. Teachings about the death penalty

Exponents of ethics based on natural law and reason as well as many Christian moralists believe that the highest authority of the state—because of its right to punish granted by natural law—has the right to impose the death penalty, primarily for murder.

To justify the death penalty they point out that only by inflicting it for certain crimes can the public welfare of the state and the human community be maintained. Because the general welfare ranks above private welfare, persons who seriously endanger the former have to be eliminated, that is, killed. For the death penalty, as well as other punishments, has these objectives: atonement for breaking the law, prevention, deterrent, and rehabilitation.

The various defenders of the death penalty—there have been and still are Christian moral theologians who deny that the death penalty is legal or appropriate—primarily try to prove that the threat of this penalty effectively deters many criminals and thus prevents crimes; and, furthermore, that if the death penalty is imposed for certain serious crimes, it serves as a guarantee that the person so punished can no longer do harm, which would be a possibility if he were kept alive and regained his freedom.

Proponents of the death penalty regard the killing of a criminal as a kind of self-defense and thus an obligation of the state on behalf of society. They view this legalized murder as a "lesser evil," compared with the "greater evil" that society would suffer if the state's authority to punish by death were restricted to cases in which there is absolutely no possibility of error.

Since many persons are deterred from committing crimes only by the fear of extreme punishments, particularly the death penalty, this ultimate form of punishment is seen as appropriate, and in fact necessary, since without it the life and property of citizens would not be sufficiently protected. It would be totally misguided only to threaten with the death penalty but not to impose it.

The decision of which crime should be punished with capital punishment must be made by state authorities only after carefully examining the circumstances. There always has to be a proportionate relationship between the crime and the punishment. Also, one has to guard against every form of sentimentality. The focus should be on the demands of justice, in light of the harm that the crime caused the general welfare, in order to see in the threat of and occasional imposition of the death penalty an appropriate and necessary method of administering justice.

Christian theologians like to quote the Old Testament, which abounds in the threat and imposition of the death penalty for many kinds of crimes. The Bible tells us that in the course of history, on the order of Yahweh, Jewish officials punitively killed hundreds of thousands in the name of religion, while thousands of others were slaughtered during wars. Readers of the Old Testament often shudder at the harshness in the administration of justice of the Jewish law, which, by means of terror, was able to deter some, but far from all, from committing crimes.

However, those favoring the death penalty are embarrassed when asked to find evidence in the New Testament that the death penalty is permitted. The principal passage they cite again and again is Paul's Letter to the Romans 13:1–7:

> Everyone is to obey the governing authorities, because there is no authority except from God and so whatever authorities exist have been appointed by God. So anyone who disobeys an authority is rebelling against God's ordinance; and rebels must expect to receive the condemnation they deserve. Magistrates bring fear not to those who do good, but to those who do evil. So if you want to live with no fear of authority, live honestly and you will have its approval; it is there to serve God for you and for your good. But if you do wrong, then you may well be afraid; because it is not for nothing that the symbol of authority is the sword; it is there to serve God, too, as his avenger, to bring retribution to wrongdoers. You must be obedient, therefore, not only because of this retribution, but also for conscience's sake. And this is why you should pay taxes, too, because the authorities are all serving God as his agents, even while they are busily occupied with that particular task. Pay to each one what is due each: taxes to the one to whom tax is due, tolls to the one to whom tolls are due, respect to the one to whom respect is due, and honor to the one to whom honor is due.

However, we would like to cite the verses that follow directly: "The only thing you should owe to anyone is love for one another, for to love the other person is to fulfill the law. All these: *You shall not commit adultery, You shall not kill, You shall not steal, You shall not covet*, and all the other commandments that there are, are summed up in this single phrase: *You must love your neighbor as yourself.* Love can cause no harm to your neighbor, and so love is the fulfillment of the law" (Rom 13:8–10).

9. Teachings about war, preparations for war, and conscription

In this section we will examine how Christian moral theologians answer the question, Does the state have the authority to defend and protect itself with violent means against an unjust, violent attack, that is, to counter it with weapons, to wage war?

This question can have diverse answers, according to one's attitude toward self-defense. Whoever believes in the right to self-defense logically grants the state the right, in certain circumstances, to arm its citizens and to wage war. However, whoever denies the right to self-defense logically has to reject war and everything connected with it, namely, arming the citizenry and compulsory military service.

However, one has to examine—from the perspective of ethics based on natural law, reason, and Christian revelation—whether the assumptions and conditions listed by those who defend the permissibility of war actually exist in a specific war. For if it can be proved that each war is reprehensible, it may not be waged under any circumstances. Since we are going to look at this more closely in the second part of our analysis, here we will only summarize without criticizing the teachings of Christian moral theologians on war. It is the generally accepted way of thinking, made sacred by being passed from generation to generation, which no one dares to criticize. This will not prevent us from examining it thoroughly, however.

Every human being, so begins the reasoning, has the right granted by natural law to life, health, and justly acquired property, especially such property necessary to maintain his life. Therefore, every person has the right to use violence to defend his life, limb, and property if no other means is available to ward off the aggressor; but in order to be just, this defense must only be sufficient to ward off the attacker. If the latter loses his life, it is his own fault because no one has the right to contest, or take by force, another's God-given right to life and property.

Whatever applies to the individual in terms of self-defense also applies to the state, for whatever is an individual's natural right is likewise the right of those united into a community. Therefore, in the case of a violent, unjust attack against a state, it has the right, granted by natural law, to use violent means to ward off the attack. Those Christians who justify war continue to emphasize, however, that every individual, as well as every state, may use violent means in defense only at the moment of an attack that cannot be averted or warded off through other methods. Furthermore, in a case of self-defense, only as much force as is absolutely necessary may be used at that moment, and only as defense.

The attitude toward war and its aims derives from this claim to self-defense. It is reasoned that every state has to protect the life and property of its citizens and to ensure justice and safety; therefore, it has the right to use any and all means to achieve these aims, and all other states have to respect this right. If another nation violates this right, the attacked state has the right to defend itself with appropriate forceful means.

However, it is obvious that before undertaking a bloody defense every nation has to try to resolve the conflict through negotiations. Only if all other means fail may war be waged.

Because every war is dreadful, it has to be prevented at any price. Therefore, the nation that starts a war incurs a heavy responsibility, because in war masses of armed men are pitted against each other, generating unspeakable horrors of every kind. We have only to consider the vast destruction of life and culture. The saddest part is that every war is unjust, that is, sinful, on at least one side. However, it can be unjust for every nation taking part.

When regarded objectively, one side always wages war unjustly, and therefore its citizens are conscience-bound to refuse military service. However, regarded subjectively, it is possible that because of ignorance or an erring conscience each warring side believes that it is fighting a just war.

To emphasize it once more, only one side can wage a just war, namely, the one that did not start the war and therefore is only defending itself. The aggressor, and in every war there is at least one, is always wrong.

Therefore, according to those Christians who justify war, only a defensive war fought in the interest of the general welfare can be a just war; and an attack aimed at forestalling another country's planned aggression is likewise viewed as a defensive war because the general welfare is seriously threatened.

For a war to be a "just defensive war," those who permit war demand that the following conditions be met:

1. The war has to be declared by the highest legitimate authority of a state.

2. A just cause has to exist, namely, a grave injustice that harms the existence and function of the state and which cannot be averted by any other means.

3. The war has to be waged with the right intention. Therefore, a war fought only for revenge, or one waged with the objective of seizing

territory, is never a "just defensive war." The right intention always has to fit into the framework of self-defense.

4. The advantages and good achieved through war clearly have to exceed the evil and horror caused by war. In other words, a defensive war, meeting all the above conditions, has to result in more good than harm for the defending state.

Every one of the above requirements advanced by supporters of a "just defensive war" has to be present. If only one condition is lacking, the war cannot qualify as just defensive. It is further taught that if a reasonable doubt exists whether a war is just or not, that war may not be waged. For whoever is willing to wage war, regardless of whether or not that war is a "just defensive war," commits a grave sin.

The fact that proponents of the "just defensive war" teach that it is not permissible to kill anyone who is not an aggressor—that is, anyone who does not participate in war, such as children, women, the aged, the ill, or prisoners—does not require further proof.

The "just defensive war," according to its supporters, is the final, indispensable, and essential method of maintaining order and security among nations. Aside from it there exists no effective method of achieving justice for an unjustly attacked state whose existence or proper function is threatened by another state. However, through international agreements attempts are made to wage war as "humanely" as possible, as the expression goes.

Those who are for war logically also support the production of armaments, instruments needed to kill and to destroy. Furthermore, they call for and consider it self-evident that the state maintain a standing army, which means that people have to be trained to use weapons and, at all times, be prepared and willing to kill and destroy on command. Governments of nations are also granted the right to legally procure all means to wage war and, therefore, to make it obligatory for every citizen to prepare for and wage war. These demands are substantiated by the claim that it is the duty of every citizen to promote the general welfare and to subordinate his personal welfare to that of the community.

This is how it happened that the representatives of the Christian churches, in a manner of speaking, placed their religious institution at the disposal of the state, and war received a moral and religious consecration. Is it not true that church authorities often use the expression "holy war"? In fact, soldiers are bound by oath to kill and destroy the enemy en masse, in blind obedience on command. It is indeed in blind obedience, for the decision and judgment whether and how war should be waged and whether a particular war is a "just defensive war" does not belong to the common man but to the state.

However, moral theologians of an older Christian school did not know anything about universal compulsory military service, which was devised only as recently as the French Revolution but since then has been instituted in nearly every country of the world, and today even the churches silently approve of it. For with only very few exceptions there exists no official objection to conscription. If, however, Christian churches would regard conscription as morally impermissible, their clergy and theologians would have to object, without fail, to the swearing in of their faithful who are forced into the military. On the contrary: in many places, parade units in complete military gear are permitted to march in Corpus Christi processions, with the soldiers carrying weapons designed to murder and destroy. Also, as of today, we do not know of one instance where clergy members of the various Christian churches have raised a clear and solemn objection to conscientious objectors being shot on the spot like criminals. In other words, so far, the churches have not officially protested against compulsory military service. Therefore, one has to assume that they have no misgivings about it. And if only a handful of churchmen occasionally object to conscription, the question is left unanswered for the faithful. Millions and millions of sincere Christians are awaiting a clear decision from the Catholic teaching authority to resolve the serious doubts of their conscience.

We have to draw the following conclusion about universal compulsory military service: The actual attitude of the Catholic Church and other Christian churches, for more than a hundred years, is that their leaders and clergy generally have not objected to conscription. To the best of our knowledge, as of today, no official position by the teaching authority of the Catholic Church exists on this issue.

Christian church leaders—with only a handful of exceptions—and the people whom they shepherd and who listen to them hold this view: *Si vis pacem, para bellum* (if you want peace, prepare for war).

Therefore, many consider armaments, compulsory military service, and war the final ethical means to keep peace among nations, and thus they regard preparations for war and conscription as necessary and effective.

Additional proof of the expression "if you want peace, prepare for war" are the chaplains whom, by agreement, churches continue to furnish the military and who usually are subordinated to a military bishop; the blessing by clergymen of soldiers marching to war and of their weapons; and the "celebrations of rejoicing" arranged by the churches after a victory of their country's armies. All the bells are rung, and before festively decorated altars the *Te Deum* ("Holy God we praise Thy name") is sung in rejoicing, as happened in Italy after her victory in the predatory war against Abyssinia and all over Germany after the destruction of Poland in the Second World War.

So much for the position of clergymen and theologians on these questions. We will return to these issues in the second part of this analysis and will discuss our point of view in more detail.

10. Teachings about total war

WE HAVE ALREADY MENTIONED that those who teach Christian ethics and morals always state clearly that neither the attacking side nor the defending side may ever kill noncombatants—that is, children, women, the ill, prisoners, and the wounded. While this seems logical to those who approve of defensive war, what about the supporters of total war? Do they believe that the entire territory of a nation waging war should be regarded as enemy territory and thus everybody indiscriminately slain and everything destroyed? Let us be clear what total war is.

The concept of total war developed only during the last few decades and is a result of modern warfare, which has managed to make technology, the economy, politics, science, and even religion, that is, the entire population and life of the state, entirely subservient to war.

The nation that wages a total war intends the complete destruction of the enemy. Only totalitarian states are able to wage a total war. They claim that the state is omnipotent and that its supreme authority can make use of everything: life and limb, livelihood and property, work and the length of the workday, the food supply, recreation, the education of children, science and art, the practice of religion, etc. The citizens of a totalitarian state exist only for the sake of the state. Absolutely everything, the individual as well as the entire nation, has to serve the nation only and to submit to its orders without objecting. The totalitarian government can place the entire state, including all of its citizens, in the service of war, employing forceful means so that everyone, either directly or indirectly, has to work for war or to produce arms.

In fact, we experienced with revulsion how National Socialism, because of its truly brilliant organization and its appallingly brutal methods, which it employed without scruples to meet its objectives, forced the entire

Greater German Reich, with its 85 million people, the other Axis powers, and the defeated nations and their peoples into the service of war. Even the Nazi demand of "children at any price" was aimed to produce soldiers, and the sole purpose of the Nazi training of youth was to militarize all of Germany's young people, beginning with the children.

The fact that total war causes everyone and everything else to suffer is of no concern to the supporters of total war since its aim is to mercilessly defeat the enemy, be it on the fighting front or at home. The entire homeland—women, children, the aged, and anyone who is still able to contribute in any way—has to work and sacrifice for the war and its needs. The state and its entire organization form a single front—united, for better or worse—which is solely engaged in the killing and destroying of whomever the leaders designate as the enemy.

It is no wonder that the opponent likewise advances with his weapons against this nation waging total war, that is, blankets the land with bombs. Did not Hitler, who was called the "*einmalige Führer*" (non-reoccurring) and "the greatest commander in history," declare during World War II, "I will eradicate their cities," which means to wipe them and all of their inhabitants from the face of the Earth? In another speech he said, "In this war there are neither victors nor defeated, but only survivors and destroyed."

Consequently, what counts in total war is who destroys the opponent first, whereby no distinction is drawn between the actual fighting front and the civilian infrastructure working for the war.

After this brief explanation of total war, it may not come as a surprise that Christian theologians and moralists, just as they reject the totalitarian state as a serious offense against natural law and Christian revelation, strongly condemn total war and label it a serious moral error. They are correct in their assessment that total war exceeds all limits of a just defense because its object is the annihilation of the opponent and disregards all human rights guaranteed by natural law.

However, those who approve of the "just defensive war" do not consider that, without wishing to do so, they are sanctioning total war and viewing it as morally permissible. For if the aggressor state wages total war without any moral restraints, one cannot expect that the attacked nation will allow itself to be annihilated. Within the parameters of the just war theory, one has to acknowledge the attacked nation's right to likewise threaten total war and to wage it mercilessly, with the objective of destroying the enemy before it itself is annihilated. Should the aggressor nation be totally destroyed in the process, it has only itself to blame—so say the supporters of self-defense.

If one state wages total war and another responds likewise, it has to be accepted as a "lesser evil," even if it seems most inhumane, because otherwise the latter would have no chance of victory.

It suffices here to point out that Christian theologians and moral philosophers reject, although not logically, total war as being morally impermissible. We, however, who regard every war as immoral do not feel it necessary to grapple with the exponents of total war, but because of the importance of the question will thoroughly examine it later.

11. Teachings about the killing of animals

The generally accepted teachings of Christian churches about the proper attitude that human beings should have toward animals can be summarized thus: God created the animals for his glory and for the benefit of man, the king of creation. In his goodness, God also takes care of the animals like a father. Animals have a soul; they have vegetative and sentient abilities that serve their perception and desires. Therefore, animals possess consciousness, feel joy and pain, and seek to be happy.

However, since the animal soul is not immortal, as opposed to the spiritual soul of human beings, animals cannot claim or assert rights before mankind, nor do they have any responsibilities before the law. Animals act neither ethically nor unethically and therefore are not responsible to anyone for their behavior. They behave according to their natural instincts.

This, however, does not mean that man should be indifferent toward animals. Rather, he should ensure that all animals in his care are healthy and should not treat them cruelly or abuse them because, in doing so, his heart hardens, likely making it easier to treat his fellow human beings similarly.

Furthermore, it is taught that it is permissible to kill an animal if one is attacked, threatened, or harmed by it, or if the animal is needed for food or other necessities of life. Consequently, most Christian theologians and teachers of ethics defend vivisection because they deem it necessary "in the interest of science" and "in the interest of suffering humanity." We are going to discuss this topic in more detail in the second part of our work and substantiate our view, which differs on many points.

PART II

Our position regarding the teachings and views of exponents of moral philosophy based on natural law and reason and Catholic (Christian) teachings of faith and morals about the commandment "You shall not kill" as presented in Part I

THE QUESTION WE ARE going to discuss in the second part of this work is, How should one view the teachings of Christian theologians and teachers of moral philosophy regarding the commandment "You shall not kill," which we presented in the first part? Does a Catholic Christian simply have to accept and observe these teachings, or may he hold another, differing view?

First of all, the following firmly applies for Catholic Christians: Whatever the Church holds as dogma, that is, a belief revealed by God, whether or not it is defined by her teaching authority, every Catholic has to accept as true, that is, to accept on faith. If he does not do so, he is likely to become a heretic who misleads others and who by this conscious rejection separates himself from the Church community.

However, we know that by far not everything the Catholic Church teaches and which the teaching authority given by Christ demands acceptance is considered a dogma. The teaching authority, in deciding whether a particular belief is a dogma or not, requires that it be infallible, that is, based on God's revelation. Here the sentence "*Roma locuta, causa finita*" (when Rome has spoken, the matter is concluded) applies. If Rome, that is the infallible teaching authority, has rendered a decision, all arguments and opinions are ended, and the Catholic Christian is obligated to accept this dogma on faith. It is another matter with teachings that have not been declared to be infallible, however.

Therefore, we have to determine whether the commandment "You shall not kill" is a revealed teaching and, therefore, has to be accepted on faith, or whether there exist disputable issues within Catholic ranks about which every person may hold his own opinion without endangering the orthodoxy of his faith.

1. Principles and rules that those who judge the teachings and opinions of Christian theologians and moral philosophers have to observe

THE TEACHING AUTHORITY OF the Church has at times entered into these disputes of opinions and, for the protection of Christian revelation, has rendered decisions that, while not infallible, Catholics have to accept. In the course of the free expression of opinions about disputed questions or at the appearance of philosophical or theological errors, it has been and continues to be necessary to declare certain views and tenets binding for Catholics and to condemn other opinions. All of this has the objective of guarding, teaching, and interpreting God's treasure of teachings on faith and morals for which Christ instituted the teaching authority.

There are "theological conclusions" about revealed truth, so-called *conclusiones theologicae*, which Catholics have to accept as "bordering on faith" (*fidei proximum*) because deviating from them would lead to errors in belief. Furthermore, there are tenets and teachings that do not give rise to doubts and are accepted as "common and universally valid teachings of the entire Catholic Church" (*sententiae communes*), so that it would be foolhardy to deviate from them. Other truths are adhered to by the teaching authority as "sure opinions" (*sententiae certae*); still others are described as "probable opinions" (*sententiae probabiles*) whose probability depends on the force of proof. Furthermore, the teaching authority has condemned a number of teachings and opinions as "heretical" (*sententiae herticae*) because they contradict revealed truths, that is, they deny them, while others are repudiated as "bordering on heresy" (*haeresi proximum*). Others are emphatically rejected as "false opinions" (*sententiae falsae*), "erroneous tenets" (*sententiae erroneae*), "improbable views" (*sententiae improbaliles*), and "faith damaging views" (*piarum aurium offensivum*). Faithful Catholics are bound by conscience to accept and obey these decisions of the teaching authority.

Besides these variously designated decisions, there are many others, often contradictory teachings and opinions, which can be described as "disputed questions." Because the teaching authority has not yet made a decision about them, Catholics are free to hold whatever opinion they consider to be correct.

In these "disputed questions" the various comments of the teaching authority apply. (Note the pronouncements of various popes on this matter.) On the "disputed questions," where opinions often clash, it is permitted to follow that particular accepted authority (theologian, ecclesiastical author, etc.) whose view appears to be the most plausible or to form one's own, well-founded view. The opinion of an ecclesiastical author counts only as much as the proof he can provide.

Keeping the above guidelines in mind, we are going to state our position on the previously advanced views of Christian theologians and teachers of moral philosophy regarding the commandment "You shall not kill" and will be particularly interested in the teachings about war. We are going to have to prove whether these teachings and views constitute dogma, that is, whether they are true and universal, or whether they are still "disputed questions." If they are unsettled issues, we are permitted to present our own, differing opinion. It is then the duty of the Church's teaching authority to examine the validity of our reasoning and to render a decision, or if it prefers, not to make a final decision at that time. In the latter instance, we clearly have the right to maintain and disseminate our opinion but may not accuse or charge with heresy those who hold differing views.

We would like to point out that in certain cases even teachings that the Church has declared to be universally true can become disputed—for example, the view that the sun revolves around the earth, which prior to Galileo was taught by referring to Holy Scripture, until it was proved that the earth actually moves around the sun. Also, at one time the Church justified the extreme measures of the Inquisition, including the killing of "heretics" and "witches." Today no theologian would dare to defend these teachings as universally true and Christian.

2. Our position regarding the teachings of Christian theologians and moral philosophers, as presented in Part I, Sections 1–4 and 6–7

THE ISSUES DISCUSSED IN the above-listed sections, with the exception of the teachings about self-defense in section 7, are not "disputed questions." They are the basic views and positions of the Catholic Church with special consideration of the fact that there is no contradiction, nor can there be, between the natural and the supernatural or between knowledge and faith. As a faithful Catholic, we share these views and positions, which are truths forming the basis for all our further remarks about the commandment "You shall not kill."

"You shall not kill" is literally a revealed moral demand made by God. Since the interpretation of all teachings on faith and morals is reserved to the Church's teaching authority, this also applies to this commandment. Of course, the interpretation has to be consistent with other revealed teachings and commandments. However, the interpretation of some teachings and demands of the Bible are still disputed; and since they are, a Catholic Christian is free to accept any one of the various opinions. A number of questions connected with and concerning the commandment "You shall not kill" are disputed questions.

To us the answer to whether the commandment "You shall not kill" is absolute or whether there can be exceptions is an undecided issue, even though today the commonly held opinion within the Catholic Church is that that there can be exceptions. Since these are explicitly taught in catechisms, which state that in certain circumstances it is permitted to kill, one takes a risk when voicing the opposite view.

Today, every student of Catholic theology and morals is taught that, if necessary, one may kill in self-defense, that in certain cases self-defense is a duty even, that there are "just defensive wars" in which a soldier may kill, and that the state has the right to impose the death penalty for certain crimes. And yet, our conscience urges us to ask, is it not high time to thoroughly scrutinize these teachings, even if there is a risk in doing so?

We dare to raise this question because within Catholic circles voices that agree with our viewpoint are being raised again and again. Therefore, we are calling into question the reasoning presented by supporters of self-defense, the "just defensive war," and the death penalty but emphasize that we are doing so in full recognition of the principle that the Church's teaching authority has to render the final decision about disputed questions. We consider it a duty of conscience to raise these issues before the public because in many circles doubts are being expressed about the justification for mass killing, a consequence of every (especially modern) war. Ordinary people continue to voice demands that the Catholic Church should forbid war and conscription and speak out against the death penalty. Convinced that this is an important and serious matter, we are going to tackle the explanation of and reasoning for our views, which differ in many fundamental points from the opinions commonly held today. We will present the result of our intensive studies, which have long occupied us, but especially since the First World War. Over several decades we have wrestled with these questions in many speeches, in various books and brochures, in newspaper articles, and especially in university lectures in moral theology and sociology classes.

3. Our position regarding the teachings about self-defense and military training

If the great commandment "You shall not kill" were to have an exception, it would surely be in the case of self-defense, provided that the right or duty of self-defense could be proved beyond a doubt. Also, an exception to this commandment could be made if God had explicitly given his permission to kill another person in special circumstances—for example, if he had permitted the imposition of the death penalty.

In this section we are going to grapple thoroughly with the issue of self-defense. In section 5 of Part I, we presented what is currently taught in all Catholic ethics and moral theology books and in catechisms.

If one recalls what was said above and considers merely how human reason justifies killing in self-defense, it would be difficult to defend an opposite view. For it seems to be almost self-evident that in situations of one life against another, the unjustly attacked person has the right to defend himself and, if he cannot protect himself otherwise, even has the right to kill the aggressor; and it is always noted that the attacker has only himself to blame if he loses his life in the process.

If the question of self-defense were simply about what is natural, it would be fruitless to deny to someone who considers only the natural and not the supernatural the right to defend himself. However, we have to view this as a supernatural issue, that is, from a Christian perspective, because humanity does not live only in a state of nature but also in a state of redemption made possible by Christ.

As Christians we have to consult revelation if we do not want to err, but the advocates of self-defense are greatly embarrassed when we ask them to support their views with the Gospels. The Old Testament, which is often cited regarding these questions, is no longer applicable to this particular one because Christ replaced the Old Testament, which often emphasized harsh, merciless, and violent means, with the New Testament, that of love, with its special emphasis on the love of enemies. We often read, "You have heard how it was said . . . but I say this to you . . ."

In place of the various Old Testament commandments on retaliation—"eye for eye, tooth for tooth, hand for hand, foot for foot, burn for burn, wound for wound, stroke for stroke" (Exod 21:24–25), or "anyone who by violence causes a death must be put to death" (Exod 21:12), or "anyone who strikes father or mother will be put to death" (Exod 21:15), or "anyone who abducts a person, whether this person has since been sold or still is held, will be put to death" (Exod 21:16)—Christ has given a new commandment. Christ demands,

> You have heard how it was said: *Eye for eye and tooth for tooth.* But I say this to you: offer no resistance to the wicked. On the contrary, if anyone hits you on the right cheek, offer him the other as well; if someone wishes to go to law with you to get your tunic, let him have your cloak as well. And if anyone requires you to go one mile, go two miles with him. Give to anyone who asks you, and if anyone wants to borrow, do not turn away. You have heard how it was said, *You will love your neighbor* and hate your enemy. But I say this to you, love your enemies and pray for those who persecute you; so that you may be children of your Father in heaven, for he causes his sun to rise on the bad as well as the good, and sends down rain to fall on the upright and the wicked alike. For if you love those who love you, what reward will you get? Do not even the tax collectors do as much? And if you save your greetings for your brothers, are you doing anything exceptional? Do not even the gentiles do as much? (Matt 5:38–47)

It is clear from the above that Christ does not approve of the right of self-defense. A true disciple of Christ should not, may not, defend himself against an aggressor. This is not merely good advice but a demand, a commandment. Likewise, do not defend yourself against someone who takes your property, even if you really need it, as someone living in the desert needs his coat to use as a blanket in the cold of night. Why all of this?

This is the reason Jesus Christ gives: "Love your enemies and pray for those who persecute you; so that you may be children of your Father in heaven."

In every case the great commandment to love your enemy, which is a strict demand, not a mere suggestion, applies. Being a child of God depends on this commandment. Therefore, whoever does not love his enemy as Christ demands, and whoever defends himself forcibly in order to protect his life, limb, or property and in the process kills the aggressor, may not say that he is a child of the heavenly Father, as every Christian should be. Or does he love the enemy or do good to him when he kills him?

However, those Christian moral philosophers and theologians who approve of self-defense grant the right of killing one's aggressor if one cannot otherwise defend oneself. They further teach that you may defend yourself forcibly if someone strikes you on the cheek or takes your coat or tunic; and if the attacker loses his life, you have not committed a wrong; he has to blame himself.

Christ demands exactly the opposite of what advocates of self-defense consider to be morally permissible. Do they regard the Sermon on the Mount as merely good advice and not as a strict and binding commandment for all followers of Christ? Or was Jesus only offering a suggestion when he commanded that his followers not resist the wicked, or when he told his disciples, "Love your enemies and do good to them, and lend without any hope of return" (Luke 6:35)? We ask once again, is one doing good or loving one's "enemy" if one mutilates or even kills him? Christ says, "Do not resist evil." If one defends oneself forcibly against an aggressor, one is thereby resisting evil.

To resist or not to resist? Which is the better course? Without doubt, the better course is what Christ requires: Do not resist. Be nonviolent. If this is so, the advocates of self-defense are wrong in saying one may kill an attacker if it is necessary, and we are right in maintaining that God's commandment "You shall not [you may not] kill" can have no exceptions—and therefore a true Christian may not kill his attacker. For a disciple of Christ not to defend himself, not to use violence, is not merely a matter for his own discretion but a serious obligation of conscience, and to do so is to be a saint and a hero. Every Christian should strive to become a saint and hero, because to the command not to resist evil and to love one's enemy Christ added, "You must therefore be perfect, just as your heavenly Father is perfect" (Matt 5:48). He also said, "Be compassionate as your Father is compassionate" (Luke 6:36). These are commands and not merely advice we may follow if convenient but not heed if inconvenient.

In order to make our position on self-defense and other questions mentioned above more understandable, we have to look at the great commandment of love, which includes all people, friend and foe alike, with special emphasis on the love of enemies. Christian teachers of morality and theologians always have to align themselves with this commandment in order to prove the correctness of the demands of ethics based on natural law and reason they advance, because whatever conflicts with Christ's command to love God and neighbor can never be consistent with natural law and ethics.

We are going to quote the most compelling passages of Holy Scripture, including the Old Testament, that forbid revenge and enmity. While they speak for themselves, taken as a whole, they shed a clear light on all the questions we will touch on.

- You will not exact vengeance on, or bear any sort of grudge against, the members of your race, but will love your neighbor as yourself. (Lev 19:18)
- Do not say, "I shall repay evil." (Prov 20:22)
- Should your enemy fall, do not rejoice, when he stumbles do not let your heart exult . . . (Prov 24:17)
- If your enemy is hungry, give him something to eat; if thirsty, something to drink. By this you will be heaping red-hot coals on his head, and Yahweh will reward you. (Prov 25:21–22)
- Do not resent your neighbor's every offense, and never act in a fit of passion. (Sir 10:6)
- Remember the last things, and stop hating. . . . Remember the commandments, and do not bear your fellow ill-will, remember the covenant of the Most High, and ignore the offense. (Sir 28:6–8)
- Whoever exacts vengeance will experience the vengeance of the Lord, who keeps strict account of sin. Pardon your neighbor any wrongs done to you, and when you pray, your sins will be forgiven. (Sir 28:1–2)
- Never try to get revenge: leave that, my dear friends, to the Retribution. As scripture says: *Vengeance is mine—I will pay them back*, the Lord promises. And more: *If your enemy is hungry, give him something to eat; if thirsty, something to drink. By this, you will be heaping red-hot coals on his head.* (Rom 12:19–20)

- Anyone who hates his brother is a murderer, and you are well aware that no murderer has eternal life remaining in him. (1 John 3:15)
- Anyone who says "I love God" and hates his brother, is a liar. (1 John 4:20)
- "But I say this to you, anyone who is angry with a brother will answer for it before the court; anyone who calls a brother 'Fool' will answer for it before the Sanhedrin; and anyone who calls him 'Traitor' will answer for it in hell fire. So then, if you are bringing your offering to the altar and there remember that your brother has something against you, leave your offering there before the altar, go and be reconciled with your brother first, and then come back and present your offering. Come to terms with your opponent in good time while you are still on the way to the court with him, or he may hand you over to the judge and the judge to the officer, and you will be thrown into prison. In truth I tell you, you will not get out till you have paid the last penny." (Matt 5:21–26)

The following passages of the New Testament make the love of enemy a strict obligation:

- "You have heard how it was said, You will love your neighbor and hate your enemy. But I say this to you, love your enemies and pray for those who persecute you; so that you may be children of your Father in heaven, for he causes his sun to rise on the bad as well as the good, and sends down rain to fall on the upright and the wicked alike." (Matt 5:43–45)
- "Yes, if you forgive others their failings, your heavenly Father will forgive you yours; but if you do not forgive others, your Father will not forgive your failings either." (Matt 6:14–15)
- Then Peter went up to him and said, "Lord, how often must I forgive my brother if he wrongs me. As often as seven times?" Jesus answered, "Not seven, I tell you, but seventy-seven times." (Matt 18:21–22)
- "Were you not bound, then, to have pity on your fellow-servant just as I had pity on you?" (Matt 18:33)
- "And when you stand in prayer, forgive whatever you have against anybody, so that your Father in heaven may forgive your failings too." (Mark 11:25–26)
- "So you should pray like this . . . forgive us our debts as we have forgiven those who are in debt to us." (Matt 6:9, 11–12)

- "Love your enemies, do good to those who hate you, bless those who curse you, pray for those who treat you badly. To anyone who slaps you on one cheek, present the other cheek as well; to anyone who takes your cloak from you, do not refuse your tunic." (Luke 6:27–29)
- ". . . all who draw the sword will die by the sword." (Matt 26:52)
- Bless your persecutors; never curse them, bless them. (Rom 12:14)
- . . . never let the sun set on your anger . . . (Eph 4:26)
- Make sure that people do not try to repay evil for evil; always aim at what is best for each other and for everyone. (1 Thess 5:15)
- Never repay one wrong with another, or one abusive word with another; instead, repay with a blessing. That is what you are called to do, so that you inherit a blessing. (1 Pet 3:9–10)
- Do not be mastered by evil, but master evil with good. (Rom 12:21)
- "So always treat others as you would like them to treat you; that is the Law and the Prophets." (Matt 7:12)
- "You shall love your neighbor as yourself." (Matt 19:19)
- "The second resembles it: 'You must love your neighbor as yourself.' On these two commandments hang the whole Law, and the Prophets too." (Matt 22:39–40)
- ". . . you must love the Lord your God with all your heart, with all your soul, with all your mind and with all your strength. The second is this: You must love your neighbor as yourself. There is no commandment greater than these." (Mark 12:30–31)
- "I give you a new commandment: love one another; you must love one another just as I have loved you. It is by your love for one another that everyone will recognize you as my disciples." (John 13:34–35)
- "This is my commandment: love one another, as I have loved you." (John 15:12)
- "My command to you is to love one another." (John 15:17)
- The only thing you should owe to anyone is love for one another, for to love the other person is to fulfill the law. All these: *You shall not commit adultery, You shall not kill, You shall not steal, You shall not covet*, and all the other commandments that there are, are summed up in this single phrase: *You must love your neighbor as yourself*. Love can cause no harm to your neighbor, and so love is the fulfillment of the Law. (Rom 13:8–10)

- . . . be servants to one another in love, since the whole of the Law is summarized in the one commandment: *You must love your neighbor as yourself.* (Gal 5:13–14)
- Well, the right thing to do is to keep the supreme Law of scripture: *you will love your neighbor as yourself*; but as soon as you make class distinctions, you are committing sin and under condemnation for breaking the Law. You see, anyone who keeps the whole of the Law but trips up on a single point, is still guilty of breaking it all. He who said, *You must not commit adultery* said also, *You must not kill.* Now if you commit murder, you need not commit adultery as well to become a breaker of the Law. (Jas 2:8–11)
- . . . do your utmost to support your faith with goodness, goodness with understanding, understanding with self-control, self-control with perseverance, perseverance with devotion, devotion with kindness to the brothers, and kindness to the brothers with love. The possession and growth of these qualities will prevent your knowledge of the Lord Jesus Christ from being ineffectual or unproductive. But without them, a person is blind or short-sighted, forgetting how the sins of the past were washed away. (2 Pet 1:5–9)
- We are well aware that we have passed over from death to life because we love our brothers. Whoever does not love, remains in death. Anyone who hates his brother is a murderer . . . (1 John 3:14–15)
- My dear friends, let us love one another, since love is from God and everyone who loves is a child of God and knows God. Whoever fails to love does not know God, because God is love. (1 John 4:7–8)
- Anyone who says "I love God" and hates his brother, is a liar, since no one who fails to love the brother whom he can see can love God whom he has not seen. Indeed this is the commandment we have received from him, that whoever loves God, must also love his brother. (1 John 4:20–21)
- Be generous to one another, sympathetic, forgiving each other as readily as God forgave you in Christ. (Eph 4:32)
- This is the proof of love, that he laid down his life for us, and we too ought to lay down our lives for our brothers. If anyone is well-off in worldly possessions and sees his brother in need but closes his heart to him, how can the love of God be remaining in him? (1 John 3:16–17)
- "But I say this to you: offer no resistance to the wicked. On the contrary, if anyone hits you on the right cheek, offer him the other as well;

if someone wishes to go to law with you to get your tunic, let him have your cloak as well." (Matt 5:39–40)

- "Be compassionate just as your Father is compassionate." (Luke 6:36)
- As God's dear children, then, take him as your pattern, and follow Christ by loving as he loved you . . . (Eph 5:1)
- "I have given you an example so that you may copy what I have done to you." (John 13:15)
- Jesus said, "Father, forgive them; they do not know what they are doing." (Luke 23:34)

To these passages we could add many similar ones or explanations, but that would only weaken their persuasive power. These excerpts from the Holy Scriptures prove clearly and unequivocally that we have to have love, including love for the enemy exactly as for the brother, relative, or friend, because every person, whether friend or foe, is our neighbor, as Jesus demonstrates so beautifully in the parable of the Good Samaritan (Luke 10:30–37). We have to love our neighbor as ourselves. Whoever has this love—and everyone who wants to please God has to have this love—will never harm even his worst enemy. Instead, as a disciple of Christ, he will give his life even for his enemy, who is his neighbor, instead of killing him in self-defense.

We have the example of Christ as a guide of what we likewise should do if we want to be his disciples. This is not left to our own discretion and is not merely good advice but the strictest command: "I have given you an example so that you may copy what I have done to you" (John 13:15). Christ, as we know, gave his life for his enemies as well as for his friends.

When anyone standing at the foot of the cross, looking up at the dying Savior, asks whether he should or may, without incurring guilt, kill an attacker in self-defense, he will immediately find the right answer in remembering the words of Christ, which he lived out on the cross: "But I say this to you: offer no resistance to the wicked. On the contrary, if anyone hits you on the right cheek, offer him the other one as well" (Matt 5:39). He will also remember how Christ acted toward his attackers when he was arrested in the garden of Gethsemane and when he was nailed to the cross. If Christ had forcibly defended himself—he certainly had the power to do so—he would have been able to prevent the most dreadful crime in history, the murder of God. Christ did not, however, defend himself by forcibly preventing his attackers from tying him up and delivering him up to death. Also, Christ admonished Peter when he wielded his sword to defend his beloved

Master: "Put your sword back, for all who draw the sword will die by the sword" (Matt 26:52).

If it were morally justifiable to defend oneself by violent means when attacked, Jesus would not have said, "All who draw the sword will die by the sword." Or did Christ mean to say, "All who unjustly draw the sword will die by the sword"? Who would argue that Peter drew the sword unjustly? Because Christ was unjustly attacked, advocates of the right of self-defense believe that Peter was justified in drawing the sword. But Christ's prohibition, "Put your sword back," applies even in the case of self-defense and permits no exceptions, "for all who draw the sword will die by the sword."

According to the words and example of Christ, we are not permitted to kill in self-defense because this violates the commandment to love. If someone were to kill his attacker, would he be acting in accordance with Christ's admonitions to "never repay one wrong with another" (1 Pet 3:9), to "offer no resistance to the wicked" (Matt 5:39), and to "love your enemies" (Luke 6:27)? Would this be the kind of love that "can cause no harm to your neighbor" (Rom 13:10)?

Certainly, an attack on life, limb, or property is a serious violation of justice, and therefore the aggressor is guilty of a grave sin. But if the injured party were to kill his attacker, the latter would presumably die with a serious sin on his conscience and lose the salvation of his soul for all eternity. In this case, the loss of earthly life stands against the everlasting perdition of a soul; and since this is out of all proportion, we have to ask: Can it be justifiable to deliver up an immortal soul to eternal damnation in order to preserve one's own, earthly life, or even to safeguard some material possession for a short period of time? If the aggressor is not killed, he still has time to repent and to convert, with God's grace. One may never accept the easily made remark used to justify killing an attacker that it is his own fault that he has been condemned to death. Instead, the Bible teaches, "This is proof of love, that he laid down his life for us, and we too ought to lay down our lives for our brothers" (1 John 3:16). We must lay down our life for them, not take their life, especially when the "brother," that is, our neighbor who is also our enemy, would be delivered up to eternal death by suffering physical death at our hand.

While the advocates of self-defense cannot support their allegation with a single relevant passage from the Gospel of Christ, we can cite many passages of Holy Scripture, especially the Gospel, to lend weight to our opposing view, unless the supporters of self-defense could prove that we are in error by citing the Gospel. However, as long as such an error has not been proved, we will adhere to our belief that self-defense is not justified and say: Since the Gospel of Christ proclaims nonviolence and, therefore, rejects self-defense, it is not morally permissible to kill one's aggressor.

As to being armed and prepared to fight, the supporters of self-defense would require that every person be trained in the use of weapons and be armed at all times, since an attack could occur anywhere and anytime. Since we reject the right of self-defense, we also have to reject the requirement of universal military preparedness. We don't need people trained to use murder weapons because this would increase insecurity and violence, not diminish it.

If today children—immature boys—are armed with daggers, as is the practice under National Socialism and fascism, it indicates a total incapacity to provide youth with a proper moral education. Of course, whoever idolizes violence recognizes only the animal nature in man, preaches hate of the enemy, and considers daggers, revolvers, hand grenades, and machine guns appropriate instruments to secure one's rights. It is a wasted effort to talk to someone with this viewpoint about love of neighbor, much less of love of enemy, and to bring up the example of Christ. While Jesus teaches "Love your enemies," the supporters of the right of self-defense preach, "Hate your enemies. Practice revenge and merciless retaliation."

According to the Graz *Tagespost* of June 1, 1943, Mussolini, while addressing disabled veterans in Predappio, said, "You have to champion holy hatred for the enemy. Every indulgence toward him is a crime and a betrayal of the fatherland." He also stated, according to a report in the *Münchner Neuesten Nachrichten*,[1] "War is as necessary for man as motherhood is for woman."

One reads in an article of the Graz *Tagespost* of July 27, 1943, "Walk through the glass-and-rubble-strewn streets of the harbor city Hamburg! Clench your teeth and do not forget who caused you this misery! Let hate burn in your hearts and stoke it to a high flame every day! Walk through the streets of Hamburg and learn from the smoldering ruins of the apartment buildings for whom our bombs and phosphorus are meant. Here forgiveness and settlement are no longer possible. The suffering of our deeply tried civilian population becomes our sacred vow to hate."

In the periodical *Das Reich* of January 9, 1944, Propaganda Minister Dr. Joseph Goebbels wrote, "Some day when our retaliation against the British Isles is put into action, our entire nation will be filled with deep satisfaction. For this we Germans are prepared to bear everything today. However this revenge may turn out, it will not stir up the least bit of sympathy in

1. No date given.

Germany." Only a man such as Goebbels could write like this. He also stated in *Das Reich* of November 29, 1942,

> In war, that side has the advantage which advances toward its goal without looking right or left and justifies its actions by success rather than by morality. . . . We as a nation have yet to learn to act strictly according to expedience in war. . . . War demands an unreserved willingness of self-denial, including giving one's life.[2] War stirs up the deepest national passions. Man reverts to the wild, original state of barbaric times.[3] It is no longer so much about what is moral or ethical but much more about what promises success. Whoever is led exclusively by what is good and advantageous for his own cause will come out ahead.

Horrified, one reads this excerpt from the newspaper *Winniza Witt* in the Graz *Tagespost* of July 9, 1943: "What was done to these martyrs of our nation (the victims slaughtered by the Soviets in the forests of Katyn and Winniza) can only be atoned for through revenge—ferocious and pitiless revenge."

Without excusing the opponents of Germany—on the contrary, we also have to condemn sharply, as base deeds of murder and inhuman crimes, the air raids of the Allies—we have to ask: Who was first to cowardly bomb defenseless cities and murder tens of thousands of men, women, and children? German bomb squadrons attacked Rotterdam, Warsaw, and Belgrade before an English airplane released one bomb over German territory.

But this is the way it is. In war every Christian country ceases to be Christian. Therefore, everything depends on convincing humanity of the power of nonviolence, which is a manifestation of love. As those who idolize violence do everything they can to spread hate, we have to exert every effort to win people over to nonviolence. It is not he who is able to use weapons who is a hero but he who has the courage to face his opponent (enemy) fearlessly with love. Any scoundrel or common criminal can wield and even master a physical weapon; but only truly saintly men and women, guided by love, can wield the spiritual weapon of nonviolence and thereby demonstrate an unparalleled heroism. To practice nonviolence does not mean merely holding still and submitting to evil; rather, nonviolence is the noblest form of action because it is motivated by love.

2. Ude remarks in parentheses: "It may be noted that Goebbels did not risk his life in the safe homeland."

3. Ude remarks in parentheses: ". . . indeed; we experienced this with horror."

Since the right of self-defense and its relationship to military training is the major theme of this work, we are here repeating some comments we cited at a public meeting in Graz in 1936.

In 1936 *Il Duce* Benito Mussolini stated at a mass meeting that for him only an "armed peace" is possible and that a disarmed peace based on nonviolence is "a utopia of utopians ignorant of the ways of the world."

Speaking in the Austrian *Bundestag* about the defense of his country, Major General Kubena demanded, as reported in the *Grazer Volksblatt* of December 5, 1936, "For the protection of the state and for the safety of the lives of its peaceful citizens—women, children, and the aged—necessary provisions have to be made." He remarked that Austria spends only 10 percent of its budget for defense, to protect its borders and its population, while other states allocate 12 percent.

The Christian (Catholic) *Grazer Volksblatt*[4] commented on this subject: "Today the peace of Europe is threatened by Bolshevism on one side and by excessive preparations for war on the other. We all hope that this threat to peace will pass without a war. However, we cannot leave to chance the fact that only a nation able to defend itself can maintain its peace. This principle, as true today as ever, applies to us as well as to every other nation; and not only the state but every responsible individual in our fatherland has to adhere to it."

According to a report in the *Neuen Freien Presse*, Vienna, March 27, 1936, D. Schmitz, the mayor of Vienna, made this remark at a public meeting while referring to Andreas Hofer: "There is no absolute pacifism. No country can renounce training its men to use weapons and kindling and nourishing love for the fatherland in the family so that in the hour of affliction everyone has the inner strength necessary."

On March 18, 1936, Schmitz stated at a convention of the Reich Youth Federation, in the presence of Cardinal Theodor Innitzer, "We do not yet have universal conscription, but it is coming. Then all of us will wear the soldier's uniform of the Austrian fatherland with pride."

According to a report of the Graz *Tagespost* of December 12, 1936, Austria's Chancellor Kurt Schuschnigg, at a meeting of the trade association of Lower Austria, said, "Preparations for an armed conflict at least are causing this time of peace to experience a more or less lasting upward swing in the economy." He eloquently described the direct and indirect benefits of defense expenditures for the Austrian economy and rejoiced over the Austrian parliament's unanimous approval of the law providing for conscription.

4. No date given.

These opinions expressed by Mussolini, Kubena, Schuschnigg, Schmitz, and the *Grazer Volksblatt* were pretty much shared by all statesmen and church representatives, Catholic as well as non-Catholic. This means nothing else but "*si vis pacem, para bellum*"—if you want peace, prepare for war; be armed! Thus weapons training, the right of self-defense—that is, repelling violence with violence—the just defensive war, and conscription are accepted as morally permissible. Much of the life of the state is centered around these precepts, with no objections raised by the Christian churches, including the Catholic Church.

The Church not only permits the swearing in of military recruits but also provides a festive setting for the ceremony, during which they have to take an oath to follow blindly and unconditionally the orders of their superiors to commit mass murder and destroy cultures. The Church blesses the soldiers as they go into battle. Priests in military uniforms—field chaplains—inflame them to attack and admonish them to do their duty, which means to mow down the enemy, to gas him, to destroy him. In churches citizens of each nation pray for victory; and when victory has been attained, and hundreds of thousands of soldiers' bodies are covering the battlefields, church bells are rung and *Te Deum laudamus* ("Holy God, we praise thy name") is sung solemnly in thanksgiving. The citizens are grateful and rejoice that the bloody struggle resulting in the death and mutilation of thousands of soldiers has led to victory. The heroes are praised from the pulpits and, in recognition for special feats in killing and destruction, are decorated with a cross. Here state and Church are staunchly and harmoniously united as they have been since the time of Emperor Constantine. And, if needed, bishops even offer their golden rings and pectoral crosses "at the altar of the endangered fatherland." The Church does not object to the state's paramilitary education of its youth. In war and preparing for war, the churches and the state work harmoniously hand in hand, and everything seems so clear and self-evident.

However, as a Christian I have to ask: Are the teachings about the morality of arming, self-defense, and the just defensive war so clear and self-evident that one cannot harbor any doubts about them? Is the viewpoint about "armed peace" and the necessity to prepare for war actually as clear as is generally taught and accepted, or is anyone who has doubts about these teachings no longer completely Christian or totally Catholic? For within the Catholic Church, with few exceptions, these precepts are taught, accepted as right, and put into practice. Conscientious objectors, however, are branded as "traitors of the fatherland," imprisoned, or, in times of war, even shot; and the churches are silent and allow it to happen.

Who is right? If a doubt arises over any view, we have the duty to resolve it because we may not act if we have any doubts. As a Christian, we have to examine which stand we must take on the question of war and peace and especially on the issues of self-defense, the "just defensive war," and arming for war, that is, the concept of "armed peace."

We understand that self-defense is resistance with physical force—for example, a fist or a weapon—at the moment of an attack on one's life, limb, or property. It is taught that it is morally permissible to repel the aggressor with a weapon, even at the risk of killing him, and that in war it is one's duty to defend oneself. This means compulsory military service. For us, only the moral demands made by Christ, especially those taught in the Sermon on the Mount and the great commandment to love, are the right way.

We can save our examination of these questions, however, if a certain Jesuit priest is right who, according to my friend Arthur von Miller, stated at a meeting of aristocrats in Vienna during World War I, "In the Sermon on the Mount Jesus did not speak as a casuist but as an orator; and therefore his rhetorical exaggerations have to be reduced to their due proportions." For us the teachings of the Sermon on the Mount are strictly obligatory commandments—not a rhetorical feat, not an oratory exercise, and still less "rhetorical exaggerations" to be "reduced to their due proportions." Such impudence has to be rejected as a most serious insult of the Son of God. As if we paltry humans had the right to censure Christ! Precisely at this occasion Christ expressed himself simply and beyond all doubt. He said, "You have heard how it was said: *Eye for eye and tooth for tooth*. But I say this to you: offer no resistance to the wicked. On the contrary, if anyone hits you on the right cheek, offer him the other as well; if someone wishes to go to law with you to get your tunic, let him have your cloak as well" (Matt 5:38–40).

Luke recorded it more briefly: "To anyone who slaps you on one cheek, present the other cheek as well; to anyone who takes your cloak from you, do not refuse your tunic" (Luke 6:29). In deliberate contrast to the brutalities and bloody horrors of the Old Testament, Christ presents his teachings about violence and self-defense: "But I say this to you . . ." Here in the Sermon on the Mount Christ refers to an attack on life and another on property—that is, two clear cases where one could respond with self-defense when life and property are endangered.

Should the person who is attacked simply consent to being struck on the cheek or to the taking of his coat, or should he, may he, defend himself (and to what extent)? It goes without saying that one may flee from the attacker. Does not Christ say this to his apostles and disciples: "If they persecute you in one town, take refuge in the next; and if they persecute you in that, take refuge in another" (Matt 10:23). But if it is not possible to flee, may the person who is attacked use violence to repel the aggressor in order to defend his life and his property, even at the risk of killing him? Because these important questions have continued to occupy humanity, Christ had to give a clear answer to remove all doubts. This he did.

That the aggressor has no right to encroach on someone else's life and property goes without saying. Such an attack is an immoral act and seriously violates justice and love of neighbor.

How then would Christ advise the person who is unjustly attacked? Would he recommend that he use violence or at least give him the option to do so? This is a matter of the greatest significance. If Christ approves of the right to self-defense, he has to say so here. Instead, he gives this unequivocal command: "Offer no resistance to the wicked" (Matt 5:38).

A disciple of Christ should not, and may not, ever respond with violence to an attacker. "On the contrary, if anyone hits you on the right cheek, offer him the other as well" (Matt 5:39). In other words, never defend yourself with violence but suffer the attack. You may defend yourself with words, that is, with spiritual weapons, as Christ did when a guard slapped his face while being questioned by the high priest. Jesus said to the guard, "If there is some offense in what I said, point it out; but if not, why do you strike me?" (John 18:23).

A slap on the cheek is a very harmful attack that may even result in death. However, a disciple of Christ should suffer such an attack, in compliance with the commandment of his Master, without becoming angry or provoked. Instead, as proof of his nonviolent attitude, he should offer his other cheek to the assailant; and if someone takes his coat, he should not meet force with force but let the attacker have his tunic as well. While this is almost incomprehensible to a person with a strictly secular outlook, it is the true Christian viewpoint. A Christian should submit to an attack without any use of violence. This is Christ's clear command and it permits no interpretations, no limitations, no "if" or "but" or "to some extent."

According to this, Christ does not grant a right of self-defense either to an individual or to a group. The same applies to both because a mass attack is merely the sum of individual attacks. Also, when Peter tried to defend his Master with his sword, Christ commanded, "Put your sword back, for all who draw the sword will die by the sword" (Matt: 26:52). All!

Every weapon and every violent defense is contrary to the teachings of Christ, which demand that we meet the assailant with goodness and love and allow him to attack us. The weapons of Christ are solely nonviolence, all-forgiving love, and forbearance, which suffer even the greatest injustice but never harm the enemy, never return evil for evil.

To avoid the slightest doubt, Christ and the apostles speaking in his name again and again emphasized love of the enemy. How can one reconcile these easily understandable commandments of Christ with the use of violence against an assailant? Who dares to claim that violence, armaments, and war are compatible with Christianity? I can only derive from Christ's commandments that they are not compatible. To be armed for war means to be always prepared to meet the enemy with violence, to harm and possibly kill him. Is this the love that Christ demands of us? To wage war means to inflict as much harm, misery, and death as possible on the enemy while claiming to bring about peace. Is this the love that Christ demands of us? How can the citizens of a warring nation say that they are obeying the great commandments to love the enemy and to repay evil with good if they stab him with a bayonet, throw hand grenades at him in order to dismember him, drop tons of bombs on him out of airplanes, and mercilessly fire cannons and machine guns into his ranks? And such people want to be called Christian and Catholic? Arming for war, training to fight, defending themselves forcibly, being soldiers and waging war—all these are incompatible with being a Christian. Whoever is a Christian, that is, whoever truly abides by Christ's teaching, may not touch a murder weapon and does not need a rifle, a revolver, a cannon, or poison gas. His defense is nonviolence, and his weapons are love, goodness, compassion, patience, and gentleness.

A Christian is also forbidden to practice revenge in response to an injustice; as Christ's apostle Paul commanded in his name, "Never try to get revenge: leave that, my dear friends, to the Retribution. As scripture says: *Vengeance is mine—I will pay them back*, the Lord promises" (Rom 12:19).

How do Catholic moral theologians, priests, and laymen justify the right of self-defense? Are they not violating the unambiguous words of Christ and his apostles when they declare arming and training for war to be acceptable and the "just defensive war" to be morally permissible? How can they, without contradicting themselves, teach that the great commandment to love includes all people, friend and foe, with no exceptions, and, on the other hand, judge the force of arms, preparations for war, and self-defense—the killing of the enemy—to be morally permissible, justified, and even a duty? For soldiers are bound by oath, at the command of their superiors, to blindly defend their fatherland and its people with murder weapons.

If someone objects and says, "If one lets the aggressor have his way, if one does not defend oneself against him, one is aiding and abetting murder and injustice."

Christ could have defended himself against his unjust assailants and thus prevented the most horrendous crime in history, the murder of God, but he allowed himself to be seized and crucified. Does this mean that Christ aided and abetted murder and crime? No; to say so would be to slander God. He simply practiced what he taught. By giving up all claims to self-defense he achieved the greatest victory in history, attaining it by means of absolute nonviolence. And, as everywhere, Christ's words are valid here: "I have given you an example so that you may copy what I have done to you" (John 13:15).

I have searched the entire New Testament but have not found a single convincing passage that permits self-defense, or that makes it a duty, or that supports armaments and war. On the contrary, I have found many passages that proclaim the exact opposite of what is generally taught today in state and church about self-defense, military preparedness, and the "just defensive war." I read in the Holy Scriptures, "*You must love your neighbor as yourself*" (Mark 12:21); "My command to you is to love one another" (John 15:17); "Anyone who hates his brother is a murderer" (1 John 3:15).

Whoever maims or kills his brother, who is his neighbor—which includes the enemy—is even more so a murderer. Still another passage reads, "Anyone who says 'I love God' and hates his brother, is a liar, since whoever does not love the brother whom he can see can love God whom he has not seen. Indeed this is the commandment we have received from him, that whoever loves God, must also love his brother" (1 John 4:20–21).

Or is the love of neighbor, the source of which is God and which is commanded by Christ, present in self-defense or the appalling struggles of war? Are the horrors of war works of love of the enemy? Does love of neighbor guide the fighting? The Apostle Paul wrote to the Romans, "Love can cause no harm to your neighbor, and so love is the fulfillment of the law" (13:10), and my church teaches me that every person, including the enemy, is my neighbor. Therefore, I am strictly obligated in conscience to conduct myself toward every person with love in my thoughts, words, and actions. The true disciple of Christ has to forego every form of violence; he has to be a conscientious objector, whatever the consequences. He is filled with the love of his heavenly Master, who says, "I give you a new commandment: love one another; you must love one another just as I have loved you. It is by your love for one another, that everyone will recognize you as my disciples" (John 13:34–35).

Not even the most worthy goal can justify war, self-defense, training, arming, and preparing for war because these glaringly contradict the commandment to love one's neighbor, especially the obligation to love one's enemy. Whatever contradicts the teaching of Christ is immoral, or someone would have to prove to me beyond a doubt that Christ recommended self-defense with violence or even made it a duty under certain circumstances.

By the way, if churches and states support self-defense, why are private individuals forbidden to carry weapons? If I have the right of self-defense, I have to be able to use a weapon. Or do only a privileged few have the right of self-defense?

However, if someone should assert that to forego self-defense is merely good advice—it is actually a Christian commandment—then the claim of universal conscription would already be proved false, and conscientious objectors would be acting entirely in accordance with Christ's teaching. With what right then are they imprisoned or even shot? Nations that have conscription and that arm themselves for war may never call themselves Christian states.

It follows from the above that renouncing the use of force against an assailant is the essence of Christianity, which makes love a duty for all human beings. However, this is not cowardice. On the contrary, it takes heroic courage to stand up against a world bristling with weapons and to choose to suffer humiliation and death instead of harming others by violence. Only Christian love originating from God makes such heroic courage possible. And if the disciple of Christ is treated violently and has to give his life for his conviction, this is not a defeat but rather a glorious victory, an eloquent witness to the power of Christianity, which is called to renew the face of the earth through love. Whoever acts in accord with this is a true hero because he has love. As the Apostle Paul said, "Love is always patient and kind; love is never jealous; love is not boastful or conceited, it is never rude and never seeks its own advantage, it does not take offense or store up grievances. Love does not rejoice at wrongdoing, but finds its joy in the truth. It is always ready to make allowances, to trust, to hope and to endure whatever comes. Love never comes to an end" (1 Cor 13:4–8).

Not without good reason did our divine Master say through the voice of his apostle, "This is the proof of love, that he laid down his life for us, and we too ought to lay down our lives for our brothers" (1 John 3:16). We should not take life, should not kill, but give our lives for our brothers and for the enemy who is also our brother.

In defiance of a world bristling with weapons, we have to be prepared to give our lives, if necessary, in order to demonstrate openly, before the whole world, the love whose source is God, because to be a Christian means to be a witness and, if need be, a martyr. Thanks be to God! There always have been and always will be conscientious objectors, honorable human beings, witnesses with the courage of Christian martyrs, who emphatically preach the great commandment of love and nonviolence to a world fallen away from Christ. They alone are the true heroes because they have an unreserved trust in the ultimate triumph of these commandments that Christ made obligatory.

If our remarks are correct, and we are deeply convinced that they are, all churches, starting with the Catholic Church, instead of supporting the right of self-defense and the right to wage war, have to forbid their members to fight in wars and to defend themselves with weapons or any kind of violence because these are incompatible with Christianity.

We have to make a decision. Either we are for cannons and renounce Christianity, or we are for Christianity and renounce cannons, self-defense, military preparations, and war. Either we are for an "armed peace," for military preparations and the use of violence—but then we may not call ourselves Christians—or we want to be true Christians—but then we have to profess nonviolence and forego self-defense. This dualism is expressed in the words of the poet Friedrich von Bodenstedt:

> You may proclaim all you wish
> The glory of war and its heroes,
> But keep still about your Christianity,
> Preached out of the mouths of cannons.
>
> Still believing, the Turkish armies
> Fight battles to glorify their Allah.
> We don't have Odin anymore,
> Dead are the gods of Valhalla.
>
> If you need to prove your courage,
> Fight as did the heroes of old,
> Shed as much blood as you must
> But don't talk about the Savior.
>
> Feel free to be whatever you wish,
> Be on this side or the other.
> Only I hate the hypocrisy
> Of the warring Nazarenes.

The belief in an "armed peace" is a grave error, irreconcilable with what Christ taught. Peace and armaments intrinsically are contradictory. Peace can only exist where moral order prevails and guides all actions, that is, where Christ's commands are fulfilled without reservation. However, a state bristling with weapons constitutes a continuous threat and provokes other nations to be on guard and to arm themselves.

Either Christ, and then this statement is unreservedly valid: If you want peace, prepare for peace, prepare for it by means of the works of peace! Achieve peace through nonviolence, born of love, and by renouncing all violent means of self-defense! No one needs to fear a truly disarmed person. Or you declare your allegiance to this tenet: If you want peace, prepare for war, be armed; and, if need be, defend your life and your property with force, even if you have to kill your assailant. Then, however, you have to give up being considered a Christian and have to expect that the explicit words of Christ will come true: "all who draw the sword will die by the sword" (Matt 26:52).

Whoever believes that military preparations help the economy is like the man who wants to heat his stove with dynamite because he thinks it has greater heating power than coal. After a war the economy is like the oven heated by dynamite: exploded and completely destroyed.

Or did a certain military vicar proclaim Christ's teachings when, according to the *Grazer Volksblatt* of September 6, 1936, in a festive address to military officers, he extolled the status of soldier as a glorious and God-pleasing profession and stated, "Military leaders are committed to the principle: 'Our hearts beat for God. Our fists beat on the enemy.'"

Or should we approve the conclusion of a lead article, about a review of young Austrian men declared fit for military service, titled "Let Us Arm," in the same newspaper on July 17, 1936? It reads, "Are not the splendid sons of our Alpine people different lads than the brainy Oxford students who declared that a strong (armed) England is a misfortune for the world and, therefore, are not inclined to fight for their country?" In response, the English minister of war called this resolution of the senior students a "foolishness of youthful stupidity." If the military vicar and the *Volksblatt* are right, then Christ is a fool—and we likewise are fools, because we call an "armed peace" a contradiction and reject self-defense, military preparations, conscription, and the "just defensive war" as incompatible with what Christ teaches.

If the supporters of war, in order to demonstrate how "Christian" they are, demand that war be waged "humanely" and form organizations that object to the various horrors of war, such people are playing a ludicrous, not to say a childish, role. When they mean war, they include total war, fought with all means, even the cruelest, in order to destroy the enemy as soon as possible. Every war is the opposite of love, and each war is brutal. If I support war, then I likewise support the cruelties committed. However, as a Christian I may not commit even the smallest brutality. A Christian has to be a conscientious objector.

Christ and Christianity may not be divided because they are one. Jesus would be contradicting himself if, on one hand, he preached unconditional love of neighbor with explicit emphasis on the unreserved love of the enemy, and, on the other hand, talked about the use of force as self-defense, considered the just defensive war moral, and permitted exceptions to the commandment "You shall not kill."

Let us summarize our remarks. An irreconcilable contradiction exists between what is generally taught in the Catholic Church about self-defense, training and arming to fight, and the "just defensive war," and Jesus' commands of love of neighbor and enemy, as recorded in the Gospels and the letters of the apostles, and demonstrated in the lives of the early Christians who refused to go to war.

We emphasize that a true Christian has no right to self-defense, to train for war, or to serve as a soldier because all of these are a flagrant contradiction of Christ's teaching about love, especially love of the enemy, which he and his apostles so often emphasized. It follows that an "armed peace" is in direct opposition to true Christianity.

We stand up against war and work for peace not by arming but by practicing justice toward all people by means of total nonviolence and even by repaying evil with good, which means doing everything in love—a love that is benevolent, includes all, and is willing to bear suffering.

Christianity and war, Christianity and armaments, Christianity and self-defense, Christianity and being a soldier are by their nature intrinsically contradictory. Therefore, the Catholic teaching authority has to examine these concepts, which we have proved to be erroneous, and has to decide whether today's generally accepted teaching about self-defense is right or whether the Gospel's admonition not to resist evil and to repay evil with good, as advocated by Christian peacemakers and conscientious objectors, is merely good advice or is a commandment of Christ that both the individual and society have to obey.

This concludes the presentation of our viewpoint, which we maintain even more firmly because of what World War II has wrought.

4. Our position regarding the teachings about the death penalty

In our book *Ethik,* published in 1912,[5] and in lectures given at the University of Graz at about that time, we defended the following thesis handed down by ethicists, moral philosophers, and theologians: The state, because of its disciplinary authority, whose purpose is to restore justice, prevent violations of the law, and rehabilitate offenders, may in particular circumstances impose the death penalty for certain crimes.

In support of this thesis, we outlined the same, entirely stereotyped reasons that the Christian ethicists and theologians were advancing. In Part I of this work we presented the justifications for imposing the death penalty that are widespread in Christian circles. At one time we also accepted uncritically the general view that the death penalty is the only effective method of prevention, deterrence, and rehabilitation and were convinced that this extreme measure is a just expiation for certain crimes. But the more we occupied ourselves with this serious issue, the more we began to question these stereotyped reasons and then to defend the opposing viewpoint.

After World War I, the "Christian" government of Dollfuss-Schuschnigg, with the consent of the bishops of Austria, reinstituted the death penalty, which had been abolished by the government led by the Social Democratic Party. The first victim of this new law was the poor, somewhat feeble-minded Peter Strauss, who was hanged in Graz on January 11, 1934, for arson and resulting damage of no more than two or three thousand *Schillinge*. This execution on the gallows made it clear to us that the death penalty violates reason, natural law, and especially Christian moral law. From then on, we considered it our duty to proclaim openly to the entire world, by writing and speaking, that the state has no right whatsoever to impose the death penalty for any crime.

This is an issue about which views differ greatly; however, every opinion is worth only as much as the reasons offered in its support. Following are our reasons for rejecting the death penalty as reprehensible.

The state is responsible for public peace, order, and safety, and anyone who violates its laws—we are assuming they are just laws—disturbs the order, peace, and safety of society. Therefore, the state has the responsibility and authority to intervene to stop violators and to punish them, if necessary, in order to safeguard the observance of the laws and the general welfare.

5. Ude, *Ethik*, 154ff.

However, we have to add that every country is composed of human beings who are fallen and corrupted by original sin (although redeemed by Christ). This means that the state in today's form constitutes an evil—although a necessary one—a kind of condition of punishment for fallen humanity. We are convinced that if our original parents had not sinned, if humanity had kept its innocence and remained connected to God, the state would still be necessary because man, by nature, is a social being. However, in that case, it would not be a necessary evil but an institution that would please all people and provide for their happiness. In this ideal state, judges and a police force would be unnecessary because no one would violate the law or cause disputes. The leadership would be just, and, in the interest of the general welfare, everyone would gladly submit to it.

However, since fallen humanity tends to cause disputes and to violate the law, at times the state has to intervene with force if the general welfare is endangered. This use of force, therefore, is a necessary evil. Since, however, government officials are also fallen human beings, they may act harshly and unjustly and misuse their authority. Thus the state itself becomes a necessary evil that at times can be oppressive to the individual and to the entire population.

Taking this into consideration, we have to examine how far the state's criminal justice system extends. It is certain that the primary rights of man, most importantly the right to life, given by God to each human being as a natural right, are guaranteed and protected by him and were bestowed prior to the existence of the state and irrespective of it. Therefore, the state has to acknowledge and respect these rights and to ensure that they are guaranteed to each citizen

When we ask for what kind of crimes the death penalty should be imposed, we receive various answers. Some insist on "eye for an eye, tooth for a tooth" and demand capital punishment only for murder, because man's most valuable possession, his life, can be protected only by the threat of the death penalty. Others go further and demand this punishment for treason and crimes against authority. Still others, like the National Socialists, demand it for every *Volksschädling* (someone considered to be harmful to the populace).[6] Who exactly is a *Volksschädling* is determined entirely by the whims of the Nazi officials. For example, they branded as such someone who stole a few parcels sent to soldiers in the field, whoever killed a cow or pig without an official permit, and, of course, anyone who refused to serve in the military, tried to flee from a prison camp, listened to a foreign radio station, or spread news that was unfavorable to the Hitler regime. Most of

6. The noun *Schädling* can be translated as pest, vermin, parasite, or vile person.

all, it was someone who held a different political opinion. Even invalids and the mentally retarded were considered *Volksschädlinge* and exterminated. In the Nazi Reich guillotines, rifles, revolvers, the gallows, and poison gas worked uninterruptedly day and night to eliminate these "harmful" persons. Spies and informers, who were accomplices of the SS and the Gestapo, saw to it that millions of their fellow citizens suffered the death penalty, not counting the millions of others who had the misfortune to have been born Jews, Czechs, Yugoslavs, or Poles, for that alone sufficed to be murdered by the Nazi state.[7]

It may be mentioned incidentally that the Bolshevik state also literally waded in the blood of millions.[8]

If one believes that the imposition of the death penalty will deter crime, one is mistaken. The theory of deterrence has failed completely. Law-abiding people need no deterrence because they are decent, and the death penalty does not deter the criminal because he is convinced that he will not be caught.

In no case are the defenders of the death penalty able to prove that the lives and property of citizens are protected effectively, or more effectively, by killing the offender. The facts prove that in countries where the death penalty exists, crimes punishable by death have increased.

For example, in the United States, where not only the legal death penalty but also lynching is practiced, in 1933 there were 12,000 murders, 3,000 kidnappings, 100,000 assaults, 50,000 robberies, and 40,000 thefts.[9] Since 1900 the murder rate has increased by 35 percent, and since 1926, the number of persons imprisoned by 50 percent. It is estimated that 12,000 murderers are still on the loose and that 400,000 persons are living only by crime.

The *Wormser Zeitung* of February 11, 1932, reported that in Poland the number of felonies and misdemeanors is steadily rising despite the increased severity of the courts.

7. According to the *Oberösterreicher Nachrichten*, Linz, of August 24, 1945, the number of murders committed by Nazi Germany was estimated at twenty-six million. Every day twelve to fourteen thousand persons were killed in the Dachau concentration camp. The same newspaper reported on August 25, 1945, that the number of Jews murdered by Hitler Germany was five to six million.

8. The *Bayrischer Kurier* of July 3, 1931, reported, "According to an official Soviet Russian statistic, the number of persons officially executed in Russia between 1917 and 1923 is at least 1,750,000. This includes 25 bishops, 1,215 members of the clergy, 6,575 professors, 8,800 physicians, 54,850 officers, 260,000 soldiers, 48,000 policemen, 12,850 government officials, 355,250 intellectuals, 815,000 farmers or farm workers, and 192,000 workers."

9. *Schönere Zukunft*, Vienna, November 18, 1934.

In a letter to the Vienna newspaper *Das kleine Blatt* of November 3, 1937, an experienced criminologist wrote,

> At one time I also defended the necessity of the death penalty (as did Justice Ratzenhofer whom you quoted). Instead, I have turned from Saul into Paul and now oppose the death penalty because it is not a deterrent. When someone is planning a crime, even if it is murder, he counts on not being caught, even at the moment the deed has been completed. Therefore, from the standpoint of officials responsible for security, the theory of deterrence has to be regarded as worthless. When the death penalty was introduced (in Austria by the Christian Democratic government of Dollfuss-Schuschnigg),[10] it undoubtedly reflected the feelings of the majority of the population. But were these the highest instincts which were given expression in this desire for the death penalty?

Those who continue to believe that society can be effectively protected only by the death penalty are wrong, and defenders of this extreme punishment will realize this after thoroughly reflecting on it, especially in the light of the teachings of Christ. The population can be protected effectively by the removal of criminals from society, their supervision, and constructive employment. These methods also allow the offender time to search inward and to reform, a fact that has to appeal to faithful Christians because in addition to God's grace, time is necessary to gain salvation of one's soul. However, a state that simply kills criminals usurps rights that belong only to God, namely, to decide the time of death and the time to impart grace.

The periodical *Der Menschheitskämpfer* states, "Every Christian should approach the death penalty with the moral seriousness which led Freiburg Unversity professor Dr. Franz Keller, a Catholic, to write the following":

> From the standpoint of the care of souls, it may be noteworthy how God cared about the soul of Cain, who murdered his brother (Gen 4:8). Tortured by his conscience, Cain, being human, counted on the possibility of being put to death for his shameful crime. The murderer of his brother is stuck in the dark precept of revenge, "eye for an eye, tooth for a tooth . . ." (which was later developed into a statute of law). In his anguish, Cain said, "Whoever encounters me can kill me." It would certainly have been a relief from the torturous pain of Cain's conscience if God had quickly executed the death sentence and ended Cain's uncertainty.

10. Kurt Schuschnigg and Engelbert Dollfuss formed a government in 1932.

> What does God do? To make us humans aware of how accursed Cain's deed is, he asks, in the powerful language of the eternal law, "What have you done? Listen! Your brother's blood is crying out to me from the ground. Now be cursed and banned from the ground that has opened its mouth to receive your brother's blood at your hands. When you till the ground it will no longer yield up its strength to you. A restless wanderer you will be on earth" (Gen 4:10–12).
>
> After these terrible words of judgment, does God call the hangman to repay evil with evil and to execute eternal justice with capital punishment? What does God, the supreme shepherd of souls and judge, do? Listen, all of you who for spiritual and other reasons are working so energetically for the retention of capital punishment in Germany! "And the LORD said, 'Whoever kills Cain will suffer a sevenfold vengeance'" (Gen 4:15). Then Yahweh made a mark on Cain so that no one who encountered him would kill him. God's intervention prevented humanity from making use of capital punishment to requite the first fratricide. In the eyes of supporters of the death penalty, however, God's method was wrong. He should have put Cain to death.[11]

We have nothing to add to Keller's serious words.

The Lord says, "Love your neighbor as yourself," "Love your enemies," "Do not return evil for evil," "Do not resist evil," "Overcome evil by good," "Vengeance is mine," and "I do not desire the death of the sinner but that he repent and live." This is how we Christians glibly talk, but at the same time we demand, in the name of the law, that the hangman put a rope around the neck of the poor criminal and break his neck. Victor Cathrein, SJ, writes, "It [the death penalty] is necessary to govern the state and maintain its unity."[12] He continues, "Let's have no false sentimentality about this important legal question."[13]

Listen, you priests and spiritual leaders of the Christian churches! Souls are at stake here, the souls of poor, unfortunate criminals who, with God's grace, can be saved for eternity if allowed to live. These are the souls of offenders whose criminal tendencies are frequently the fault of society, above and below, because the source and cause of so-called death-deserving crimes may be traced to the lack or inadequacy of housing, alcoholism, capitalistic exploitation, unemployment, lack of education, being led astray,

11. Keller, *Der Menschheitskämpfer*, 10.

12. Cathrein, *Moralphilosophie*, 2:639.

13. Ibid., 647.

bad examples, poverty, hunger, depraved sexuality, wastefulness, lack of religion, bad books, the glorification of vice, immoral movies, etc. Is it not the duty of every faithful Christian, who is filled with sincere love of God and neighbor and knows the value of each human soul, to do everything in his power to save these offenders at any price? But this is not so!

Christians who support capital punishment and who like Cathrein "know no sentimentality regarding this important legal question" reply coldly that the death penalty is necessary and that the criminal must die. If, however, the offender thereby loses his soul for all eternity, "this is not the fault of the authorities, who are only doing their duty, but he himself is to blame."[14] It is incomprehensible to us that a Catholic priest can say this.

What if the state, claiming to be authorized by God to impose the death penalty, executes an innocent person, which, indeed, has happened? How can such a fatal error ever be corrected? Cathrein dismisses the issue with the remark that "the possibility that an innocent person is put to death cannot be denied, but this has to be considered a much lesser evil than the great evils to which society would be exposed if the death penalty were imposed only in cases where an error would be absolutely impossible. This would defeat the purpose of capital punishment."[15]

In response, we can only comment that a Christian who is indifferent to judicial murder and agrees with Cathrein can ultimately say, "*Sic volo, sic jubeo, stat pro ratione voluntas*" (thus I will, thus I command; the will stands in place of reason).

However, Cathrein and his supporters offer a consolation to the innocent person who is executed: "He who is innocent and put to death has it in his power, by patiently submitting, to transform this bitter misfortune which Providence has permitted into an everlasting crown."[16]

But does this justify or excuse a judicial murder? Or are the gallows, the guillotine, the sword, the revolver, the gas chamber, and other instruments of murder—is quartering and disembowelment—the *ultima ratio* for those whose duty it is to ensure the general welfare? It is certainly easier to simply hang or shoot an offender without hesitation than to create, by years of painstaking work, social conditions in which the causes and sources of crime decrease and, consequently, the number of crimes diminishes.

As long as the entire community and, above all, the government do nothing to create better social conditions to stem the causes and sources of crime—that is, as long as society itself is responsible for so many people

14. Ibid.

15. Ibid., 651.

16. Ibid., 652.

becoming criminals—we, even if we were to agree to the use of the death penalty in certain serious cases, must flatly deny the state the right to kill an unfortunate offender.

If, however, the death penalty is in fact as indispensable and important a method for promoting the public welfare as its supporters maintain, then the executioner would be one of the most important and esteemed persons in society, one we would look upon with reverence, respect, and gratitude. Why then does hardly anyone, including Cathrein himself, choose the profession of executioner?

As their trump card, supporters of the death penalty cite Paul's Letter to the Romans:

> Let every person be subordinate to the higher authorities, for there is no authority except from God, and those that exist have been established by God. Therefore, whoever resists authority opposes what God has appointed, and those who oppose it will bring judgment upon themselves. For rulers are not a cause of fear to good conduct but to evil. Do you wish to have no fear of authority? Then do what is good and you will receive approval from it, for it is a servant of God for your good. But if you do evil, be afraid, for it does not bear the sword without purpose; it is the servant of God to inflict wrath on the evildoer. Therefore, it is necessary to be subject not only because of the wrath but also because of conscience. (Rom 13:1–5)[17]

It is clearly evident from the above, as well as from the following verses from the First Letter of Peter, that a state is entitled to punish and that it is indeed necessary: "For the sake of the Lord, accept the authority of every human institution: the emperor, as the supreme authority, and the governors as commissioned by him to punish criminals and praise those who do good" (1 Pet 2:13–14).

However, Paul's words in his Letter to the Romans, "for it does not bear the sword without purpose," which defenders of capital punishment cite to support their view, are, in effect, only a side remark. By no means does this short sentence prove that God has granted the state the authority to impose the death penalty. Of course, a sword can also be used to kill, but this does not mean that officials may, or must, behead a criminal or a petty offender. If the supporters of the death penalty accept this sentence verbatim, then decapitation would be the only permissible method of punishment, not crucifixion or hanging. Whoever proves too much proves nothing.

17. Here the translator used the New American Bible (1991 edition), because the rendition of this passage corresponded more closely to the one Ude had used.

For if this passage proves beyond a doubt that supporters of the death penalty are correct, then those who believe in the sword would maintain that the state can punish any offense, regardless how small or serious, by means of the sword, by killing the perpetrator. For Paul's Letter to the Romans states without reservation, "But if you do evil be afraid, for it does not bear the sword without purpose . . ." If the Apostle Paul wished to prove with this sentence the right to impose the death penalty, then even the person who commits the slightest wrong would have to be executed.

This sword, carried by authorities not "without purpose," having become sacred by being passed down for thousands of years, is, in our opinion, an ill-chosen symbol, like the fascist symbol of a bundle of rods and an axe, which makes visible the state's power to punish.

It does not follow from his reference to the sword that Paul agrees that the right of the death penalty has been granted by God. The apostle simply states that the sword expresses the state's authority to punish, nothing more, nothing less.

If, in support of Rom 13:4, one often cites Acts 25:11, this also does not prove that Paul accepts the death penalty as an expressly God-given right. In this passage Paul defends himself before the Roman governor: "If I am guilty of committing any capital crime, I do not ask to be spared the death penalty."

Paul, who knew everything Jesus had taught about love of neighbor and enemy, counseled us, "Do not be mastered by evil, but master evil with good" (Rom 12:21); "love can cause no harm to your neighbor" (Rom 13:10); "be generous to one another, sympathetic, forgiving each other as readily as God forgave you in Christ" (Eph 4:32); and "make sure that people do not try to repay evil for evil; always aim at what is best for each other and for everyone" (1 Thess 5:15). This apostle, for whom the teaching of his Master—"love your enemies"—was not a mere phrase but the essence of life, would not suddenly turn around and permit the rendering of evil for evil and killing. Just as Paul's sending back the slave Onesimus to his master, Philemon, does not mean that he approved of slavery, so Rom 13:1–5 and Acts 25:11 should not be interpreted to mean that Paul grants the state the right to impose the death penalty. He is simply saying that if he is wrong and has committed what the pagan Roman official Festus considers a capital crime, he does not refuse to die. This is not about whether or not the authorities have the right to impose the death penalty. Paul is simply taking into account the conditions under which the Roman state assumed the right to impose the death penalty for certain crimes; he is not making a judgment whether or not this punishment is permissible. As a faithful disciple of his

Master, Paul is ready to suffer injustice and submit to violence, even if it is imposed unjustly.

The above-cited teachings of Jesus and Paul are applicable not only to personal relationships but also to public life. They concern everyone, including those who exercise authority in a state. If Christ's commandment to love, including the enemy, does not apply to persons who exercise authority, the Gospels would have stated this at least once. They did not.

Therefore, those favoring capital punishment may not conclude from Rom 13:1–5 and Acts 25:11 that the death penalty is justified beyond any reasonable doubt. Reference to the Old Testament also fails on this issue, in light of the numerous passages of revelation cited above from the New Testament, and partially even from the Old Testament. There is only one moral law, and the commandment "you shall not kill" allows for no exceptions, not even for authorities of the state.

Therefore, our viewpoint, which denies the state the right to impose the death penalty, is well founded and corresponds to the demands of Christianity (note the declaration of Lactantius in Part II, Section 5).

It is of the utmost importance to enlighten humanity, by the spoken and written word, in speeches and sermons, and to reform all nations so that after nineteen hundred years of Christianity this pagan, totally unchristian barbarity and disgrace to civilization might finally be abolished and never again instituted.

Moreover, which human being (are those who exercise government authority not human beings?) has the right to condemn his unfortunate brothers and sisters and take their lives, over which only God may dispose, just because they had the misfortune to become criminals? Only he does who is totally free from every sin and failure. But which human being can claim this, or say that he has never given a bad example and, therefore, has had no part in the misdeeds of others? However, if we share in the guilt, if we are poor sinners and so dependent on God's grace and mercy, if our society shares the responsibility for many people becoming criminals, what right does such a society have to judge a misfortunate offender and deprive him of his life? But if someone were completely free of all sin and failings, he would be even less likely to condemn anyone but, like Christ, would have mercy on all fallen human beings.

It is with good reason that the Holy Scriptures include the story of the adulteress (John 8:1–11). Among the Jews, the punishment for adultery was death by stoning. Jesus says to the hypocritical Pharisees who desire to stone her, "Let the one among you who is guiltless be the first to throw a stone." Ashamed and aware of their guilt the Pharisees go away. Then Jesus says to the woman, "Has no one condemned you?" She replies, "No one, sir."

"Neither do I condemn you," says Jesus. "Go away, and from this moment sin no more."

Salvation is not found in the gallows or in the sword but in the cross. In the face of the cross of Christ our eyes are opened and we poor human beings are speechless. We realize the flimsiness of all the excuses and reasons given to try to justify the right of self-defense and the death penalty.

Furthermore, today's prison system, whose inhumanity we have experienced ourselves, needs to be totally reformed. Especially shaming to our culture are the concentration camps. No words can express the inhumanity of the Nazi concentration camp in Dachau, where an average of twelve to fourteen thousand people were murdered every day, or the fact that millions of others perished in the other camps because of hunger and torture. However, despite these atrocities and crimes which cry to the high heavens, some of the cruel methods that Nazi Germany employed against those holding differing political views are still being used by Germany's conquorers, instead of letting love and forgiveness rule to pave the way toward peaceful understanding. Because evil is being repaid for evil, hate and revenge are sown; and thus the next world war is being prepared. Justice demands that Nazi Germany recognize its errors and acknowledge its guilt.

In the name of Christianity, we have to demand the abolition of concentration camps, espionage services, and secret police organizations (Gestapo, secret services, CIC, etc.) in every country. Peace on earth will never be achieved by brutal force, violent methods, or anything that serves to promote violence.

5. Our position regarding the teachings about war

Earlier we briefly presented the teachings on war, armaments, and conscription defended by the Catholic Church. At first glance it seems as if these teachings are generally accepted and thought to be certain, carrying in the Church nearly the weight of dogma. However, in our opinion, and as we will prove, these teachings are not at all certain but are debatable. At the very least, one has to acknowledge our good intentions and before rejecting our opinion has to study and analyze our reasoning.

We venture to say that the currently prevalent teachings about war are incorrect, and we advance the proposition that since Christianity and war are totally irreconcilable, there is no such thing as a "just war," that every Christian should be a conscientious objector, and that, logically, conscription has to be flatly rejected.

As a consequence of our above-stated position regarding self-defense and being armed and trained in the use of weapons, our position on war, armaments, and conscription has been unequivocally decided. For if a Christian, following Christ's teaching and example, rejects forcible self-defense—in fact, has to reject it—and therefore cannot bear arms, that is, return violence for violence, this firm conviction defeats the entire "just war" ideology worked out extravagantly by Christian theologians. Also, arming for war has lost all meaning, and every form of obligatory military service has to be rejected. Because of this attitude, the Christian who rejects the right to wage war has to be a conscientious objector.

This sober assessment makes unnecessary any further analysis of the requirements that from a Christian viepoint have to be met for a war to be "just defensive," in which the conscripted soldier is bound by oath to kill the enemy, in blind obedience to an order of the state.

However, because of the great importance of this issue, we are going to examine the arguments of the Christian defenders of the "just defensive war" in order to determine whether their reasoning rules out every doubt about their validity. We will prove that under today's conditions there cannot be a "just defensive war." But first, as an introduction to our remarks, we will give a brief summary of the book *The Church and Peace*, by Hermann Hoffmann.

a. The Church and Peace, *by Hermann Hoffmann*

The title of this section refers to the Roman Catholic Church. The Catholic theologian Hermann Hoffmann gave his book *The Church and Peace* the subtitle *From the Peace Church to a World of Peace*, pointing out the purpose of his work.

Hoffmann's remarks begin with an excellent, brief overview of the efforts made by Catholic popes, bishops, theologians, and writers to prevent war and to work for peace. The Church of Christ, purely and simply, has in its teachings again and again met its obligations to proclaim and negotiate peace, as Hoffmann proves in the first part of his work.

The author concludes that because the Church is a peace church and opposed to war, Christians have to work for peace, and he briefly shows how this can be done. In the first part of his book Hoffmann includes a number of statements from papal encyclicals and pastoral letters of bishops.

He presents the opinions of Catholic theologians and guiding principles of peace groups to erase any doubt that the Church of Christ can rightfully be regarded as a peace church and that she has again and again fulfilled her duty to work for peace.

Following is a short summary of this very important book. We will point out a number of passages that illuminate our own comments but, above all, will prove that many of the questions regarding the commandment "you shall not kill" are still contested. Therefore, no one may challenge our right to express our views on these questions in an effort to work toward a final resolution. Our goal is solely to stimulate the development and deepening of Christian teachings about war, and it is the responsibility of our Church's teaching authority to render a final decision on these contested questions and to end this dispute.

Hoffmann's book begins with an essay by Cardinal Theodor Innitzer of Vienna, titled "The Holy Year and Peace," which presents evidence that the Catholic Church has always been a leader regarding the issue of peace, and that wars can only be prevented where justice and peace reign. After citing several relevant biblical passages, the cardinal states, "Jesus has rejected every war,"[18] and "like our Master Jesus, his apostles also proclaim the good news of peace and emphasize that true peace can only be found in a relationship with God."[19] Innitzer also states,

> There can be no peace without justice and love. There can be no true, lasting peace when freedom and natural law, when the conditions essential for the life of a nation are disregarded or thwarted. For the command to give or to let everyone have what belongs to him, and thereby create or maintain peace, applies not only to the individual but also to nations. For the sake of justice, peace and peacefulness is an obligatory commandment. There will always be differences of opinions and interests between individuals and groups, but their settlement should never result in forgetting that all people are brothers and sisters and that they should all pray to the same God: "Our Father!"[20]

Innitzer also writes, "Tertullian, Origen and Lactantius were absolutely opposed to war,"[21] and "while the Church itself did not forbid military service, the spirit of the early Church was without a doubt strongly unfavorably disposed toward war and warlike ways. The holy fathers Cyprian, Chrys-

18. Hoffmann, *Kirche und der Friede*, 4.

19. Ibid., 6.

20. Ibid., 17–18.

21. Ibid., 7.

ostomus, and Ambrose clearly point this out."[22] He continues, "Since there was no compulsory military service in the Roman Empire, there no controversy existed about being a soldier. A baptized Christian did not become a soldier."[23] Also, "we should not try to apologetically justify everything that happens in the Church. While a shadow remains a shadow, still the idea of the Church as bearer of the spirit of Christ remains, even though her actions often deviated greatly."[24] Here the cardinal mentioned the Crusades and said that "their kind of warfare far overshadows the boundaries of justice and love."[25]

To support his view, Innitzer cites various authorities. The first is Origen (d. 254), from *Apology against Celsus* (8, 73): "In overcoming the demons which stir up war and disturb peace, we render better service to the rulers than those who carry the sword. . . . We do not march into battle with the emperor, even if he demands it (conscientious objection!),[26] but we fight for him in that we establish our own camp, a camp of prayer, from where we send our prayer to God."[27]

From Lactantius (d. 340), *Divine Institutes* (6, 18, 20): "A righteous man is not permitted to bear arms. His duty is justice. He may not even accuse a felon, because there is little difference in whether someone kills with the sword or a word because killing is forbidden. Not the slightest exception from God's commandment should be made."[28]

From the letter of St. Cyprian (d. 258), a bishop, to Donatus: "While murder is a crime if committed by an individual, it is honored as a virtue and as bravery if committed by many. Thus it is not innocence that merits immunity from criminal proceedings but the large scale of the crime."[29]

From *The City of God*, by St. Augustine (d. 430), the great Doctor of the Church: "Whoever can think about war without feeling deep pain must have lost all human emotion. We must consider peace more precious than anything. There is no greater glory than to keep peace. How despicable is the glory of victory achieved by atrocities! It is more praiseworthy to kill

22. Ibid., 9.
23. Ibid., 8.
24. Ibid., 12ff.
25. Ibid., 14.
26. Translator's note: phrase in parentheses was inserted by Ude.
27. Hoffmann, *Kirche und der Friede*, 7.
28. Ibid.
29. Ibid., 9.

war with words than human beings with a sword, to win peace by means of peace and not by war" (69, 70).[30]

From an encyclical by Pope Leo XIII issued in June 1894: "Nothing is more necessary than to struggle against war, and everything done in this direction can be regarded not only as a great advancement of the Christian idea but also of the common welfare."[31]

From the comments of Cardinal Michael von Faulhaber of Munich, on the occasion of a disarmament conference: "The old saying 'if you want peace, arm for war' has to be eliminated. Today's endless armaments offer no protection against war and no guarantee of peace. Instead of 'prepare for war,' we say today, 'if you want peace, mobilize for peace.'"[32]

From *Militia Christi*, by Professor Adolf von Harnack, a Lutheran theologian: "No further words are needed to determine that the Gospel permits no form of violence, is in no way warlike, or permits bellicose actions."[33]

In the chapters that follow, Hoffmann elaborates on how the idea of peace and the desire to abolish war appear already in the writings of the prophets of the old covenant, how Christ makes them the essence of his teaching, and how the Catholic Church, from the Middle Ages to modern times, has promoted the idea of peace through its popes, bishops, theologians, and religious writers. He states,

> It is true that Christ has never explicitly forbidden war. Neither has he expressly forbidden slavery, or excess profiteering from land, or the exploitation of colonies, or morphine addiction. Therefore, should all of these be allowed? Instead, do we not have to find the answer to these and all other questions in the spirit of the Lord? Since Christ did not forbid war, the early Church did not do so either. Because during his time on earth Christ was not confronted with this question, he did not address it. The same holds true for the Church in its beginnings. Because the Roman Empire was at peace at the time the Church was developing, the latter neither approved nor disapproved defensive war. We cannot definitely determine whether before Emperor Constantine a Christian was ever a soldier, but it is doubtful.[34]

Among others, Hoffmann cites Tertullian (d. 240), a staunch opponent of war: "They are not compatible, the banner of God and the banner of

30. Ibid., 10.
31. Ibid., 13–14.
32. Ibid., 16.
33. Ibid., 5–6.
34. Ibid., 45–46.

men, the commander-in-chief symbol of Christ and the commander-in-chief symbol of the devil. A Christian can only wage war without a sword, because the Lord has abolished the sword."[35]

Hoffmann then quotes St. Justin (d. 166): "We had become experts in murder and every evil, but we all have exchanged our weapons. We have traded in our swords for plowshares and our lances for farming tools. Now we practice the fear of God, justice, kindness to others, faith and anticipation of the future, as they were given to us by God the Father through the Crucified One."[36]

Hippolytus (d. 235) gave this advice: "The soldier serving as a gendarme is forbidden to kill; and if ordered to kill, he may not do so."[37]

St. Basilius of Caeserea (d. 379) instructed all who had taken part in war to refrain from receiving Holy Communion for three years because of "the blood that had soiled their hands."[38]

Hoffmann points out that in the Middle Ages, the following popes worked for peace: Leo IV (d. 855), Gregory VII (d. 1085), Alexander III (d. 1181), and Innocent III (d. 1216). Innocent wrote to the king of France, "To bring mercy and peace to mankind is the first duty on earth of the worthy deputy of Jesus."[39]

Hoffmann notes that the great Church councils also acted to prevent and oppose war, including the Council of Limoges (1031), which condemned war with the following words: "Cursed are they and their accomplices because of the evil that they do, cursed be their weapons. Let them be like Cain, the murderer of his brother, like Judas, the betrayer . . . their joy should be wiped out in the face of the holy angels."[40]

The Lateran Council of 1514 explained that "in the community of the Christian nations, the *res publica christiana*, nothing is more injurious, nothing more heinous than war."[41]

Hoffmann comments accurately on the Crusades: "The Crusades demonstrate how the power of war almost cannot be resisted. First one defends oneself, then one conquers, and then one has to defend the conquered

35. Ibid., 47.
36. Ibid., 48.
37. Ibid.
38. Ibid., 49–50.
39. Ibid.,52.
40. Ibid., 55.
41. Ibid., 56.

peoples."[42] In the process the most despicable atrocities are committed, and much injustice is perpetrated.

Hoffmann reminds the reader that St. Francis of Assisi (d. 1226) forbade the members of his Third Order to carry weapons and to swear the oath of fealty that would have obligated them to bear arms.[43]

Then Hoffmann describes the efforts on behalf of peace by Popes Pius IX (d. 1878), Leo XIII (d. 1903), Pius X (d. 1914), Benedict XV (d. 1922), and Pius XI (d. 1939).[44] Prior to the outbreak of the Franco-Prussian War, Pius XI wrote to King Wilhelm I of Prussia, "Our most urgent desire is to live to see that armaments and war vanish and that the abominable suffering they cause is prevented."[45]

Leo XIII expressed his opinion in a speech in consistory on February 11, 1889: "Nothing is more urgent, nothing is more necessary than to work against war, and every effort in this direction has to be regarded as laudatory in the Christian spirit and for the benefit of all."[46]

In his Christmas address of December 23, 1894, Leo XIII said, "Since the highest priest is the incorruptible guardian of the faith and the defender of justice, he is to be regarded as the apostle of unity and world peace."[47]

Following this Hoffmann writes, "This presents us with the old question: First peace and then justice, or first justice and then peace? Leo, the apostle of world peace, did not believe that war creates justice. His famous encyclical of June 20, 1894, called the prevailing peace merely a pretense. He condemned the armaments race, decried conscription, and declared the struggle for justice to be the only method of eradicating the causes of war: 'ambition, greed for the property of others, and jealousy.'"[48]

In 1895 Leo XIII said, "How great it would be if the era of true peace would dawn, if cannons and rifles would be tossed aside, and if international questions would be decided by the open consultation of the rulers and the pope."[49]

In 1899 Leo wrote to Nicholas II, the czar of Russia, "One has wanted to manage the relationship between nations by a new law, based on the principle of utility, the right of the stronger, the success of *faits accomplis*, and on

42. Hoffmann, *Kirche und Friede*, 58.
43. Ibid., 60.
44. Ibid., 67–75.
45. Ibid., 62.
46. Ibid., 63–64.
47. Ibid., 64.
48. Ibid., 64–65.
49. Ibid., 65.

other points of view that deny the eternal and unchangeable principles of justice. This is the principal error that has led Europe into such a condition of discord."[50]

Pope Pius X wrote to his nuncio to the United States, "It is a highly noble task to work for the harmony of souls, to restrain belligerent tendencies, to fend off the dangers of war, and even to portray the so-called armed peace as uncalled for. Everything done to reach this goal, even if not done immediately or completely, demonstrates a noble attitude, serves the general welfare, and is worthy of praise. And this even more so in our age when the size of armies, the power of weapons, and the advancements in military science, foreboding the potentials of war, instill serious concerns in even the mightiest ruler."[51]

Hoffmann writes that Benedict XV "lives in history as the pope who, while maintaining total neutrality, again and again urged peace and did everything he could to relieve the horrors of the suffering caused by war. His first pastoral message was a call to peace. His words on the first Christmas of the war (1914) were very moving, but even more so was the admonition to peace he addressed to the warring nations and their rulers in July 1915."[52]

> In the sacred name of God, in the name of our Heavenly Father and Lord, for the sake of the blessed blood of Jesus, which he shed as ransom for mankind, we beseech you, whom God's providence has called to govern the nations now at war, to put an end to this horrible slaughter which has disgraced Europe for an entire year. The blood being shed is the blood of brothers. The most beautiful regions of Europe, this garden of the world, are covered with corpses and rubble. It is you who, before God and men, carry the dreadful responsibility for war and peace. Listen to our pleas, to the paternal voice of the deputy of the Eternal and Supreme Judge, to whom you must answer for the acts of the state as well as for the deeds of your personal life. It should not be said that this enormous conflict cannot be resolved without the force of weapons. It is necessary to abandon the plans of mutual destruction. Let us consider that nations do not die; humiliated and oppressed, grinding their teeth, they bear the yoke forced upon them while preparing to shake it off, while passing down hate and revenge from generation to generation. From now on, with a clear conscience, why not examine and consider the rights and just aspirations of the nations? Why

50. Ibid., 66.
51. Ibid., 68–69.
52. Ibid., 71.

> not enter into a direct or indirect exchange of ideas with an open mind, with the intent, within the realm of possibility, of achieving these rights and aspirations and thus ending this terrible struggle, as has happened in similar situations? Blessed is he who first raises the olive branch and holds out the hand to his enemy with the offer of reasonable terms of peace. The balance of power of the world and the thriving and guaranteed peace of the nations are based much more on mutual goodwill and respect of the rights and dignity of others than on mass armies and huge chains of fortresses.[53]

Hoffmann relates that on August 1, 1915, Pope Benedict picked up the olive branch and made his famous peace offer:

> He demanded that the moral power of law take the place of the material force of weapons. Consequently, all nations should come to an understanding about simultaneous and mutual disarmament according to agreed-upon rules and guarantees as to what is sufficient to keep public order in each nation. Armies would be replaced with a court of arbitration charged with the task of maintaining peace. The court would reach decisions according to agreed-upon criteria and guarantees if a state refused to submit international questions to this court or to accept its decisions.
>
> The pope called for freedom and shared control of the oceans. As for reparations for war damages and the cost of war, he proposed full and mutual renunciation, pointing out that this would be justified by the enormous advantages of disarmament, even more so because people would not understand that the slaughter was being continued for purely economic reasons.
>
> Pope Benedict further demanded the mutual return of occupied territories, the restoration of Belgium, the return of colonies, an investigation of territorial questions—for example, between Italy and Austria and between Germany and France—in a spirit of reconciliation because a lasting peace with disarmament would bring immense advantages. Finally, he urged an investigation of the questions of Armenia and Poland.[54]

Such a farsighted peace, founded on justice, would have saved the world incalculable mistakes and troubles in national, economic, and social matters. This appeal for peace is and remains forever the charter of the Catholic peace movement.

53. Ibid., 71–72.
54. Ibid., 72–73.

Hoffmann points out that Pope Pius XI continued the labors of his predecessor on behalf of peace by continually raising his voice "for the peace of Christ in the kingdom of Christ."[55]

From these various peace offers Hoffmann draws the conclusion that "it is not the Church that has failed, but we Catholics who have not paid attention to the papal peace messages. It is our fault that the peace popes have far too long remained commanders-in-chief without officers and armies."[56]

As for the frequently raised assertion that there will always be wars because of the depravity of mankind, Hoffmann comments astutely,

> We have no peace, and no one knows when peace will come. But no one may say that because there is no peace there will never be peace, and we will always have wars. This is completely wrong! The conclusion can only be: There will always be conflicts, but conflicts and war are two very different things. War is but one form of conflict. We have to strive to wage these conflicts in ways worthy of human beings and Christians. Our goal has to be to eliminate war as a form of conflict because it is unworthy of human beings and Christians. In the Kellogg-Briand Pact, statesmen have outlawed war as the Gospels did long ago. When will Christians outlaw it?[57]

Hoffmann mentions various other Church writers and theologians who have witnessed to Catholic peace efforts and the condemnation of war. These include the Doctors of the Church St. Augustine (d. 430) and St. Thomas Aquinas (d. 1274); the theologians Francisco de Vitoria (d. 1546), Vanderpol, Suárez, Bellarmine, F. Stratmann, Busenbaum (d. 1668), Gousset (d. 1866), St. Alphonsus Liguori (d. 1787), Molina (d. 1600), Konrad Martin (d. 1879), Franz X. Linsenmann (d. 1848), Anton Koch (d. 1915), and J. B. Hirscher (d. 1865). Hoffmann describes the views these men held about war and how these attitudes gradually led to the development of "the just defensive war," which today is regarded as permissible by the great majority of Catholics.

F. Stratmann, OP, summarized the "classical teaching of Catholic theology" in ten points. If every one of these ten conditions is present, a war is judged to be a "just defensive war," and it is morally permissible to wage it:

1. Serious injustice suffered by one or both of the contending parties.
2. A serious moral offense committed by one party.

55. Hoffmann, *Kirche und Friede*, 74.

56. Ibid., 75.

57. Ibid., 37.

3. Evidence beyond all doubt of this offense.
4. War is unavoidable after all serious attempts of conciliation have failed.
5. Proportionality of offense and methods of punishment—the war is unjust and impermissible if the punishment outweighs the offense.
6. Moral certainty that the just side will win.
7. Right intention that the war will promote what is good and avoid what is evil. The good that the war will achieve for a state must outweigh the harm it is expected to cause.
8. Right method of waging war—observing the bounds of justice and love.
9. Prevention of serious upheaval of non-belligerent states and the entire Christian community.
10. Declaration of war by a legally authorized government that in the name of God may enforce his justice.[58]

Hoffmann comments, "These ten demands formulated by Stratmann brand every war of conquest, every war of revenge, and every imperialistic war as unjust."[59]

Hoffmann does not fail to prove that the above-named theologians—Busenbaum, Gousset, St. Alphonsus Liguori, Molina, Martin, Linsenmann, Koch, and Hirscher—have more or less watered down the strict Catholic teaching about the legitimacy of the "just defensive war." However, whenever any of these theologians adopt this stricter viewpoint of the Church, they are still inclined to assume that it is nearly impossible to secure reliable evidence in order to make a judgment as to whether a war is permissible. Since the common soldier is not able to judge whether a war is just or unjust, he may serve, except in a clearly and unquestionably unjust war.

Following the chapter about the teachings of theologians on war, Hoffmann presents the opinions of several generals of modern times. Their views demonstrate that the politics of nations no longer pay heed to the teaching of the Church on the just defensive war. He writes, "War becomes a duel fought with lethal weapons until one side is no longer able to fight. The difference is that in a duel one or the other of the opponents falls or is no longer able to fight. In combat between nations the statesmen or generals do not fall. Neither do those who profit from war nor the industrialists who

58. Ibid., 80–81.

59. Cited in ibid., 82.

produce armaments. The people and the unknown masses suffer and shed their blood until they can no longer fight."[60]

Hoffmann continues,

> The duel cannot determine who is right, cannot restore honor, and cannot be a satisfaction for an insult to one's honor. It can only determine who can shoot, strike, wound, and kill better and more cruelly. The same is true of war. . . . The duel has long been forbidden by the Church and the Catholic conscience. War, which has been declared illegal by a number of statesmen, likewise has to be outlawed by the state and society, by the Church, Christianity, and the Christian conscience. This moral banishment of war must lead to its elimination from the thoughts, imagination, and emotions of human beings because it is an indecent, dishonorable, and morally unjustifiable method of governing nations. The conscience of the Christian outlaws war.[61]

In the following chapter, titled "Today's War," Hoffmann presents convincing evidence that one should no longer be able to use the term "just defensive war," either now or in the future. He writes, "We know from the last war [World War I] and even more so from the approaching one [World War II] that war is not compatible with the spirit of Christianity."[62] He comments, "If Jesus wants to recognize us as his disciples by the way we love one another as he loved us, can anyone who throws hand grenades or gas bombs hope to be identified as his disciple? . . . In shooting to pieces, mutilating, and poisoning our human brother, we murder also our holy brother Jesus. . . . Our yes to our brother Christ demands that we say no to war."[63] Hoffmann writes further, "War is no longer confined to one country. Today the issue is much more serious and fundamental. It is whether all of us—whether we be German, French, British, American, Polish, or Czech—want, for reasons of state, to continue to justify a system sanctioned, taught, and practiced in Christendom that flatly contradicts the most fundamental Christian rules of life."[64]

"It would be seemly for Christians to let the Gospels be the judge of war, but it should not be forgotten that other factors can force us to revise our views about war, which lost its meaning and its dignity in World War I.

60. Ibid., 92.
61. Ibid., 93–94.
62. Ibid, 95.
63. Ibid., 97–98.
64. Ibid., 98–99.

A strictly defensive war no longer exists. War ruins what it seeks to defend. . . . War of today and tomorrow is no longer war but, to use papal words, 'an inhuman slaughter and a horrible bloodbath.'"[65]

Hoffmann writes, "Today a defensive rampart can no longer serve as protection against the modern technology of destruction, which neither defends nor makes defense possible any longer and which will turn the next war into the murder of Europe. Today's warfare includes confusing and deceiving public opinion. Cardinal Faulhaber writes that modern technology has produced methods, especially aerial combat and the use of gas, which are no longer human, much less Christian."

From the above comments, Hoffmann draws conclusions that arise for the individual believer from the Christian teaching about war. He points out the recent accomplishments of theologians, peace groups, and representatives of churches working to prevent war. The author believes that disarmament and the elimination of universal conscription are necessary, especially since many well-known Church leaders have long demanded these—for example, Cardinal Benoît-Marie Langénieux, who described conscription as "godless and destructive of the freedom of conscience"; Bishop Wilhelm Ketteler of Mainz; Monsignor d'Hulst; and Bishop Michael Keller of Münster.[66]

We agree with Hoffmann that conscientious objection is an "international obligation," as does the earlier quoted moral theologian Franz Keller of Freiburg.

Hoffmann draws the conclusion that "a new encounter of politics and morality is necessary" and that "a complete end has to be made to the absolute state."[67] He demands that "we purify the concepts of nation and fatherland and regard nationalism as the heresy of our age. Besides justifiable nationalism, we must foster international relations and work toward a community of nations."

He again quotes Cardinal Faulhaber: "The love for one's own nation should not be based on hate and the mania to reduce the territory of other nations. . . . We will have to learn that we also have made and can make mistakes." Faulhaber demanded just rights and protection for minorities and called for the reduction of the excessive claims of sovereignty by the nations; he said, "The following words of Christ have to become part of the common consciousness of all citizens: 'Do not do to others whatever you

65. Ibid., 101, 104.

66. Ibid., 122.

67. Ibid., 124.

would not want them to do to you, and do to others whatever you would have them do to you.'"[68]

Hoffmann writes,

> The era of colonies has passed. All countries having colonies are guilty because the colonial peoples want freedom and should be permitted to demand it. Instead of colonies there should be "an inner colonization" as well as "continuing education for peace." Unfortunately, Catholics have failed substantially in this regard by not having adopted the spirit of peace of the Church of Christ. The nations, especially their youth, have to be shown that working for peace is true heroism, a much greater heroism than to murder in battle. Especially the mothers of our nation should think about what Bishop Burger of Freiburg said: "Love of the fatherland is not demonstrated only in exercises on the battlefield. We cry out: War never again! Women especially cry out. They did not give birth to their children so that they could be torn to pieces on the battlefield but so that they could live and work."[69]

Hoffmann relates that the papal nuncio Orsenigo told members of the press in Berlin on May 9, 1931, "Today, more than ever, it is the duty of the journalist to direct his conscience toward the ideas of justice and peace in order, with untiring effort, to instill this attitude in his readers."[70]

The final part of Hoffmann's book briefly describes the work of various Catholic peace organizations and champions of peace and offers a short list of important books and pamphlets that cover the issue of war and peace. The appendix consists of relevant statements by popes, bishops, theologians, and peace associations cited by Hoffmann. We are going to quote from a few of them:

Pope Leo XIII commented on the dangers of military service in his letter of June 20, 1894, to all of the world's rulers and peoples: "The inexperienced youth are thrown into the dangers of military life where they are deprived of the counsel of their parents and removed from their authority. In their bloom and vigor, young men are called from farms, beneficial studies, commerce and trades to bear arms. Things have gone so far that the armed peace has gradually become unbearable."[71]

68. Hoffmann, *Kirche und Friede*, 129–30.

69. Ibid., 131.

70. Ibid., 141.

71. Ibid., 161–62

Writing to the journalist W. T. Stead on January 12, 1899, Pope Leo expressed this opinion: "Securing peace has to become the noblest goal of human aspirations. Accordingly, the Holy See, if it wishes to remain faithful to its tradition, cannot desire anything more ardently than that all nations are united as brothers in a league of peace and that justice reign in international relations."[72]

In his peace encyclical of May 23, 1920, Pope Benedict XV emphasized the love of neighbor, and of the enemy, with the following words:

> It is our wish that you bishops urge especially your priests, as servants of peace, to zealously stand up for what constitutes the essence of human life, namely, the love of neighbor, including of one's enemies. By becoming everything for everyone, may they be a shining example and resolutely "wage war" against enmity and hate. . . . We wish that our reminder of the duty of the individual to practice love would be extended to those nations that fought in the Great War so that, as far as possible, every cause for strife will be removed, justice served, and these countries again resume relations of friendship. For the Gospel's commandment of love among individuals differs in no way from what should hold true for states and nations, since they are nothing but the collection of human beings. In this era of fascists, national socialists, communists, imperialists, capitalists, and plutocrats double attention should be paid to these last words.[73]

We cite the following statement from the joint pastoral letter of the Austrian bishops of August 4, 1918, which concisely explains the causes of World War I:

> Science, alienated from God, believes in unending progress and rejects every supernatural truth. Technology, with its unlimited possibilities, has achieved much and dreams of a kind of omnipotence. Because of the international communications and commerce that this proud generation has created, it presumes that the plea "Our Father, give us today our daily bread" is unnecessary and that hunger and misery have been eliminated forever. A social welfare system insuring everyone against hail and fire is intended to substitute for God's divine providence. This unforeseen secular advancement has fostered the delusion of autonomy and self-aggrandizement in relation to God and his revelation imparted to us by the Church. And since false ideas logically have to lead to calamitous actions, this

72. Ibid., 163.

73. Ibid., 164–65.

> self-aggrandizement, which denies the boundaries of Christian justice, has dragged "politics without morals," "the will to power," and "the right of the stronger" into the economic and national competition of nations. But wherever the principle of the right of the stronger exists, wars are unavoidable. The only source of justice is God, and justice cannot be established the way laws are made. Only the will of God creates justice.[74]

In his appeal for peace of August 1, 1917, Pope Benedict XV called for mutual disarmament and a court of arbitration. He demanded that "the raw force of weapons be vanquished by the ethical power of justice" and suggested that "there are other methods to restore violated rights between nations than violence and destruction."[75]

Under the chairmanship of Bishop Besson, a theological verdict about the ethical permissibility of war was hammered out in Freiburg, Switzerland. It states, "Modern war, because of its mechanization and lack of restraint, causes such tremendous material and spiritual damages to the individual, the family, society, and even religion, and is such a terrible world catastrophe, that it ceases to be an appropriate means of securing order and peace."[76]

Hoffmann's book *The Church and Peace* proves clearly that today's view of war (discussed here in Part I, section 9), widely held in Catholic circles, is no longer reconcilable with Christian teaching. His work shows us clearly that an encouraging tendency can be observed—a striving to do more justice to God's great commandment "You shall not kill" and to strengthen the teachings about war and peace in the spirit of Christ's words and example. This will help get rid of the traditional, often thoughtlessly accepted patterns of thinking of earlier times.

The continuing development of Christian teaching about war seems to be directed toward outlawing war all down the line. At the very least, however, influential authorities are leaning toward a stricter interpretation of the questions connected with war so that we no longer have to fear that our comments will be rejected from the start. On the contrary, Hoffmann's presentation raised our courage to claim the authorities he cited, develop them further, summarize them systematically, and use them to support our own arguments. The terrible experiences of World War II virtually cry out for a thorough examination of the war ideology Christian churches have championed until now.

74.. Hoffmann, *Kirche und der Friede*, 176–77.

75. Ibid., 191.

76. Ibid., 111, 194–201.

b. There is no "just defensive war"

We tend to disregard that today, as always, every warring side, including the unjust aggressor, has time and time again claimed that it was conducting a just war.

The Christian supporters of self-defense and the "just defensive war" are theoretically correct when teaching that every war is unjust on at least one side but that it cannot be unjust on both sides. Therefore, in every war, the entire population of at least one side should refuse to take part because it is taught correctly that even when there is a doubt about whether or not a war is just, one should refuse to serve in it. Even though this teaching is logical, it has never been put into practice. Rather, both sides pray for victory. "God, punish England," Christians prayed here, and there Christians prayed, "God, destroy Germany." Each country wanted to have God on its side so that with his help it would be able to defeat the other, which, of course, can only be achieved by means of killing and destruction. Thus God should take part extensively and earnestly in this mass murder. Therefore, on all sides the weapons are expressly blessed so that the soldiers commanded to commit mass murder may kill and destroy successfully and render the enemy harmless.

Here we must ask: Of what use is a theory or a teaching that since the beginning of mankind has never been, and probably never will be, put into action? And if need be, who should render a clear-cut decision as to which side's claims are just? Such a decision should be made about every war so that the Christian churches could remind their faithful on the side of the unjust aggressor of their duty of conscientious objection. Only, as far as we know, this has never occurred. After the horrors of war have passed, a condemnation no longer serves a purpose. Even the most ardent supporters of self-defense and the "just defensive war" cannot deny that every war is dreadful and un-Christian.

Everyone who defends war believes that the statement "If you want peace, prepare for war; arm yourself and be ready to fight" is reasonable and that armaments—and, in specific cases, even war—may be able to guarantee peace. Furthermore, the defenders of war (here we mean a "just defensive war") must always believe that peace is guaranteed and safeguarded best if an enemy is completely destroyed and rendered innocuous. This idea is logically accurate. However, if the unjust aggressor intends to annihilate the opponent, the unjustly attacked side can only defend itself by doing everything possible to destroy the aggressor first.

Does such a theory not lead to the conclusion that whoever is unjustly attacked is permitted to wage total war? Whoever thinks logically has to approve of total war and the destruction it wreaks as the only effective method of waging war if the aggressor wages total war. For, as we have experienced in World War II, if one warring side decides on total war, the other side is forced to do likewise unless it wants to surrender immediately. After all, the supporters of self-defense justify that the individual may, if necessary, kill the unjust aggressor. In war, numerous individuals over here face many individuals over there. If, for example, those over there favor total war, they are determined to annihilate those over here. However, if those over here do not want to be totally destroyed first—since the theory that self-defense is justified—they seek to beat those over there to the punch by annihilating them first, that is, by destroying an entire nation.

For in total war the entire population works only for war, according to a plan. No one may remain neutral in a nation waging total war. Men, women, the aged, and children participate in one way or another, directly or indirectly. In total war one entire population sides against another entire population. All of the so-called fatherland helps relentlessly to keep the war of annihilation going. If the attacked nation succeeds in destroying the aggressor in his hinterland, the latter's army fighting on the front will soon be finished. Then the attacked country, having accomplished its goal of total destruction, finally has its desired peace and tranquility.

We have to ask whether those who advocate war do not dread such conclusions. However, they have to draw them because total war has already become a reality. With great horror we experienced it firsthand. If the aggressor wages total war, what else can an unjustly attacked state do but to act likewise and attempt to destroy the other first?

Or do the supporters of the "just defensive war" suddenly want to deny the right of self-defense to the attacked side because the aggressor is waging total war? A determination by one side to annihilate the other can only be met with a similar determination by the other side if the latter's defense is to have any chance of success.

What else does this mean than that the entire Christian war ideology, as presented by Christian moral philosophers and theologians, simply does not hold its own against the realities of modern warfare but breaks down completely? Is the total destruction of the opponent the utmost wisdom? However, we also have to consider that today no nation can ever assert justifiably that it is waging a "just defensive war," because all of the following poison both the life of nations and international relations: lies, incitement, hate, the most brutal violence, exploitation, expropriation, deceit, hypocrisy, bad example, violation of all human rights, denial of God, exaggerated nationalism, the mania of sovereignty, wrong conduct of life, and rejection of Christianity and Church.

Therefore, no nation may justifiably say that it had no part in the outbreak of war and thus waged a just defensive war. For only that country which can say without reservation that God's Ten Commandments (which agree with ethics and morals based on natural law and reason) and the ethical demands of Christianity have been kept in the lives of individual citizens as well as in civic, economic, political, and international affairs may say with a clear conscience that it had no part in the outbreak of war. Which nation is justified in doing so? The facts prove that any state claiming this is lying.

The above reflection proves that the war ideology of the Christian nations breaks down because, considering modern methods of waging war, there can be no "just defensive war" in the face of the great collective guilt of every nation participating in international relations. Today all wars are, on one hand, economic enterprises of internationally organized capitalism, which is exploiting the people of the world in order to produce huge gains for those who benefit from war. Another principal cause of war, besides private or state investments, is fascistic, national socialistic, communistic, and imperialistic organizations, at the mercy of the despotism of shameless dictators and political parties, which employ raw violence, trample on all human rights, and enslave peoples and nations.

Exaggerated nationalism, combined with the principle that everything that benefits the state (read: party bosses) is permissible and that the individual exists only for the sake of the nation, meaning that everyone and everything has to serve the leaders unconditionally and without criticism, has created the atmosphere that made World War II possible. In this, the most dreadful of all previous wars, states that were more or less totalitarian waged total war in which self-defense no longer acted as the motivating factor, but rather the sadistic determination to achieve the total, merciless destruction of the enemy by every possible means.

This war ideology of Christians who believe that self-defense is justifiable and who thus support war fails and is completely irrelevant when applied to total war because the enormously developed technology of war cannot be turned back. On the contrary, in the next war, efforts will be directed to surpass the methods of World War II. This is proven by the atom bomb that ended that war. Even in war one never learns.

Therefore, the only thing that Christian churches—above all, the Catholic Church—can do and should do is to trust in the eventual victory of Christian moral teaching and simply forbid their faithful to take part in any war. They should do this because, on one hand, the Christian moral law rejects the totalitarian state as well as total war and, on the other hand, because today a "just defensive war" does not exist. Only a firm faith in the unreserved validity of the commandment "you should not, you may not kill" has the power to liberate humanity from the tyranny of war.

After these general comments we turn to a critical examination of the reasons and conditions advanced by supporters of the "just defensive war" (again, we do not agree that there is such a thing) in order to prove that it is morally permissible. As we have noted earlier, the following four major conditions, as well as other minor ones, have to exist for a war to be called a "just defensive war." It has to be declared by the proper authority of a nation; a just cause has to exist; it has to be waged with the right intention; and the good to be achieved must be greater than the harm the war will cause. (Earlier, we listed the ten conditions delineated by P. Stratmann.)

First of all, the war has to be declared by the proper authority.

If a nation directly, by voting, or indirectly through its elected representatives, decides on war, it is the general population that desires the war and thus as a whole bears the responsibility. The matter becomes more difficult if a single individual endowed with full authority, such as an emperor, a king, or an absolute ruler, decides to fight a war. In this case the people are not consulted and, certainly, the absolute ruler bears full responsibility for his grave decision. However, in this instance, where compulsory military service exists, the entire population has to submit without resistance and has to be available to commit mass murder upon command. Whoever refuses is simply shot. The dictator holds every means of force in his hand and uses it ruthlessly.

In the above case, what should citizens do who are conscientious objectors? Supporters of the "just defensive war" theory simply say that the ordinary citizen may not presume to make a judgment about whether a war is justified. He simply has to acquiesce in the government's interpretation of the political situation because that authority claims to be better informed. Such an assertion is clearly a rape of conscience because, in the final analysis, only the individual conscience should determine whether to act upon the order of an authority.

However, supporters of the "just defensive war" go much further. They permit the authority of the state to bind individuals by oath to kill and destroy if commanded by military superiors. Thus far, however, the Church has been able to keep priests free of the obligation to fight in war because of the dignity conferred by their ordination. Several modern nations have disregarded this exception and called clerics and theologians to war service because they are also citizens. And when conscription was legalized, the Church never objected to the governments of Europe. On the contrary, the actual behavior of Church authorities approved of it. And if it is morally acceptable to kill and destroy in a "just defensive war," we cannot see why priests and bishops, like their fellow countrymen, should not offer their lives for their nation if its highest official, who alone has the supposedly correct understanding and is responsible for military preparedness, decides to go to war.

The correct understanding! That is what it is all about. But what guarantee is there that he, who because of his character and abilities alone has the decisive power over war and peace, is able to render the right judgment in the serious matter of whether or not a conflict would be a "just defensive war"? For the mere claim by the supreme state authority that he is waging a "just defensive war" and is assuming total responsibility for it does not guarantee that this is actually the case. Here we are thinking about Adolf Hitler, the "Führer" of the German nation.

However, what can be done if reasonable doubts exist about whether the war the highest government authority has decided to wage is just? Do millions of the country's inhabitants have to pick up weapons and other millions work to support the war effort only because one person believes he is fighting a just war and even escalates it into a total war?

We know that supporters of the "just defensive war" are right when they teach that if valid doubts exist about whether a war is morally permissible, it may never be waged; and whoever is ready to go to war, whether or not the conflict is just, sins gravely.

Without a doubt, Church authorities on both sides viewed World War II, a total war, as just. For had they regarded it as unjust, or even merely doubted whether it was justified, Christian churches would have had to forbid their faithful to participate in it. Church officials would have made conscientious objection obligatory, even at the risk of the faithful being killed because of that conviction, which surely would have been the case. To view such a monstrous war as World War II as unjust and still fight in it or merely remain silent would be to share in the guilt of all the horrors and injustices of this war and to betray Christianity. How does our divine Savior put it? "Anyone who wants to save his life will lose it; but anyone who loses his life for my sake will find it. What, then, will anyone gain by winning the whole world and forfeiting his life?" (Matt 16:25–26). And again: "Do not be afraid of those who kill the body but cannot kill the soul; fear him rather who can destroy both body and soul in hell" (Matt 10:28).

While we do not wish to accuse leaders of Christian churches of intentionally betraying Christ and his teachings, we must assume, much to our regret, that World Wars I and II were regarded by both sides as "just defensive wars." In World War II church leaders in the Allied countries clearly stated that they were waging a "just," a "holy" war. By their silence about Word War II and by raising no objections to the war service of the clergy and laymen, leaders of Christian churches in Nazi Germany and the other Axis powers demonstrated clearly that they considered it a "just defensive war." To say it once again: If there was any doubt about the justice of this war waged by the National Socialists, the spiritual authorities of the various Christian denominations were obligated to raise objections; but this did not happen. Therefore, our assumption is correct.

A pamphlet titled "What Are the World Churches Saying about This War?"[77] by Dr. Matthes Ziegler, NSDAP[78] director of supervision of ideological training and education of party members, includes the following statements by officials of Christian denominations justifying the war waged by the Allies. Unfortunately, other documents were unavailable to us. Although it was impossible to check their accuracy, we assume that the following quotations from the Ziegler pamphlet are accurate.

The Vatican's daily newspaper, *L'Osservatore Romano*, reported on September 13, 1939, "It has been said: 'A nation that does not defend itself does not deserve to exist.' There is even more truth in the statement: Nations which defend themselves have the right to live. This is the case with Poland, which deserves it doubly due to its heroically resisting simultaneously on two fronts. This is the desire and firm belief of those sharing the same faith, which is also the faith of Poland, because they realize that danger to Poland also threatens Catholicism itself."[79]

On May 11, 1940, after the German invasion of Holland and Belgium, Pope Pius XII sent the following telegram of sympathy to the king of Belgium: "At the moment that the Belgian people, for the second time, are exposed unjustly and against their will to the horrors of war, we assure you and the beloved Belgian people of our affection. We pray to God that this difficult trial will end with the restoration of complete freedom and independence. We extend our apostolic blessing to you and the Belgian people."[80]

This message received the warmest approval of the *Manchester Guardian*, which commented on May 5, 1940, "Germany has created such an atmosphere of fear in the entire world that few rulers dare to express their opinion about her criminal behavior. In many regions the mood of this time is silent horror. Therefore, those raising their voice in witness to the public conscience and in support of Germany's victims deserve our gratitude. . . .

77. Ziegler, *Was sagen die Weltkirchen zu diesem Krieg?*

78. *Nationalsozialistische Deutsche Arbeiterpartei.*

79. Ziegler, *Was sagen die Weltkirchen*, 26.

80. Ibid., 30–31.

The message of the pope will give courage to those who still safeguard and value Christian virtues."[81]

The bishops of England and Wales stated in a joint declaration on September 13, 1939, "This conflict was forced upon us by those who are indifferent to world unity and the peace of Christ. We, the Catholic hierarchy of England and Wales, at this time of national trials and efforts, urge all the faithful to fulfill their duty of laudable obedience to His Majesty the King and contribute enthusiastically to all aspects of national service. . . . No country has a greater claim to our efforts than Poland, which throughout the centuries has played a significant part in defending our mutual Catholic heritage."[82]

Archbishop Dorney of Liverpool wrote in a pastoral letter,

> We are entering a war whose duration no one can predict. However, we can be at peace because we are certain that this war is not our doing but that it was forced upon our nation by the unrelenting aggression of a man driven by insatiable ambition. Through our prime minister our country has done everything possible to avoid this war. Up to the last moment he tried to find a peaceful solution to the international problems. It appears that the chancellor of the German nation has decided upon war and deliberately sought to provoke it by attacking a neighboring country after, only twelve months earlier, having assured it of Germany's desire to live with it in friendship. The Catholics of this country are going to take part faithfully in this crusade by responding to this appeal directed to them as citizens: to preserve the principles of freedom and justice and to defend their fatherland against a fate of slavery which has already befallen other countries. We cannot forget how the German government has persecuted religion, especially the Catholic religion.[83]

Cardinal Arthur Hinsley, archbishop of Westminster, commented in a radio address of December 9, 1939, according to a report in the *Baseler Nachrichten*, "True freedom and true peace can only be won with the sword of the Spirit. The spiritual works are truth, justice, and charity. Therefore, above everything else, Great Britain picked up weapons in order to defend these values. During the last critical years, the current British government has done everything to keep the peace by freely negotiating past injustices. The direct causes of the current war are the cynical and systematic disregard

81. Ibid., n.p.

82. Ibid., 75.

83. Ibid., 75–76.

of truth, the ruthless breaking of promises, brutal violence, and inhuman persecution. Great Britain is innocent of all of these violations."[84]

In his radio address of August 3, 1940, Cardinal Hinsley expressed this opinion: "It seems to me to be a poor argument to point to our old sins in order to debate our active resistance against the injustice already inflicted upon Poland, Finland, Norway, Denmark, Holland, Belgium, and Luxembourg. As I look upon this as an immense struggle between light and darkness, a neutrality of the heart is impossible for me."[85]

The Swiss Catholic news service *Kipa* reported on February 20, 1940, that the Australian Bishop of Maitland bid farewell to Catholics serving in his country's expeditionary forces with the following words: "Your task is noble even though it means entering into a war. Pacifists, or at least a group of them, are condemning you. But we are all pacifists of sterling worth. We have prayed and worked for peace and hoped it would become a reality, but we have been unsuccessful. So now you must take leave of us in order to seek peace through war."[86]

France's Catholic daily *La Croix* wrote in its October 13, 1939, issue, "It is clear from pastoral letters and articles in Catholic publications that Catholics agree completely on these three points: (1) The present war is a true crusade. (2) We can only emerge victorious from this crusade. (3) However, spiritual mobilization is absolutely necessary. The present war is not only just but also a holy crusade—a moral and, therefore, a religious necessity—like the erstwhile struggle of Christianity against the threat of Islam."[87]

Cardinal Jean Verdier, archbishop of Paris, commented in his Lenten letter of 1940, "Our history has known no struggle whose mission was more spiritual, moral, and Christian except for the Crusades. This assessment makes the present war truly consecrated and fills our souls with unshakable confidence and the greatest courage. The victory that we anticipate must be the victory of all."[88]

As is well known, Pope Pius XII, in his encyclical *Summi Pontificatus* of October 20, 1939, published in seven languages, stated his opinion about the violation of Poland by Nazi Germany and pointed out that the life and peace of nations are greatly endangered by Nazi racist propaganda and the

84. Ibid., 76–77.
85. Ibid., 82.
86. Ibid., 83.
87. Ibid., 95–96.
88. Ibid., 104.

concept of the total state, as noted by Ziegler in quoting the following passage of this encyclical:

> To insure peaceful co-existence and fruitful relations between countries, it is an indispensable prerequisite that the nations honor and conduct themselves according to natural law on which international relations are based. This alone can assure that these relations are maintained and are effective. This natural law includes respect for the rights of existence, independence, and cultural advancement. It also includes the adherence to agreements entered into in accordance with international law. Without a doubt, a prerequisite for the peaceful co-existence of nations—so to speak the soul of all lawful relations between them—is mutual trust. This includes the assurance that promises are kept by both sides; that all parties are convinced that wisdom is much better than the force of weapons (Eccl 9:18); and the willingness to negotiate before proceeding to the use of force whenever obstruction, impediments, changes, or other disagreements occur, as these may not necessarily derive from evil intentions but could be caused by changed conditions or by opposing interests. If, however, one wanted to separate international law from divine law in order to make it conform to the will of the state, one would diminish it and cause it to lose its strong and noble mooring. Then it would succumb to the fatal dynamic force of private interests and collective selfishness which seek to secure their own rights at the expense of others.[89]

Regarding this encyclical, Cardinal Verdier of Paris commented in the journal *Semaine Religieuse*,

> The pope has addressed the Catholic and indeed the entire world. He shines light on the bloody conflict in which millions of people are opposing each other. This encyclical clearly points out the ultimate causes of the war, namely, the struggle for power, raw violence, the breaking of promises and treaty obligations, systematic lies, and all inhumane and immoral ideas which our enemies employ and with which they endanger our culture. The pope condemns all of these so clearly and forcefully, thereby greatly relieving the human conscience. How touching is the way in which the pontiff embraces his beloved and unfortunate Poland and discusses its restoration in the future. Pius XII has shined the light of purity and fidelity on humanity.[90]

89. Ziegler, *Was sagen die Weltkirchen*, 15ff.

90. Ibid., 12–13.

All of the above statements by authorities of the Christian churches on the side of the Allies demonstrate clearly that they were convinced they were fighting a "just defensive war" and, like the aggressor, Germany, and the other Axis powers, could wage it as a total war of annihilation. How very deeply I regret this.

All protestations of the Allies that they are innocent regarding World War II must be rejected as false, however. While the immediate, direct cause of this war was Hitler's Germany, the other Axis powers as well as the Allies are likewise guilty. Or have the Allies already forgotten the existence of the treaties of Versailles and St. Germain? Or are they free from capitalism, fascism, imperialism, the quest for world power, hate, a propaganda of lies, or loathsome espionage services? Is the "Secret Service," which stealthily employs murder, bribery, and defamation, only a figment of the German imagination, or is it as real as the Nazi Gestapo, the German SS, and the Russian GPU?

Is communism not a continual threat to world peace? Furthermore, how can the Allies justify the undeniable cruelties they inflicted in waging war? We recall the inhumane slaughter caused by the phosphor bombs dropped on German cities. We ourselves experienced these while imprisoned in Linz and Wels. Can these attacks be justified by saying that Hitler first perpetrated such cruelties on the civil populations of Rotterdam, Warsaw, and Belgrade? If, as a Christian, one desires to follow without reservation the great commandment to love one's enemy, can one justify such cruelties by saying that the other side has also committed them? And the Christian churches, including the Catholic Church, call their war "a holy war," "a holy crusade," a war they claim to be completely innocent of causing, and one that, they maintain, they are waging in the name of culture, civilization, and Christianity? Do these allegations not prove how religion is frightfully misused for political purposes?

But why waste any more words? Just as Nazi Germany and the states aligned with her may not claim that they are innocent regarding this war, the countries attacked by Germany may not say so either. All peoples and nations of the world, without exception, are complicit. And Christians especially have to strike their breast and confess, "Our guilt, our guilt, our great guilt."

The following has to be said about the previously listed conditions by advocates of the "just defensive war." The only cause warranting a defensive war is a serious injustice perpetrated by one state on another that cannot be redressed by any other means. Furthermore, the good that this defensive war seeks to achieve has to be greater than the evil and horrors it would cause. In other words, this defensive war, meeting all other conditions, has to be more beneficial than harmful; for every war, even the just defensive war, is unspeakably dreadful and frightful.

Earlier, we tried to prove that there is no such thing as a "just defensive war," if for no other reason than that all nations share in the responsibility for a war. Therefore, we concluded that fighting a war is morally impermissible in every case. This is even more evident if we keep in mind that, as we maintained earlier, a Christian may never kill in so-called self-defense.

Therefore, the Christian churches have to reject war as irreconcilable with Christianity and to convince their faithful to refuse war service. In addition, the ideology about war maintained in Christian circles has to be abandoned as being false. Because Christianity and war are incompatible, every Christian is bound by his conscience to refuse to serve in war. It is an international, holy duty, as we preached to all the world after World War I.

A further task of Christian churches is to continually educate the nations, especially their youth, in this spirit, which means they should cry out fearlessly, to all authorities preparing for war, "*Non licet*": "This is not permitted." It will be much easier for Christian leaders to call out like this if we consider that the fourth condition advanced by advocates of a "just defensive war" is never met because the evils that modern total war causes far exceed the good it seeks to accomplish.

One only has to recall the Second World War's destruction on both sides—the millions of murdered people and the criminal destruction on the ground, below the ground, in the air, and in the water. No one will dare to maintain seriously that the good that was achieved equaled or exceeded the evil caused, if one stands in front of the ruins and rubble of bombed-out cities or observes the collapse of morals, the hardening of hearts, the loss of a sense of justice above and below. One has to reflect on the destruction of irreplaceable cultural treasures and how many years of hard work it will take to repair the material, intellectual, and religious losses. Even the most adamant racist and defender of blood and soil will have to admit that this war destroyed the best of our "noble German race" and that, in many cases, only the weaker people have remained. What sorry prospects for the future, and how long will it take for the mutual hatred that was cultivated by every possible method everywhere to fade away?

Every war is a serious aberration by nations and peoples. And unless they oppose war, the leaders of Christian churches share in the guilt for this most heinous going astray of the human spirit. It is no disgrace to admit one's error, however, to renounce it as soon as one recognizes it, and then to follow courageously a more enlightened persuasion.

How impressed the entire world would be if all Christian churches—and first of all the Roman Catholic Church—would condemn war without exception, that is, would stigmatize war, armaments, and conscription as irreconcilable with the Christian spirit. How all nations on earth would listen and breathe a sigh of relief!

For everyone who lived through World War II has to say: Not only are armaments, the willingness to go to war, and war necessitating conscription not morally justifiable methods of securing and maintaining peace, but conscription and arming for war, especially, combined with a declaration of total war, create a continual opportunity for a new war as well as fear among all nations of becoming entangled in the next armed conflict, for which a cause is most often intentionally sought and found. Because conscription demands that citizens surrender their will, they are being transformed into unaccountable, soulless automatons. This is a serious moral violation of their conscience. Christian churches should again and again drum this into the minds of their faithful.

This violation of conscience by the completely morally reprehensible system of conscription can be quickly ended by the nations themselves by immediately legalizing conscientious objection. If no one follows the call to arms and nobody lends himself to shooting or to imprisoning conscientious objectors, militarism will suffer the death it deserves.

Mothers and young women must show their contempt for the uniforms of soldiers instead of running after them, for women bear some of the responsibility for today's glorification of militarism, and with it, glorification of war. Women and mothers have to seriously consider this question: "Did we give birth to our sons and raise them with much effort and sacrifice, only for the monster state to slaughter them in war?"

Is it really the sole and highest duty of the sons of a nation to be soldiers? It almost seems that you mothers think so; for if you were convinced otherwise, you would not give your boys toy soldiers to play with. Do you want your nation to expose your sons and husbands again and again to the mouths of cannons and machine guns, to grenades, tanks, and deadly air attacks so that they can breathe their last on battlefields, be torn to pieces, or turned into cripples? If you do not want this to happen—and no loving wife and mother could—you must join us who are opponents of war and fight against it by ridding the world of its causes. You must speak out against war and work for peace in the nursery, in the family, and everywhere the opportunity presents itself.

In order to prevent any misunderstanding, we want to make it clear that it is not our intention to demean, insult, or deny the Christian conviction of those soldiers on every side who did not deliberately and intentionally commit cruelties but believed in good faith that it was their duty to do as ordered. Many of them, perhaps most, simply followed their certain conscience even if this personal conscience erred. For we cannot say often enough that every human being is obligated to follow his certain conscience even if it is essentially in error.

However, from what we have said about war not being permissible, it can be concluded that the conscience of all those who went to war in good faith seriously erred. Yet those who for good reasons consider self-defense, the "just defensive war," and the death penalty to be morally permissible cannot be called un-Christian. Yet for reasons we have stated and believe to be sound, they are mistaken and violate the Christian teaching about love, especially that of loving one's enemies.

The main task now is to enlighten humanity and to prove again and again that the prevailing Christian war ideology is erroneous. It is the duty of representatives of the Christian churches to boldly organize and lead this campaign. It appears that World War II has made the hearts of all peoples receptive to this enlightenment. Millions are waiting in eager expectation for the churches, in the name of Christ, to exclaim clearly and emphatically to the entire world the unconditional "You shall not, you may not kill." Not even in war.

c. Military preparedness, conscription, and Christianity

In this section we repeat a public speech we made in 1936 at the time of the Abyssinian War. For this speech and for an open letter to Benito Mussolini, published in several Swiss and other foreign newspapers, in which we held him responsible for this war, we were severely reprimanded and punished by the Austrian government, which at that time was friendly to the Italian dictator.

This speech dealt with the position Christianity should take regarding military training and conscription and the consequences resulting for a Christian. We have previously dealt with these issues and have rejected conscription on the basis of ethics founded on natural law and reason as well as on Christian morality. Because of the importance of this question, however, we consider it necessary to repeat these remarks. Following is the speech as it was given:

The Holy Scriptures tell us that nineteen hundred years ago a man walked on this earth, doing good and proclaiming his great commandment of love: "You must love your neighbor as yourself" (Mark 12:31); "This is my commandment: love one another as I have loved you" (John 15:12). Jesus did not want anyone excluded from this love. Our neighbor is every human being, even someone from another race, as is expressed so beautifully in the marvelous parable of the Good Samaritan. It is this commandment, the unreserved love of the enemy, which Christ and, in his name, the apostles emphasized again and again.

"You shall love your enemy" is not merely good advice, nor is it intended only for the perfect, but is a strict obligation of conscience for everyone, without exception. Whoever does not observe it cannot be a disciple of Christ. A true disciple of Christ does not wield a weapon. His only weapon is love, the kind of love that does not practice self-defense; if struck on one cheek, he offers the other. It is the kind of love that does not use violence to counter violence but that would rather be crucified than kill the crucifiers. This strict command to love one's enemy applies to private as well as to public life and also to international relations. A faithful Christian has to keep it unconditionally.

For nineteen hundred years Christianity has again and again seriously sinned against this great commandment, which today is especially trampled underfoot. Church and state officials are vying with one another in justifying and glorifying war, this organized mass murder, and praising it as if it were something great and holy. Thus Christian churches, including the Catholic Church, have become helpers' helpers. Catholic men, as well as other men, have to swear a sacred oath to be always ready to murder and destroy the enemy wherever and whenever national leaders say so. What a dreadful contrast there is between the demands of the Sermon on the Mount and the behavior of so many members and responsible authorities of Christian churches, including in Christian nations.

Nations and their citizens consider military preparedness primary and most important. Thus, without any opposition, both houses of Congress of the United States appropriated $1,100 million for military preparations, according to the *Grazer Tagespost* of March 4, 1936. The largest portion of taxes and the gross national product is sacrificed for the military. The matter of organized mass murder keeps the entire world constantly breathless and anxious and characterizes all politics. The profession of soldier is the most esteemed social status. The final and supreme wisdom of all statesmen consists in this: to be prepared for war.

It is no wonder that the ideas of military training and compulsory military service constantly occupy the minds of all statesmen, so that we live in an age of militarization of the nations. For in their relations with other states all nations of the world operate according to this principle: If you want peace, be armed to the teeth. And the leaders of nations reiterate: Only a state that is militarily prepared will be able to exist and keep the peace.

Poor Jesus! Today there is no room for you and your teaching in the world, not even in countries that pretend to rule in the name of God the Almighty, from whom all justice originates. What if you returned today and proclaimed in public assemblies and from pulpits, "all who draw the sword will die by the sword" (Matt 26:52), insisted that all who call themselves Christians should keep your law of nonviolence, and demanded that we should respond only with love to violence and unjust attacks, that is, that we conquer evil—the enemy—only with good? Jesus, if you were to come and publicly demand this, you would be considered a fool and locked up in a mental institution, forbidden to preach, judged to be a traitor and imprisoned, or regarded as an antisocial element and most likely killed.

For if you are right, there would be no military training or conscription. However, conscription has been legalized everywhere. Even the youth is taught to fight, and the ability to use arms is considered the highest virtue of the citizen. Love of the fatherland without military service has become inconceivable. To be a soldier, to be able to stab and shoot and take part in military drills, has become the alpha and omega of political wisdom.

Jesus, if I want to follow you, I have to become nonviolent like you, condemn the force of weapons, and object to military preparedness. Jesus, nowhere do you advise countering the violence of the unjust aggressor with violence. On the contrary, we are only your true disciples if, according to the principles of the Sermon on the Mount, we answer even the most unjust violence with love and do not defend ourselves with force. According to your teaching, we should be willing to sacrifice our lives. For "no one can have greater love than to lay down his life for his friends" (John 15:13). This is a command binding on all Christians; for as you showed your love by giving your life for us, we also must lay down our lives for our brothers. We should never take a life but should meet the aggressor unarmed, according to Christ's example. According to the words of the Lord, we should flee if we are unjustly persecuted: "If they persecute you in one town, take refuge in the next" (Matt 10:23). The true disciple of Christ should be unarmed and nonviolent. His only weapons are truth, love, and unconditional trust in God, and his trust is his only victorious weapon. If justice is on our side and we have love, we do not have to fear "those who kill the body but cannot kill the soul" (Matt 10:28). The only Christlike way to conquer evil, that is, the enemy, is with good, meaning with love. "Never try to get revenge; leave that, my dear friends, to the Retribution. As scripture says: *Vengeance is mine—I will pay them back*, the Lord promises. And more: *If your enemy is hungry, give him something to eat; if thirsty, something to drink. By this you will be heaping red-hot coals on his head.* Do not be mastered by evil, but master evil with good" (Rom 12:19–21). A Christian should be armed only with these words, never with a weapon that could render his enemy harmless or even take his life.

Let me say only this: Poison gas bombs render all soldiers defenseless. These bombs, hurled suddenly and unexpectedly from roaring airplanes, kill the most proficient soldiers, along with women, children, and the aged. Whoever talks about the ability to defend oneself, in this age of poison gas bombs, is either an idle chatterer or a calculating beneficiary from war. Poison gas warfare [and especially the atomic bomb!][91] makes all military preparadness irrelevant and useless.

Self-defense is never justified for a Christian. Instead, with childlike trust he submits to the teachings of the Sermon on the Mount and obeys them unconditionally. A true Christian has complete and unreserved trust in the enormous power that derives from literally abiding by Christ's clear teachings. We, however, often do not follow these teachings because of a lack of trust or our weak faith. We may agree theoretically that these teachings are true and right and will achieve victory, but our actions often betray our conviction. We Christians of today are largely a cowardly generation.

Therefore, there should be no military preparations, especially not according to the godless principle "if you want peace, prepare for war." Wherever we see soldiers marching and youths being subjected to pre-military training, there Christ and his Sermon on the Mount are not known. Or, if they are known, they are either denied or ignored.

If Christ supports military preparedness, why does he send his apostles and disciples unarmed into a world that opposes Christianity, where lies, injustice, hate, and violence prevail? The disciple of Christ does not need a weapon, nor should he have one, because Jesus says, "I am sending you out like lambs among wolves" (Luke 10:3). We should only wear the "armament of God," as Paul invites us: "So stand your ground, with truth *a belt round your waist*, and *uprightness* a *breastplate*, wearing for shoes on your feet *the eagerness to spread the gospel of peace* and always carrying the shield of faith so that you can use it to quench the burning arrows of the Evil One. And then you must take *salvation as your helmet* and the sword of the Spirit, that is, the word of God" (Eph 6:14–17).

Armed with such weapons, we have nothing to fear, for Christ himself encourages us when he says, "Be courageous: I have conquered the world" (John 16:33). Christ conquered the world and all opponents solely by his

91. Comment by the publisher, Hanns Kobinger.

witness to the truth, his love and his goodness, demonstrated by the supreme triumph of nonviolence on the cross.

"Jesus went about doing good . . ." (Acts 10:38). Therefore, the poet writes so convincingly,

> This is the sorrow of Good Friday:
> That the wicked world,
> Which is full of hate,
> Kills the best and the purest.
>
> This is the lesson of Good Friday:
> That He who overcomes the world
> For the salvation of humanity
> Is He who sacrifices Himself.
>
> This is the faith of Good Friday
> Which blazes brightly from the cross
> To die—to rise again
> It is death that gives new life.

This is Christian military preparedness, which, totally disarmed, never repays evil with evil but is always ready to offer the other cheek. This Christian way of "fighting" continues to blaze a trail in Christendom even though the world and many Christians do not want to have anything to do with it. Again and again, Christian voices can be heard that advocate for unarmed defense, that is, for nonviolence.

On March 12 the Catholic Church celebrates the feast of the holy martyr Maximilian of Tebessa, in North Africa, who was beheaded in 295 AD because he renounced military service and refused to fight, as he considered doing so to be unchristian. The *Acta Martyrum* describes Maximilian's interrogation by the proconsul Dion. Here is their dialogue.

> After Maximilian was recruited and judged to be fit for military service, the proconsul addressed him: "What is your name?"
>
> Maximilian answered, "Why do you want to know my name? I cannot be a soldier because I am a Christian."
>
> The proconsul ordered, "Let him be killed!"
>
> Maximilian replied, "I cannot serve in war. I cannot do anything unjust because I am a Christian."
>
> The proconsul ordered, "Measure him!"

He was measured, and it was reported, "He is 5 feet and 10 inches tall."

Dion ordered, "Give him the insignia!"

Maximilian refused, and said once more, "I cannot serve in war."

Dion: "Become a soldier, or you will die."

Maximilian: "I will not serve. Cut off my head. I serve no worldly power. I serve my God."

The proconsul asked, "Who taught you this?"

Maximilian: "My will and God who called me."

Now Dion said to Maximilian's father, Victor, "You persuade your son!"

Victor replied, "He understands enough to know what is good for him."

Dion said to Maximilian, "You must serve and take this insignia."

Maximilian: "I will not take this insignia because I am already marked with the sign of Christ, my God."

Dion ordered the officials, "He should be marked as a soldier!"

Maximilian resisted: "I want no worldly insignia, and if you place it around my neck, I will not be obligated by it. I am a Christian and may not wear a lead medallion after being signed with the mark of salvation of my Lord Jesus Christ. He is the son of the living God whom you do not know, who suffered for our salvation. God sacrificed him for our sins. All of us Christians serve and follow him, the source of our life and our salvation."

Dion commanded, "Become a soldier, take this insignia, or you will perish miserably."

Maximilian: "I will not perish. My name is already inscribed by the Lord. I cannot become a soldier."

Dion: "Think about how young you are and serve. This is fitting for a young man."

Maximilian: "My service is intended for the Lord. I cannot serve the world. I have already said: I am a Christian."

Dion: "There are Christians who served Diocletian, Maximian, Constantine, and Maximus as soldiers."

Maximilian: "They must have known what is good for them. As for me, I am a Christian and may not commit evil."

Dion: "What injustice do they commit who render military service?"

Maximilian: "You know that yourself."

Dion: "Become a soldier! If you scorn military service, you will perish miserably."

> Maximilian: "I will not perish. If I have to leave this world, my soul will live with Christ, my Lord."
>
> Dion ordered, "Write down his name!" When this was done, he said, "Because you have refused to become a soldier because of your pride, you shall become a terrifying example for others and receive the appropriate punishment."
>
> Then he read the judgment from a tablet: "Maximilian should be executed with a sword. He has been insubordinate and refused to render the oath of allegiance."
>
> Maximilian exclaimed joyously, "Deo gratias!"
>
> Maximilian lived twenty-one years, three months, and eighteen days on this earth. When led to the place of execution he said, "Beloved brothers, strive with your entire strength and longing, that it will be granted you to gaze upon the Lord and that he will give you a glorious crown."
>
> With a joyful countenance he addressed his father: "Give the new robe you had made for my enlistment to the executioner. Having been compensated a hundredfold, I will see you again, and together we will rejoice in the Lord."
>
> Convinced of this, he soon suffered a martyr's death.

If we did not know that this happened in 295 AD we could easily think that Dion is heading a military tribunal today and considers military service the highest honor for a young man but conscientious objection a crime deserving death.

Who is right? Is it Maximilian, who believes military service to be incompatible with the essence of Christianity, dies for his belief, and is honored by the Church as a holy martyr? Or are today's defenders and advocates of military service right? Which view is right? Maximilian's conviction that he cannot serve in war or do anything unjust because he is a Christian, or the view of those who believe that bearing arms and military service are sacred obligations of love for the fatherland?

The answer is not difficult. Maximilian is right. Bearing arms and serving in the military are incompatible with the true nature of Christianity, for the Church would never have been able to declare Maximilian a saint had he advocated an unchristian opinion, that is, had he given his life for an erroneous idea. It follows that those Christian nations that have instituted conscription are in the wrong. In the name of Christianity we have to object particularly to the pre-military training of youth and reject it as unchristian.

Or did Pope Leo XIII violate Christian teaching when he objected to universal military service and called it "an assassination of the self-determination of the moral personality"? Or when, protesting the military training of young people, in his encyclical *Praeclarae gratulationis publicae* of 1894 he wrote, "Inexperienced young people are removed from the counsel of parents and teachers and subjected to the dangers of military barracks"?

We all know how life in these barracks seriously endangers morality.

Furthermore, Pope Benedict XV, in his splendid call for peace of 1917—which, unfortunately, is totally forgotten today—appealed to the nations to abolish conscription. In 1890 Archbishop Benoît-Marie Langénieux of Reims described universal military service as "godless in principle and destructive of the freedom of conscience."

On March 25, 1922, Pope Pius XI reproached the victorious powers for being on the warpath because of their rearmament, thus preventing the flowering of their youth and poisoning and clouding the best sources of their physical, mental, religious, and moral life.

What splendid testimonies these are from the treasury of Christian ideas, from the mouths of the Church's highest teaching authority. Only: Where is the action? Why does the entire Catholic clergy not adopt these papal words, unanimously oppose conscription, and call their faithful to conscientious objection? The attitude of today's Christendom proves just the opposite. Here the words of our Lord apply: "You must therefore do and observe what they tell you; but do not be guided by what they do" (Matt 23:3); "But alas for you Pharisees, because you pay your tithe of mint and rue and all sorts of garden herbs and neglect justice and the love of God! These you should have practiced, without neglecting the others" (Luke 11:42).

The terrible events during the Abyssinian War, regardless of how other states conducted themselves, prove that the Sermon on the Mount is no longer relevant, even in countries calling themselves Christian and Catholic. (This is precisely what we said while that war was raging.)

According to the report of *L'Osservatore Romano* of April 2, 1935, Pope Pius XI stated in a secret consistory, "If the nations were again to capitulate to destruction, this would be such an unspeakable crime and the raging of an insane spirit that we consider it simply out of the question, according to the old saying: 'One should consider whatever is opposed to justice simply out of the question.' We cannot share the view that those who attach great importance to the success and fortune of the nations should drive not only the country entrusted to them but all of humanity into decline, destruction, and extermination.

"However, if someone—may God prevent it, and we hope it will never happen—should plan such an abominable crime or even commit it, then even with a sorrow-filled heart, we will not keep from asking God to destroy those nations which desire war. Our words refer to the fact that every new war is morally unacceptable . Besides, considering the present troubled conditions, a new war seems to us, and many who share our view, morally and physically out of the question."

Thus wrote the pope in 1935. However, the actions of Benito Mussolini prove how greatly Pope Pius XI was misled that war was impossible in those hard times.

According to the *Grazer Volksblatt* of November 5, 1928, Mussolini addressed his nation on the Piazza Venezia in Rome on the tenth anniversary of World War I. He stated that the war had not been forced upon the Italian people by a sudden attack but that they had deliberately desired the conflict. He called the war a free act of the conscious will of the Italian nation and recalled that the first part had been very severe, with six hundred thousand people killed, four hundred thousand disabled, and millions wounded. He concluded his address with the question, "Should it become necessary tomorrow, will you do everything all of us did yesterday?" The crowd responded with a resounding yes.

This same Mussolini, who had professed the most ruthless militancy, with cold-blooded deliberation and the use of the most modern technology of war, in 1935 attacked the Abyssinian people, even though he was fully aware that this was a raid on the defenseless.

If Mussolini continues like this, the Abyssinian people will soon be exterminated. Those who excel in this human slaughter are called "heroes," and, as a sign of great appreciation, a cross is pinned to their chest. The cross, this holy symbol of the greatest and most merciful love, is thus most shamefully misused in order to inflame the lowest human instinct, which is called the highest virtue.

The world's nations and Christian churches are watching this terrible, human slaughter and shameless, flagrant raid and are remaining silent. Rome, too, is silent. Those in authority lack the courage in the name of Christ to oppose this satanic activity in Abyssinia and to shout, "*Non licet*!" (this is not permitted).

Because of the discrepancy between its teaching and action the Church becomes a laughtingstock and a serious cause for anger in the eyes of many. The conduct of statesmen in the inhumane and unchristian horrors of the Abyssinian War is either scorned as "a farce" or viewed with approval.

Only one thing can change this moral collapse of the entire culture of the world: the unconditional assertion of nonviolence according to Christ's Sermon on the Mount. The armament capitalists and their beneficiaries do not want to hear this, however. They see to it that their well-paid accomplices always extoll man's ability to defend himself, ensure that our young people receive a pre-military education, and work energetically so that armies of millions will always be ready to fight wars in order to secure, from this bloody war business, huge profits for them.

Intoxicated by their Caesarean mania, the rulers will again and again appeal to the desire of man, tainted by original sin, to defend himself. These rulers will surround themselves with soldiers in order to assert their authority. "For God," "for the nation," "for freedom," etc., are the slogans by which idealistic young people let themselves be deluded to pick up weapons by those who reap benefits from war. Totally ignorant of the true cost of military preparedness, armament capitalists and rulers will again and again persuade nations to offer bloody sacrifices to the idol of military readiness and to make available the largest part of the national income for organized mass murder and destruction. If, for example, the $4,126 million that the nations now spend each year for this would be used to promote the general welfare, how much good and happiness could be created!

Even though this statement has to be welcomed for itself, what good is it if, not long ago (February 1936), George Lansbury, a member of the Labor Party, declared in the Lower House of the British Parliament that war, because it is opposed to morality and God, is totally inappropriate for solving any problem? However well intentioned, what good does such a statement do if one does not outlaw the root cause, the erroneous understanding of military preparedness?

Either Christ is right in his Sermon on the Mount, and then all efforts to defend military readiness and militarism are wrong, or one dares to reinterpret the Sermon on the Mount or to declare it to be erroneous. In the latter case, one may defend the training and arming of men and compulsory military service, but one should cease to call these activities Christian. Training and arming men to fight are incompatible with Christianity. If they are compatible, St. Maximilian died for a false belief, we should not honor him as a holy martyr, and the Church was seriously mistaken when it proclaimed him a saint. However, as long as the Sermon on the Mount is a part of the Gospel, this truth remains: The training and arming of men is incompatible with Christianity. Therefore, the establishment of conscription is a crime against the people.

It is high time that the truth is honored and that at last the authorities of the Church call to mind the Sermon of the Mount and act accordingly. Therefore, there should be neither training and arming to fight nor support for these measures but adhering to truth, which has nothing to do with military preparedness. From the Christian viewpoint, we have to reject military training and conscription as serious moral errors. As Christians, as Catholics, we are bound by our conscience to refuse military service.[92]

92. Following the collapse of the Nazi German Reich, several newspapers reported that U.S. President Harry S. Truman recommended and demanded that universal military service, which was established by the United States during World War II, be continued in order to maintain peace and protect the United States. According to a report in the *Salzburger Nachrichten* of October 29, 1945, Truman made the following points in a speech delivered in New York City's Central Park: "1. Our Army, Navy, and Air Force, in collaboration with our Allies, must enforce the terms of peace imposed upon our defeated enemies. 2. We must fulfill the military obligations which we are undertaking as a member of the United Nations Organization—to support a lasting peace, by force if necessary. 3. [Text not relevant.] 4. In this troubled and uncertain world, our military forces must be adequate to discharge the fundamental mission laid upon them by the Constitution of the United States—to 'provide for the common defense' of the United States."

"These four military tasks," President Truman said, "are not directed toward war—not toward conquest—but toward peace." In Point 12 of the United States foreign policy he stated, "We are convinced that the preservation of peace between nations requires a United Nations Organization composed of all the peace-loving nations of the world who are willing jointly to use force if necessary to insure peace."

In the United States, as well as in other states, conscription is regarded as the appropriate means for safeguarding freedom and maintaining peace. Unfortunately, this is a way of thinking that America and those holding responsibility developed without regard to the teaching of Christ. For this the American people will have to pay a bitter penalty, since Christ's words are true: "all who draw the sword will die by the sword" (Matt 26:52). Neither conscription nor the atomic bomb—which America wants to keep secret for herself as a special method to secure world peace—will be able to guarantee it. On the contrary: it is precisely the top-secret atomic bomb—in spite of the good intentions we believe Truman has—that will seduce the United States into striving to become a capitalistic dictatorship and thus to amass fuel for the third and, most likely, last world war. Let us create peace by eradicating the causes of war!

Therefore, we have to agree with Vyacheslav Molotov, the Russian foreign minister, when he stated in a speech commemorating the twenty-eighth anniversary of the October Revolution (according to a report in the *Salzburger Nachrichten* of November 7, 1945), "It [the atomic bomb] may neither remain the sole property of one country nor be used as a method of pressure in foreign policy. No power should exert a decisive influence on world politics. Only cooperation is justified. . . . For this reason the invention of nuclear energy has to be rejected as an instrument in the power game of foreign policy and to assure the security of peace-loving nations."

We cannot judge whether Molotov harbored ulterior motives and, if so, of what kind. However, what he said is correct. Therefore, we warmly welcome the following report of October 25, 1945, of the *Demokratische Volksblatt*: "Representative Joseph Martin, the leader of the Republican minority in the United States Congress, has proposed an international agreement under which all nations would abolish conscription during peace time. . . . Such an agreement would be a giant step toward the goal of achieving enduring peace, would reduce the incentive for war, and would save billions of dollars, which could be used to improve conditions in the world for the benefit of millions of people on earth."

d. Total war

A man named Claus Schrempf wrote the following in the *Grazer Tagespost* of September 7, 1943: "Since World War I (1918) it has been known that every future armed conflict would be a total war in which not army against army but nation against nation would enter into a struggle for existence. In this fight each side, in order to defeat the enemy, would make use of its total national energy in the form of weapons, economic resources, all human and material reserves, as well as every possible method of warfare."

This statement is correct, at least in relation to how the Nazi leadership waged World War II. They prepared for total war as soon as they seized power. However, Germany's opponents also engaged in total war.

National Socialist speakers and newspapers candidly told what total war consists of. For example, First Lieutenant Julius Ringel described it with candor in a speech he gave in Graz on December 16, 1937, to the Austrian Soldiers' Front, to which we immediately expressed our disapproval from a Christian viewpoint based on natural law and reason. Here are the major statements of his speech:

> An armament frenzy has gripped the entire world. Therefore, now it is already necessary to be concerned about the type of war of tomorrow. The general principles of waging war are always the same, but the face of war is subject to constant changes. In the war of the future all energy, every institution of the nation, and its people will systematically be made available to the service of the fatherland. Total war is going to involve everyone and everything—that is why it is called total war. The "front" will be everywhere. Besides the war of weapons, a psychological and economic war will be fought.
>
> Decisive for the outcome of the war is the actual fighting as well as the attitude of the people. In the future war, everyone—man and woman—will become a soldier, and all young people will have to be trained for war from earliest childhood. The will of one's own people for war has to be strengthened, and one must seek to prejudice the rest of the world toward one's foe and to win neutral states to one's side in order to defeat the enemy's will to fight. To achieve this, massive oral and written propaganda has to be developed, and every means is good enough if it serves the purpose.
>
> The air force will play a decisive role. It will seek to destroy the enemy's war industry, transportation system, barracks, and entire economy. Therefore, care must be taken to protect one's country, especially against the enemy's air force.

> The entire economy has to become a defense economy and regulated to meet military needs. All economic energies have to be systematically combined to make the nation's fighting power as great as possible. As soon as a war nears, the economic freedom of the individual has to be restricted by the government, especially by military authorities, for the benefit of the state. And once the war has begun, the entire economy has to be completely adapted to the war effort, with the needs of the individual subordinated. Public and private resources have to be confiscated to serve the war, and labor adapted to warfare. All persons of both genders who are able to work have to serve the war effort, and all available raw materials claimed for the war. Only after the conflict has ended will the war economy be reconverted to meet peacetime conditions.[93]

We remarked already, in 1937, "provided that not everything—people, animals, cultural treasures, and the countryside—has been destroyed."

Preparations of the war economy, as Ringel explains, consist of distributing "human material" and deploying it to wage war on fronts abroad and at home. Human beings are regarded only as material for the war effort, of course, material controlled by the few who make decisions about the war.

Both genders have to be placed wherever they can be most useful to meet the war objectives, and the decision for this rests, so it is declared, solely on the supreme authority. Furthermore, the services of every citizen who has the necessary knowledge are requisitioned for military science and defense research because war encompasses every field of knowledge, particularly technology and chemistry. Capable young people, especially, have to be educated for this effort. And for the advocates of total war it goes without saying that theology also has to serve the aims of war.

Lieutenant Riegel continued,

> Already in peacetime, the entire food industry has to be organized to serve the requirements of war without friction, and, as far as possible, the nation must become self-sufficient. From what has been stated, there is no question that all extraction and reclamation of resources have to be viewed from the angle of preparing for and waging war. Heaven, earth, air, land, water, minerals, and all human resources have meaning only in regard to the coming war and have to serve it. Industry already has to be organized during peacetime so that it can be changed immediately to war production, not to mention that sufficient military goods should already be produced during peacetime.

93. *Grazer Volksblatt*, December 16, 1936.

> It follows that the idea of war has to dominate all work during peacetime.
>
> In total war, armed conflict between armies becomes a spiritual and material struggle of the nations. This is how the necessary link between the actual military leadership, government authorities, and citizens' organizations is achieved. Everyone becomes a soldier and a fighter, whether on the front or at home. Deciding on the war aims is reserved only to the nation's military leadership, which has to ensure that the weapons for the psychological and economic war are as powerful as the weapons of the army.[94]

We were greatly shocked when we read this report in the Catholic *Grazer Volksblatt*—shocked that something like this could be said in a Christian nation, which I have always considered Austria to be, and shocked that these remarks were "honored with deserved applause," as the *Volksblatt* commented. But we were even more surprised that no one, neither Christian church leaders nor the "Christian" *Grazer Volksblatt*, raised even the slightest objection. Ringel's comments seem to have been accepted everywhere as correct, without any disagreement. Surely Ringel, against whom I, personally, do not have the slightest objection, is the spokesman for those who regard total war as being justified. From their standpoint, he is perfectly correct in supporting total war. This reasoning is open, honest, and logical, and is exactly how the Nazi leadership is operating.

However, from the viewpoint of ethics based on natural law, reason, and Christian moral law, we have to flatly reject total war. First of all, we point to our earlier comments about the permissibility of self-defense from the standpoint of morality and that whoever rejects the right to self-defense (justifiable homicide) logically has to reject war as morally impermissible.

But let us examine more closely the claims of those favoring total war. We refrain, however, from saying that the assumption on which they base their stand is incorrect. As we have proved above, the teaching that justified homicide is permissible is wrong. Here we are going to concentrate only on Ringel's statements and principles. We can summarize his speech in the following sentences: Already in peacetime the entire nation, the government, and citizens of both genders and their ideas about intellectual and material matters have to be directed entirely and systematically toward the next war and be subservient to it without reservation. All organizations and the entire private and public economy have to be subordinated to military considerations. While there is peace, all work has to serve solely the next war. The

94. *Grazer Volksblatt*, December 16, 1936.

highest officials of the state and the entire nation have to be completely and unreservedly at the disposal of the military leadership and to submit to it.

We ask: Is it true that the noblest and first duty of the state is to prepare for war even in peacetime? Is total war compatible with the mission of the state according to ethics based on natural law and reason? Is it the duty of the state, that is, of the government and citizens, to plan and prepare for war and consequently to subordinate the entire life of a nation, of its citizens and economy, to serve the next war?

Supporters of total war regard the state as a community whose purpose is to direct its economy, people, and all governmental activities to the service of the coming war so that all can work for it. Yet the Christian concept of the mission of the state differs in that it teaches that the state is a community whose duty it is to achieve the common welfare. Further, by the joint efforts of government and citizens, laws and regulations should be established so that all individuals, without discrimination, can achieve a dignified existence in tranquility and peace.

The purpose of the state is not to wage war but to work to provide for the common good and to safeguard justice. To achieve this goal, which should control everything that occurs in a state, leaders and citizens have to work together systematically. Creating a dignified existence for every citizen first of all requires such orderly conditions that the possibility of a future war can be avoided. This will be even more true where justice is allowed to flourish. Each person should be guaranteed that which is his own or that to which he is entitled by natural law.

If all people have adequate means for a dignified existence, the danger of war is considerably reduced. However, the less the general welfare is promoted, the more the individual nations count on war and prepare for it the closer draws the reality that a war will start. For the more a country occupies itself with preparations for war, and the more time, work, resources, and people are used for these measures, the less time, work, resources, and people remain to further the general welfare.

War preparations and armaments always harm the general welfare and are incompatible with it. If the entire state is engaged in total war, if men and women, the aged, children, and everything else is serving organized mass murder and the destruction of culture, and if all intellectual efforts are systematically directed solely from the viewpoint of war, then the state betrays the purpose that God has assigned to it. A nation that agrees to total war has entirely lost its purpose. It no longer is a state, as required by natural law and Christian ethics, but more correctly can be called an agent for systematic human slaughter and the destruction of culture.

However, the supporters of total war believe they are serving peace in a special way with the realization of their ideas. They are convinced that the statement "if you want peace, prepare for war" is morally irreproachable. But we consider this statement to be morally wrong and, above all, in contradiction to the Christian commandment to love one's enemy. We say simply that if all nations would systematically use all their activities, institutions, and revenues for the realization of peace instead of for wars, we would have peace. For we believe this statement to be correct: "If you want peace, prepare for peace by promoting the works of peace."

Therefore, not total war but total peace. If the first is possible, so is the second, only with the difference that total war, in all aspects, slaps the demands of natural law in the face and contradicts Christian moral law, while total peace is completely in the spirit of natural law and Christian moral law.

Natural law obligates leaders and citizens of nations to work for peace by promoting the general welfare in accordance with the requirements of natural law, which means to eliminate everything that endangers peace. This, first of all, means a reorganization of the currency and proper legislation regarding land so that by the elimination of the capitalistic economy, that is, an interest economy, every citizen is guaranteed the means necessary for a dignified existence. In agreement with natural law, besides the right to life, each citizen has to be guaranteed the right to use and own material goods, and it is the duty of the state to do so.

The more workers, the more time, the more land and its produce, the more money, and the more intellectual efforts are used to prepare for and wage wars, the less of these remain for the proper duties of the state, that is, for peace.

A few words have to be said about the allegation by supporters of total war that the entire economy must serve the next war and be controlled by it. According to economics based on natural law, reason, and Christian teachings, the primary goal of the economy is to make use of all available material goods so that every person who fulfills his duty to work can realize a dignified existence. According to the teachings of those who support total war, the economy must serve, completely and exclusively, the aims of war. This purpose, even if it were legitimate, would only partially and subordinately benefit the highest goal of the economy. The supporters of total war are seriously mistaken when they portray war as an end in itself and subordinate to it every function of the nation, that is, the community, the economy, personal freedom, and even the life of every citizen. Thus militarism becomes the highest idol of the state. For supporters of total war, the state exists only to be militarily prepared under all circumstances, as if not being prepared were impossible and foolish.

Downright outrageous and presumptuous is the claim that the military leadership alone has the right—actually the duty—to determine the objectives of a war and, therefore, to make sure that the weapons for the psychological and economic war are as powerful as those of the army. If we suppose, but not grant, that militarism is legitimate, the military leadership would constitute only part of the highest government authority and would be subordinated to it.

If the supporters of total war were right, all of the teachings of natural law and Christian ethics, up to now, would have been wrong, and new ethics and morals would have to be developed from the position that war controls everything. But this assumption of the supporters of war has to be promptly confronted by church leaders. The concept of total war has to be stigmatized and rejected as a very serious error before the entire world. To remain silent would be to betray the teachings of Christ.

Therefore, not total war but total peace! This we have to demand in the name of morality based on natural law, reason, and Christianity. If the 5.4 billion gold dollars that, according to the Secretariat of the League of Nations, the world's nations spent on armaments in 1935 had been used to build up and improve the community and the economy according to the demands of justice, how much could have been accomplished for peace! Yet the armaments race achieved only this: that the outbreak of a war could be expected any moment. One has to consider that in a war, the armaments capitalists are the primary beneficiaries and will do everything so that their bloody business flourishes, that is, so that a war breaks out. While in 1935 the world's total expenditures for armaments already amounted to 5.4 billion gold dollars (about 38 billion gold *Schillinge*), at the beginning of 1936 they rose every day at an average of 470 million gold *Schillinge*.[95] Assuming that this rate continued during the entire year, the nations of the world spent 172 billion gold *Schillinge* in a single year for preparations of organized mass murder and destruction.

Is this not madness? In view of such facts, where are reason and moral responsibility? Is total war really the greatest and ultimate political wisdom? Are human beings really born only to become soldiers, that is, to slaughter others in order to finally be slaughtered themselves? When are political leaders finally going to wake up?

If only the leaders of Christian churches would at last come to understand this and have the courage to outlaw war in the name of Christ! But they remain silent and continue to support the "just defensive war." However,

95. *Die Geissel* (Vienna), no. 3, March 1936, n.p.

Even if others, guilty like Pilate,
Cowardly, remain silent,
We, nevertheless, will bear witness
To Christ and His kingdom of peace!

We profess loudly before the whole world bristling with weapons: Total war is a crime against the mission of the state. It is an everlasting perpetuation of war. As Christians we should work only for total peace. For Christ, you teach us to love our fellowman. You teach us to do good to all. You teach us to also love our enemy. You command us to repay evil with good, to not resist him who does evil, to offer the other cheek to him who strikes us. You teach us to forgive the enemy and never to practice revenge against him. You teach us not to counter violence with violence but with nonviolence. Only the supporters of total war—and war in general—direct us to hate the enemy, to turn the entire world against him, to ponder day and night how to destroy him, and to make all resources, the life of the nation and of every citizen, available for murder and destruction. This means making war and military preparations the essence of life.

If supporters of total war deny life after death, that is, believe that human beings live only for this world, what right do they have to demand that the members of the living generation sacrifice themselves only for the life of the future generations, instead of enjoying the short life they have on earth? Here we can see how thoroughly the materialistic, Darwinian view has corroded the brains and hearts of today's human beings. Instead of God's Ten Commandments it is proclaimed: Right belongs to the stronger, and everything is permitted that is useful to the state.

Who is right? Christ or those who support war?

Our answer, short and to the point, can only be this: "Then Simon Peter spoke up, 'You are the Christ,' he said, 'the Son of the living God. To whom shall we go? You have the words of eternal life'" (Matt 16:16).

Therefore, the supporters of total war, as well as of war in general, are wrong.

We who have perceived this truth will witness to it with the courage of our convictions and that of the martyrs.

Today, after the experiences of the second disastrous world war, we have to call total war a crime of a nation against its people, and the coming generations will have to bear the terrible results and horrors. Particularly in the final years of World War II, total war was translated into reality with sheer fathomless brutality on both sides.

As Gauleiter Sauckel stated at a conference in Weimar on January 6, 1943, on the side of Nazi Germany, all possible production reserves were mobilized for the war on a gigantic scale, unheard of in history. According to a newspaper report, Sauckel said, "It is clear even to the last German that the war has reached a stage that will relentlessly put an end to the few remaining comforts and diversions and will direct the life of the individual as well as that of the entire nation toward one goal, a war of victory. In view of this, all other considerations subside totally and are no longer valid today. We have to adapt totally and exclusively to the demands of a war whose dimensions, forms, and locations we cannot yet know."

Therefore, we have to note: Certain of victory, Hitler always contended and declared to the entire world—and his helpers' helpers have always insisted—that he, the "greatest commander of all time," decides on the place and time of an attack and forces his will on the enemy so that no territory on which a German soldier has set foot will ever be surrendered again. However, the war's events of 1943–45 have shown how one should regard the prophecies of the *Führer* of the German nation (and of other leaders). Even the total war Hitler waged with all means could not prevent the Russians from reconquering the entire Ukraine and the Allies from ultimately occupying all of Germany.

No National Socialist ever considered that a total war could also lead to a total defeat. Or did what we have to call the irresponsible, criminal leadership of Nazi Germany realize this? Did it perhaps deliver up the entire German nation to the terrors of total war because it did not wish a single German to remain who could raise the accusation against National Socialism that it caused the total ruin of the German people? For, surely, those Germans who survived this war are ashamed to belong to the German people. Yet this may not keep us from setting everything in motion to help our poor, deeply humiliated country to get up again and, first of all, to bring it to realize its guilt.

What a disgraceful end Nazi Germany experienced! How cowardly did the Nazi high authorities, beginning with the *Führer*, abandon their people, whom they had lied to, deceived, and betrayed? But, likewise, every decent Englishman, American, Russian, and Frenchman will be ashamed of how the Allies also waged total war.

e. Capitalism: One of the major causes of war

In our book *Soziologie* we dealt with the question of "war or peace" from the viewpoint of ethics based on natural law and stated,

> In the final analysis, today all wars between our modern civilized nations are merely business ventures of internationally

> organized investment capital. Our modern governments are often taken advantage of by capitalism. For example, let us consider the armaments industry, which stirs up the nations to war by means of deceitful slogans such as "for the threatened fatherland," or "for God, emperor and nation," whenever capitalism finds it necessary to serve its interests. In addition, leaders ambitious for power, or political parties, use the warlike atmosphere—for whose existence all civilized countries must share the guilt—in order to materialize their plans by getting involved in war, whereby they are calculatingly used as tools by the capitalists for their financial interests.[96]

We are thinking first of all of Adolf Hitler and his Nazi party, whom the armaments capitalists used as a welcome tool in order to hurl the torch of war into the world. For this, as has been proved, the best prospects were Hitler, with his—we are convinced—schizophrenic nature, and the National Socialist party because of its *Weltanschauung*, severed from all Christian principles.

In the year 1932, with the intercession of Franz von Papen, representing the German general staff, which was calling for revenge, Hitler met in Essen with Fritz Thyssen, a leading industrialist, and Kurt von Schröder, a prominent banker. These two men financed the enormous propaganda effort of the Nazi Party, while Hitler, ambitious to be the "greatest commander-in-chief of all time," paved the way for the militarization of Germany for total war, after seizing power in 1933.

However, the unfortunate nations, who had to sacrifice blood, life, and property, sadly do not grasp that for the interests of only a few capitalists and the ambition of only a few men, on both sides, they had to sacrifice life and property. Had they realized this, millions of human beings would not have allowed themselves to be misused but in solidarity would have refused to serve in war. On the contrary, these millions produced the atmosphere that made it possible for capitalists and mad, ambitious men to realize their self-seeking plans.

In our book *Money: Its Influence on Society, Economy, and Culture*,[97] which we wrote at the request of the International Liberation League, we explained in detail how the capitalistic economy causes wars. We wrote that we are firmly convinced that all struggle against war and every effort on behalf of peace will only have a chance of being realized if we succeed in abolishing capitalism, that is, an economy based on interest, including

96. Ude, *Soziologie*, 111.

97. Ude, *Das Geld*, 149–58.

money backed by gold, by giving money a worldwide stable purchasing power, forcing money to remain in circulation, and putting an end to the capitalistic exploitation of land.

We will try to prove that today wars are the last expedient of our politicians demonstrating their inability to put an end, rationally and effectively, to the economic crises caused by capitalism. Wars are always diversionary maneuvers from the actual enemy. They plunge nations into misery and purposely prevent and destroy the general welfare.

Today the issue of war and peace includes these tasks: How do we get the failed, collapsed economy going again? How do we provide sufficient work and bread for all people? How do we prevent the exploitation of workers through interest? How do we firmly establish individuals and families in the soil of their homeland?

When people can again lead a dignified existence, they and their government will not think about war. On the contrary, they will leave no stone unturned to prevent anything that may lead to war so that a well-functioning economy will not be destroyed. For everyone has to realize that armed conflicts between nations, especially modern, total wars, are nothing but a senseless destruction of life, the economy, and culture. Wars, again and again proposed and induced by capitalists and a few ambitious men, benefit only their originators, enabling them to realize their sordid goals, to gain wealth, and to satisfy their limitless ambition.

Whoever is for war may not hide behind the claim of espousing a "humane" conduct of war, as do all Christian moral philosophers and theologians who support "just defensive war." Instead, we have to agree with Japanese Minister Yukio Ozaki when he admits frankly, in his book *Japan at the Crossroad*, what war is really like: "Victory is achieved quickly if one demoralizes and destroys the enemy by ruthlessly killing all civilians, old or young, man, woman, or child. . . . It is absurd to discuss whether the use of poison gas, bacteria, and air attacks on unfortified cities should be prohibited. As long as there are wars, no one can prevent these methods, for, obviously, the most effective weapons will be used whether they are prohibited or not."

We have a choice: Either we succeed in putting the economy on its feet again and eliminate unemployment by ethical means, which we can achieve only by reforming money, or one war of total destruction will follow another. What we said before World War II we say again now that it has ended: Unless all countries of the world work together to restructure the economy according to economics based on natural law and reason, as we explained in our *Soziologie*,[98] a third, even more terrible total war is imminent. A heinous human talent of invention will ensure this, and again capitalists will benefit while ambitious leaders compete for the glory of being the "unsurpassed and greatest commander of all time." Truly we will not be envious of this title, especially if these leaders withdraw from their command in the manner Hitler did. Already, atom bombs and other terrible weapons stand ready for a third world war.

At this time of economic crises caused by a failed monetary system, accompanied by terrible unemployment because of deflation, many feel that there are just too many people living in Germany. Therefore, they wish to enlarge their territory; they clamor for colonies. This desire was openly and clearly stated by Hitler's right hand, Reichsminister Dr. Joseph Goebbels, in Munich, as reported by the Graz *Tagespost* of October 19, 1942:

> Everything that may oppress us has to be steadfastly shouldered, not only because we, as a nation and Reich, are fighting for existence or nonexistence, but also because in all of history we never had a more favorable moment than now, with our right of existence and its possibilities, to secure and utilize the appropriate territory for eternity. This struggle is not about make-believe goals or mere idols, nor is it about the prestige of the state or nation, nor about throne and altar. Instead, this time we are fighting for what is important and necessary: coal, iron, oil, and, especially, wheat for the daily bread on the tables of our people. We fight so that the standard of living of our people will be changed and improved, so that the German people can finally sit at the fat pots of the world.

Dr. Goebbels also summarized in one sentence the results of the war up to then: "that we, the former have-nots, have become owners while the former owners continue to collapse to have-nots." With this statement Goebbels admitted frankly that this was an obvious *Raubkrieg* (predatory war). One could laugh about these remarks if they had not been so serious.

But as later events prove, Dr. Goebbels gloated much too early; he had computed the bill without the host. His statements clearly implied that the Nazi leadership was not capable of organizing the German economy so that each citizen could achieve a dignified existence, that Germany needed the war to gain "a place in the sun," with the needed living space, and proceeded to seize by force everything splendid this space had to offer.

Of course, besides economic causes leading to war, there are others: exaggerated nationalism, the extreme claims of sovereignty of nations, the

98. Ude, *Soziologie*, 167.

insane worship of race, and the megalomania of government leaders. In the final analysis, however, the economic causes are always decisive that war breaks out.

We cannot forego to mention the book *The Fight for the World Power—Oil*, by Anton Zischka.[99] Based on uncontestable facts, the author grippingly describes how the competition for oil, that is, for the petroleum fields of the world and the sale of petroleum by the few oil magnates of the world—Rockefeller, Deterding, Marcus Samuel, Zaharoff, etc.—is controlled and will continue to be so by the world powers backing these capitalists.

Dr. Goebbels stated above that Germany was also competing for oil and, therefore, waging war. Now, in the aftermath of World War II, oil again is playing a major role in the struggle between communism and capitalism for domination of the world. For whoever controls the oil fields can dictate terms to other nations and has won the next war from the start. Without gasoline and raw oil automobiles can't run, airplanes can't fly, tanks can't move, and modern warships and submarines fail to work. Therefore, the world powers shun no means, even war, to get possession of this zealously desired oil. Capitalism's struggle for oil is especially a fight for oil's high earnings and at the same time for political supremacy of the world in order to exploit other nations.

Therefore, whoever is a sincere, unshakable opponent of war and wants to work effectively for peace has to pledge that all people are again ensured a dignified existence. They must be able to earn enough money to buy what they need, and there must always be a sufficient supply of all necessary goods and services. This, however, is impossible as long as working human beings are cheated by capitalism, through interest, out of money and land, and by communism, through expropriation, of the fruits of their labor. The capitalistic economy has no use for the permanent prosperity of all of humanity since interest can only be extorted by an economy of scarcity. Communism, on the other hand, by means of expropriation, sees to it that workers cannot even acquire property.

Inflation, deflation, and money backed by gold always prevent all citizens from attaining lasting prosperity. Everything—money, land, machines, houses, and all that is necessary to sustain life—is turned into capital, that is, into interest-extorting goods.

War breaks out when the collaborating international financiers, or thoroughly militarized communism, consider it to be a favorable time, namely, when the magnates of the armaments industry—one of the most profitable industries—have completed preparations for war. Capitalists

99. Zischka, *Der Kampf um die Weltmacht Öl.*

of some countries, by clever money maneuvers, disrupt the economy of other countries and see to it that war breaks out, availing themselves of any means, even criminal means, like the assassination in Sarajevo. Once war has begun, international capitalism, working together, makes sure that the conflict lasts as long as armaments and other capitalists profit. For example, did World War I not cost 3,072 billion RM (Reichsmark), spent purely for mass murder and destruction, a sum that, for the most part, landed in the pockets of armament magnates and others who benefited from the war? In the carnage, which lasted four years, three months, and ten days, around twelve million soldiers died on all fronts. The killing of one soldier cost an average of 100,000 RM, of which the armaments industry pocketed 60,000 RM as clear profit.[100]

100. From reports of several newspapers available to us following the end of World War II, we can report these facts: in total, the Allies (the United States, England, Russia, and France) mobilized more than 62 million persons; Hitler's Germany and her allies, 30 million (*Salzburger Nachrichten*, Salzburg, October 11, 1945). According to a report of the *Oberösterreichischen Nachrichten*, Linz, September 27, 1945, the number of people directly harmed by the war and its consequences is estimated at 60 million. According to British Prime Minister Clement Attlee, the losses of the German fighting forces amounted to about 3,000,000 killed and 3,400,000 wounded, not including the missing (*Demokratisches Volksblatt*, Salzburg, October 24, 1945). As reported by the *Oberösterreichischen Nachrichten* of October 30, 1945, the air war cost the United States the lives of 79,265 airmen and 18,000 planes; Great Britain, 79,281 airmen and 22,000 planes. The air attacks of the Allies killed 300,000 Germans, destroyed 3,600,000 buildings in German towns and other inhabited areas, and turned the most important German cities into rubble.

As we learned from a report of the *Oberösterreichischen Nachrichten* of October 11, 1945, the U.S. portion of the world's war industry production for the year 1941 was only 12 percent. However, in 1945 it amounted to 45 percent of the world's total of 110 billion dollars spent for military goods (according to the currency value of August 1942). Since the summer of 1943 the United States supplied more than 5 billion dollars' worth of ammunition every month. According to Russian foreign minister Molotov, Russia's war damages are valued at 679 billion rubles (*Salzburger Nachrichten*, November 7, 1945).

Below the terrible statistics of World War II, as far as they were available from various newspapers, are estimated in round numbers:

- 15,000,000 soldiers killed on both sides;
- 3,000,000 killed by bomb attacks;
- 26,000,000 murdered by the accomplices of National Socialism, including 11,000,000 in concentration camps;
- 5,500,000 additional human beings murdered.

This totals approximately 50,000,000 deaths. We were unable to find out how many deaths during this war can be attributed to Bolshevism in Russia. Furthermore, the war is responsible for

- 29,650,000 disabled;
- 21,240,000 homeless;

The goal of vommunism, by demanding the "dictatorship of the armed proletariat," is revolution, turmoil, and war, and it makes sure that its agents foment these.

In view of such facts, even the most inveterate supporter of war and the most dimwitted citizen must realize how wars are made and who benefits from them. The laboring population has to sacrifice life, body, and possessions on orders from above—and at the conclusion of the war the people inherit misery, while the capitalists, victorious autocrats, and bigwigs enjoy the gigantic returns of their profitable, bloody business.

No less prominent an organization than the League of Nations carefully studied the intrigues of the armament industry in World War I and concluded, in 1921,

> The armament firms fanned the politics of war and persuaded their own countries to pursue war politics and to increase their armaments. At home and abroad the armaments industries spread false information about the army and navy programs of various countries in order to drive up military expenditures. By controlling their own as well as foreign newspapers these firms sought to influence public opinion. They organized international rings that fostered an armaments competition by playing off one country against another. International armaments trusts were organized that drove up prices.

The League of Nations, surely a trustworthy witness, discovered the truth and wanted to make it known.

Surely the nations' statesmen desire to create order and peace but frequently want to do so without removing the causes of disorder and those disrupting peace. These causes are not eliminated because it is not understood that the relationship between the supply of goods and the demand for money has to be properly regulated, which would overpower the capitalistic economy, one of the main causes of wars. In every economy the circulation of money has to and can be regulated according to the principle of equal value so that one contribution equals the one made in return, so that the purchasing power of money is always the same. An end has to be made to the hoarding of money so that it, and consequently goods, can no longer be misused to extort interest. This can be achieved if laws are passed to tax the circulation of money.

- 20,000,000 displaced persons seeking refuge all over the world, including 15,000,000 Germans.

In causing all of these deaths, this vast destruction and misery, the warring states sacrificed approximately 630 billion dollars.

We presented all of the above and a few other ideas in the earlier mentioned books, *Soziologie* and *Das Geld, sein Einfluss auf Gesellschaft, Wirtschaft und Kultur*, and in several small pamphlets. Those of us who oppose war and are friends of peace have to know these ideas and translate them into reality if we do not merely want to talk about peace but wish sincerely to work for peace and to prevent war.

Or what can a pacifist reply when reading the following in the major newspaper of Norway's conservative party, *Morgenblatt*, November 25, 1931?

> Is there going to be war in the East? It may sound cruel, but a war would be desirable for business trends. The world of today is no different than before. A war would increase the demand for ship tonnage. The risk of transporting goods would rise, as would prices and with them speculation. This means a readjustment of foreign trade to the advantage of the neutral countries and increased orders for their industries. Therefore, the entire world is following the developments in Manchuria with great interest. The market of goods and the stock market register everything that is happening. It cannot be denied that, should the situation become serious, it would mean a gigantic stimulation of the economy of the entire world. However, if this situation does not result in war, the world will have to wait for a long time for a natural recovery, because this is still far away.

This is surely a candid but shameless declaration, however logical it may be from a capitalistic viewpoint because the armaments industry produces a profit three or four times higher than other industries.

In the following section we present various facts and details that seriously incriminate the armaments industry and expose it as the sector most interested in war.

f. War and expenditures for armaments; the high treason of the defense industry in World War I

It is understandable that while working on this book during World War II, the statistics for that war were still unavailable. However, it is certain that the figures for World War II far exceed those of World War I. Therefore, we had to rely on earlier facts, but even these are shocking in their enormity. Whosoever permits himself to be impartially affected by them will be readily struck by the crime of war and armaments.

According to the *Friedensfront*,[101] Germany's expenditures during the Weimar Republic were for

1. the standing army;
2. war pensions;
3. hidden costs for the army;
4. construction of railroads, harbors, roads, etc., for military purposes;
5. investments of the private war industry;
6. interest for domestic and foreign loans taken out to cover the costs resulting from the war.

For 1928–29, Germany's total expenditures (minus payments to individual countries): 8,375,100,000 RM (*Reichsmark*), broken down into

- expenditures for the military forces 875,000,000 RM
- domestic war expenditures 2,314,900,000 RM
- foreign war expenditures 2,178,500,000 RM
- remaining expenditures 3,054,700,000 RM

This means that of the Reich's total expenditures, 63.5 percent were used to cover the consequences of the last war and to prepare for the next one. Thus, 5.3 billion RM were spent for war, while the remaining three billion had to cover all other expenses: the foreign office, administration of justice, education, welfare, the economy, transportation, service of the debt, etc. The amount spent for education amounted to only 1 percent of what was spent for war because, according to a report of *Das Neue Volk*,[102] of every 100 RM were spent

- 42.42 RM for costs resulting from WWI and for war preparations;
- 23.60 RM for welfare;
- 15.02 RM for service on debts;
- 12.08 RM for administration;
- 5.65 RM for floating debts;
- 0.81 RM for housing and developments;
- 0.42 RM for education.

During the 1930s, 76.5 percent of France's government expenditures were for war-related costs. In the United States the figure was 72.2 percent.

101. *Friedensfront*, Heide in Holstein, May, 15, 1932, n.p.

102. *Das Neue Volk*, Würzburg, October 15, 1932, n.p.

England, France, Japan, Italy, Russia, North America, and Germany spent a total of 12 billion RM for armaments only. The regular expenditures for armaments of all nations of the world amounted to around 20 billion RM annually. In the fifteen years before 1933, England spent an average of £250 for weapons every minute.

These figures cry to the high heavens. The nations of the world have fallen prey to madness. They believe that they advance peace and security with their armaments, but they only promote war. Insecurity in the world is growing, and by means of the proliferation of armaments the next war is being prepared.

L'Osservatore Romano, the Vatican newspaper, declared on December 29, 1928, "To arm for war no longer means to promote peace but war. . . . Just as it is not possible to want truth if one lies, it is not possible to want peace if one supports the statement that everyone has the right to be armed to the teeth. Mistrust not only prevents the unity of the West but will ultimately totally destroy its culture."

If armaments would at least promote the public welfare! However, the army, navy, and all military equipment are nothing more than a means for the highly treasonous, internationally connected armaments industry to reap gigantic profits and to secure positions of status for various others who benefit from militarism. Above all, armaments capitalism is responsible in a special way for rearmament and war. In these devilish international enterprises of the arms industry the fatherland and its people are clearly betrayed.

The German press did not attempt to refute the shocking facts presented in the German pamphlet "The Bloody International Armaments Industry,"[103] which has just published its fifth edition of forty thousand copies, and from which we draw the following facts.

Between 1914 and 1918 the directors of some of Germany's large industries sent thousands of tons of iron ore, steel, armored shields, etc., to the enemy. Before the outbreak of World War I, the firm of Krupp A. G. sold a grenade detonator patent to Vickers of England for a share in the profit on each grenade produced, for which Krupp A. G. received 123 million RM after the war! This was a truly bloody deal at the cost of German soldiers. A German court ordered the German armaments firm Thyssen to pay 100,000 RM because in 1917 it supplied France with armored shields for her infantry and even had the audacity to charge only 68 RM per item, while the German army had to pay 117 RM per piece. Before the war, Krupp supplied the United States Navy with nickel-steel plated panels for 800 RM less per ton than it did the German Navy.

103. Lehmann-Rußbüldt, *Die blutige Internationale*, n.p.

All poison gas patents of the I. G. Farbenwerke were sold to a French chemical combine, and factories producing poison gas were established in France under the supervision of German experts. For the largest poison gas factory in the world, established in Poland, not only did I. G. Farbenwerke supply patents and instruction, but Krupp furnished what were guaranteed as the most efficient compressors. The French firm Schneider in Creusot took part in this bloody business. Thus German, Polish, and French armament capitalists united like brothers to produce poison gas with which their three countries could destroy each other—and, as World War II proved, this they did.

This is how it was. Thus the nations of the world are cheated and misused by the international armaments industry, which has no conscience and practices high treason, and, bribed by this industry, the leaders of nations lie to their people that their country should be armed for "God" and "the fatherland." With the slogan "you must become trained to be ready to fight" one seeks to capture the youth. One states that the people should again be filled with a military spirit, discipline, and order. Therefore, politicians, leaders as well as the press, largely bought off by armaments capitalism, are spreading propaganda for conscription. Also, protection against poison gas is zealously promoted. Of course! If the armaments industry produces gas, one needs gas masks for protection. Considerable money is earned with these, just as with poison gas and other instruments of murder. There is no question that all this protection against gas is nothing but fraud and rubbish.

Or does anyone believe that all of this is done out of true love for the fatherland, and to protect it? Whoever believes this must have a very limited critical ability.

As stated repeatedly, above all, modern wars are purely capitalistic business ventures of internationally organized high finance. The armaments industry and its investors, as well as their political and nonpolitical promoters, are the only ones benefiting from war. For the general public, particularly for the working masses, war brings only death and destruction, suffering, privation, and terrible misery. Therefore, it is incomprehensible how willingly the soldiers of every participating country allowed themselves to be taken advantage of by their leaders in World War II.

To emphasize once again, we do not want to be accused of degrading and condemning our soldiers and those of our opponents who did their duty during World War II. On the contrary, we appreciate their superhuman efforts. Most of them gave their life and blood in good faith, but they were misused by those who benefited from the war.

Despite these disturbing facts, our statesmen, prominent persons, and even clergymen have dared to plead for a reinstatement of conscription.

For example, Austria's minister of war, Carl Vaugoin, had the audacity to declare in a public address that "a state will be more respected, secure, and economically strong as its ability to defend itself is developed."[104] In other words, the more a state is delivered into the hands of armaments capitalists, the more favorable is its position.

Germany's Chancellor Kurt von Schleicher, in a speech in the Kyffhäuserbund, on January 15, 1933, called the reinstatement of conscription the most important goal of Germany's security. Dr. Hecht, a government section head, representing Austria at a meeting of the disarmament commission in Geneva, declared, "The Austrian government regards a conscripted army as a fundamental requirement for the security of the country. On the other hand, the government and the population also desire the establishment of the new defense system for idealistic reasons, because an army based on conscription trains its soldiers especially in love for the fatherland, unity, and discipline. It is for these considerations and by no means for aims of rearmament that we see the establishment of the militia system as necessary for the state."[105]

The above contains almost as many lies as sentences!

The Austrian people were not asked at all what they want. Rather, the political parties simply agreed to issue an order! Although the government does nothing to relieve the misery of the unemployed and of seniors with small pensions, at least by means of the military system, for which there is enough money, love for the fatherland should be drummed in by military drills.

At a rally of the German association of veterans in Berlin, on September 4, 1932, a speaker named Seldte said, "Today, military thinking and attitude are once again prevalent in Germany. Even though the old German army no longer exists, the spirit of discipline, of serving all, and of sacrificing for the community—this spirit of the old army and the front—is arising anew."[106]

In other words, this means that the more a nation is a weak-willed, blindly obedient military mass—which, when ordered, in mindless submission is always ready to murder human beings and, if need be, themselves be torn to pieces or gassed—and the higher are the contracts and dividends of the war industry, the better off is a nation. Let him who can believe this do so.[107]

104. *Grazer Volksblatt*, January 1, 1933.

105. *Uhr-Blatt*, Graz, February 8, 1933.

106. *Grazer Morgenzeitung*, September 5, 1932.

107. Ude: Now, as we are looking over this manuscript, only two years since the

Therefore, the armaments industry is the most shameful, bloody, capitalistic business, operated at the expense of the poor nations, which are, consciously or unconsciously, deliberately incited to war by political leaders paid off by the armaments capitalists and by the press controlled by these leaders. Military expenditures are contrary to the general welfare.

Do we need further proof to make clear to the peoples of the world just who it is they are waging wars for, who stirs up wars, and who abuses the patriotic enthusiasm of the masses?

The nations, suffering great hardships, neither need war nor want poison bombs, cannons, machine guns, pocket battleships, submarines, gas masks, or squadrons of airplanes. They need and want work and bread. They want peace, and to own homes and land. For this they do not need weapons, a people's militia, or a war department, but a department of peace.

Whoever advocates military training and defends war, whether he occupies a high or low position, whether he is a man or woman, priest or layman, subordinate or executive, let him make his body, life, and possessions available and permit himself to be drilled to commit organized mass murder. Then let him, along with the armaments capitalists, go to the battle front and murder to his heart's content. We others, however, who have seen through the trickery of military preparedness and war, are staying at home. We have something better to do than to be misused and induced to commit mass murder by the international arms industry, our leaders and political parties. We refuse resolutely to support the bloody business of the criminal arms industry, and we flatly deny the state the right to institute universal military service or a people's militia. We are conscientious objectors because as Christians we have to reject conscription as immoral.

Therefore, we also are unwilling to accept the unreasonable demand to bind unfortunate, conscripted young people by oath to promise blind obedience and to train them to commit organized murder. We stand by Christ and his teaching. Let the world's peoples decide freely whether they want

---

collapse of the Nazi rule of terror, the newspapers report that the Austrian government and the Allies, convening at a so-called peace conference, are considering the establishment of an Austrian army. This means it is expected of Austria—impoverished, ransacked, and economically on her knees—to deliver herself up anew to the monster that is militarism. However, neither the Allies nor our government are asking whether or not the people approve of this. It is simply dictated—even though, supposedly, Austria is now a democracy. Two attempts by the Austrian Peace Organization (Östereichische Friedensgesellschaft) to hold a public discussion of this question were forbidden immediately by the police. Let us hope that, by appealing to democracy, the Austrian people will not submit to such a dictatorial measure in a question that so seriously affects their lives but will prevail so that they themselves will be able to decide this issue in a free election.

war or peace. We are convinced that they would vote against every war and all armaments. Only those who profit from arms capitalism are for war, as are ambitious and power-hungry nations, especially if their leaders believe they can shine as "the greatest commanders of all time." This includes communism with its concept of the "dictatorship of the armed proletariat."

All the leaders of the world's Christian churches should at last acknowledge their duty to teach and influence the souls entrusted to their care—that is, in the manner we have explained, to turn them into firm opponents of war, and conscientious objectors.

g. Permanent readiness for war as cause of serious spiritual and ethical disorders of the nations

In 1937 we gave an address about how the permanent preparedness for war is a cause of the serious spiritual and moral disorders of the nations. The truly insane actions of the nations during World War II, which broke out shortly thereafter and caused unspeakable horrors and misery, prove that the remarks we made in 1937 were accurate. We would like to acquaint our readers with our speech and repeat it in its entirety:

We read in the *Grazer Mittag* of January 20, 1937, that in the previous day's session of England's Lower House of Parliament, Foreign Minister Anthony Eden pointed out with satisfaction the great interest in peace demonstrated by the people of England as well as by those of numerous other countries. He said, "We are convinced that the yearning for peace among the nations of the world is so irresistible that if all barriers to the freedom of international relations and of speech were removed, the danger to peace would be largely eliminated. . . . Every month gained for freedom is to our advantage."

According to a report in the *Grazer Volksblatt* of February 6, 1936, George Lansbury, a member of the Labour Party, in an address in the British Parliament, stated, "War is totally inappropriate to solve any issue because it is opposed to morality and to God."

The same newspaper, in its January 13, 1937, issue, quoted from an address by Austrian President Wilhelm Miklas to the diplomatic corps at the New Year's reception:

> I have been deeply touched by the words of sincere sympathy that in your behalf the papal nuncio dedicated to my fatherland

> and the warm appreciation for the unrelenting efforts of the Austrian government and people on behalf of the welfare of our country and peace in the world. . . . Situated in the heart of Europe, where the important lines of political and cultural development cross each other, our state is able to fulfill and realize its natural mission only in peace and with international cooperation. . . . Mr. Nuncio, I especially welcomed to hear you express that in other states, too, leading personalities and powerful forces are at work to safeguard the structure of peace from every harm.

According to the *Grazer Volksblatt* of April 25, 1936, Austrian chancellor Kurt von Schuschnigg said to a representative of the *Morning-Post*, "Our goal is to support peaceful collaboration among nations."[108]

Dr. Edvard Beneš, at that time foreign minister of Czechoslovakia, speaking to university students in Prague, according to the *Grazer Volksblatt* of November 24, 1935, stated, "I regard wars as inhumane and as the most terrible insult to the most humane teaching, that of Christ. . . . The development of a nation could also be fostered splendidly without war because today's method of bacteriological and chemical warfare has absolutely nothing to do with heroism. The question of war and peace is above all one of the will, the conviction, and the energy of the leading personalities. I am fighting for the most lasting peace for reasons of the practical necessity to guard against the horrors of war."

In a radio address to the Eucharistic Congress in Lima on October 27, 1937, Pope Pius XI said, "May it please God that the Christian spirit of peace, the only source of true peace, spread across all of the Earth and as soon as possible reach many hearts so that they be moved and reconciled, including in those places in Europe and Africa where, unfortunately, peace is greatly disturbed and could even be further damaged. For this peace, which has to be joined with justice, truth and love, we, my dear sons, will implore the Prince of Peace in the Eucharist."[109]

Cardinal Michael von Faulhaber of Munich wrote to the Women's International League of Peace and Freedom, "In fact, another war, with new technological means of destruction, would result in such misery and distress to the warring nations that all who are sympathetic with human culture have to raise their voice against war beforehand."[110]

108. *Grazer Volksblatt*, April 25, 1936.

109. *Wiener Kirchenblatt*, November 17, 1935.

110. *Das Neue Volk*, Würzburg, March 30, 1929.

Hungary's foreign minister Kálmán Kanya responded to a toast by the Austrian chancellor at a meeting of Hungarian and Austrian foreign policy leaders, "Above all, I would like to express my joy that the signatories of the Protocol of Rome are meeting already for a second time, working seriously and selflessly to build peace and progress. . . . Certainly, it is a laborious but, at the same time, a good and rewarding task to vigorously promote this evolutionary process in the hope that, even if only slowly and little by little, the condition of true peace that we yearn for can be realized."[111]

Franklin D. Roosevelt, president of the United States of America, expressed this opinion at the opening of the Panamanian Conference: "I trust that the republics of the New World will support the Old World to prevent the catastrophe of war. I am convinced that everywhere ordinary people want to live in peace, while leaders and governments resort to war. Peace can only be achieved by laborious effort, and millions of people hope for it."[112]

France's foreign minister Delbos explained in a radio address given on the occasion of a memorial celebration of the World War I victory of November 11, 1918, "After all, you, the soldiers of the world war, also died for peace, and it is our duty to preserve it. It is the fervent wish of all Frenchmen on this November 11th that we, and the generations that will come after us, will never again see a return of the horrors we experienced. Peace is also a victory, one that is very hard to achieve. One has to struggle against hate that divides the nations, against the blindness and untruthfulness of those who insist that wars are unavoidable, and against the threats that keep the world in a constant state of mobilization."[113]

According to the *Grazer Volksblatt* of March 4, 1936, the British White Paper on the defense of the empire commented, "It is also a fact that the general increase of the level of armaments does not guarantee peace."

Austria's state secretary Guido Schmidt expressed the following point of view to a representative of the *Giornale d'Italia*: "The Schuschnigg government, desiring to serve the European peace and a settlement of economic interests in Europe, is in complete agreement with Mussolini, the head of the Italian government. The Austrian government regards the Italian-Austrian friendship as one of the most important pillars of these constructive politics."[114]

111. *Wiener Reichspost*, November 12, 1936.
112. *Grazer Tagespost*, December 2, 1936.
113. *Grazer Mittag*, November 12, 1936.
114. *Grazer Mittag*, September 17, 1936.

Adolf Hitler, the *Führer* of the German Reich, stated on May 1, 1935, "Just as we established peace in our own nation, we desire nothing else than peace in the world because we know that important work can only succeed in a time of peace."[115]

And on May 21 he told the *Reichstag*, "National Socialistic Germany desires peace out of the deepest inner ideological convictions. It also wants it because of the simple realization that no war would alleviate the prevailing common European troubles but, instead, would increase them. . . . Whoever raises the torch of war can only wish for chaos."[116]

When we hear these and similar statements—and we could quote hundreds of them—a joyful hope must fill our hearts that peace will come soon. Only we will be bitterly disappointed if day after day the newspapers report ever more sinister types of armaments and continuous preparations for war by these same nations, whose statesmen talk so beautifully about peace.

According to the *Grazer Mittag* of January 13, 1937, English Prime Minister Anthony Eden declared in a speech, "In a world which is rapidly rearming, we can pursue no other politics than those of rearmament."

As early as January 20, 1937, the *Grazer Volksblatt* reported that the British Parliament voted to increase the military budget by £50 million to £210 million and to borrow £200 million for this purpose. The same article stated that England will institute general conscription if war breaks out. In no time all able-bodied men will be forced to join the army and participate in the murder and destruction organized by the government.

Austria's chancellor Kurt von Schuschnigg declared to a representative of the *Morning-Post*, "In order to do this [the work of peaceful cooperation among nations] and to fulfill our will, we have to organize our defense forces. We have to explain once and for all: The reorganization of the Austrian defense system not only guarantees the peace of Austria but the peace of all of central Europe."[117]

Schuschnigg also commented at a plenary meeting of the Lower Austrian trade associations, "From what we see, it appears there is every reason to believe that it is merely a beautiful dream when peace is talked about. It seems that war, the scourge of God, is one of the unavoidable blows of the fate of nations."[118]

The Catholic Diocese of Seckau issued the following order from its seat in Graz, Austria, on October 10, 1936: "The ministry of defense will hold a

115. *Die Heimat,* news service of Germans living in Austria, June, 1935.

116. *Die Heimat,* June, 1935.

117. *Grazer Volksblatt*, April 25, 1936.

118. *Grazer Tagespost*, December 12, 1936.

collection beginning September 30, 1936, entitled, 'National Collection for the Army and for Airplanes.' The reverend clergy is herewith informed of this collection and invited, if possible, to support it."[119]

The archbishops of Bologna and Trento donated their golden episcopal chains to finance Italy's war against Abyssinia, according to a report in the *Grazer Mittag* of November 25, 1935.

Il Duce, Benito Mussolini, said the following in Venice on the tenth anniversary of Italy's victory (read: betrayal) in World War I: "The war was not forced upon the Italian nation by a sudden attack, but she deliberately wished for it. It was a spontaneous act of her conscious will. Initially, the war in Italy was especially severe, which is confirmed by the terrible yet sublime figure of 600,000 soldiers killed, 400,000 disabled, and millions injured."[120]

And when Mussolini asked his listeners whether, should it become necessary, they would once again go to war, the assembly of several thousand replied with a tumultuous "yes!"

According to newspaper reports, the Swiss Catholic bishops recommended to their faithful that they subscribe to their country's defense bonds. Subsequently, these actually became oversubscribed. This event was celebrated by the ringing of church bells, as had been Italy's victory over Abyssinia.

Bishop Kepler once said, "In war, religion celebrates its silent and public triumphs. Here she takes noble, loving revenge for often being badly treated in peacetime. . . . She conquers many hearts that had been closed to her, sees the churches once again filled, consecrates the army before it marches to war, and accompanies it with invisible, piously praying multitudes. She consecrates the war itself and provides it with means of grace for its victories and defeats."[121]

(We add that in Vienna, for example, following War I, during the years 1919–26, 85,620 Catholics left the Church. In 1927, 20,000 withdrew within four months.)

From a November 28, 1936, report from Tokyo we learn that of a total government income of just over three billion yen, half was used for defense purposes. The French Cabinet appropriated five billion Francs only for air defense,[122]and China plans to institute conscription.[123]

119. *Grazer Volksblatt*, October 13, 1936.
120. *Grazer Volksblatt*, November 5, 1928.
121. *Grazer Volksblatt*, February 14, 1915.
122. *Grazer Volksblatt*, October 28, 1936.
123. *Grazer Volksblatt*, March 4, 1936.

Hitler, the Führer of the German Reich, declared at the 1935 Party Day of Freedom, "The readiness of our army provides Germany with the necessary protection on land. The establishment of our air force protects the German homeland from fire and gas. . . . The fact that we have again instituted conscription is a wonderful education that we are bestowing on the coming young German generation. . . . Our nation must make great sacrifices and does so gladly, for it does not want its sons to be poorly prepared and, secondly, does not want to see Germany continue to be defenseless."[124]

No more needs to be said.

If we call to mind what we said earlier about total war, is it any wonder that the entire world has been gripped by a widespread militarization fever and is terrified of an even more horrible world war than the previous one? Should we believe statesmen when they talk ingratiatingly about peace and incessantly emphasize how much they desire it? Or should we entrust ourselves to them when they prepare for war? How can the desire for peace be reconciled with the constant readiness for war?

Here two views clash irreconcilably: "If you want peace, prepare for war," and the opinion of the few who say with Christ, "Be just and kind, do not counter force with force, but conquer evil with good. Do not resist him who does you harm."

The question about which view is right has already been decided because Christ has solved the issue of war and peace unequivocally and clearly—and he is always right. The great commandment to love one's neighbor, including one's enemy, which Christ made a duty of conscience, is what is final here. This commandment silences on the spot every objection by the advocates of self-defense, conscription, and preparing for war.

Thus all those who defend war and want to keep peace by means of armaments are wrong. It is impossible to be for peace and for war at the same time because whoever arms, whoever champions military preparedness, whoever teaches the moral necessity of self-defense by forceful means and advocates preparedness for war is for war and, therefore, in conflict with the commandment to love one's enemy. Human beings, however, are created for truth, not for deceit or hypocrisy.

Therefore, everyone who does not side with truth and is not honest is divided within himself. He carries within a serious contradiction that has a most destructive and disastrous effect on his personal and public life. Truth

124. Eher, *Hitler's Speeches on the Party Day of Freedom*, n.p.

cannot be suppressed as long as reason is awake. However, whoever tries to cast the truth aside does violence to himself. Sooner or later such a person will have emotional problems that will have damaging physical effects.

Likewise, human beings are created for life, and the law of self-preservation is present in every healthy man and woman. Only the person who is very tense and emotionally ill is tortured by thoughts of suicide until, under certain circumstances, he succumbs to these. Healthy people say yes to life. However, war is the planned mutual destruction of life, but with more or less hope that oneself will not be killed but will succeed in destroying the so-called enemy. This is playing with life. One has to lie to oneself to some extent that to preserve one's own life one has to kill the opponent, but always with the realization that one could also be killed.

This results in an inner conflict of which one is more or less conscious. To think constantly about one's willingness to take part in war conflicts with the healthy instinct of self-preservation. This applies to the individual as well as to entire nations. By always affirming war and preparing for it, the desire of nations to destroy each other is kept alive and by means of the armaments race is immensely increased. This results in enormous mental and spiritual tension and fear. The idea of "the enemy," against whom one has to defend oneself without fail if he threatens with death and destruction, and the desire to render the foe harmless before he can strike, in time deprive one of every rational deliberation and awaken animal instincts that conflict with the rational free will, that is, the moral will.

The consequence is mental and moral confusion. Individual human beings and entire nations become mentally ill. Being always ready for war creates a condition that is anything but peace. It is a so-called psychosis, that is, a mental illness, combined with a more or less serious lack of judgment from whose consequences one can no longer turn away.

General Jan Christiaan Smuts, a prominent South African and British Commonwealth statesman, was right when he said, "The rumors circulating about a coming war create an atmosphere of war that is more apt to bring about a war than anything else. These rumors appear highly irresponsible and dangerous to me."[125]

But who, we have to ask, is responsible for the rise and spread of such dangerous rumors? They are, in the first place, the representatives of the armaments industry, those statesmen they have bought, the nations with their arms race and their press, as well as the people who champion and glorify war and depict military training, conscription, and self-defense as moral duties.

125. *Neue Freie Presse*, Vienna, November 13, 1934, 3.

This is how far present humanity has come with its constant readiness to wage war, so that even "total war" is taken for granted and justified. The desire to destroy—which is not only approved by statesmen but also sanctioned and even presented as a moral duty by church officials who endorse "just defensive war"—is honored as a moral deed under the slogan "for God, emperor, and fatherland," without considering that even the noblest end never justifies evil means. However, one also shares in the guilt for the sinister growth of the spirit of war by merely keeping silent when one should speak up loudly.

What moral confusion must be caused to the minds of children, as here in Austria, when the Catechism, which is approved by the Church and the Ministry of Education, on the one hand teaches that they are to practice love of neighbor, including their enemy, and that they are strictly bound in conscience to keep Christ's commandment to return good for evil and not to resist him who does evil, but if struck on one cheek, to offer the other—while, on the other hand, this same Catechism depicts killing and destroying in war as a moral and heroic duty; and when, contrary to the Ministry of Education, the Ministry of War subjects even children to pre-military training, that is, educates them to kill and destroy the enemy.

It is no wonder that a spirit of insincerity, religious hypocrisy, and indifference captures the hearts of people and that they no longer have any use for the Church but lose all respect for religious as well as secular authority. Thus force replaces law, hate of all for all casts aside love of neighbor, and a sense of and appreciation for justice have disappeared.

We cannot close these remarks more effectively than by citing an open letter that 339 psychiatrists from all over the world sent to the world's statesmen in October 1935. We would like to familiarize all bishops and priests with this letter, which states,

> We psychiatrists, whose task it is to probe the mental and spiritual life of healthy and sick human beings and to serve them with our knowledge, as physicians feel it is our duty to speak to you in all seriousness.
>
> Presently there prevails a way of thinking in the world that threatens the life of nations with enormous dangers that can lead to a definite war psychosis. War means to summon up all forces of destruction against humanity and signifies the destruction of humankind through technology. As in all human events, in the complex problem of war, the spiritual condition of nations is highly important.

In order for war to be prevented, the nations and their leaders have to be aware of their attitude toward war. Only self-awareness can prevent a world catastrophe.

Basic to this awareness is the following discernment:

1. Apparently there exists a contrast between the conscious aversion of the individual toward war and a willingness of the whole to wage it because human beings think and feel differently as individuals than as part of the whole. In civilized men and women of the twentieth century there persist the wild and destructive instincts of prehistoric humans, instincts that have not yet been refined. These manifest themselves without restraint when danger threatens the community. This unconscious desire to live out these primitive instincts without being punished, but rather being rewarded, greatly furthers the willingness to wage war. It is important to be always aware that only the mind can keep these bellicose instincts in check. Guided into good paths, these instincts provide powers that can be a blessing for humanity, the same powers that, untamed, lead to chaos.

2. The national lack of a sense of reality is frightening. Concepts of war expressing themselves in parade uniforms have nothing to do with the reality of war. Also astonishing is the indifference to the criminal activities and intrigues of the international armaments industry. It is madness to allow a very few to realize personal profits from the slaughter of millions. The sense of reality and the instinct of self-preservation of the masses have to be roused because these instincts are the strongest allies against war, as is strengthening the moral and religious feelings of the people.

3. The speeches of well-known statesmen frequently show that their ideas about war are primitive and no different from those of the average citizen. Because of the modern methods of waging war, expressions like "War is the necessary consequence of Darwin's teaching" and "Mars is the supreme lord of war" are false and dangerous. They veil primitive bellicose and controlling instincts and serve only to incite the desire for war of one's own people. These speeches contain tremendous powers of suggestion. Once inflamed, the spirit of war can no longer be suppressed. Let us be reminded of the 1914 slogan "the fatherland is in danger" and its effect on the nations. As with the individual, entire nations can become neurotic under the influence of such suggestions and by means of fear and irrational ideas can be driven to adventures that portend their own demise and that of others. We psychiatrists declare that today's science is able to differentiate between real, pretended, and unconscious motives,

> including those of statesmen. History will judge those who subject their people to military drills and at the same time always talk about peace. It is they who will be judged guilty of causing the unspeakable misery that a new war will bring.
>
> We state emphatically that international relations on behalf of peace, even if sincere, still do not guarantee the sacrificial will required to ensure lasting peace—if necessary, at the cost of national sacrifices. We are of the opinion that those organizations furthering the common interests of the nations are well enough developed to make it possible for their leaders, in concerted action, to prevent every war.
>
> However, should some leaders believe that the organizations dedicated to peace are not yet adequately prepared to secure lasting peace, we suggest they spend as much energy and money for this effort as is being spent to arm their nations.
>
> We close by saying that we bow down with admiration before those statesmen who, with a superior morality and culture, guide their nations into the path of peace. They alone can call themselves "leaders of nations."

We completely approve of the content of this open letter to statesmen, signed by 339 psychiatrists, and wholeheartedly thank these fearless men for issuing it.

Nations and statesmen play with war and thus incur tremendous responsibility. It seems that today the willingness to go to war is cultivated under slogans such as "against Bolshevism," "against communism," "against fascism," and others, but many statesmen use these to hide self-serving, power-political intentions. Capitalism, communism, Bolshevism, and fascism are not fought with cannons and machine guns, not with bombs and poison gas, but only with efforts to provide poor people who are suffering and deprived of their rights with a dignified existence, based on justice and love of neighbor. This means assuring them of decent wages for their work. To achieve this, church and state, each in its own domain, should work harmoniously together.

It is a crime when churches summon their faithful to a "crusade" against Bolshevism, as once they summoned them to a crusade against the Turks under the slogan "it is the will of God" and thus brought death and misery to hundreds of thousand lives.

Such an invitation to a settlement by means of weapons seems to be made in an article in *L'Osservatore Romano* in an attempt to answer the question, how should one fight communism? It stated, "This communism [meaning Bolshevism], as it is raging in Spain, is to be fought as the facts necessitate, and this fight is a crusade of the decent people who do not rise up against authority but against criminality and barbarism. Everyone who does not get involved is guilty, every excuse given is unjust, and every capitulation is criminal. Crime should not triumph. Virtues should not be undervalued."[126]

We say again: It would be inexcusable if such words would demand fighting communism with weapons. Even at the risk of being blamed, we have to admit that if Franco and his cronies had not initiated the fight against the Spanish government, there would never have occurred the many atrocities in Spain that we are witnessing today with deep sorrow. Therefore, never this: "If you want peace, prepare for war," but only this: "If you want peace, prepare for peace!" Not force, or hate, or militarization, but solely justice and love of neighbor. These alone create and secure peace. The path in this direction was shown for society and the economy in the two papal encyclicals *Rerum novarum*, issued by Leo XIII in 1891, and *Quadragesimo anno*, issued by Pius XI in 1931.

Therefore, it is our task to inform others of our ideas so that they can form their conscience accordingly and so that statesmen, nations, and all people finally realize that they do not serve peace by being prepared for war but by being ready to serve peace without reservation.

As we explained above, our convictions lead us to the following view: The teaching of the *Kathechismus der katholischen Religion*, approved by the bishops of Austria in 1930,[127] which permits the killing of a human being in self-defense, such as when a soldier is defending his fatherland, is opposed to the teaching of Christ to love one's enemy. The teaching that self-defense is morally permissible is largely responsible for humanity's rigid attitude that always being ready for war will secure peace.

The nations of the world support the necessity of being prepared for war by citing self-defense, and from this logically reach the point of demanding total war! We, however, without reservation, stand with Christ when he demanded in the Sermon on the Mount, "To anyone who slaps you on one cheek, present the other cheek as well; to anyone who takes your cloak from you, do not refuse your tunic" (Luke 6:29). We want to follow the commands of Christ word for word: "Love your enemies and pray for those who persecute you" (Matt 5:44); "Never pay back evil with evil" (Rom 12:17); "But I say to you: offer no resistance to the wicked" (Matt 5:39); "Do not be mastered by evil, but master evil with good" (Rom 12:21); "This is my commandment: love one another as I have loved you" (John 15:12); "Love

126. *Grazer Volksblatt*, January 9, 1937.

127. *Kathechismus der katholischen Religion*, 90.

can cause no harm to your neighbor" (Rom 13:10); "Anyone who hates his brother is a murderer" (1 John 3:15); "If your enemy is hungry, give him something to eat; if thirsty, something to drink" (Prov 25:21).[128]

Therefore, we reject the moral justification of self-defense and advocate complete nonviolence because only it agrees with the demand of Christ to love one's enemy. This is incomprehensible for the person who likens humans to animals and takes only original sin into account. But it is comprehensible for him who, sanctified by the grace of Christ, conducts his life according to Christ's teaching. For wherever there is peace, there is no hatred but only pure, benevolent love and justice which acts in accordance with love.

Only in this way do we reach the demand: "Total peace!" And this peace is the peace of Christ in the kingdom of Christ. Only this is a true, joy-giving peace—though one we gain only by making sacrifices. But it is possible and will be safeguarded by the works of justice and love Only this peace meets the words of our Lord: "Happy the peacemakers: they shall be called sons of God" (Matt 5:9).

h. Militarism, war, and public morality

Whoever loves his country, whoever sees the family as the nucleus of the state, and whoever sees an invaluable national treasure in a healthy and morally governed sexual life must be an opponent of war and must deplore and condemn militarism. For the facts prove that times of war are times of the worst immorality and extensive infection with sexual diseases, which are harmful to the race. Also, during war prostitution thrives. But even in peacetime, military life is a constant source of opportunity for young people, both officers and enlisted men, to stray in various ways, and a school for perversities, especially homosexual offenses. This nadir is being fostered especially by brothels and prostitutes, who are carefully looked after and regulated by the state.

The head physician of the Imperial and Royal War College, Dr. Franz Hirz, commented in a flyer directed at young soldiers, "The frighteningly high number of officers who quickly died after being paralyzed can be explained by the extensive spread of syphilis. This also applies to the frequency of syphilitc myelopathy."

For example, before its loss of territory in 1919, the old Austria had no fewer than 551 brothels—tolerated by the government—which were under medical and police supervision, with 6,797 licensed prostitutes—besides,

128. See other passages from the Holy Scriptures quoted in Part II, section 3 above.

of course, the unofficial prostitutes, of which there were about 40,000 in Vienna alone. It was no coincidence that towns with military bases had been provided with such establishments and with prostitutes, and during the war more and more such shameful places were established almost as close as the front.

The above applied not only to the old Austrian military but also to the military in other countries. In times of war, when millions of married and unmarried men are torn from their families for extensive periods, there exists, in a sense, a sexual state of distress, which ministries of war seek to meet by establishing brothels as far as the front and supplying them with licensed prostitutes.

Here are some facts from World War I. New recruits were supplied with prophylactics, and instructions on how to use them, and were taught disinfection procedures. Boxes and boxes of these preventatives were delivered to the front. The men either had to disinfect themselves, or this was done by medics especially employed for this task. There were separate brothels for officers and enlisted men, and men visiting these establishments had to follow special regulations.

In the July 1917 issue of the medical journal of the Austrian imperial and royal Army, a Dr. Moldavan praised these measures as if they were highly important moral achievements. He wrote, "We have established brothels with satisfactory material [read: prostitutes], under strict military control, and, as far as possible, we supply officers and enlisted men with prophylactics at no cost."

And what was achieved by these "exemplary" measures?

Professor Dr. Finger provided the following information at the German-Austrian Convention for the Welfare of the Nation in March 1916: in the Austrian army approximately 800,000 soldiers were infected with venereal disease. A third of these were married men. In September 1917, of the troops stationed in Sternthal, near Pettau in Steiermark, soldiers admitted for venereal diseases already reached 32,000, and that in a single hospital.

What an appalling prospect, from a strictly racial hygienic and population-political viewpoint, is the return of all these infected men to their families. For even if after the disarmament, the strictest measures for the prevention and spread of venereal diseases had been enforced, renowned medical experts do not believe that these diseases can be completely cured. For example, Professor Stern stated, "It is also true for syphilis that the earlier we can detect the first symptoms, which today is not difficult, the earlier we can mitigate the dangers. I expressly say 'mitigate' and purposely avoid talking about curing because even with our new methods of treatment this cannot be guaranteed to the extent that is often assumed."[129]

Dr. Zweifel writes in his work *The Problem of Prostitution in Switzerland*, "It is a sad truth that a person with syphilis may not be regarded as cured even if the sores are healed. Almost without exception, the disease spreads stealthily and attacks inner organs . . . and anyone carrying this disease continues to endanger others, who may become infected."[130]

Already in times of peace, 31 percent of all illnesses in the Austro-Hungarian Army were venereal diseases. This means that daily 1,748 men suffered, as many as two regiments in peacetime. Official statistics list 61.6 soldiers with venereal diseases per 1,000 men.

In World War I the increase of venereal diseases among youth was striking. In Vienna, during peacetime, of 1,000 youth aged fifteen, one was afflicted; aged sixteen, three; aged seventeen, eleven; aged eighteen, twenty-seven. During World War I the figures rose: of those aged fifteen, eight were afflicted; aged sixteen, nine; aged seventeen, twenty-six; and aged eighteen, sixty-eight.[131]

It was estimated that these diseases cost the German Reich 90 million Reichsmark annually and that in Prussia alone the cost was 410,000 RM daily, totaling 150 million yearly.[132]

The following document shows that all these measures taken by military authorities during war were "shamelessly promoting whoring on a large scale." It cannot be called anything else. This document was issued by the German military authority, which controlled the operation and hygienic measures of a public brothel in München-Gladbach during World War I. The following passage excerpted from this document, which is truly a document of the Nazi "civilization," is taken from the book *War to War!*, by Ernst Friedrich.[133]

> The two women who make up the entire personnel of the public house (Gasthausstr. 2) explained that they are unable to satisfy the great number of visitors who swamp the house, in front of which numerous groups of sex-starved clients are usually waiting. The women explained that, in view of the service they owe to their Belgian and German regular subscribers, they are unable to grant the division more than twenty visits a day, ten

129. Fassbender, *Des deutschen Volkes*, 675–76.
130. Zweifel, *Die Prostitutionsfrage*, 78–79.
131. Finger, *Der Krieg und die Bekämpfung*, 20.
132. Ibid.
133. Friedrich, *Krieg dem Krieg*, 160.

> for each regiment. This establishment does not operate at night and strictly observes Sunday rest. On the other hand, the city authorities do not permit increasing the personnel. In order to prevent disorder and to keep these women from working beyond their strength, the following order was issued:
>
> Work days: Every day except Sunday.
>
> Maximum work: Every woman serves ten men daily, 20 for two women, totaling 120 visits during one work week.
>
> Time of operation: 5:30 p.m. to 9 p.m.
>
> No visits are permitted outside these hours.
>
> Rates: Five Mark for a visit of one quarter hour, which includes entering and leaving the establishment.
>
> Refreshments: The house sells no beverages. There is no waiting room. Only two visitors are allowed inside the house at one time.
>
> Schedule: The six days of the week are arranged like this:

Monday:	1st Battalion of the 164th Regiment
Tuesday:	1st Battalion of the 169th Regiment
Wednesday:	2nd Battalion of the 164th Regiment
Thursday:	2nd Battalion of the 169th Regiment
Friday:	3rd Battalion of the 164th Regiment
Saturday:	3rd Battalion of the 169th Regiment

> In the office of the sergeant major of each of these battalions there are twenty admission tickets available for the designated day, five for each company. The soldiers who want to visit the establishment receive a ticket that gives them the right of priority.
>
> Following are further regulations for those men who have the right to visit when the women are not occupied. It is recommended that the officers on duty on the Gasthaus Strasse see that everything is in order.[134]

From a Christian viewpoint, this document of military measures to prevent venereal diseases can only be called disgraceful. And the nation that is responsible for it calls itself a "*Kulturvolk*." This is the moral condition of an army highly glorified for its "heroism," of an army of which the Führer and the people, and not least our women and girls, are proud. The military is praised as an "eminent factor of national education and formation of character." However, the opposite is true.

In this connection, we cannot refrain from making the public acquainted with a second "cultural document" that seems to be almost more atrocious than the one above. Titled "SS Order for the Entire SS and the Police," it was issued in Berlin on October 28, 1939, by the Reich Department

134. Ibid.

for Domestic Affairs and signed by *Reichsführer* of the SS (*Schutzstaffel*) and head of the German police Heinrich Himmler. A war measure, this document provides evidence of the low regard in Nazi Germany for the relationship between the genders.

This order culminated in the Nazi aspiration for children at any price so that the state will always have enough soldiers at its disposal. In the Nazi state, based on force, only the man who could fight, the soldier, counted—and to become such a man was the highest goal to which one could aspire. The Nazi leaders incessantly drummed this message into people's minds in meetings and in newspapers, radio, and film. Here are only a few examples:

Artur Axmann, the youth leader of the German Reich, received a telegram from Führer Adolf Hitler on the occasion of the Day of Paramilitary Training of the German Youth, which read, "The goal of this training[135] is to achieve soldier-like thinking and action on a National Socialistic foundation. . . . The front expects that the Hitler Youth, in its most difficult trials, continues to regard providing the fighting troops with a steady flow of recruits as its highest duty."[136]

And Wilhelm Schepmann, chief of staff of the SA (*Sturmabteilung*), commented on the Nazi concept of fighting ability and military aptitude:

> The important task of the SA, in accordance with the will of the Führer, is to convey the National Socialistic spirit to the German men trained for the military and to strengthen the National Socialistic concept of defense. Our future is only guaranteed if the cultivation of military virtue always ranks first. Whatever may come, we follow Adolf Hitler through thick and thin. . . . A National Socialist bows down only before eternal providence and Adolf Hitler and before nothing else. . . . Our entire life has to be a passionate devotion to the soldier at the front. . . . The highest duty of the SA remains to keep German manhood free from disloyalty and to inspire it to bravely wield the sword for honor, freedom, nation, and Führer.[137]

The effect of the constant propaganda to promote military training and the profession of soldier can be seen in the following birth notice from the *Münchner Neuesten Nachrichten*: "NSFK[138] Obersturmbannführer

135. Author's note: This means the training of young people by soldiers well tried on the front, with the goal of turning children into soldiers.

136. *Tagespost*, Graz, September 4–5, 1943.

137. *Tagespost*, Graz, November 16, 1943.

138. Author's comment: I do not care at all what these letters mean, but by this and other word formations like "Gestapo"=*Geheime Schutz Polizei* and "Kripo"=*Kriminal Polizei*, the German language was severely mutilated.

Wolfgang Voigtländer announces the birth of a son on May 15, 1943, with the words: 'Airforce recruit has arrived'"—as though German male children were predetermined to join a certain armed service.

German youth and young people of all nations, let us tell you what is meant by cultivating "soldier-like youth" and what it means to be a soldier. Let us tell you in the words of the author of a book most worthy of reading, which, however, is strictly forbidden in the Nazi state: *All Quiet on the Western Front*. Erich Maria Remarque states most accurately,

> We had ten weeks of basic training, and that changed us more radically than ten years at school. We learnt that a polished button is more important than four volumes of Schopenhauer. We came to realize—first with astonishment, then bitterness, and finally with indifference—that the mind apparently wasn't of prime importance, but the boot brush; not ideas, but the system; not freedom, but drill. We had joined up with enthusiasm and goodwill; but they did everything to drive that out of us. After three weeks it no longer struck us as odd that a postman with a couple of stripes should have more power over us than our parents ever had, or our teachers, or all of civilization from Plato to Goethe. With our young, wide-open eyes we saw that the classical concept of patriotism of our teachers, for the time being, was realized by surrendering our individual personalities more completely than we would ever have expected from the most lowly errand boy. Saluting, snapping to attention, marching, presenting arms, right about, left about, clicking the heels, insults and a thousand varieties of chicanery. We had imagined that our task would be different and discovered that we were being trained for heroism the way they train circus horses . . .[139]

Here is another excerpt:

> I ask you: Whatever a man may be in civilian life, in which occupation could he afford that sort of behavior[140] without getting punched out? He can do this only in the army. You see, this always goes to his head. And the less someone was in civilian life, the more it goes to his head now.[141]

Remarque describes the conscripted army thus:

139. Remarque, *Im Westen nichts Neues*, 27–28.

140. Ude: Meaning arbitrarily oppressing and tormenting their subordinates, insulting them, and demanding everything possible and impossible from them.

141. Remarque, *All Quiet on the Western Front*, 49.

> It is a great brotherhood which combines the good fellowship of the folk song, the solidarity among convicts, and the desperate clinging together of those condemned to die into a condition of life which, in the midst of danger, rises above the tension and abandonment of death to a fleeting grasping of every hour won, in the most dispassionate way. It is heroic and banal, if you want to evaluate it—but who wants to do that?[142]

In order to have many soldiers available, *Reichsführer* Heinrich Himmler issued the above-mentioned "SS Order":

> In every war the finest blood is shed. Many a victory of weapons was at the same time a devastating defeat of the nation's vitality and its blood. But the unfortunately necessary death of the best men, as worthy as it is to be mourned, is still not the worst. Much worse is the loss of the children who were not produced by the living during the war and by those who died after the war.
>
> The old wisdom that only the person who has produced sons and daughters can die in peace [author's note: how will the *Führer* of the German nation die since he has no sons and daughters?] has to be true in this war especially for the *Schutzstaffel*. He can die peacefully who knows that his kin, that everything his ancestors and he have desired and aspired to will be continued by his children. The greatest treasure the widow of a fallen soldier has is always the child of the man whom she loved.
>
> Beyond the boundaries of otherwise necessary civil laws and customs, it can be a noble mission for German women and girls of good blood, even outside of marriage, not rashly but with deep moral seriousness, to become mothers of children of soldiers going to war, as only fate knows whether they will return or will fall for Germany.
>
> Especially in these times it is also a sacred duty for the fathers and mothers whom the state has ordered to remain in the homeland to continue to produce children.
>
> We should never forget that the victory of the sword and of the blood shed by our soldiers would have no meaning if not followed by the victory of the child and the settlement of new territory.
>
> In the last war, many a soldier, because of his concern that if his wife were to have an additional child, she would be left in need and with worries, decided not to father any more children during the war itself. You SS men do not need to have such

142. Ibid., 267.

> concerns because the following regulations take these worries from your shoulders:
>
> For all legitimate and illegitimate children of good blood[143] whose fathers died in war, special representatives, personally selected by me, will take over the guardianship in the name of the *Reichsführer* of the SS. We stand by these mothers and will be responsible for the upbringing and material needs of these children until they reach majority so that no mother and widow has to worry about any necessities.
>
> The SS will provide for all legitimate and illegitimate children fathered during the war and for the expectant mothers if they need help. After the war, when the fathers return, the SS will provide generous material assistance to anyone who applies.
>
> You SS men and mothers of these children hoped for by Germany, based on your belief in the *Führer* and in the desire for eternal life of our blood and our nation, should demonstrate that just as you know how to fight and die courageously for Germany, you are willing to pass on life for Germany!
>
> *Reichsführer* SS H. Himmler

A document with such an outrageous demand, never heard of before, directed to a nation of eighty-five million, could only have been devised by a Nazi mind like Himmler's, and only SS men could have been expected to translate it into reality. Or, perhaps many German women and girls? Himmler regards his SS men, whom he orders to produce children, no matter whether legitimate or illegitimate, as simply Aryan breeding animals, to whom German women and girls should be subjugated indiscriminately, in order to have the SS take charge of the education of these children. This is most likely because Himmler regards this organization as especially suited to raise children according to the Nazi Weltanschauung.

However, Himmler and his associates are not troubled that the family life of Germany is thoroughly destroyed and rendered superfluous and that the entire Greater German Reich is turned into a single rabbit hutch, with Himmler as supervisor. The Nazi state needs soldiers, nothing but soldiers at any price, and also willing party members. A method that, at least for the moment, promises success is to categorically obey the above-mentioned SS order, with which, generally, sexually maturing young people, especially, like to comply with because it relieves them of every responsibility for raising their children.

143. Author's note: The fact that in the Hitler-Himmler Reich, children not having "good blood," that is, those mentally challenged, those with incurable diseases, etc., were simply killed in the interest of breeding a superior race is a reality that makes each decent German deeply ashamed.

That Himmler, with this order, overrules the natural right that grants parents the inalienable right and duty to raise their children seems to cause him not the least pangs of conscience because he rationalizes thus: Whatever helps the German nation to victory is morally permissible, even if it violates "the boundaries of otherwise necessary laws and customs" a hundred times. For the Nazis, the ends justify any means.

At the end of this section we would like to impress upon the reader the undeniable fact that in times of war the military exceedingly endangers the morals and health of the population and radically poisons family life in every nation. For this reason alone we have to reject totally the military and war. The military and war provide opportunities for transgressing the Sixth Commandment on a grand scale. To prove this point, we cite the dreadful raping of girls and women by members of the troops who "freed" Austria.

"What, then, will anyone gain by winning the whole world and forfeiting his life?" (Matt 16:26). Infinitely superior to the life of the body is the life of the soul, which can be lost by committing serious sins. General Helmuth von Moltke, who certainly was not fundamentally opposed to war, stated in a Reichstag session on April 24, 1877, "Even a successful military campaign costs more than it gains, for to pay for material goods with human lives cannot be regarded as a victory." Thus, if it is not acceptable to sacrifice the mortal, physical life of soldiers for the conquest of material goods, even less so may the life of immortal souls be risked by the military or by war!

Experience proves that in war, the military provides a ready opportunity for many of its members to commit constant, grave offenses against the Sixth Commandment of God, namely, the opportunity for serious sins, while dangerously damaging the health of the nation by contagious venereal diseases. The serious, irreparable effects on the family life of the entire nation by no means are offset by the gains the government expects the military to achieve. Because the military, with everything accompanying it, materially and morally, is a gigantic losing business for every nation, it should be abolished.

After all we have said about them, the military and the profession of soldier are not achievements of which a nation can be proud. However, it is up to the people whether they will continue to put up with being forced into the military.

Every rational and morally serious, that is, firm Christian believer will agree when we say: The morality of the nation categorically demands that war be outlawed and, consequently, that all militarism be eliminated because it is essentially evil and severely damages the general welfare, not only economically but also morally and sociopolitically. The wounds it inflicts on the nation cannot be healed. The military and the general welfare of the population are diametrically opposed to each other.

6. Violence or nonviolence?

a. Heroes and heroism

Historians, the press—unfortunately including self-improvement publications—and, almost without exception, schools, film, radio, and here and there the pulpit and the churches falsify public opinion to a vast extent by glorifying war.

Soldiers are celebrated as heroes; war songs are composed; the horror of killing is glorified with the halo of "martyrdom for God, for Kaiser, for the people, and for the fatherland," and epic poems ensure that heroic deeds are not forgotten. The enormous lie that "it is sweet to die for the fatherland," used since prehistoric times, continues to be employed today in many ways. Again and again, even God is made into an ally of war by all sides. "God with us" was engraved on the pack buckles of Hitler's soldiers in the most horrible of all wars. Racial hatred, wars of retaliation and revenge, and no less wars of conquest are praised as being honorable. Vivid pictures are painted of what would have been if this or that war had not been waged. Lies, violence, brutality of every kind, and atrocious espionage are rampant in every war. And after a victory, thanks to better technical equipment or a superior ability to murder and destroy mercilessly—which often is achieved by distributing alcohol to the soldiers—government authorities talk about "the gratitude of the fatherland" and pin crosses and medals embellished with colorful ribbons and jewels to the chest of the "heroes." Generally, the more decorations a soldier displays on his uniform, the more he has murdered and destroyed. The churches hold worship services to thank God for "the victory he helped them achieve"; and the people, in their incredibly blissful submissiveness, even if they are tired of war, are always ready to be led again to the slaughter, convinced that wars are necessary and that there is nothing that can be done.

But what is this glorified "heroism" of war really like?

Outdoors in the dirt, in the slaughter fields, plowed up by exploding bullets, are mountains of dismembered bodies, the bodies of the fallen "heroes." Millions bled to death and breathed their last, lonely and abandoned, in excruciating pain, torn to pieces, mutilated, gassed, covered with rubble. Some were "fortunate" enough to be thrown together into mass graves and covered with dirt, as is done with carrion. The bodies of other hundreds of thousands of these "heroes" are decomposing unburied, their odor polluting the air. Hundreds of thousands of others ended up on the bottom of the ocean or became food for fish, while still others died of hunger, froze to death, or perished in prison camps, far from their homeland and their loved ones. Fathers and mothers, women and children are grieving inconsolably for all of these "heroes" who lost their lives so wretchedly for "nation and fatherland," whose deaths "for *Führer* and fatherland" are announced by their relatives in the newspaper obituaries with "proud sorrow."

Still other millions of these glorified "heroes" returned as wretched cripples, without a hand or a foot, many blind, others with jaws shot to pieces, all sick or disabled for the rest of their lives. They are living witnesses to a "glorious victory" or an "unfortunate defeat."

Still others caught syphilis or gonorrhea in the brothels provided by the military and upon their return infected their wives and their children.

Millions of these "heroes" demonstrated their heroism by indiscriminately leading astray, dishonoring, and even raping women and girls, even school-age girls, in enemy countries and also at home while on leave. But, no, not always "led astray," because many girls and women proudly gave themselves, even forced themselves on these men. No wonder that many a man returning from war as "hero" found an unfaithful wife or bride, and many a father, a dishonored daughter.

And the ruins of cities and villages destroyed by these "heroes," in blind obedience to their commanders, rise up to the high heavens. Often they also killed the inhabitants and destroyed cultural treasures while the high command of the army reported this "heroism" with jubilation in newspapers and on the radio, and the people rejoiced. This happened on all sides.

What glorious "heroism," in which death, agony, crime, rape, murder, destruction, horror, and brutality of every kind play the leading role! And such heroism is celebrated and decorated.

Oh, you poor, abused and deluded "heroes"!

We cannot find words to portray the so-called heroism of war as it really is because it often hides cowardice, brutality, crime, vile acts, sadism, and sheer animal instincts.

It has to be noted in their defense, however, that in war all soldiers are constantly under the pressure of tremendously brutal violence. For if a soldier refuses to execute on command the "heroic deeds" of war, namely, murder and destruction, he is simply shot on the spot. What choice does he have but to become a "hero" whether he wants to or not? If he is lucky to escape alive, he is celebrated as a "hero" who splendidly proved his worth. If he is unlucky, however, and remains behind on the "field of honor," he is likewise praised as a "hero" who joyfully gave his life in the belief that it is sweet to die for his countrymen and his fatherland. That is how they talk at victory celebrations and lie that they will never forget these "heroes" in all eternity. That the death of each one is frequently a dreadful process and has nothing to do with "heroism" is not considered, however.

All of this is only possible because the people, laboring under the constant psychological pressure of conscription, long ago gave up thinking independently, acting rationally, and courageously opposing violence. For at the moment when all the people of a nation—men, women, and young people—having understood the impotence of violence, no longer pick up a weapon and simply refuse to serve in war, militarism and war are finished simultaneously. For how could the leader of a nation wage war by himself when the people do not join in and no one in the entire country is willing, when ordered, to shoot his fellow citizen who refuses to go to war?

This brief reflection shows that the most brutal and seemingly strongest and invincible force can be overcome immediately without weapons by total nonviolence and that the greatest force is simply powerless against correctly applied nonviolence. However, that brutal force, which turns soldiers into "heroes," reigns today proves that because they fear that violent means will be used against them if they refuse to go to war, people do not trust their own thinking but are willing to commit violence. They are not aware of the power of nonviolence and so permit themselves to be misused by those who by chance are in power.

Thus, by means of nonviolence, which is much superior to raw, physical force, the immense and brazen lie of the authorities regarding the necessity of armaments and "heroism" would be at once exposed as a lie, and the weakness, powerlessness, and hypocrisy of raw force would be established. Then the nations and all citizens would be truly free, whereas today they are forced to serve like slaves. Therefore, as soon as the nations would be convinced of the powerlessness of raw violence and of the invincible power of nonviolence, militarism and its illusory "heroism" and hero worship would be finished, and the authorities would have more than enough time and means to reflect on and carry out whatever truly promotes peace.

Since we are discussing heroism, we have to call heroes, without reservation, those conscientious objectors who, convinced that it is never permitted to kill, even on the highest command, were shot as "traitors" to the fatherland. By their example they demonstrated that under no circumstances, not even on the highest command, may one do what is immoral, regardless of the consequences. God has to be obeyed more than man.

Therefore, no soldier may excuse the atrocities he committed by saying that he was commanded to do so. However, the freedom of the will can be very much impaired by the threat that he who refuses to obey an order will be shot. We will discuss this further in the following section.

b. What is violence and how does it work?

The question at hand is, what is the relationship of violence and nonviolence? Here we take the Christian position which can never disagree with morality based on natural law and reason. First we will answer the question, what is violence? Then we will discuss how it works.

The amount of force secular authorities may use is determined by the objectives of the state, whose duty it is to promote and guarantee the general welfare. This means the state has to issue regulations, create institutions, and provide the necessary means to secure for all citizens the rights to which they are entitled by nature and by God. These include the right to life, the right to own and use property, and the right of freedom of religion. All these rights guarantee a dignified existence, and the officials of the state, in cooperation with the citizens, are responsible for ensuring that no one is prevented from realizing these absolute rights and that they are not contested. Whenever these rights are violated or impeded, the government has to do whatever is necessary to effectively stop these infractions. As much as possible, measures should be taken to prevent crimes against life, property, and freedom of conscience. To carry out all of these duties, the government cannot dispense with a certain amount of physical force, that is, coercion; but in no case does it have the right to enact the death penalty, as we proved earlier. There are other effective methods to safeguard society and prevent criminals from doing harm. However, there is no state with perfect justice, nor will there ever be one, because human beings are flawed as a result of original sin.

What is violence? In *Violence and Nonviolence*,[144] Dr. Kobler calls violence "an encroachment on order by force." Below is a summary of his comments.

Violence can go so far as to cause the deprivation of rights or even death. Violence can also serve coercion, that is, to force someone to agree to do whatever the coercer wants. Violence can destroy order but can also serve to restore it, that is, to force opposing wills back within the realm of order. Violence can also be used to destroy the established system of life and existence in order to institute the kind of system desired. Again and again

144. Kogler, *Gewalt und Gewaltlosigkeit*, n.p.

in the course of history, social, intellectual, and even religious systems have been created by means of violence, which was regarded as a suitable means to create the envisioned system. For example, religious inquisitors who employed torture were convinced they were serving the purity of the Christian faith. If deemed necessary, violence was seen as a method pleasing to God; that it had exactly the opposite effect was not realized. Government authorities continually employ violence in order to uphold social, economic, and judicial systems, to stabilize and expand them, and to defend them against injurious infringements.

This concludes our summary of Dr. Kobler's thoughts.

Violence can be applied by brutal physical means—by chaining, wounding, imprisoning, torturing, killing, withholding food and water, and by burning—as well as by ethical psychological means—by persuasion, instruction, warnings, kindness, and forgiveness, that is, by influencing the will, which means by applying moral pressure.

Every time a person uses forceful means his own goal-oriented will is involved. If the goal is appropriate, he is justified in using forceful means—as, for example, parents in the interest of training their children or government officials in the interest of maintaining the general welfare. If these forcible means do not violate natural rights—to life, to own and use property—the force is justified and permissible. However, killing is morally reprehensible in every instance and may never be used, as we explained above.

As we proved when we discussed self-defense, as a private individual, a Christian may never resort to physical, brutal means to secure his rights or to defend them if violent means are used against him. Nonviolence is the only (and in every case triumphant) weapon that the individual may and should employ. Only government authorities have the right and duty to enforce social justice with morally permissible means and to safeguard and protect it effectively against all violators, even with violent means, if other methods prove unsuccessful.

It should always be remembered that the state is necessary for humanity flawed by original sin; human beings, because of their tendency to sin, can impede the purpose of the state, which is to promote the general welfare, or may not be able to adapt themselves.

It is important to note that the exercise of people's free will as such can never suffer physical violence, while physical functions governed by the will can. For example, someone who is chained cannot move his limbs as he wishes or could if he were not in chains. By the use of physical force, or even only the threat of it, a person can be frightened, often to the point of being robbed of his clear ability to reason, and thus under pressure may do something that he never would have done with a free, clear mind. The use of physical force can influence a person's free will to the degree that the fear induced by violence or the threat of violence affects his ability to reason.

The observance of government laws as well as the enforcement of legal claims can, to a certain extent—even if not always—be achieved by physical force. For example, an imprisoned thief is prevented from stealing again. Or the mere threat of physical punishment can prevent the breaking of laws.

Violent means are not part of the nature of justice, for justice is justice even when it cannot be obtained by force. The rightful owner of an object remains its owner even if it is not possible to prosecute the thief and force him to give back the stolen item. Violence does not have precedence over justice. The two should never be confused. If they were, then the cause of the stronger, not of the weaker, of the cunning, not the less clever, would always be just. Then justice stops being justice.

Let us establish that the free will, as such, can never be coerced, even by the most brutal force or the strongest pressure. However, human physical activities that are subject to the will can be coerced. Above all, fear induced by the threat and use of violent means—as by punitive laws—can compel someone's will to do whatever the person using violence wants to attain. In this way, a few people are able to avail themselves of the state's means of force and by abusing their authority can scare the population of an entire nation, make it submissive, and thus serve their criminal objectives.

We recall the horrible acts of violence and unprecedented bloody crimes of various police institutions by which a handful of irresponsible autocrats in the fascistic-dictatorial countries were able to do violence to entire nations and make them serve their criminal objectives. If we consider the last war, a total war, we have to shudder at the virtual frenzy of violence with which it raged in nearly the entire world, causing death and destruction to an extent never before seen in history.

Using violence in the most callous manner, a few autocrats without moral restraints forced their citizens to commit mass murder, the most terrible cruelty, and senseless destruction. They commanded, "Murder and destroy, and whoever refuses to do so will himself be murdered."

When the history of the Nazi epoch is written, the judgment of history will most likely be this: It was a time during which a nation of eighty-five million people, led by a schizophrenic man with horrendous delusions of grandeur and a few criminals just as deluded and sadistic, by the use of raw violence, was ravished and destroyed politically, economically, culturally, morally, and racially in a few years, and the entire world thrown into confusion. The other governments that participated in World War II will not be judged much differently.

The primary and most important duty of the executive of a state is not the application of violence but to govern, which means to create, according to a plan, all necessary instruments to provide for the general welfare.

c. The abuse of the authority of the state by means of the theory of state utilitarianism

The total state, which we described earlier, lays claim to unrestrained power and, therefore, also to unlimited use of violence in the arbitrary disposition over life and death. The concept of entitlement to unlimited use of violence is connected with the theory of state utilitarianism and logically derives from it. For this theory teaches that everything that benefits the state is permitted, and this is determined only by the will of the head of the state. "My will is your creed," Hitler told the German people. Everything has to conform unconditionally to the will of this leader alone.

If this arbitrary will of the leader knows no moral restraints, is always focused only on what is useful at the moment, and is the highest authority which cannot be appealed, then, as we have witnessed, the world experiences all the horrors of fascistic, communistic, and national socialistic states, supported by the imperialistic-capitalistic states with divers forms of dictatorships. The respective leaders of these dictatorships, at any given time, put their plans into effect by brutal force.

The consequence of the nations governed according to state utilitarianism and founded on violence was total war and will always be total war and never peace. However, the victim, affected by this violence, will always strive to have so many methods of violence at his disposal as to be able to overcome his enemy or, by using even more violence than the enemy, to subjugate him.

Whoever permits the principles of state utilitarianism to guide his moral behavior logically will approve of everything leading to his goal, such as lies, hypocrisy, theft, plunder, destruction, the use of the most brutal force, and murder, if these allegedly benefit the state. Surely, such methods may achieve momentary successes, but whether these are true successes remains to be seen.

We will prove later that nonviolence, and only nonviolence, triumphs over every form of unjustified violence. We emphasize: *unjustified* violence because the use of force by government officials can be justified in certain cases, although within strictly defined limits. However, as a private person, an individual has no right to use violent means, as we explained when discussing self-defense; and, if he does, he is not following Christ's Sermon on the Mount. However, as the Holy Scriptures teach, parents have the right of correction, which means that they may use force when their children are disobedient. True to the saying "He who does not obey has to feel it," Prov 13:24 states, "Whoever fails to use the stick, hates his child; whoever is free with his correction loves him." In Prov 23:13 we read, "Do not be chary of correcting a child, a stroke of the cane is not likely to be fatal." This does not mean that one may beat children for any reason, however.

To prevent his disciples from having to encounter situations in which they may be tempted to defend themselves by using force, Christ advised them, "If they persecute you in one town, take refuge in the next; and if they persecute you in that, take refuge in another" (Matt 10:23). Jesus does not say that they may or should defend themselves with violent means against an attacker.

However, the state and its officials may employ a limited amount of force, as stated in the Scriptures cited above and also in Rom 13:1–5 and 1 Pet 2:13ff. But government authorities do not have the right to impose the death penalty, to wage war, or to institute conscription. If they, entirely unjustly, assume these rights, the words of Christ, spoken in the Garden of Gethsemane, are relevant: "Put your sword back, for all who draw the sword will die by the sword" (Matt 26:52). The poet implies the same: "Every misdeed will be avenged on earth." These words will come true if citizens use violent means to oppose their government's abuse of power. It is a fact that tyrants seldom died a natural death and many governments using violence were brought down by bloody revolutions. Even the murder of a tyrant is never justified, nor is any other political murder, because each murder is a base crime, condemned by the great commandment that allows no exception: "You shall not, you may not kill!"

As with every war, a war of conquest is above all an abuse by holders of executive power who subscribe to the theory of state utilitarianism. Of course, those who wage a war of conquest deceive by calling it a "just defensive war" and readily note that it is being fought for "a place in the sun" that an "evil" neighbor is contesting, and that it is a duty to take up weapons so that one's country is not condemned for all eternity to be a nation of "have-nots."

In this connection we point out what the German *Reichsminister* for propaganda, Joseph Goebbels, said in Munich on October 19, 1942. He implied clearly that Hitler's attack of Russia was strictly predatory, like that of Mussolini against Abyssinia.

As shamelessly as Goebbels, *Reichsmarshall* Göring asserted in an address in Berlin on October 5, 1942, "I am very much in favor that the inhabitants of the territories we have taken under our protection and those we have conquered do not suffer from hunger. However, if the actions of the opponent cause difficulties in providing sufficient food, everyone should know: If there is hunger, by no means in Germany."[145]

This means that the people of other countries may hunger and starve but not the Germans, which will be accomplished by the force of weapons, and whatever more is needed is stolen from a neighbor.

Thus, it is brute force that determines the behavior of those in power, not only in Germany but also in some other nations. That is how it has been and presumably will be for a long time. If the Nazi dictators had their wish, it would be so forever; for, in their opinion, Nazi Germany was to last for all eternity, or its existence guaranteed for at least a thousand years.

Trusting in the victory and truth of the words of Christ, we can guarantee to those in the world who abuse their authority that "all who draw the sword will die by the sword" (Matt 26:52). These words have already come true in a dreadful way for Italy, Germany, and Japan and, unfailingly, will come true for every other country that believes it has to safeguard its existence with weapons.

d. Violence and Christian churches

Christ endowed the Church he founded with only spiritual weapons in order to establish the kingdom of God on earth. These are priestly authority, teaching authority, and the authority to bind and loose. Christ gave these to the Church because it is her mission to lead souls to heaven.

When asked by Pilate whether he is the king of the Jews, Jesus replies, "Mine is not a kingdom of this world; if my kingdom were of this world, my men would have fought to prevent my being surrendered to the Jews. As it is, my kingdom does not belong here" (John 18:36).

When Peter, who had completely misunderstood his master and had armed himself with a sword, wields it and strikes one of the men who want to arrest Jesus, he is admonished by Christ: "Put your sword back, for all who draw the sword will die by the sword" (Matt 26:52).

Christ stands before us unarmed, and that is how he sends his apostles into a world bristling with weapons and full of violence: "Look, I am sending you out like sheep among wolves . . ." (Matt 10:16). However: "Do not be afraid of those who kill the body but cannot kill the soul; fear him rather who can destroy both body and soul in hell" (Matt 10:28). But he also remarks, "Anyone who finds his life will lose it; anyone who loses his life for my sake will find it" (Matt 10:39).

145. *Tagespost*, Graz, October 6, 1942.

Therefore, the use of physical force or coercion has no part in the authority (sphere of influence) of the church of Christ, especially because every individual is free to choose his religion according to his conscience. No one should be forced to practice any religion, for Christ gave his followers always and everywhere free will—aside from the grace of God, which is absolutely necessary and available to every human being. The Gospels state over and over "if you want"—for example, "If anyone wants to be a follower of mine, let him renounce himself and take up his cross and follow me" (Matt 16:24); "But if you wish to enter into life, keep the commandments" (Matt 19:17); "If you wish to be perfect, go and sell you possessions and give the money to the poor, and you will have treasure in heaven; then come, follow me" (Matt 19:21); "Anyone who wants to be great among you must be your servant, and anyone who wants to be first among you must be your slave" (Matt 20:26–28). Never is there the least coercion in Christ's admonitions.

If, in the interest of Christianity, anyone in authority in a Christian church uses force, it is an abuse that cannot strongly enough be condemned. Unfortunately, so many Christian churches, including the Catholic Church, have not hesitated to use brutal violence and various methods of cruelty to force those with differing beliefs to give up their convictions and adopt the religious views of those using these violent methods.

The actions of Charlemagne against the pagan Saxons, the brutal torture of the Inquisition, the burning at the stake of witches and heretics, the confiscation of property, the exiling, imprisonment, or even killing of those with differing beliefs raise the most serious indictment against those who employed these violent methods and disdained the freedom of conscience of others. Also there was the totally unchristian principle of cuius regio, *eius religio*, which means that whoever holds political power has the right to compel his subjects to follow his religion and to use force against those who do not comply. During the Reformation and Counter-Reformation this principle, appealed to by both Protestants and Catholics, led to many brutal acts of violence and greatly harmed the churches of Christ. Also, the various religious wars, including the Crusades, are and will remain a disgrace that has brought Christianity, a religion of love, into disrepute.

In the name of Christ and for him, and in the interests of his kingdom, against his clear command not to resist evil, not to return evil for evil but to overcome evil with good, violent means have been used that, without exception, have to be rejected. To determine whether and to what extent those who used violent means acted out of an insurmountably erring conscience and therefore may personally be excused is not within the realm of this analysis.

In compliance with the will of Jesus, the church of Christ is a social institution founded absolutely on total nonviolence. Therefore, a follower of Christ may never resort to violence or believe that physical means of force serve the interests of the kingdom of God.

In compliance with the teaching and example of Christ, in every situation the weapon of the true Christian is and will remain total nonviolence, which acts through love and is love's crowning achievement. For only he who has love and fashions his entire life and behavior toward every person out of love is able to act unconditionally in the spirit of nonviolence. Therefore, Christian nonviolence is the highest endeavor; this does not, however, mean submitting passively to everything, as is mistakenly believed. Even the enemy is not excluded from the loving actions of the servant of Christ.

Therefore, no true Christian who lives by the love of God and so practices love of neighbor may make himself available to commit acts of violence such as occur during every war. Whenever it is demanded that he participate in a violent action, the true follower of Christ must decide according to this principle: "Obedience to God comes before obedience to men" (Acts 5:29); and if his decision to act as Christ taught has the most dire consequences, he will accept them without hesitating. Therefore, a true Christian, filled completely with the love of Christ, will never support any effort to try to prove that under certain circumstances one may or even must kill.

The more the individual Christian as a citizen tries to embody the nonviolence of the kingdom of God, that is, the more he is inspired by Christian love, the less the use of violence by government officials is necessary. For the more a person tries to be nonviolent, the more he helps prepare the end time that the two great prophets Isaiah and Micah predicted:

> It will happen in the final days that the mountain of Yahweh's house will rise higher than the mountains and tower above the heights. Then all the nations will stream to it, many peoples will come to it and say, "Come, let us go up to the mountain of Yahweh, to the house of the God of Jacob that he may teach us his ways so that we may walk in his paths." For the Law will issue from Zion and the word of Yahweh from Jerusalem. Then he will judge between the nations and arbitrate between many peoples. They will hammer their swords into ploughshares and their spears into sickles. Nation will not lift sword against nation, no longer will they learn how to make war. (Isa 2:2–4; cf. Mic 4:1–3)

The mission of the leaders of the church of Christ, as well as of the faithful in their care, is to prepare for the peace that these two great prophets predicted will exist at the end time; church leaders should teach nonviolence and train their faithful to boycott war, the embodiment of the most brutal use of violence, and also endorse conscientious objection as a duty of love.

Here we would like to point to an ancient custom in the Vatican that we believe should be discontinued, namely, the Papal Guard, which includes the Guard of Nobles, the Swiss Guard, the Palace Honor Guard, and the Papal Gendarmerie. During festive occasions these guards put on a military show. For example, when a pope declares a new saint, they march to St. Peter's Basilica under military command and in colorful uniforms, with helmets and revolvers, spears and lances, rattling sabers and modern rifles. They are usually greeted with frenetic applause by the multitude of Italians and pilgrims from all over the world.

It is impossible to imagine our divine Lord in such a military procession, as it is he who said, "Mine is not a kingdom of this world; if my kingdom were of this world, my men would have fought to prevent my being surrendered to the Jews. As it is, my kingdom does not belong here" (John 18:36).

The pope, who represents Christ on earth, should abolish all military pageantry, whichs bring to mind killing and destruction, using Christ's words, "Put your sword back, for all who draw the sword will die by the sword" (Matt 26:52). For no murder weapons are needed to make known the great message of love, including love of one's enemy. On the contrary, wherever murder weapons are carried and armies raised and trained, it automatically brings to mind that these weapons are not merely toys but can be used to kill and destroy.

As deputy of the Lord of love and trustee of his teaching, the pope should avoid everything that in the eyes of the world gives even the slightest appearance that militarism with its brutal use of violence is sacred and pleasing to God and is absolutely necessary because it is approved of, tolerated, and practiced by most Christians. We believe that Christ's deputy never needs a sword in order to carry out the mission entrusted to him by Christ and to bring about the peace of Christ in his kingdom. *Pax vobis*—peace be with you—should always be on the lips of the deputy of Christ. How peculiar to hear these words from him who is surrounded by military units with the latest killing equipment; nearly everyone who sees this will automatically think of the slogan "If you want peace, be armed." If, however, the pope, as Christ's representative on earth, advocates, "If you want peace, prepare for peace by the works of peace," why then, on the most sacred occasions, have a military cohort and displays of murder weapons?

e. "This does not concern me!" How everyone shares in the responsibility for the violence in the world

In ordinary life one often hears the expression "this does not concern me." With these words we tend to dismiss any blame or responsibility for something or for an event. When a war starts, it is always the fault of others who now are the "enemy," or specific individuals far and near are held responsible for the outbreak.

If, however, a war lasts longer and one is affected by it and comes to know how dreadful war can be, one may become indignant and even ask, "Why does God permit these injustices and horrors?" Others go even further and say, "If God were just, he should never have allowed this to happen." These and similar statements prove that people do not think rationally, because a thoughtful person will conclude that everything that happens in the world concerns every single human being and that all of our actions, even our most secret thoughts, and all that it is our duty to do but we omit to do, in time will take on an importance beyond the purely personal. In other words, everything that we do or fail to do affects our society because, according to God's plan, the entire universe is a unified entity with thousands and thousands of relationships into which every being is incorporated. Man, however, as a rational and free being, occupies an exceptional position in the universe because he has been given freedom and thus is able to adapt to and advance or to disrupt the order ordained and desired by God.

Every one of our thoughts, words, and actions is significant first of all to the immediate surroundings in which we live. Every one of us influences our environment either positively or negatively. Whatever we do or omit to do draws wider and wider circles, just like a stone tossed into a lake. This is how every person makes history. Long after we are gone, everything we did, either good or bad, continues to have repercussions and, over time, ever wider radiating consequences, possibly even of worldwide importance. Every one of us is always in the center of everything that happens in the world, constantly has an effect on others, and is always affected by others. There is a constant give and take between all people. In this manner, every member of a family, individual families, communities, nations, and finally all continents are connected.

Therefore, it is never inconsequential whether our actions are good or bad or whether we act or fail to act. Every one of us is always responsible for everything he does and does not do. The fact that we all constantly mutually affect one another has a collective impact. If this impact is adverse and involves violence, it results in collective guilt, which produces collective responsibility.

Therefore, whoever says, "This does not concern me" should immediately search his conscience to find out whether he is totally free of all violence. For only he who never had an evil thought, never uttered a bad word, never did anything wrong but always did his duty may say that evil with all of its violence (the good is never violent) does not concern him, meaning that he did everything in his power to prevent evil and to abolish it on earth.

Only he who is totally nonviolent, that is, he who lives out of love, bears no responsibility for the violence committed by others. However, whoever does not help prevent and abolish evil wherever he can—that is, as a Christian, does not "overcome evil with good"—already shares in the responsibility that this evil exists, and he may never justifiably say, "This does not concern me."

A truly unique example of how everything a single person does affects all of humanity and makes history is, in the truest sense of the word, the life of Jesus Christ. Everything that Christ did or refrained from doing has had a perceptible influence until the present and is always in the center of all that happens in the world. What Christ thought, taught, and did continues to influence the entire world, affects the formation of conscience among all people, and obliges them to take a stand.

Jesus Christ, the nonviolent One, is actively among us: "And look, I am with you always; yes, to the end of time" (Matt 28:20). Christ always stands against the world hostile to him and that always resorts to violence, but he tells us, "Be courageous: I have conquered the world" (John 16:33). By his nonviolence Christ conquered the world, that is, violence. Irrefutable proof for this is the cross on Golgotha, as it loudly announces—today just as 1900 years ago—the victory of the spirit, aligned with the holy will of God, over all violence, the triumph of truth over lies, of justice over injustice, of love over hatred.

Stronger than all the hate in the world is the love of Jesus Christ, who "went about doing good" (Acts 10:38) and was completely without sin, and therefore could ask, "Can any of you convict me of a sin?" (John 8:46). This is how Christ conquered the world—or, which is the same, violence—the violence that knows nothing but to persecute the good, that is, to use violence against anyone who does good. Christ tells his apostles and disciples, "If they persecuted me, they will persecute you too" (John 15:20); "but be courageous: I have conquered the world" (John 16:33).

Therefore, if we follow Christ, we can and will conquer the violent world with nonviolence. For "this is what the love of God is: keeping his commandments. Nor are his commandments burdensome, because every child of God overcomes the world. And this is the victory that has overcome the world—our faith" (1 John 5:3–4). This is the living faith that acts through love, the kind of love that never returns evil for evil but always and everywhere overcomes evil with good, following the example of him about whom Isaiah prophesied, "I have offered my back to those who struck me, my cheeks to those who plucked my beard; I have not turned my face away from insult and spitting" (Isa 50:6). And who, while hanging on the cross, instead of punishing and destroying his executioners as they deserved, prays for them: "Father, forgive them; they do not know what they are doing" (Luke 23:34).

The nonviolence inspired by the love of Christ is the highest form of active love—not merely a dull, passive acceptance of whatever happens but a nonviolence that always and everywhere is eager to do good to him who uses violence. This love resists evil only inasmuch as it never lets itself be tempted by even the greatest use of unjust violence to do something evil and fend off violence with violence. This kind of love knows no fear, as it is mindful of the words of Christ: "Do not be afraid of those who kill the body but cannot kill the soul; fear him rather who can destroy both body and soul in hell" (Matt 10:28).

Therefore, this love is never silent where truth, justice, and love, in short, where God's holy will is offended, as when the servant of the high priest slapped Jesus in the face, and Christ countered, "If there is some offense in what I said, point it out; but if not, why do you strike me?" (John 18:23). With this attitude Christ revealed his heroism, a greatness of soul that renders us silent and awestruck. Or would our divine Lord and Master appear greater to us if, in order to vindicate his divine honor, he had in return slapped the servant and acted like those who believe in self-defense?

All of us, the entire human family, have to come to terms with Christ until the end of time. His teaching and example always remind us of the eternal conflict between violence and nonviolence and make us keenly aware of the great truth that this concerns every one of us. Therefore, no one may say that he is not responsible for war or that he suffers innocently. He deserves the most severe reprimand who dares to ask, "Why does God permit war and all of its cruelties? Why does he permit that millions are mercilessly slaughtered?"

All of us have to share the guilt for the war we just experienced, the most horrible of all wars. We are responsible for much that happened because we helped create an atmosphere in which the spirit of violence could grow and finally culminate in war. We did this by our insincerity, by our small and big acts of injustice and unkindness, by our wrath and impatience, by our hatred, our indifference and insincerity regarding religion, and especially by neglecting to care for those among us who are physically, spiritually, and morally impaired. We did it by our faulty and unnatural lifestyle, by craving pleasure, by the improper use of resources, by misuse of work, by exploitation, by causing annoyance, by wrongful accusation and slander, by neglect of our vocational duties, by our silence when we should have spoken, and by our cowardice and fear of others.

Whenever the "I" stands against the "you," whenever we do and emphasize only that which separates, provokes, divides people and not that which unifies and reconciles them, we all share in the responsibility for the existence of cannons, grenades, torpedoes, tanks, bomber squadrons, and the atomic bomb. It is because all, without exception, are to blame that concentrated violence bursts forth like an avalanche that, once set in motion, mercilessly demolishes and buries everything.

It is generally believed that by means of raw violence we can remedy the deplorable state of affairs that we ourselves have caused and that we can solve national and international problems by means of the horrors of war. To this solution the words of Christ apply: "All who draw the sword will die by the sword" (Matt 26:52). Not only does violence not solve anything, but it turns against those who use it, as we who experienced the unspeakable, wretched end of National Socialism and other ideologies can attest. Rather, violence always lays the groundwork for the next, even more violent attempt to solve problems. Violence begets vindictiveness, hostility, and schemes for revenge, unless the victim, conscious of his own guilt, decides to try the nonviolence Christ taught and modeled.

However, once a war, long prepared for by arming nations, has begun, no one wants to be responsible for its outbreak, and all of the warring nations begin to blame one another. Their "White, Blue, Brown and Black Papers" try to prove that they themselves are completely innocent and that war was forced upon them.

In World War I, Germany and Austria were accused by the Entente of being the only countries to blame for the outbreak. In World War II, the Führer of the German nation proclaimed at every opportunity—in his name and that of his followers—that the Jews alone were to blame for that war and that Germany was only waging a war forced upon her by England, America, and Russia, while the president of the United States, in his White Paper, placed the entire blame on the German people.

In order to be just, we have to differentiate between direct and indirect causes. From what we said earlier, we can conclude that all of us caused the war and paved the way for it long ago, especially by our exploitative capitalistic economy, our party organizations that employed the most brutal violence, our unnatural way of life, as well as the exaggerated nationalism of the sovereign nation-states.

The actions of individuals, of prevailing responsible politicians, but also of persons not in politics are among the direct causes of the war. Above all, there are the deceitful and hypocritical intrigues—which cannot be condemned enough—of diplomats everywhere. As hirelings of capitalism they have to see to it that the heaps of inflammatory material, so often disseminated everywhere by an irresponsible and bribable press, are ignited here or there. Cleverly, they make sure that there are scapegoats to blame for the outbreak of the war, if in no other way than by barefaced lies.

The following remarks show that Germany alone was not responsible for the outbreak of World Wars I and II, but rather that she shares in the direct and indirect blame, as do all the other warring states and even the neutral ones, as we will note briefly below:

The Nazi pagan-centralist nationalities principle of a pure culture, empowered by the heavily armed Prussian-German militarism always ready to retaliate and fight, misled influential men of Germany to create—by all available methods—a national German state based on pan-Germanism, under the leadership of Prussia, in opposition to the just as reprehensible pan-Slavism led by Russia. It was seen as a downright betrayal of the German people to come to a friendly supranational understanding and to work toward a European federation with the Slavs, that is, with Russia, Poland, Czechoslovakia, and the Balkan nations. The "German thinkers," first of all the German philosophers—not to speak of the entire German press, which, of course, is always an organ of those in power—have, by their false and corrupt theories and dogmas, laid the foundation for such ideas.

Following are three points of evidence that the principle of nationalities, supported by Prussian militarism, was the prevailing principle of German politicians and diplomats. As a solution to the Polish question, the well-known German philosopher Eduard von Hartmann advised his countrymen to "annihilate the Poles." The Nazi Third Reich tried to put his advice into action in the most brutal manner. The French statesman Georges Clemenceau believed that there are twenty million Germans too many and that they should be eradicated. The celebrated German historian Theodor Mommsen expressed the view that the only language the Czechs understand is being hit vigorously on their skulls. Kaiser Wilhelm II stated in Bremen in 1906, "It is the responsibility of the German merchant all over the world to pound in the nail on which we (the Germans) can hang our armor."

In addition there is the hatred of the Jews, which is constantly and vigorously being hammered into the minds of the German people through inflammatory speeches. Under the leadership of Hitler and his henchmen—Himmler, Göring, and Goebbels—this hatred led to the slaughter and annihilation of Jews living in Germany, Austria, and in the countries Germany conquered and occupied. One struggles against having to relate the horrendously diabolic inhumanities that the German people committed (yes, the entire German population, because people either participated or remained silent out of cowardice or fear, even if they did not approve of these shameful deeds) in order to literally annihilate Jews, Poles, Czechs, and Slovenes.

Everyone who is not a prejudiced, diehard Nazi can readily understand that this racial hatred, which raged like an orgy, was perceived by the entire world as a constant disturbance of the peace.

The world was also provoked by the slogan, made sickening by its being endlessly repeated, "The world shall be healed by the German character," as well as by the catchphrase, shouted by old and young alike, "Today Germany is ours, tomorrow the whole world." Another provocation was the constant claim that the German people are the "master race" and the foremost representative of the "purest race of the world," the Aryan race.

We have to ask further why in 1914, after Austria had issued the ultimatum to Serbia, Germany and Austria refused any mediation by other powers and avoided any agreement. Most likely it was because they wanted war and let brutal violence decide. For that they had conspicuously armed in previous years. The bloody outcome was four and a half years of organized mass murder and destruction. This confirmed for Germany and Austria, and not less so for the Entente, the truth of the Lord's words: "For all who draw the sword will die by the sword" (Matt 26:52).

Lloyd George was right when he said, "The outbreak of the world war accurately reflects everything that happened, was permitted, talked, and written about in Germany since 1866." However, this statement also applies without exception to all other nations involved in the war and also to the neutral states.

For example, England should remind herself how she established her world empire. The road of her colonization is marked with blood and dead bodies, with murder and corruption, and with the various horrors of war. Directed by heartless capitalism, the British Empire was created by bringing four-fifths of the earth's land mass with its rich resources under England's control. This nation's politics often consisted of entangling other states in wars according to the maxim "When two argue, the third one delights." Further, England, along with the other Entente powers—France, the United States, and Russia—dictated the criminal and disgraceful peace treaties of Versailles and St. Germain in order to completely subject Germany and Austria economically, intending to enslave the German people. If the Entente had made a truly ethical peace, we would have been saved from the second, even more devastating world war, and there would have been no Hitler and no Nazi party. Therefore, England, the United States, Russia, and Italy should keep silent instead of holding Germany solely responsible for the outbreak of World War II. The facts prove that violence always produces counterviolence. If the so-called victors of World War II (we are writing this while the war is still raging) commit the same error as the "victors" of World War I and again dictate a "violent peace," that is, grant the chairmanship of the peace talks to capitalism and violence instead of to Christ and nonviolence, then woe to the world! Then they are already paving the way for the third world war, and that humanity could not bear.

Many books could be written about how much the so-called intelligentsia, namely, university scientists and scholars, as well as the press of every political orientation, shared in the guilt for all recent wars. Whenever scientists or scholars indirectly aid in fighting against religion, faith, and morality—as, for example the French Encyclopedists or various English and German philosophers of the Enlightenment, beginning with Charles Darwin, down to Ernst Haeckel, Friedrich Nietzsche, and the Nazi pen-pushers—direction is given to the unfolding of violence, to lies, injustice, and hate, and the people's hearts are made receptive for war.

Frequently this godless, corruptive seed sown by these scholars and scientists does not sprout until centuries later. For example, even Christian scholars lent themselves to justifying the capitalistic economy—an economy based on interest—as well as killing in self-defense. Thus one should not be surprised that now we have a second world war.

Or when we consider the warring popes who employed armies of mercenaries; when we recall the militant bishops of the Middle Ages who strutted around in helmet and armor; when we think about the cardinals of the Catholic Church who were wardens of the horrible dungeons in the Angels' Castle on the Tiber; when we recall the Italian bishops and cardinals who donated their golden pectoral crosses to support Mussolini in his war against Abyssinia; when we consider those Italian bishops who congratulated him on his "victory" in that predatory war; and when we ponder that in all Christian and non-Christian schools in the world children are already inoculated with the spirit of war, then we understand that the ideas of military readiness, war, and heroism have literally corroded the minds of all of humanity and prepared the nations to institute universal military service, by which the entire world has been transformed into a perpetual war camp. Therefore, it is pure hypocrisy if any country waging war says it is not responsible for the war.

To continue: Why do all nations establish such extensive and expensive espionage agencies all over the world if not to search out the weaknesses of their opponents and to cleverly use them in war? And yet the individual nations dare to claim that they are in no way responsible for the outbreak of the war, and the Nazi state least of all should incessantly assert its innocence. Did not Hitler in his book *Mein Kampf* advise lying to one's enemy in order to lay the entire blame for the outbreak of the war on one's opponents and to paint oneself as innocent? We quote his exact words: "It is totally wrong to discuss the blame for the war [World War I] from the standpoint that Germany alone is made responsible for the outbreak of this catastrophe, but it would have been more correct to lay the entire blame on the opponent, even if this did not really correspond to the actual events."

I would like to remind the French of Clemenceau's statement, quoted earlier, and of the Treaty of Versailles, which France and the other members of the Entente dictated, by which Clemenceau's wish to get rid of the twenty million Germans he believed were too many was to be realized.

People go even further, however, and blame God in heaven. Suddenly he is to blame for all the horrors and crimes committed by warring states everywhere, by soldiers and civilians, because he could have prevented these evil deeds but did not. We have to ask, does God wage war? Rather, is it not human beings themselves who make war with their lies, injustice, and hate, their exploitation of one another, their faulty lifestyles, their pleasure-seeking, passions, delusions, and lust for power—in short, do not human beings, through their collective guilt, do that which necessarily leads to the use of violence and, therefore, always to war? If, in accordance with the commandments of Christ, human beings would forego every kind of violence, there would be peace among the nations of the world. For if all people, faithful to what Christ commanded in the Sermon on the Mount, would follow what he said—"Set your hearts on his kingdom first, and on God's saving justice"—then, as he assured them, "all these other things"—whatever is needed for a dignified existence—"will be given you as well" (Matt 6:33). Then militarism, war, conscription, the death penalty, concentration camps, prisons, etc., would be unnecessary. Human beings, however, do not do what God commands and guarantees peace.

Do not parents give their very young children war toys and thus poison their gentle souls with the notion of the most brutal violence and prepare them for the "heroism" of war? Is not the goal of the so-called pre-military education of youth that the entire population take up the yoke of conscription and make it willing to fight a total war? Do not our girls and women literally chase after soldiers in uniform, and is it not the case that in the world of men the "soldier ideal," that is, the constant willingness to murder and destroy, is made to appear as something extremely desirable and as the noblest profession a man can have? Is it not true that all nations take part in capitalistic exploitation—an economy based on usury—that is, seek to appropriate the fruits of others' labors without rendering any service in return, thus endangering the right to use one's possessions and the right of property of untold millions of people?

Is it not the case that the foolish, unnatural lifestyle, especially the highly destructive and antisocial poisoning by substances like alcohol and nicotine, already seriously damages offspring in the embryonic stage and consequently passes a criminal disposition to many? Is it not the bad example of religious hypocrisy and civic insincerity that removes moral inhibitions and paves the way for unrestrained acts of violence? We ask, did God command that we simply kill political opponents, the poor, the weak, the old, people with incurable diseases, the mentally disabled, those unable to work, and even mercilessly annihilate entire races? Rather, is it not a prejudiced, one-party, exaggerated nationalism, is it not a "gospel" focused on blood, race, and soil along with racial hatred preached by those who expound this "gospel," and also the exploitative capitalistic economy, which has given rise to unspeakable crimes and brutalities such as the world has never before experienced to this extent? Is it not the spirit of revenge and the ingrained belief in "an eye for an eye and a tooth for a tooth" that results in an incessant arms race and a willingness to go to war? And have not the cruelties toward and torture of animals and their murder by the hundreds of thousands made human hearts hard, merciless, and savage? In one word: Is not the cause of all of these brutalities the defection from Christ and from the great commandment to love always?

It is no wonder that the entire world has been turned into a bloodstained battlefield covered with ruins, a devastation freely acquiesced to by humanity. Every person possesses free will and can choose between violence and nonviolencee. Each individual is personally responsible for his choice. Therefore, if people freely do that which leads to war, they will have war; but if they do not want war, they have to choose the path Christ taught, namely, the path of nonviolence which acts out of love.

What right does man have to accuse God by asking, why does God permit all the injustice and horrors of war? Rather, we humans with our free will produce the many infractions discussed above that result in the collective guilt that leads to war.

At the very least, people share in the responsibility for the horrors of war by not resisting the commands to take part in mass murder and destruction but permitting themselves to be misused to commit these crimes because of conscription, and by remaining silent in the face of horror and injustice when they should consider it their duty to speak out against them.

It is up to each of us whether there is peace or war, nonviolence or violence on earth. If we were serious about not wanting war, then we would have to be on the side of those who practice nonviolence and, therefore, we would unreservedly refuse to participate in war. But whoever expects that the sword will decide, and whoever uses it—or, being conscripted, permits himself to be convinced to use the sword—should not complain if, in one way or another, the words of Christ come true: "all who draw the sword will die by the sword" (Matt 26:52). The untold millions whose bones are rotting on battlefields, all revolutions that toppled tyrants and rulers from their thrones, and all murders of revenge and measures of retribution prove the validity of this sentence: "All who draw the sword will die by the sword."

Therefore, every one of us is responsible for everything that happens in the world and has to suffer the consequences. For that reason everything concerns everyone. God, however, is just and allows people to have free will and does not rescind the law of cause and effect. Consequently, everyone has to be responsible for what he does or fails to do with his free will. Therefore, no one is justified in saying "this or that does not concern me" unless he can prove that he does not share in any way in the collective guilt.

Therefore, to those who say that the innocent have to suffer with the guilty, we have to reply first of all that, regrettably, none of us pitiable human beings is totally innocent. Each one of us shares in the world's collective guilt. However, children, as far as they are not already responsible for their actions, suffer innocently and do so because we have created social conditions leading to violence. Therefore, we have to make every effort to reduce our part of the collective guilt by admitting that we are to blame and then completely refrain from violence and substitute nonviolence inspired by love.

If, however, an innocent person has to suffer with the guilty—that is, if he must bear the consequences of some violent action committed by others without himself having caused it—we, as faithful Christians, know that a completely just settlement will take place in the afterlife, where each person will be rewarded for everything good he did but will have to atone for the bad, as far as he did not already atone here on earth. This is not so for the nations and states, however, with their collective guilt, for in eternity there will be no nations or states. God in his justice provides that these are already rewarded on earth for all good and punished for all evil. That this punishment often consists of wars and revolutions, of economic distress that frequently leads to epidemics, etc., is an easily understood natural consequence of the disorder created by using their free will to trespass God's commandments.

f. "There is nothing that can be done about it!"

On par with the above-mentioned expression, "This does not concern me," there is another one: "There is nothing that can be done about it." Whoever uses the latter thinks he can thereby justifiably reject all responsibility and complicity for any matter being called into question.

Regarding war, one hears repeatedly, "There is nothing that can be done about it." That is, one simply has to let the murder and destruction happen since one is powerless in face of them. However, especially when it concerns war, the statement "there is nothing that can be done about it" is always unwarranted. This saying is only justified where something happens totally independent of the decision of our free will or against our free will. There is nothing one can do, for example, about an eclipse of the sun, about the arrival of winter, about humans having to die, etc. Whenever something depends on the decision of our free will, however, it is up to us to do or not do this or that, to let something happen or prevent it from happening.

If it is one's moral duty to act or to refrain from acting, one is not justified in saying, "There is nothing that can be done about it" or, more accurately, "There is nothing I can do about this." On the contrary, as long as our action or nonaction depends on our free will, we should act, refrain from acting, or prevent something. We are responsible for the consequences.

If it concerns so-called positive commandments (moral mandates), we are usually duty-bound to comply with them, but not always. For example, we should always follow the advice of St. Luke to "pray continually and never lose heart" (Luke 18:1). Yet this does not mean that we should spend our entire life only in church and in prayer. In the case of so-called negative commandments, however, we are duty-bound to observe these always and without exception. This includes the commandments "you shall not bear false witness against your neighbor," "you shall not kill," and "you shall not steal."

We already know that wars are the result of collective guilt to which individual human beings contribute to the extent that they do not conform their lives to the demands of the Ten Commandments; for wars are not natural phenomena that have to occur but are born in human hearts. Wars come about because the moral code is voluntarily disturbed, that is, freely willed acts of violence take place whose avoidance depends as much on the decision of the free will of individual human beings as does approving of or committing them. If human beings did not want wars, there would be no wars. They are waged because people freely desire them.

If humanity would obey the Ten Commandments without reservation, there would be no wars. To say this is not being utopian, for every human being is bound by his conscience to obey all moral commandments because God demands it. Next to God's help, which is always available to everyone, it depends only on people's free will whether they want to obey God's commandments or not. Yet one cannot expect of human beings who are already poisoned and damaged in their embryonic stage, physically and mentally infected because of their own actions, and ruled and weakened by their passions that they will immediately regulate their lives according to the Ten Commandments and, consequently, according to nonviolence motivated by love, as Christ demanded. One has to remember that often parents, ancestors, and government officials are responsible for inflicting great harm and for influencing decisions.

Therefore, the following statement continues to be true: Wars can and should be prevented and made impossible by the actions of the free will of individual human beings. Every person should do what he can and what his conscience requires of him. No one can shake off his responsibility for the outbreak of a war by saying, "There is nothing that can be done about it," but everyone should say, "I can and I must do my part to prevent wars."

Our entire life and everything we do either promotes or prevents war. We promote it whenever we disturb the natural, moral, and Christian order of life, and we prevent it whenever we try to fashion our entire private and public life in accordance with God's commandments.

One can oppose and prevent wars—indeed, it is one's duty. Every Christian will and must readily understand this in light of Christ's great primary commandment, "You must love your neighbor as yourself," which includes, "love your enemies."

However, since the right willingness always has to be preceded by the right knowledge, first, we have to provide the right education. Excellent opportunities for this are the spoken and written word, radio and film, the nursery, school, pulpit, and meeting hall. The author hopes that this work will contribute in a modest way to providing this urgently needed education so that the nations will finally regain their clear vision. Yet how can they see if the leaders fail and, constrained by old methods of thinking, continue to opt for militarism?

We need men and women leaders who possess the requisite knowledge and courage to enlighten the nations enslaved by the bitter yoke of militarism to have the right will. By means of this enlightenment, all citizens should come to realize how much irresistible power each individual has to free himself from the slavery of militarism. Each person, however, whether young or old, whether man or woman, has to be taught convincingly that he or she, by the moral conduct of his or her private and public life, has the power to overthrow and abolish militarism and to conquer raw violence with nonviolence, even against the will of those in power, as we will prove in the following sections.

Something can be done, that is, everyone can do something as far as is possible for him or her—indeed, it is always his or her duty—to make the crime of future wars impossible. Whoever does not do this is partly responsible for all the horrors of future wars. How many opportunities present themselves every day for parents in the nursery, for teachers in school, for priests in the pulpit, for officials in their office, for workers in the factory, for scholars at their desk, for scientists in the laboratory, for artists and artisans, farmers and especially government leaders to banish the spirit of war from people's minds and to promote nonviolence. Again, whoever stands idly by and does not take part in this struggle is partly responsible that the seeds remain for future wars and the atrocities these perpetrate.

How much the faithful of the various Christian churches could accomplish in this regard if their leaders and every believer would always work to oppose war and to establish peace! Unfortunately, many have instead worked astutely to develop a war ideology they believe to be as compatible as possible with the demands of Christianity. This is a thankless and, as World War II proves, totally unsuccessful task that has failed in every respect. However, that here and there, now and then, a Christian voice had the courage and continues to have the courage to speak out candidly against this commonly held view proves how urgent it is to examine this untenable war ideology and to revise it to comply with Christ's teaching about love of neighbor and enemy.

When, prior to the outbreak of World War II, a Catholic priest, Leopold Schwarz, in his work *Stand Firmly by Your Faith*,[146] exuberantly approved the justification of war, one wanted to shout at him, and to all who agree with him, the words of Pope Pius X of August 4, 1903: "Woe, too many spiritual shepherds waste their efforts on seemingly important instead of on truly important matters. The children ask for bread, and no one wants to break it for them."

Abbé Demulier writes in his essay "War and Church," in the international collection of essays *Catholic Voices against War*, that "the faithful are sufficiently educated about their anti-military responsibilities by the reigning popes' repeated teachings, transmitted to them by their bishops and priests."[147]

Thanks be to God that there are opponents of war among popes, bishops, and priests as well as among Catholic laymen, but this is far from

146. Schwarz, *Stehe fest im Glauben.*

147. Demulier, "Kirche und Krieg."

common. The prevailing opinion among Catholics everywhere is that soldiers simply have to obey the call of conscription and are obliged in conscience to render war service. The decision whether there will be a war or not does not belong to common soldiers. They have to render an oath that they will blindly follow the orders of the government in power, which alone has the right to decide whether or not a war is just. Therefore, we hardly believe that Demulier would maintain his assertion regarding the total war we have just experienced. Rather, we believe that he especially would share our viewpoint that all of this cannot be discussed often or thoroughly enough because when a war breaks out, the majority of church officials on every side usually remain silent—if they are not actually promoting the spirit of war—and let the faithful struggle alone with their troubled conscience. They do not have the courage to condemn conscription as unchristian, most likely because they do not want to provoke the vengeance of the brutal men in power.

The objection that nations and governments will not heed the teachings and demands of a pope or bishop is so trivial and meaningless that one has to be utterly ashamed that such an objection is raised by people who call themselves Catholic. Nations and governments are themselves responsible whether or not they want to obey the teachings of Christ, while popes, bishops, and priests are responsible for proclaiming the gospel of Christ regardless of whether it is welcome or not. Did not Paul, the apostle to the nations, command his disciple Bishop Timothy to "proclaim the message and, welcome or unwelcome, insist on it. Refute falsehood, correct error, provide encouragement, but do all with patience and with care to instruct" (2 Tim 4:2).

How many opportunities, unfortunately, are missed in which one should do something, while, on the other hand, Leopold Schwarz ventured to write, and that in the year 1938, shortly before the outbreak of World War II, "In the extraordinary times of war, which open up the depths of souls, people either grow spiritually or reveal their weaknesses. All things, but especially the teachings and institutions of religious, cultural, and social life, have to stand the test in war; otherwise they will be cast aside. Whether something stands the test is related to training, education, and selection. War is generally seen as positive, and without ignoring its evils many believe to see an element of progress in it."[148]

Professor Spann described in detail the test of war and its beneficial effects on religion and culture, the community, and the individual. It is his opinion that whoever says no to war betrays civilization. For him war is "the

148. Schwarz, *Stehe fest im Glauben*, 626.

midwife of every development of the state and all culture, which, however, can develop fully only when there is peace everywhere."

Schwarz also writes,

> It is clear that man is tested in war. The soldier has to exert himself to the utmost, both spiritually and physically; the inventor has to give his last for the defense of the fatherland;[149] the laborer has to accomplish the extraordinary, working day and night shifts; the Caritas has to double its impact; the writer has to create gripping words and pictures; and the church has to open the deepest fount of religion. Great sacrifices are demanded, and the entire nation has to stretch itself if it wants to endure the struggle.[150]

He also maintains that "the government of a country determines war and peace. It must know whether justice will win out or whether only the fight remains. However, if those in power decide on war, it is all the more the duty of everyone to be obedient, brave, and loyal, for in war the existence or nonexistence of a nation is determined."[151]

Schwarz believes that war does not contradict the law of love. It is very difficult to restrain oneself in face of his statements. We can only comment that if what he proclaims is truly the teaching of Christ on war, the teaching of Christianity, then it is no wonder that many people refuse to accept this religion. We have to reject flatly Schwarz' opinions because all of the more than two hundred thousand soldiers who were surrounded by the Russians at Stalingrad would indignantly reject them if they were to return—those two hundred thousand victims who, at the order of Hitler, had to let themselves be massacred to the last man instead of surrendering as the whole world (except the Nazis) expected.

Our motto must be this: "Never again war!" We can and should do something. Our Christian conscience demands it. However, "never again war" is ineffective if the causes of war are not removed and we do not work unrelentingly to translate into reality those social, economic, national, and international conditions that bring about peace.

Above all, those called by God to proclaim the truths of Christianity have to lead the way and enlighten their faithful. In view of the two world wars, even the most obstinate defenders of war will admit that Catholics and, actually, all Christians finally want to hear unequivocally from the highest officials of the Catholic Church which view it is that agrees with the

149. Ude: for example, atom bombs, poison gas, guided missiles.

150. Schwarz, *Stehe fest im Glauben*, 627.

151. Ibid., 639.

teaching of Christ: the one that justifies war and, consequently, conscription, or the one that does not. Both opinions cannot be true at the same time. The leadership of the Church, without fail, is urged to reach a decision whether we who outrightly reject war and conscription as unchristian are wrong or whether the defenders of war and conscription are in error.

The often used saying "*consulantur probati auctores*"—one should consult the authoritative teachers of the Church—is of no use to us because these questions have never been conclusively decided by the Church. We already know, without asking the teaching authority, that two contradicting views or teachings cannot be true at the same time. Both views can be wrong, or one false and the other one true. We would like to know, and as Catholics we ask that the infallible teaching authority decide and thereby help resolve the uncertainty of conscience among millions of Catholics. We Catholics have a right to find this out so that our troubled consciences can be relieved, and we urgently ask for a conclusive decision in this great and very important matter that deeply affects all citizens of the world. May the highest teaching authority of our Catholic Church become persuaded that something can and must be done.

g. The abolishment of armaments, conscription, and war by means of nonviolence

Among reasoning people, negotiations are the only proper and reliable means to solve and eliminate opposing views, provided that the negotiators are willing to let justice alone rule. Whether someone is in the right can never be decided by the use of raw force because justice is not a matter of the fist or of superior weapons but a matter of the will guided by moral law. Justice consists in the resolute determination to accord to everyone that which he or she is entitled to.

There will only be complete justice in every case if all people are inspired by the love of neighbor. Whoever seeks only his own advantage, without concern for whether this is just, and whoever believes that justice is on the side of the stronger has only one method to enforce his will, namely, raw violence—but only if he is stronger and more clever than his opponent.

It cannot be pointed out emphatically enough that the use of violence alone and the victory of violence over the opponent never prove that justice is on the side of the so-called victor. Rather, justice and injustice are spiritual and moral values that can never be proved by the sharpness of the sword, or by other weapons technology provides, but only by a will guided by moral principles. Such a will takes care never to be unjust and is always willing to make amends for any injustice inflicted.

Today, however, all states jealously defend their sovereignty and believe in and practice violence. There is no more convincing proof of this than the fact that all nations in the world are arming for war, even though their representatives solemnly assure again and again that they do not want war but peace. But if every nation is sincerely ready not to wage war, why then do we have the armaments race, in which every nation tries to surpass all others? Each one arms because no nation or government trusts another. Every one insists that violence will bring about justice and subscribes to the principle "If you want peace, prepare for war. Be armed!"

Every nation has the kind of government it deserves and wants. If a nation's entire population would agree not to wage war, its government could never go to war in opposition to the will of all of its citizens. However, as long as governments without opposition from their citizens sacrifice the greater portion of the national income for these insane armaments, and as long as the citizens submit to conscription and let themselves be coerced to serve in war—that is, as long as militarism carries on its orgies—the nations will have war.

However, how could it come to war where citizens by common consent refuse the means for armaments and for waging war, and all simply refuse to be conscripted and to put on a uniform? But where this does not happen, where the citizens dutifully permit themselves to be drafted, no nation can complain when a war breaks out and becomes a total war, as we have experienced. For nations do not arm merely for pure enjoyment but because they calculate that the weapons readied for mass murder and destruction will be used. A government would be plainly stupid if it militarized without intending to use the armaments, but only let them get old and then replaced them with new weapons. Besides, the generals and officers also want to demonstrate what they can do.

Up to now no nation has seriously considered liberating itself from the senseless and criminal yoke of militarism by which all nations are incessantly enslaved—or if a country had occasionally considered it, it did not find the courage to throw off this heavy yoke. Indeed, all people could relatively easily force their governments to disarm, to abolish conscription, and to solve all political, economic, national, and international disputes not by the use of violence but by negotiations. Only impeccably ethical, that is, nonviolent means should be used to resolve disputes. How this can happen will be demonstrated in the following paragraphs.

A most important challenge, blessed by ethics based on natural law and reason as well as by Christian moral law, is that one may never cooperate with anything evil; if forced to do so, one is obligated to refuse, whatever the consequences. Another challenge is that every citizen is obligated in conscience to translate into reality the purpose of the state, which is to establish and ensure the general welfare, and to do so with irreproachably ethical means.

We have shown above that every war and all preparations for war as well as conscription contradict the great, universal commandment of God: "You should not (may not) kill!" This means that it is not morally permitted to take part in war or preparations for war or to let oneself be directly or indirectly forced to serve in war by means of conscription. It is the duty of every citizen to break the morally reprehensible yoke of militarism, aside from the fact that armaments, war, and conscription seriously endanger the general welfare and often even make it impossible.

According to the demands of Christian love, active nonviolence is the only moral and effective means to abolish armaments, conscription, and wars, even against violent opposition and the determination of governments to rely on violence. Therefore, all Christians are obligated in conscience to practice nonviolence.

Next we have to establish what we mean by nonviolence. As true peace activists and pacifists (*pacem facientes*—those who make peace) understand nonviolence, it means the absence of brute physical force and of the threat of violence, and, at the same time, the greatest desire to work for peace—that is, to establish conditions in which, instead of brute physical force, spiritual and moral forces may work to create social commitments.

Therefore, what is most important is to convince people that the totally immoral use of physical force, whether in private, public, social, national, or international life, never brings blessings and happiness. On the contrary, violence always turns against those who use it. We have to convince mankind that in contrast to brutal, physical force, the spiritual-ethical powers acting by means of justice and love of neighbor are indeed capable of renewing the face of the earth because their goal is to establish and maintain order in all relationships. To be nonviolent does not only mean to abstain from the use of force but also to let love reign and thus effectively overcome with good the evil caused by violence.

Let us consider Oskar Ewald's comments on this matter:

> Another paradox (that is, a curiously surprising, apparent contradiction) is the demand of Christ's Sermon on the Mount not to resist evil, to offer the left cheek if one is struck on the right one. Of course, this is not a question of allowing evil or even encouraging it, because then one would also be guilty, but it is a

> matter of overcoming it by another method than physical force, hate, or hostility. We could state this demand more concisely: It is necessary to overcome evil, but it is not possible to do so by means of evil but only by means of good. And what is good? It is not only the removal of and absence of evil, otherwise it could also be nothing. But it is the good which is the gauge of itself and also of its opposite—all viciousness, degeneration, and depravity. There exists not only physical force and nonviolence but also supra-force, which is the most important because it is a spiritual force, the power of love which is creative, constructive, and uniting. That is the task Christ assigned to human beings by expressing it as a paradox.[152]

We have nothing to add to Ewald's excellent comments.

Of course, National Socialism, communism, and fascism as well as capitalism and imperialism—that is, all present forms of government and economics, not excluding the existing democracies because and inasmuch as they champion capitalism—can ever adopt our point of view because then they would have to renounce themselves. Above all, because National Socialism, communism, and fascism personify entrenched violence they must logically reject and persecute natural law and Christianity. It is self-evident that capitalism, imperialism, and Bolshevistic communism cannot pass muster before the tribunals of natural law and Christianity.

Instead of further arguments we cite here the comments of Dr. Robert Ley, Nazi minister of labor, made to political leaders in June 1942:

> Four thousand years ago, humanity left its barbarous condition and entered into the state of cultural development, into the era of striving for the beautiful. Two thousand years ago there occurred a revolution in favor of a Weltanschauung of the inferior, a Weltanschauung based on compassion and mercy, a Weltanschauung of weakness based on man's guilt in the eyes of God. This is the world of Judaism [author's note: Dr. Ley also includes Christianity], and this world Germany opposes. The German man or woman aspires to the world of the will [read: unrestrained force and arbitrariness], which the Führer personifies most purely and radiantly. This struggle between the world of the weak [read: love of neighbor] and the world of the will [read: most brutal force] has to be fought out.[153]

152. Ewald, *Gewalt und Gewaltlosigkeit*, 49.

153. *Neues Wiener Tageblatt*, June 10, 1942.

We can assure the Nazi minister that this struggle will indeed be fought out and that the brutal force that sanctions all methods, even the meanest and most criminal, has to be (and will be) overcome and replaced by nonviolence, inspired by Christian love, if the world is not to perish.

We already predicted in our writings the humiliating collapse of the Nazi system based on force two years before it occurred. May the fate that has overtaken National Socialism serve as a deterrent for all those who believe that they can establish a peaceful new order in Europe by force!

Only he who knows nothing about the nature of nonviolence inspired by love can deny that nonviolence is always superior to violence. We refer again to Oskar Ewald, who writes,

> In a world in which the most important duty of Christians would be to gratefully accept a blow on the cheek, scoundrels would win hands down, and whatever they sowed would flourish, so that it would overgrow all that is good. Infallible evidence proves that Christ wanted exactly the opposite. The goal is not the destruction or suppression of the opponent but his transformation. Whoever desires love may not realize it by physical force, which by its nature includes hate, malice, and hostility. If we desire love, we have no use for violence, which contradicts love because love is the power of the promptings of the heart, not that of physical force. We have to remove a maximum of opposition with a maximum of solidarity. If we merely reduce the conflict, we do not abolish it. . . . If we do not remove it with a spirit of solidarity, we call forth the demons of hate, violence, and revenge. . . . We are never completely right, and our opponent is never completely wrong. . . . Only virtue endures which takes on the struggle with vice . . . We have to understand that the issue of violence cannot be dealt with in isolation but only in connection with all of life's questions because it is central to them. The answer depends on to what extent human beings have the capacity to be divinely inspired, which means it is a matter of religion. . . . Finally, the challenge of nonviolence is nothing but the challenge of true, perfect love.[154]

Ewald is perfectly right, for Paul, apostle to the nations, writes in 1 Cor 13:1–14,

> Though I command languages both human and angelic—if I speak without love, I am no more than a gong booming or a cymbal clashing. And though I have the power of prophecy, to

154. *Gewalt und Gewaltlosigkeit*, 50–51.

> penetrate all the mysteries and knowledge, and though I have all the faith necessary to move mountains—if I am without love, I am nothing. Though I should give away to the poor all that I possess, and if I even give my body to be burned—if I am without love, it will do me no good whatever.
>
> Love is always patient and kind; love is never jealous; love is not boastful or conceited, it is never rude and never seeks its own advantage, it does not take offense or store up grievances. Love does not rejoice at wrongdoing, but finds its joy in the truth. It is always ready to make allowances, to trust, to hope and to endure whatever comes.
>
> Love never comes to an end. But if there are prophecies, they will be done away with; if tongues, they will fall silent; and if knowledge, it will be done away with. For we know only imperfectly, and we prophesy imperfectly; but once perfection comes, all imperfect things will be done away with. When I was a child, I used to talk like a child, and see things as a child does, and think like a child; but now that I have become an adult, I have finished with all childish ways. Now we see only reflections in a mirror, mere riddles, but then we shall be seeing face to face. Now I can know only imperfectly; but then I shall know just as fully as I am myself known.
>
> As it is, these remain: faith, hope and love, the three of them; and the greatest of them is love.

Such love as Paul describes indeed does overcome evil with good. It is the serving, sacrificial, untiring, active, conquering love that surpasses everything when it is confronted with injustice and violence because it has not only the strength to suffer any injustice but also the willingness to work to do good to anyone who acts unjustly, in order to win him over to the good. Only truly great people are able to rise to such high-mindedness, people who are saints and therefore heroes, while every scoundrel and criminal and anyone lacking in character is able to strike down his opponent if he is merely stronger or cleverer and has a better weapon. To struggle against oneself is the most difficult battle, and to conquer oneself is the greatest victory.

Because Christ possesses to the highest degree this love which expresses itself in nonviolence, he is the greatest of all; or, more accurately, because Christ was and is the greatest among all, he possesses to the highest degree serving, self-sacrificing love. Jesus told his disciples, "You know that among the Gentiles the rulers lord it over them, and great men make their authority felt. Among you this is not to happen. No; anyone who wants to become great among you must be your servant, and anyone who wants to be first among you must be your slave, just as the Son of Man came not to be served but to serve, and to give his life as ransom for many" (Matt 20:25–28). These words describe the kingdom where love, that is, serving one another, is most important. Instead of violence there is serving, always-forgiving, self-sacrificing love.

In addition to the Scripture passages quoted above, Jesus commands, "Offer no resistance to the wicked. On the contrary, if anyone hits you on the right cheek, offer him the other as well; if someone wishes to go to law with you to get your tunic, let him have your cloak as well" (Matt 5:39–40). With these words Jesus condemns revenge by means of blind, brutal force as well as living only for one's own interests.

Ragaz describes this idea splendidly in the collection *Violence and Nonviolence*:

> Here in the death of Christ on the cross is revealed the divine mystery of sacrifice, the profundity and glory of the kingdom of God compared with all the glitter of the world. Christ knows by what means the kingdom of God conquers—as contrasted with the means used by the kingdom of the world—by drinking his cup and being baptized with his baptism. This means that one does not practice violence or pay back injustice with injustice but by suffering and sacrifice transforms evil into good, the curse into a blessing, and hate into love; by not baptizing others with blood shed by the sword but by taking upon oneself the baptism of blood—even if it isn't the actual blood of the heart. The freely accepted cross is the eternal condemnation of violence. It is the turning point of history. Whoever proclaims one's allegiance to the cross condemns the world as being un-godly. The cross is the incomparable, eternal sermon of nonviolence.[155]

On the other hand, Robert Ley and cronies use coercion to govern and hope to achieve everything with raw violence (which reveals their weakness), and therefore they have to reject Christ and Christianity. How pitifully this Reich ended which at the beginning was seemingly so gloriously organized and intended by their Nazi founders to exist for at least a thousand years. In its use of violence these words of the Lord were literally fulfilled: "For all who draw the sword will die by the sword" (Matt 26:52).

Using physical force with brutal coercion to counter an opponent or an actual injustice would be appropriate only if it were the sole method by which to achieve and safeguard justice. Violence is not the last method, however, because how can one establish justice by committing injustice?

155. Ragaz, "Jesus Christus und die Gewaltlosigkeit," 72.

Instead, we have to examine the causes that lead to the use of force. By doing so we will find that war, the most horrible form of the use of force, has its roots in adverse social conditions: first of all, in the exploitation by capitalism; in the newest political party organizations—fascism, communism, and National Socialism—which by their nature are completely unchristian, as well as the false appraisal of nationalism; further, in an erroneous lifestyle, that is, in the wrongful manner of acquiring and using luxury goods; in short, in not obeying the Creator's Ten Commandments, and thereby disturbing the harmony desired by God, which alone guarantees the order of the world.

In order to make wars impossible, we do not need to reach for a sword but rather to eliminate the causes that inevitably lead to war. This, of course, requires a vast amount of personal and social work. We also have to consider that in this sinful world, despite all sacrifices and efforts, we can substitute for the means of violence a much stronger and better way, namely, acts of justice, based on Christian, nonviolent love.

Therefore, we have to ensure that we do not eventually have to face the choice of violence or nonviolence, but that we prevent war by creating and improving social and economic conditions in accordance with individual and public justice and true love of our neighbor. We have to force upon matter the laws of the spirit by letting the spirit, guided by moral law, control matter. Of course, this cannot be done immediately but necessitates continuous, thorough work, based on a goal-oriented religious and civic education.

Consequently, making violence unnecessary is the primary and best method by which to prevent war, but this can only be achieved by eliminating the causes that lead to the use of force and by thoroughly enlightening the nations. This enlightenment has to be based on the warning of John the apostle, who tells us, "Do not love the world or what is in the world. If anyone does love the world, the love of the Father finds no place in him, because everything there is in the world—disordered bodily desires, disordered desires of the eyes, pride in possession—is not from the Father but is from the world. And the world, with all its disordered desires, is passing away"(1 John 2:15–17).

Therefore, it is necessary that a public opinion be created that deliberately opposes war and everything connected with or leading to it. At the same time, however, we have to demonstrate ways that lead to and guarantee peace; but first we have to have the right knowledge, and then the corresponding action will follow.

Militarism has to be thoroughly ostracized in the eyes of the nations. The futility of using violence has to be pointed out to everyone, beginning with the young. The more people become convinced that armaments and wars not only do not succeed to achieve and keep peace but, on the contrary, continually threaten and disturb the peace, the more they will become convinced that having to render blind obedience to organized murder in war on the command of a few violates one's personal conscience and is something unspeakably horrible. The more people become convinced that every soldier is forced by his government to be a blind tool in the hands of those who support and benefit from war, the more people will realize that the question of "war and peace" is a matter of education, religion, and morality. The more people examine and see through the lie of bellicose agitators that every war is about nation and fatherland, existence and nonexistence, freedom, and even religion, and rather about money, power, and the satisfaction of personal ambition, the more people will be clear about the causes of war—and will refuse to render military service and thus make war impossible in the future, even against the will of government officials prone to using force.

We only have to consider the huge amount of mental and physical energy, of time, money, raw materials, and labor, of patience, endurance, and willpower that is expended by the leaders of nations and their citizens forced to wage war in order to prepare for organized mass murder and destruction, and then to execute it on command.

A simple, self-evident law of economics states that the more labor, time, money, land, and raw materials are used for the production of damaging, antisocial goods (this includes harmful substances like alcohol and tobacco, as well as armaments, luxury items, and fashions), the less labor, time, money, land, and raw materials remain to produce necessary, useful, goods.

To accept this principle means to utterly condemn armaments, war, and universal conscription from an economic view and to point out that those who maintain the opposite are harming society. For no evil one wants to prevent by waging war is greater than the war itself.

We have to agree with what Father Rostworowski, SJ, wrote right after having experienced World War I: "Besides the tremendous material damage, the destruction of entire countries and millions of lives, a future war would cause a total moral collapse. . . . Honor to those who accept the consequences, those heroes who have the courage to say: We will not serve this crime. . . . It is they who destroy the old illusion. To them be honor because they have proclaimed a Christianity of action."

With Father Rostworowski we have to profess, "Blessed are they who open the eyes of the blind! Blessed are they who rise above savage nationalism and with their mind and heart try to embrace the entire human family."

For Christ says, "Blessed are the peacemakers: they shall be recognized as children of God" (Matt 5:9).

Exactly as is presently done for war, from now on, all energy and means should be made available unreservedly to serve peace and to maintain life in an ethical manner.

However, since governments all over the world, despite constant assurances that they do not want war, will not voluntarily give up violence or relinquish militarism, they will have to be forced—of course with nonviolent means—to give up their preparations for war. The instrument for this is the so-called noncooperation movement, which, at the same time, has to be a nonviolence movement. The people of the world should immediately enact this movement without, and even in opposition to, the will of their governments.

People only have to be willing to liberate themselves at last from the traditional patterns of thinking and stock phrases, accepted without criticism, which cannot be condemned enough. One should not think that by not serving in war one is abandoning the fatherland in its hour of need or that as an opponent of war one is a traitor to fatherland or nation, as those who favor the use of force keep insisting.

It is not we who oppose war with every ethical means and work for peace who are traitors to fatherland and nation but those who instigate, support, defend, and benefit from war, and all who pick up weapons and wage war and by their participation make wars possible. They plunge fatherland and nation into peril and cause dreadful destruction and millions of deaths.

h. The noncooperation, nonresistance, and nonviolence movements and the Satyagraha movement of Mahatma Gandhi

We have already pointed out the moral command that one may never participate in anything inherently bad, just as one may not try to achieve a good goal with immoral means, because even the noblest goal does not sanctify inherently unethical means. We also stated that if forced to participate in an inherently immoral action, one may not, under any circumstances, give in to coercion. Finally, we noted that it is the duty of every citizen to participate in promoting the general welfare.

These principles and everything discussed here about violence and nonviolence have led to the formation of the movements listed in the heading of this section, whose goal is to overcome brutal force with nonviolence. In actuality, all are only a single movement with the same goal and methods, a movement that we can call "overcoming violence with nonviolence."

The term "passive resistance," often used to describe this movement, is inaccurate because "resistance" implies an action, while the word "passive" implies mere submission and suffering. This movement advocates the most energetic action but without the use of brutal, physical force. When physical force is used against them, the members of this movement must endure it and not inflict it in return.

We will briefly describe the Satyagraha movement founded by the Indian apostle of peace, Mahatma Gandhi, who based his idea on Christ's Sermon on the Mount. Gandhi, a lawyer, came to Natal in South Africa in order to resolve a legal case for his firm. On that occasion he learned about the aggression and suffering to which his Indian countrymen living in Natal were being subjected by the colonial English government. When asked by his countrymen, Gandhi decided to lead their efforts to achieve justice. First he sent various petitions to the English government seeking to abolish the intolerable conditions. Since that was unsuccessful, he organized the Satyagraha movement of nonresistance among his countrymen.

Working energetically between 1893 and 1915, Gandhi succeeded in persuading the Indians to give up all violent means of resistance against the British government but not to submit in any way to unjust laws. Arrests followed. Thousands joyfully went to jail without offering the least resistance. Finally, the government knew no way out, for it could not jail all the Indians living in Natal, and had no choice but to give in and to rescind the oppressive, unjust laws.

It took twenty-two years for this movement of nonresistance to reach its goal, and the Indians had to endure much suffering and injustice until their patience and faithfulness finally won out over violence. This is truly a heroic example! It is shows that nonviolent means are indeed able to force those using violence to give in, but it takes much determination, patience, and perseverance.

In 1915 Gandhi returned to India to organize the Satyagraha movement in order to work for political freedom for India and its people who were oppressed by the English government. By means of zealous and untiring education and meetings, our apostle of peace succeeded in convincing many of his countrymen to give up every kind of force against the government, to practice political disobedience by noncooperation, and to refuse to obey all unjust laws whenever this could be done in an ethical manner. The English government used various methods of force against the lawbreakers and filled the jails. Without resisting the government's force, the members of this movement walked into prisons, and neither hunger nor death could break their nonviolent resistance. Gandhi himself was arrested and imprisoned. Yet, the movement spread.

Directed at the brutal English government, the Satyagraha movement operated by these principles: Every member foregoes all government titles and honors. No one buys government bonds. Lawyers strike and refuse to work on any litigation. All disputes among Indians are settled by mediation. No member sends his children to government-operated schools. The government-appointed committee for constitutional reform is boycotted. No Indian takes part in official government receptions and functions. English goods are boycotted so that economic independence among Indians is promoted.

The more the movement spread, the harder the English government punished the nonviolent Indians struggling for their freedom. Very quickly the prisons filled up. What could a government do? It could not possibly imprison a nation of a hundred million or annihilate it. What action was left to such a government, rendered helpless by nonviolence, but to give in and grant the Indian nation freedom and independence?

A government, even the most violent, is only possible as long as the people support it, either voluntarily or involuntarily. However, when the people want to compel their government to rescind illegal laws, that is, those that obligate them to participate in a bad cause (for example, laws enacting universal conscription, the death penalty, serving in war, the use of taxes for armaments, etc.), they can do one of two things: use force when the government tries to compel obedience to these laws, or simply refuse to obey and accept the punishment for noncompliance, without countering with violence.

What will a government do if the entire population refuses to obey such laws? Even the most brutal government is powerless against the people joined in noncooperation, nonviolence, and nonresistance. If it does not want to perish along with the people and cause complete disorder or even the disintegration of the entire economic, social, and political life, the government has to give in and abolish the unjust laws in question. For example, if the people no longer pay taxes, if the laborers in the munitions factories refuse to work, if those eligible for military service no longer comply, if the soldiers no longer pick up weapons, if the administrators no longer go to their offices, if parents no longer send their children to school because there the youngsters are educated in the ways of violence and war—if everyone does all this without the least violent resistance, even if threatened with punishment, then we would like to see the government that, faced with such an extensive resistance movement, would imprison or annihilate its entire population. Surrounded by such nonviolence, a government would not at all be able to use brute force.

Of course, the participants in such a movement must face the possibility that, especially when first organizing, their goods may be expropriated, or those taking part may be exiled or jailed, or could even lose their lives. However, once the entire population has become part of this effort, the unjust, brutal government has lost.[156]

Necessary for the man or woman who is part of such a movement is a fundamental power of the soul derived from love, that love which empowers one to give one's life for others, if necessary, according to the words of Jesus: "No one can have greater love than to lay down his life for his friends" (John 15:13). This sacrifice cannot frighten the person who desires to obey God more than man.

Therefore, we who are convinced of the irresistible power of nonviolence have decided to fashion our life accordingly. We who earnestly desire an end to war should lead and educate the people and not worry about any possible personal consequences.

Of course, it seems it will take years of strenuous work to firmly establish this nonresistance movement in the thoughts and actions of the nations. At first only individual leading personalities will work creatively for the great idea of nonviolence, supply supportive arguments for it, and communicate it to other prominent individuals. Then, convincing speakers and organizers will have to convey this idea to the people by means of the spoken and written word. Obviously, the concept will be opposed here and there, but convincing arguments and counterarguments will dissolve this opposition. The more people become captivated by this idea—it will take years of work—the more strength its proponents will gain. Finally, there has to be someone whose leadership will enable this idea to be victorious and to dominate.

This work of educating must start early in a child's life. He or she has to be taught to oppose all causes leading to violence and to abhor all ideas and institutions violence employs. At the same time the child's soul has to be filled with love for all those who use forceful means because Christianity commands us to love, not to hate, our enemies, including those who use violence against us. The human being has to be trained already in his youth to use those powers of the soul that alone will conquer violence, that is, to practice the strictest justice and all-encompassing love of the enemy.

Also, the more the individual is taught to create conditions that, as much as possible, make the use of force unnecessary from the start, the more

156. Ude: For example, if the Allies and the Austrian government were to establish an Austrian army and universal conscription without allowing the Austrian people to vote on these issues, the most effective means for preventing such a measure would be the Satyagraha movement.

the victory of nonviolence is assured, so that the people and the government will at last ostracize militarism as the most cunning agent of the meanest and most brutal force, will abolish it, and never let it be revived. If, however, a government does not want to do this, Satyagraha must be employed or else the nations will be eternally dominated and enslaved by violence.

The nonviolent movement to abolish war is not merely the responsibility of a single country but has to be organized nation by nation, and the opponents of war will have to work in unison so that this movement becomes worldwide.

How we envision this movement is demonstrated by the open letter we directed to all friends of peace in the world following World War I. It concisely summarizes what we previously wrote about overcoming violence with nonviolence. This letter, cited below, answers the question, how do the nations attain universal disarmament? For we want that all armaments should disappear; and if they disappear, so will all wars.

i. How can the nations of the world attain general disarmament?

The nations of the world can only attain universal disarmament by changing their way of thinking. They will disarm only when they realize how reprehensible war is and focus all of their thoughts and endeavors toward educating for peace, that is, the elimination of the causes of war. Armaments will only disappear when the causes of war have been eliminated. The time for general disarmament will only come when statesmen and citizens will be convinced that the statement "if you want peace, prepare for war" is wrong, but that "if you want peace, prepare for peace" is right.

Therefore, everything depends on convincing people of the value of peace and showing them the way that inevitably leads to it, which is to govern all social, economic, political, national, and international relations by means of justice and love of neighbor, since right action derives only from right inner conviction. Therefore, the home, school, church, private and public life, and especially the press have to participate in the important task of educating for peace. The true attitude toward peace has to be taught by the spoken and written word and especially by example, which will naturally result in disarmament.

We will briefly note the fundamental guiding principles that point the way that leads to peace, that is, to disarmament.

All of today's wars are, first of all, calculated, systematically organized business ventures of the international, collaborating capital of the whole world. The capitalistic economy, that is, the interest or profit economy, has been and is a main cause of wars, and so a constant danger to peace. Therefore, there will be no peace or disarmament as long as interest slavery exists.

The proper solution to the problem of war and peace lies in arriving at the right answer to this question: How do we abolish the capitalistic economy? With its abolishment, the rug is also pulled out from under communism.

When all people can again enjoy a dignified existence—that is, when everyone has a job; when import and export in international trade takes place without friction; when the exploitation of the laboring classes by interest is ended; when a satisfactory right to housing is established; when there is neither inflation nor deflation; when the entire economy is based on the principle of equivalence, that is, when compensation is equal to the work or product provided; when always and everywhere there exists individual and social justice; in a word, when the capitalistic profit economy is replaced by a morally regulated economy of need, that is, when only necessary and useful goods are produced, never useless and superfluous ones; when everyone has what he needs for a dignified existence—only then can and will there be peace. For we always have to hold fast the principles based on natural law and, therefore, on Christian moral teaching, without which the struggle against armaments, universal conscription, and war will be hopeless, and there never will be peace.

These are the principles held by opponents of war:

1. Every human being has a right to life and the responsibility to preserve it. The right to life is inviolable. ("You should not, you may not kill.")

2. Every human being has the duty to practice a religion. Religion and religious persuasion are subject to a free decision based on individual conscience. Religious sincerity is demanded from everyone. ("You should not, you may not lie.") Therefore, the question of peace is not only a purely political and economic matter, but primarily a religious-moral one.

3. God gave the earth and all its resources to all people, without distinction, to use without cost so that all human beings, without discrimination, can lead a dignified existence and fulfill the task God gave them—to contribute to civilization.

4. Besides the right to use the earth's resources, every human being has the right of ownership, that is, to acquire goods and to own what he obtains by honest means, to manage these goods as he likes, but only to the extent that the rights of others are not violated. There is only the right to good use, not to misuse of property.

5. Every human being has the right to his or her earned income and to acquire private property, because usually it guarantees the social order,

peace, and, generally, an individual's joy in his or her work, better than common ownership (common property, collective ownership, communism).

6. The right to property is not self-glorifying, independent, or without responsibilities, but human beings are only beneficiaries and fief holders. God is the feudal lord. Property obligates a person to work.

7. Property and the rights to ownership apply, first of all, only to the acquisition of goods not claimed by anyone else and to what is obtained by morally irreproachable means. Only work entitles to income, except for the acquisition of unclaimed goods. Therefore, every worker has a right to all the fruits of his labor, that is, the right to full compensation according to the principle of equivalency (the amount of work rendered and the compensation should be of equal value). ("You should not, you may not steal.")

8. Every human being has a duty to work and, therefore, also the right to work, that is, he has the direct or indirect right to the necessary resources required for his work. Or if he is unable to obtain these, he has at least the right that those who have more than enough resources for work share them. Because it is a matter of social justice, it is the duty of him who has an excess to make it available to those without possessions and to the unemployed. However, man does not live to work but has to work in order to be able to lead a moral and dignified existence.

9. The demand "to every family its own house and land" is based on natural law. Every person has the right to use his land appropriately.

10. The excess that someone has produced honestly by his work does belong to him, but in accordance with social justice, he is strictly obligated to turn over his surplus to those who own nothing or are unemployed, preferably by providing them with opportunities for work. Each person possessing a surplus is obliged to give as many goods as they need to live to those unable to work who have nothing. (Justice: to give or to let each person have what is his.)

11. Never should harmful, unnecessary, and superfluous things be produced or used in the economy, because this is always done at the cost of necessary and useful goods. Armaments and wars, especially—not to mention all damages caused by wars—are a senseless robbery of a country's wealth.

12. The general welfare may never be harmed or endangered by private property. Therefore, the state may and should socialize, with compensation, property that harms the general welfare.

13. It is the duty of every government to guide the economy according to the principles stated here and to plan so that there are enough necessary goods to ensure a dignified existence for everyone. However, this

should not be the kind of planned economy as demanded by socialism and communism.

14. Every economic system or party organization that deprives the worker of the fruits of his labor or makes it impossible for him to fulfill his obligation to work and, therefore, to acquire necessary goods is inherently immoral and has to be abolished. Every gain without work (interest) is an exploitation of the work of others and unjust. Therefore, the interest economy (capitalism) is intrinsically immoral ("You should, you may not steal").

15. People create the kind of economy they have by the decision of their free will. Therefore, it is wrong to maintain that the economy has its own law, to which human beings simply have to accommodate themselves. The demands of moral law also apply to all economic and political activities.

16. Just as every individual and each nation has its God-given rights and duties, every nationality—even if it constitutes only a minority in a country—has the right to use and cultivate its language, customs, religion, and culture, as well as the right to all physical means necessary for a dignified existence. There are no master races and slave races. All nations and states have equal rights.

17. No nation has the right to dominate another one. Instead, the nations should help one another with love and justice and should not hate or make difficulties for each other.

18. States and churches do not exist for individual human beings; rather, human beings exist for states and churches. States are responsible for man's earthly well-being and have to provide the physical means, while churches are responsible for the welfare of the soul and have to create the moral foundation needed to make it possible for each human being to lead a dignified existence. Using church and religion for political and other non-church purposes constitutes an abuse of religion. While religious tolerance has to be rejected, all persons and states have the duty to practice civic tolerance for persons of other religious persuasions. Religious sincerity is demanded from everyone.

19. Because the nations of the world have the responsibility to ensure that all human beings on earth may lead a dignified existence, the advancement of national sovereignty is subordinated to the advancement of the general welfare. Those states that consider it their primary mission to advance national sovereignty violate natural law, in accordance with which God gave all the land and resources of the earth to all people to use without cost. Therefore, every state is obligated to renounce absolute sovereignty and to establish a guided and planned economy to cover the needs of all people.

20. It is the duty of state and church to combat exaggerated nationalism, the interest economy, and all other causes leading to war.

21. Politics is the art of ensuring the general welfare with ethical means, according to the demands of justice.

22. Public or private disagreements and conflicts may not be resolved by violent means but by rational negotiations based on justice.

We can summarize all of these principles in one demand: In all personal, social, political, and economic affairs there has to be complete individual and social justice, that is, to let each person have what is his, what is due to him according to natural law and the Christian worldview. However, justice is only truly justice when it is inspired by all-embracing love of neighbor. Whatever is immoral (unchristian) can never be politically, economically, medically, or legally right.

For a complete discussion of the above principles we refer to our pamphlet "The Way to Civil and International Peace," presented in consideration of the papal social encyclicals *Rerum novarum* and *Quadragesimo anno,* as well as to our book *Soziologie.* This book demonstrates, from the viewpoint of natural law, how society, the economy, and national and international life have to be ordered so that there can be peace on earth, and answers the question, what do we have to do to prevent wars and to create the kind of order that we call peace? *Du sollst nich töten!* and *Soziologie* are related and complementary works.

The above principles reveal the conviction that makes us determined to abolish the capitalistic economy unconditionally and to prepare the way for peace. These principles show us the way to break the slavery of interest, which is gain without work; getting rid of interest is the key to the solution of the social question. Without abolishing interest we cannot eradicate the misery and poverty of society, which must be eliminated if we want to have peace because they are the fertile soil for militarization and war, and again and again they provide opportunities for power-hungry dictators and political parties to pursue imperialistic goals with weapons and to enslave people.

As just human beings, we are obligated in conscience to abolish interest and with it the capitalistic profit economy and to use our influence so that in all aspects of life the principle of equivalency (the value of work and its compensation are equivalent) will be operative.

If we seriously desire this, as all serious pacifists do, then we have to change completely the monetary system and the law governing land ownership. We have to see that money constantly circulates instead of being hoarded, to the detriment of the economy. Furthermore, we have to ensure that always as much money circulates and is used for purchases as there are necessary goods offered. We must also see to it that, on the average, the price of all goods always remains the same, that prices do not rise and fall. We also have to ensure that the shortage of apartments and abysmal conditions of many dwellings are eliminated, that is, that speculating with and demanding exorbitant prices for housing are stopped so that every person's right to own a home and land can be realized. We have to demand all of this for the sake of justice.

We, the supporters of the "theory of a free economy,"[157] believe we can realize the above demands, which are absolutely necessary to maintain peace, by means of the principles of "free money," "a stable currency," and "free land."[158]

We demand "free money" and, therefore, the abolition of all gold reserves because the value of money is guaranteed by the goods produced in a respective economy. We ask that money be assessed a hoarding tax, which would automatically increase the amount in circulation, so that money cannot be arbitrarily kept without a penalty but always has to circulate and buy goods. This would stimulate the production of needed goods until interest vanishes with the abundance of goods produced.

We also demand a stable currency, that is, the so-called index currency which alone would make it possible that money has and maintains a stable purchasing power, thus preventing both inflation and deflation, which cause unemployment.

Finally, we demand "free land," which means that land no longer remains private property and is misused to coerce interest but becomes common property owned by the nation, so that everyone has the opportunity to lease as much land as he needs for a dignified existence for himself and his family.

We cannot elaborate here on the theory of the "free economy" but have to refer to the prolific writings on this subject. If anyone can demonstrate better ways to establish a just economy, we will readily assist in translating these into reality.

If we are peace activists according to the principles stated above, especially if we are true Christians and fashion our entire life according to these tenets, we will certainly also be conscientious objectors, regardless of any possible consequences. We will be staunch opponents of military training and will counter violence with nonviolence, even when ill-advised Christians teach that self-defense is justified. If struck on the right cheek, for the sake of love, we will also offer the other one.

Remembering the commands "You shall not kill" and "You shall not steal," our thoughts will not be turned toward the destruction of life or the acquisition of someone else's property but toward the preservation of life.

157. "Freiwirtschaftslehre."

158. "Freigeld, Festwährung, Freiland."

We will also see to it that, in goodness and love, every living being is happy because he has everything he needs to live. Therefore, it is understandable that some dedicated peace activists are also vegetarians.

And if someone should ask, "Do you believe that there will ever be peace all over the world?" we will answer, "We do not know whether there will ever be complete peace or universal disarmament. We know this, however: The more people accept and live according to the ideas we have set forth here, the sooner there will be peace, the more readily and gladly people will renounce weapons and armaments, and the closer we will come to the time of peace as prophesied by Isaiah and Micah."

Therefore, this is entirely up to each one of us. Of course, everyone has to decide freely whether to adopt the proper attitude toward peace and to work actively to achieve it. If one wants to, one can immediately work for peace and contribute to general disarmament. Then the words of our Savior will apply to him or her: "Blessed are the peacemakers: they shall be recognized as the children of God" (Matt 5:9).

If the ruling powers want to play their evil game, however, we should not be scared off by their threats or use of violence because we know that as peacemakers we have justice on our side and also that the days of violence are numbered because of the nonviolence movement. Keeping our eyes on the cross of Christ will give us courage and strength for our work.

A life with such a purpose is true, active, Christian heroism and is incomparably greater than the treacherous and cowardly massacre of one's opponent with machine guns, bombs, or poison gas. The death of Christ on the cross is the victory of the heroic efforts for peace, inspired by love and justice, over brutal force. By his death Christ rendered a scathing judgment on militarism as well as on every other unjust use of force. First, Good Friday, but Easter morning will surely follow!

The thoughts developed in this section led to the writing of the open letter to friends of peace all over the world that follows here verbatim:

"A wish as introduction: May this letter reach all friends of peace in the world, regardless of their religion, race, language, and political views, and may it be read carefully. All friends of peace agree that we all want peace.

However, views differ immediately when these questions are raised: How do we bring peace to the world? What should we do so that peace will actually come? What has to be done so that the nations will actually disarm? For if we cannot achieve the disarmament of all nations, working for peace has lost its significance.

One thing is certain: If we, the world's friends of peace, do not work together toward the same goal and cannot understand one another, then there will never be peace. For we face a relatively small, unified, deliberate international group that endorses war—people who derive great benefits from armaments and war. These know exactly what they want while we, the friends of peace, have almost as many different programs for peace as there are peace organizations in the world, and these do not work in a unified fashion but often fight or even reject one another.

The question 'why do we want peace'? often reveals fundamentally different attitudes. Many want peace only because it is beneficial to them or to their countrymen. They are pacifists because they are utilitarian. However, true work for peace is nothing but altruism translated into action, or, in other words, the realization of love of neighbor, based on justice for all people and nations. Therefore, as true friends of peace, we have to direct everything we do toward ordering society and creating social and economic conditions in such a way that every person, regardless of religion, political views, race, or language, is guaranteed the right to life and, consequently, the right to work and the right to property. For if human beings are not able to lead a dignified existence, then society will be in disorder and thus become a cauldron for unrest and violence.

The more favorable the social and economic conditions, the easier it is for each person to lead a dignified existence. If everyone is guaranteed a sufficient income so that he can have a dignified existence according to his station in life, then wars for economic reasons are impossible.

Now we are confronted with the serious and crucial question, How do we create social and economic conditions that guarantee a dignified existence to every human being? We, the friends of peace, have to come up with a united answer because only a unified inner attitude will result in joined action. Will it be possible to unite all friends of peace in such an action? If not, our work is for naught. If we look at the economic conditions in the world, we face the following facts:

Because of the capitalistic economy, humanity is divided into two large camps of proletarians and capitalists, into two classes, the exploited and the exploiters, regardless of whether the exploiters are private persons, privately owned companies, or states. Therefore, on one side we have economic deprivation, great misery, and inhumane conditions because of unemployment and lack of the means necessary for a dignified life; and, on the other side, we have an accumulation of huge riches, which are used to further exploit the laborers. The capitalistic economy is nothing but an economy based on interest. Capital extorts interest, which is usury: profit without work, which the capitalist takes from the people without an equivalent return.

In a capitalistic economy, which severely violates justice and causes disordered conditions, the just economic principle of equivalency is constantly seriously violated, resulting in a struggle in private and in public life, as well as in economic, political, and international affairs.

Therefore we, the friends of peace, have to answer these questions: How do we conquer the interest economy? How do we abolish interest? We find an unequivocal answer when we examine this economy and how it is being practiced all over the world.

The following facts are evident: In order to exploit human labor, which, besides nature, alone produces value, capitalists use primarily money and land as means of exploitation by interest. Today, money—and the gold reserves in its service—extorts interest by hook or by crook by withholding it from the economy and hoarding it until the demanded interest is paid. In addition, capitalists systematically plan inflation and deflation in order to realize profits—without working themselves—from the laboring classes. In an interest economy, money, which in its essence should be only a means of exchange, becomes a means of exploitation. The pursuit of money and gold has largely captured and contaminated the hearts of most people, including many who call themselves friends of peace. But he who is exploiting another may not at the same time insist that he is seeking peace.

Besides money, land as private property is used by its owners to extort interest, that is, to exploit the work of the laboring classes. The substandard conditions or outright lack of housing, the wild speculation and appalling usury with land, the competition for colonies, and the crimes and atrocities to which many natives have been subjected—all are consequences of the misuse of land by a few with the ability to acquire it and to exploit millions of human beings who do not even own as much as a foot of land. Land has been turned into capital, and owning it, just as having money and gold, has brought tremendous power and domination over those who do not own land. It is no wonder that such unjust economic conditions cause socialism and communism to arise, with their promises to regain the rights stolen by capitalism from the exploited and disinherited masses. Thus, in a sense, socialism and communism, which also immensely disrupt the peace, are the children of capitalism.

We should not be surprised at all that capitalists use militarism and support armaments to safeguard the robbery they execute systematically and cooperatively all over the world. We have to bear in mind that armaments and war are planned and organized business ventures of the collaborating international investment capital, yielding huge profits. The capitalist does not ask whether certain goods are necessary but only whether they yield profit (interest). And the masses are lied to, told that wars are a natural necessity and have to be waged for God, for emperor, for fatherland, and for nation. Since governments and statesmen often benefit from the capitalistic economy, they institute universal military service and force men to wage war. Even Christian clergymen provide their assistance by proclaiming to their faithful that they are obligated by oath to take part in the legally organized mass murder.

We friends of peace are now faced with this important question: How do we effectively prevent money and land from becoming capital? Only if we succeed in this can we hope that dignified living conditions for all people will return and that peace will be guaranteed.

From the standpoint of justice—which has to be of prime importance to true friends of peace—we have to ensure that money cannot be withheld at will from the economy but that there is always as much money in circulation as there are goods available. Otherwise, there is disorder in the economy. At the same time, a just economy plans for the just distribution of necessary goods to assure a dignified existence for all.

Therefore we, the friends of peace, also have to answer these questions: How do we make sure that money has a stable purchasing power? How do we prevent inflation and deflation? How do we provide for a just distribution of the goods an economy produces?

As long as we do not succeed in removing the interest-extorting characteristic from money by abolishing interest—which, unfortunately, has become legal in every nation—and in providing for a just distribution of goods essential for a dignified existence for all people, peace is not possible. Capitalists cannot be, nor will they ever be, true friends of peace, and even less so true peace activists. Neither can communists, because they demand a 'dictatorship of the armed proletariat' and renounce private property in that they consign all of it to the 'monster' state by means of nationalization.

In addition, we, as true friends of peace, have to see to it that land, the foundation of all personal, national, and cultural development, becomes subject to a law that ensures that every person may use it. The claim "for every family its own home and the necessary land" is a demand that we have to raise steadfastly. The issue that faces us is this: How do we guarantee every human being, every family, and every nation its right to land?

Some of us friends of peace advocate a 'free economy' based on 'free money,' 'a stable currency,' and 'free land'[159] in order to effectively combat capitalistic exploitation

'Free money' assures that it is forced to circulate. 'A stable currency' gives money a stable domestic purchasing power, prevents inflation and deflation, and guarantees stable prices and full, just wages. 'Free land' removes land from private ownership, stops it from extorting interest, and ensures

159. FFF: Freigeld, Festwährung, Freiland.

that land becomes the communal property of all people so that every human being is able to receive a sufficient amount for his use, as hereditary leasehold.

However, should anyone show us a better and more effective method to abolish the interest economy, we are immediately ready to accept it. As friends of peace we are convinced that we will fight in vain for peace as long as we are unable to force all money to circulate, give it a stable purchasing power, and guarantee the use of land to all people. At the same time, we have to regulate the production of goods and their consumption according to a plan that assures that in every economy only necessary, useful, and pleasant goods are produced and consumed, never harmful, useless, or superfluous products. In place of the exaggerated efforts to produce everything domestically in order to be totally independent from other countries, there should be a planned, cooperative world economy that will truly meet all needs. This will happen because the interest economy will be defeated by the economic order we have described above. By overcoming capitalism, we will pull the rug out from under communism.

We, the world's friends of peace, are faced with these questions: Can we adopt the ideas presented in this open letter? In this sprit should we systematically organize a unified, planned peace movement all over the world? Will we be able to unite all friends of peace in a joint attack on the interest economy? If not, we will be unable to work effectively for peace.

Of course, the peace movement has to pay attention to the problem of nationalities, and every true friend of peace will most likely agree with the following statement: Every nationality, regardless of whether it constitutes a majority or minority in a state, should have a right to its national characteristics, language, and culture and should be guaranteed its right to land and all that the land produces so that its people can develop and have a dignified existence. The distinction of master races and slave races has to be abolished. But all of this can be accomplished only if we solve the social questions as outlined.

From the above we can draw the following self-evident conclusion: Young people who have been taught properly by their parents since childhood and have adopted the nonviolent viewpoint will refuse to go to war. We would like to see what governments and their officials would do about millions of confirmed conscientious objectors. It is important that the friends of peace all over the world work together in this spirit.

Every friend of peace has to be willing to refuse nonviolently to obey all unjust demands and orders of militaristic governments, especially to refuse to pay taxes and to produce weapons; to simply ignore orders for enlistment; and to no longer send his or her children to schools that subject them to a military education. If the millions of friends of peace in all countries work together in the same spirit, then I would like to see the government that would not consent to our politics of nonviolence.

Then education, starting in the nursery, will be entirely different than it is today. Military toys will disappear. History books and school texts will no longer celebrate the waging of war as heroic. Instead of conscription and military service a new public service will be established. All of the money, labor, and time now being sacrificed to militarism, that is, to organized mass murder and destruction, will be freed to serve the social and cultural edification of the people. Instead of the widely accepted slogan 'if you want peace, prepare for war—be armed,' the principle will be, 'if you want peace, prepare for peace.' Prepare for peace by removing the causes of war and practicing justice and love of neighbor.

When we friends of peace fight against capitalism and communism, we do not fight against capitalists and communists but only against capitalistic and communistic ideas and institutions. We do not struggle against the advocates of war as persons but only against the spirit of war and its manifestations. The multitude of friends of peace and advocates of nonviolence should be organized internationally in order to drive from the field the relatively few who champion violence and fight consciously for death and destruction, while we struggle on behalf of life and the improvement of society.

Dear friends of peace in the whole world! What I would not give to bring us all closer to understanding that peace on earth can happen only if we work purposefully together as one. Therefore, I ask each individual to seriously grapple with my ideas and to consider if, based on these, the international work on behalf of peace could be organized in a unified fashion.

Above all, we who work for peace based on a Christian foundation have to insist resolutely that the blatant contradiction within the Christian churches be removed, or we will never succeed. As we know, on one hand theologians and clergymen teach unconditional love of the enemy, in accordance with Christ's gospel, while, on the other hand, they maintain that self-defense—that is, killing with a weapon—is morally permissible, as are the 'just defensive war,' the death penalty, military training of youth, conscription, and war.

Christians are taught: 'You shall not kill'; 'if struck on one cheek, offer the other one as well'; 'if someone takes your tunic, do not refuse your cloak as well.' In the same breath, however, they are taught that you may kill; in fact, in certain circumstances, you must kill! Who is right? With whom should we Christian friends of peace stand?

Therefore, to achieve our goal, I encourage the creation of a worldwide peace ministry to lead the civil, nonviolent resistance of all friends of peace against militarily minded governments. Nothing for war! Everything for peace! Everything: time, money, labor, resources only for peace, because we Christian friends of peace have no doubt that the following are incompatible: Christianity and self-defense with a weapon, Christianity and conscription, Christianity and war. There is no such thing as a "just defensive war." Because we as Christians are obligated to love our enemy, we can only attain the peace we all so fervently desire with nonviolence, since Christ's words are true: "Set your hearts on his kingdom first, and God's saving justice, and all these other things will be given you as well" (Matt 6:33).

Unfortunately, this letter sent to friends of peace in the world went unanswered. We assume it is because of the difficult conditions at that time. But how can we achieve disarmament if not by action? Just talking about peace, violence, and nonviolence, as is customary at so many meetings of "parlor pacifists," will never bring peace. Even references to the Bible are not able to do so if, at the same time, we do not effectively oppose the causes that lead to armaments and war and force government officials to disarm and to abolish conscription.

Do citizens exist for states and governments, or do states and governments exist for their citizens? Are states not institutions that should enable cooperation, based on justice, between leaders and citizens so that everyone can earn and secure a dignified existence, or are states merely institutions that force millions to kill and destroy in blind obedience upon command? Is it not absurd that so many are forced by so few to commit the most horrible deeds and that they submit without asserting their will, without resisting? Something is definitely amiss in the minds of all these millions. In an instance the armies could throw away their weapons, disarm and go home to participate in works of peace. But they do not do so because they are not aware of their strength or of the invincible power of the statement "I will!" "I would like to" does not work, but only a courageous "I will!"

If many millions let themselves be forced voluntarily—yes, voluntarily—to go to war; if year after year, under great deprivation, day and night, under the threat of dying, they willingly and without resisting shed blood and commit the most horrible deeds, they should not complain that there is war. If they seriously desired that there be no war, there would not be. That again and again nations arm themselves for wars and fight them and that conscription exists proves that almost all countries on earth want war, because if they really did not, who then would force men to let themselves be trained for the organized slaughter of human beings and destruction and to kill upon command? And, especially, if these men were supported by women and girls who would not allow their husbands, sons, and brothers to be forced into the military in order to destroy life, then the nations' leaders would have to pay for the weapons out of their own pockets and go to war, instead of ordering their citizens to face the enemy's guns while they preserve their own "valuable" lives far from the front.

However, if someone suggests that what we desire is impossible, he should kindly tell us how else wars could be prevented. Whoever has no other or even better suggestions should remain silent or be satisfied with the position of all fatalists that there always will be wars. We who want to be true Christians must and will firmly support the ideas stated here and strive to win ever more people for them. Every human being has a free will and can use it either to work for war or for peace.

Yet we have to take account of the tremendous fear and cowardice of people as well as the laziness of the frequently indifferent masses that think only in old, entrenched patterns. It is largely a mental battle to educate the people of the world and persuade them to think, while those who believe in violence, conscious of their own weakness, try to prevent the masses from thinking. We purposely say "conscious of their own weakness"; otherwise the authorities would not strictly forbid—even threaten with the death penalty—the educational work of the opponents of war. They are afraid of our work because our reasons are so convincing that all nations, if they permitted our educational efforts, would soon be forced to end their militarism.

The entrenched patterns of thought with which those who support violence continually befuddle the minds of the masses would be recognized as such and indignantly rejected by the people.[160]

160. In this age of atom bombs, which, according to nuclear physicists, destroy all life within six hundred square kilometers; in this age of technology, which informs us that already huge areas of the earth could be destroyed by powerful radioactive rays, all of humanity, leaders, and followers, should finally realize that in light of modern weapons of destruction, waging war has become totally senseless, that is, militarism has completely failed. Nevertheless, the world continues to arm.

At the peace negotiations following World War II, the representatives of the individual nations are expecting everything from an "armed peace," are preparing for it, but are not considering that by doing so they are risking not only the existence of their nations but also of their own lives. Even poor, totally plundered Austria is supposed to again maintain an army, as the Allies and Austrian government want. However, no one is asking the people whether they want an army or universal conscription, although the Allies and Austrian government constantly assure them that Austria is a democratic republic.

The Austrian government even forbade several meetings of the Austrian League for Peace, scheduled to be held in Vienna, at which the subject of the new army was to be discussed.

If Austria and other nations consent to such a dictatorship, there will definitely be a third world war that will be waged between the two fronts, which already have their marching orders—the front of capitalism, with America in the lead, and the front of

Therefore, everything depends on uniting the undaunted supporters of nonviolence all over the world, of which there are more than a few, in order to spread the idea of nonviolence to more and more groups, despite every kind of violence used against those who champion nonviolence.

The basic question that the supporters of nonviolence—as well as the opponents of self-defense, the death penalty, armaments, and war—first have to answer is, violence or nonviolence?

Depending on whether one is on the side of violence or that of nonviolence, one accepts the commandment "You shall not kill," with or without reservation; and, conversely, whoever accepts this commandment only with exceptions has to oppose nonviolence. However, the latter must prove that Christianity is compatible with violence and war and that God approves organized killing, destruction, and a "just defensive war," that is, that the field commander and his soldiers who wage such a war are pleasing God. Or, perhaps we conscientious objectors and opponents of war are right to believe that Christianity is incompatible with killing and Christianity.

If the teaching authority of the Catholic Church, by virtue of its infallibility, decided to declare that, in agreement with the spirit of Christianity, in certain situations one may, even should, kill, and that therefore an exception exists to these words of Christ, "for all who draw the sword will die by the sword" (Matt 26:52), then the supporters of violence could lay claim to the Catholic Church for themselves in certain cases, while we Catholic supporters of nonviolence could no longer say that Christ taught and demanded nonviolence without exception. Accordingly, we also could no longer say that God's commandment "You shall not kill" permits no exceptions and that Christ's words, "for all who draw the sword will die by the sword," can be interpreted without reservation. In that case, we also could interpret with reservation all commandments about love of neighbor, especially Christ's explicit commandments to love our enemies. Where would such an interpretation lead if the teachings of our Divine Savior, and precisely, the most fundamental ones, were to be understood only with reservation? Then we would have to give up on Christianity.

j. Misuse of technology and the economy by advocates of violence

Someone coined the statement "war is the father of everything." Many millions have since repeated this idea and believe firmly that it is true. They are convinced that all of life in nature is to be understood only as struggle, and

communism, led by Russia. Then woe to the whole world!

war, with mutual destruction, as a struggle in which the stronger pushes the weaker aside, destroys, kills, survives, and is victorious.

The facts prove such a worldview to be superficial and false, however; it is not mutual killing and destruction that create and bring about progress, improvement, and development or raise the cultural level but living and working together cooperatively and harmoniously. It is the mutual support of all of nature in the entire cosmos that produces common progress in cosmic life, just as in the personal and social life of human beings.

Inanimate matter and living nature—plants, animals, and human beings—make up the wonderfully constructed cosmos, form a harmoniously organized, mutually dependent whole that operates according to natural law. The only difference is that man, having free will, is able to interfere violently in this whole, while all other beings adapt to it according to the natural course of their being, development, and function. Therefore, struggle and war never create but only destroy and annihilate.

It is correct to say that there always have been wars. But humanity usually forgets that wars have always brought only poverty, misery, destruction, and the deaths of millions. If after a war there was some advancement, it was not the result of the war but of peaceful and creative energies. The wars that seemingly were a prerequisite for peace, and the violence that was practiced in order to safeguard the "achievements" of war, caused only further violence and finally other wars, murder, and revolution, according to the principle that violence always begets violence. Since every "victor" again and again uses the same methods of violence against the "defeated," war follows upon war, the nations rise and fall, and one or another social group or political party emerges on top.

As time went on, mutual slaughter and destruction by means of ever more advanced technological inventions had ever more drastic and dreadful consequences, up to our era when war is nothing more than a mutual race toward destruction in which it is only important to beat one's enemy in the production of more effective and technically advanced weapons and to see that one's own military is better trained in their use. We mention only incidentally that all this war technology only serves capitalism, plutocratic and one-sided party interests, as well as communism with its "dictatorship of the armed proletariat."

This manner of waging war seriously disturbs and violates cosmic laws and the moral order and eventually turns against the perpetrators. God designated man as ruler over creation and intended him to govern in the ways of God, who is justice and love, and in whose image man was made. Man should rule creatively and not destructively, support and not destroy life, and observe all cosmic laws and moral demands. Man may make use of all of creation but should never abuse it.

The purpose of creation, of the great cosmos, according to God's holy will, is to serve human beings so that, assisted by its resources and energy, they can create for themselves a dignified existence. However, in order to understand the enormity and senselessness of the misuse that war-waging human beings make of available resources, we begin with these comments:

In order to manage the economy, human beings need, besides mental and physical energy, resources such as land, raw materials, plants, animals, light, air, sun, water, steam, electricity, tools, machines, and money. Since the earth's resources are limited, however, human beings have to manage them according to a plan and, of course, should first produce all necessary goods, then useful goods, and finally, luxury goods. Never should harmful or unnecessary goods be produced or consumed. The goal of every economy—private as well as national—is to meet all needs in an ethical manner.

According to Scripture, human beings received the following instruction from their Creator: "Be fruitful, multiply, fill the earth and subdue it" (Gen 1:28). Therefore, man is, in fact, king of creation, which is at his disposal, and just as God himself, man should rule creation with justice and love and fully obey the natural law and moral laws and thus observe the order established by God.

However, this obligation to rule the earth by means of man's mental and physical energy is not easy but requires effort and exertion according to the words of the Creator to the first human beings on their pilgrimage, after their fall: "Accursed be the soil because of you! Painfully will you get your food from it as long as you live. It will yield you brambles and thistles . . . By the sweat of your face will you earn your food, until you return to the ground, as you were taken from it" (Gen 3:17–19).

The history of mankind tells us how hard humans have struggled until this day to subject the earth and also relates their extensive misuses and enormous failures. We only mention: slavery, capitalism (the interest economy), communism, war. There is no need of proof of what enormous crimes and unspeakable cruelties these four words encompass.

Man has always understood how to place technical progress in the service of wars in order to make the organized business of killing and destruction ever easier and more thorough and to do so before the enemy is able to do likewise. However, all progress of technology, all inventions and machines, as well as everything in the cosmos should serve only to make every human being's existence easier, not harder or even impossible.

For example, every machine should lighten man's burden of extracting and processing raw materials to meet all needs, should relieve him of dirty and cumbersome work, and should help him gain time for cultural pursuits. The machine should not be used to exploit people, that is, it should not become capital, an interest-coercing object, and should be used even less for mass murder and destruction.

World War II, a total war, demonstrated how appallingly the machine has been misused. All factories worked day and night with their machines for war alone instead of for the production of necessary goods, which the rulers simply cut back, thus literally organizing for hunger in favor of the war aims. The most cunning murder weapons were invented, and, gradually, the entire national wealth was sacrificed to produce murder weapons—not to mention the millions of human beings who were sacrificed with cold calculation by the leaders. They did not give any thought to what happens if everything—people and wealth—is sacrificed to the war monster. Telling is the statement that Hitler, the *Führer* and commander of the German people, made in Munich on November 8, 1939. He said, "We can imagine everything but never capitulating. If someone tells me that the war will last three years, I will answer that it makes no difference how long it lasts. Germany will never capitulate, not now, and not in the future!"

It is not technology, especially not the machine as such, that harms humanity but its abuse, above all its misuse for the most brutal oppression of nations by "capitalism," "communism," and "militarism." It is not technology that exploits the laborers and creates the misery of the proletariat, but the capitalist who uses the goods produced by the machine to coerce, without his own labor, profit and interest from workers and consumers. It is not technology or the machine that murder and destroy but the nations' leaders—whom capitalists and communists use as their tools—who abuse the technological inventions for mass murder and destruction, and thereby enable the capitalists to realize huge profits. In war, especially in total war, the production of even the most needed consumer goods is significantly reduced. The largest part of the available labor force is engaged in killing and destruction or in producing the instruments to kill and destroy and still must produce the goods needed by the military and the people at home for their existence.

Therefore, the entire technological operation of a warring state constitutes a huge budget deficit that grows daily like an avalanche and has to result in economic chaos. The dead alone, on both sides, represent a loss of the labor force that can never be made up, especially if we also calculate the potential loss of offspring caused by the deaths of the strongest and most virile men.

Destroyed cities can eventually be rebuilt, though not, as some people brag, in three years and more beautiful than they were before. The wrecked economy can in time be running again, but the millions of victims cannot be revived nor the destroyed cultural treasures re-created. Also, irreparable damage is caused in warring countries by hunger and malnutrition as well as by the moral and religious collapse.

We refer to the comments we made earlier about war and expenditures for armaments, about the betrayal by the armaments industry, and about militarism, war, and public morality.The figures mentioned in those passages cry to high heaven that the nations have become mad. They were convinced and still are that they are serving peace with their huge armaments, with one state always trying to surpass the others. Instead, they only encourage war and by continually preparing for war contribute to the serious mental and moral disturbances we described earlier. The steady arming of nations all over the world was precisely the cause of the growing insecurity in the 1930s and World War II.

The resources of the economy and the achievements of technology will only be available to meet the needs of the people when the exploitation of the working people by the capitalistic economy, the expropriation of all honestly acquired property sought by communism, and the enslavement of nations by party organizations established by means of brutal violence have been abolished. In the future it will be the obligation of a just government leadership to prevent the exploitation of workers and, by proper management of the economy, to assure that there are enough needed goods produced and distributed to all.

The distribution of the annual income in Austria before World War I can be regarded as nothing but a serious crime: 660,000 people had a monthly income of about 303 *Schillinge* per capita; 2,640,000 persons received 61 *Schillinge* per month; and 3,300,000 people—half of the inhabitants—had to get along on 12 *Schillinge* a month. For these deplorable conditions, which cry to high heaven, we blame not Austria but capitalism, which dominates the world and, unfortunately, is supported and legally protected by all governments.

Therefore, it has to be ensured that the capitalistic profit economy, where goods are always short in supply, is transformed into a well-managed economy of need; that technology, machines, and land no longer become capital used to coerce interest; and that private property is effectively protected against appropriation by communism. However, if a government employing violence does not voluntarily meet its obligation to serve the general welfare, a united nation can nonviolently force it to do so, as we explained earlier.

Technology, machines, and other inventions that serve war and armaments should no longer be used, and armaments works have to be turned into factories producing useful goods. Ministries of war have to be abolished, and professional officers no longer able to adapt to nonmilitary jobs have to retire. Of course, the government has to provide for soldiers returning from war who can no longer earn a living and also for all civilians who have incurred injury as a result of bombing campaigns.

In order to regulate the economy systematically so that all necessary goods are produced and justly distributed to all citizens, the following sociological facts have to be considered. The proper maintenance of the life of a nation requires that every two persons able to work support a third one no longer able to work. Of every sixty-six persons there are forty-four able to work, fifteen children not yet able to work, and seven people no longer able to work. Of those forty-four able to work, 58 percent (twenty-five) have to produce the food necessary for all inhabitants. Only 38 percent (seventeen persons) are needed to produce all other goods necessary for a dignified existence for everyone. Of the forty-four able to work, 4 percent are unemployed at any given time. They should be recruited for public works like street construction, to build housing developments, or for artistic and academic endeavors.

In such an economy, governed according to social justice, nothing is left over for armaments or war, and if these are desired, it will be at the cost of essential commodities because the expenditures for armaments and war are always in an inverted relationship to the money needed for goods to ensure a dignified existence for everyone. A nation that allocates more of its budget for armaments and war will have less money available for all other needs.

Therefore, armaments and war are like thieves when it comes to the general welfare of a country. However, if an entire nation seriously wished it, all armaments would be done for. This would happen by nonviolent noncooperation, by the refusal to work for any company producing armaments. Every person who works for such a firm helps prepare for war. Also sharing in the guilt is anyone who stands by passively saying that it is none of his concern what others or his government do. Every citizen shares in the responsibility for the actions of his government because every government is only possible with the will of the people. For example, did not the great majority of the German people want the Nazi government? Everyone who perceives armaments and war as a crime committed on the entire nation is duty-bound by his conscience to oppose them and should join the nonviolence movement.

The comment that a country has to be armed because other nations are arming is not valid because if it were attacked, a state would have much less to fear or suffer if it were to face the enemy's violence with nonviolence.

Saying that a country should be armed for self-defense has no validity in view of the immense progress of the technology of murder and destruction. Self-defense has lost all significance in modern war—waged with fighter planes, phosphor, flame throwers, tanks, submarines, poison gas, and finally the atom bomb—because it is no longer desirable to wait until the point of self-defense but to beat the enemy to the punch and totally destroy him.

This writer wonders whether during World War II there were Catholic and Protestant clergymen who, like their counterparts in World War I, glorified the horrors of war and encouraged soldiers to perpetrate them or even called this a service pleasing to God. A Catholic priest and well-known poet spurred on the soldiers of the First World War like this:

> Styrian woodcutters, cut down the Serbian rabble with your gun,
> Styrian hunters, hit the Russian bear right on target,
> Styrian vintners, press the Welsh fruit to blood-red wine.

A member of a Catholic religious order implored the Mother of God,

> Victor over the Turks, bless the bayonets,
> Bless their blades which dig into lying flesh,
> Spread your wings over our soldiers
> So that their eye is clear, their hand does not shake,
> And their heart has been well advised
> Why they are crushing the harvest.
> Sink their iron spades deep into Christ's furrows!
> Mother of God, we sing battle psalms to you.

A Protestant pastor stated in a homily, "Germany, which goes to war armed with such virtues and powers, is ready to experience the war as a worship service. Certainly a bold but also a truly Protestant thought." Another pastor said, "Christ also belongs in war, especially with His highest demands to love, because what better, all-embracing occasion is there than war to practice love?"

Enough! Shuddering, we have to turn from such enthusiasm for war. If this is Christianity, if love of the fatherland consists of such thoughts and feelings, then we no longer want to be Christians and will forego Christianity and fatherland.

It is high time that at least the servants of our Christian churches finally begin to understand their Christ correctly. It is time to let go of the worn-out platitudes and outdated ideology of war that so many theologians keep expounding.

Of course, we Catholics are grateful for the two papal encyclicals *Rerum novarum* and *Quadragesimo anno*, but we are still waiting for the final, liberating word that clearly and concisely, without any ambiguity, rejects the interest economy—regardless of the guise it wears while carrying out its robberies—be it exploitation by private capitalism or the various forms of state capitalism, or exploitation and enslavement by fascist, communist, or national socialist parties. At last we want to hear from the proper authorities that there is no such thing as "good capitalism," that even today money itself is not fruitful, that every economic means used to acquire the fruits of others' labor without anything in return is capital, that is, interest-coercing property. We would also like to hear that, without exception, today's wars are profitable ventures for capitalists and for this reason alone are reprehensible. All this is the necessary preliminary work for an effective campaign against violence and for abolishing it nonviolently by means of Christian love, because without overcoming capitalism, as well as communism with its demand of a "dictatorship of the armed proletariat," we can never stand up effectively against war, as we have explained in our book *Soziologie* and in other writings.

k. The Quakers, the Doukhobors, and the No-Conscription Fellowship

In the middle of the seventeenth century, George Fox founded the family of Quakers in England. They, an offshoot of the Puritan movement that separated from the Church of England, rely on the "inner light." Right from the beginning they refused to serve in the king's army, and because Fox had refused military service in 1650, he was thrown into prison.

In 1660 the Quakers wrote to King Charles II, "We refuse all exterior wars and battles and fighting with exterior weapons, regardless for what goal or pretext. This is our testimony before the whole world. . . . We know for certain and bear witness to the world that the Spirit of Christ, which leads us in truth, will never command us to fight or to wage war with exterior weapons against anyone, whether for the kingdom of Christ or for the kingdoms of the world."

William Penn, a pioneer of the Quaker movement, coined the phrase "no fighting but suffering" as a principle to which the members of this Christian family remained faithful. He immigrated to America, where Pennsylvania was deeded to him as a settlement in return for a debt the English government owed him. The Quaker movement spread and founded peace organizations. Many members had to suffer imprisonment and numerous persecutions for their refusal to participate in wars. Even today they are unshakable conscientious objectors and try to win others to their conviction by word and deed. Faithful to the principle of Christ's teaching of love of neighbor, they have endeavored by their unselfish charity to heal the hardships and misery of wars.

The Doukhobors were a Russian-Christian peasant sect that for reasons of conscience literally obeyed the commandment "you shall not kill" and, therefore, refused military service. Consequently, they had to suffer terrible persecutions under the tsarist governments. After Leo Tolstoy obtained permission for them to emigrate, seven thousand left their homeland for America, where they still live in economically thriving communities, in which all property is shared, remaining always faithful to their conviction, derived from Christianity, to practice conscientious objection.

Another example worthy of emulation is the No-Conscription Fellowship movement founded by Fenner Brockway in England in 1914. It describes itself thus:

> The No-Conscription Fellowship is an alliance of men who expect to be called to military service and who for reasons of conscience will refuse to carry weapons because they consider human life to be sacred and, therefore, do not want to assume the responsibility of killing. They deny governments the right to command "You shall bear weapons" and will firmly oppose every attempt to introduce general military service in England. However, should this happen, they will obey their conscience and not the orders of government, regardless of the consequences.

We believe that all of Christendom, including the Catholic Church, which constitutes 47 percent, in agreement with the Sermon on the Mount, should unanimously sign such a declaration and act accordingly. If it were possible to turn all people who call themselves Christians into conscientious objectors, 820 million people—438 of 469 million in Europe alone—would refuse military service. If this were the case, every war would be impossible, and the Hitlers, Mussolinis, and whatever their names, would have to prepare themselves for war and fight personally against one another.

All of Christianity stands embarrassed by this band of men united in the No-Conscription Fellowship, six thousand of whom already have had to endure prison. They are so firmly convinced that they do not shrink from becoming martyrs. In all modern wars there also have been individuals here and there who have refused to participate because of their convictions, some of whom were shot on the spot as traitors of their country and people.

The question is, whom do we regard more highly? The men who did not hesitate to sacrifice even their lives for having become conscientious objectors out of obedience to the teaching of Christ, or the many Christian ideologists who, using the same teaching, argue that the bloody acts of violence in war are not only justified and but are a duty and who *ad infinitum* repeat the outdated platitudes used throughout history to justify war?

If these and others could refuse to go to war, why can't we also do so? Therefore, the question, "Violence or nonviolence?" can no longer be ignored but demands an answer from church leaders, whom God has called to work for the salvation of souls. We should no longer be denied the answer to this urgent question, which concerns more than two billion people on the earth: Does going to war and killing in blind obedience agree with Christ's command to love one's neighbor, including one's enemy—and is it therefore pleasing to God—or not? Christianity is faced with great responsibility.

l. Conscientious objection is an international obligation

Earlier we explained our views about military training and conscription and concluded that every Christian—indeed, every reasonable human being—should refuse to serve in war and should reject militarism. We cited the holy martyr Maximilian of Tebessa as an example of Christian conscientious objection. He sacrificed his life for his conviction and demonstrated heroic courage that merited sainthood. For his declaration "as a Christian you may not go to war" he became a martyr, while today millions of Catholic and other Christians—some because of ignorance due to a lack of proper instruction, others because of fear or cowardice, some even contrary to their conviction, or at least with an uncertain conscience—allow themselves to be forced to go to war because conscientious objection is usually punished by death.

Yet no one would have to fear being killed for being a conscientious objector if, united, all followed their inner convictions and refused to serve in war. This would be a glorious victory of nonviolence over violence. For example, what in Germany could the brutal violence of a *Führer* and his few hundred closest followers, or even the few thousand supporters scattered throughout the country do against eighty million convinced of conscientious objection? The most brutal violence would be rendered powerless by the entire nation united in conscientious objection.

It is psychologically very stimulating to take a closer look at the conflicted conscience of men who within themselves, for the most part, reject and condemn war and conscription, but who still voluntarily submit to conscription and then, on command, in slavish obedience, participate in mass murder and destruction.

Let us consider how conscription is accomplished. The leader of a nation and a few like-minded officials decide on conscription and threaten that "whoever refuses to become a soldier or to serve in war will be shot." It is relatively easy for these men to institute such a law because when a war breaks out that they decided on, they themselves usually do not have to face machine guns, go on patrols, or lie in the muck of trenches day after day, always aware that they could lose their life at any moment. Instead, these men, almost without exception, know that their precious life is secure in headquarters far behind the front lines. They do not have to enter the battlefield but only issue commands, and millions of others have to go to war, under this terrible threat: "Whoever refuses will be shot on the spot."

This brutal threat is the main reason that millions of men, despite wanting to refuse, cave in, that is, suffer a psychological shock. Worried that they might lose their lives if they refuse to fight, they pick up weapons, contrary to their conviction, and tell themselves, "If I have to be on the battlefield, I just may escape being hit." No one loses the hope of saving his own skin unless he is already very apathetic or, prior to the bloody action, was artificially stirred up to become a "blindly attacking hero."

It is every person's immensely strong will to survive and to resist violent death to the utmost, which causes the usually young, inexperienced recruit, threatened with certain violent death if he refuses to fight, to comply with conscription. The soldier, despite his dread and reluctance, throws himself as ordered into the battle, where he very likely could be killed, while continuing to hope that he will not be killed and, after the war, will be celebrated as a hero.

This will to live and the fear of being shot upon refusal to fight are so powerful that they force almost all men, whether old or young, who are coerced by conscription to move in a vicious circle. Every single one tells himself, "You will certainly be shot if you do not report for duty or if you refuse to go to war, and you will also be shot if you refuse to shoot your comrade who was sentenced to death." So, he concludes: "Instead of being shot, I had better become a soldier, go to war, and shoot my comrade, if necessary," soothing his conscience with the unoriginal thought, "There is nothing one can do if so ordered from above."

But no one says, "If everyone refused to become a soldier, to go to war, and, if ordered, to shoot even his comrade, everyone would stay alive, and no one would be shot." If everyone thought and acted in this way, conscription and all militarism would quickly meet their demise because no one would carry out the punishment threatened by those trying to enforce universal military service.

It is apathy, cowardice, and lack of principles that cause millions of people—despite the general aversion to conscription—to betray their innermost conviction and become slaves of a few cunning and brutal people, even though it would be so easy to make conscription impossible and, with it, armaments and war.

Therefore, the great question is, How do we persuade all of our fellow citizens, men and women, old and young, to accept the idea of conscientious objection? This will be possible only by an unrelenting campaign to educate the people and by permanent banishment of conscription and war. It is a question of producing a mass effect, a literal psychosis, because the individual feels safer within the multitude. The government's threat of force must be revealed to be only a scarecrow of which no one needs to be frightened, if all think and act alike. A drop of water does not drive a mill wheel, but millions or billions of drops together. It takes some "civil courage" to bring about the downfall of military training and conscription all over the world. The spiritual leaders of every nation, above all, those of the Christian churches, united in one movement, have to muster the courage, by means of the spoken and written word, to open a unified barrage on the seemingly invincible barricades of conscription, erected by a few interest groups advocating violent means. This barrage would have a surprising effect, and a lost war presents a favorable opportunity in which people would joyfully participate.

Many say that this is utopian thinking. It is not utopian. We are completely serious. Above all, we are thinking about the pope in Rome who, as the highest teaching authority, has the power one day to proclaim, openly before all the world, from every Catholic pulpit—that is, to all 450 million Roman Catholics—the Christian message that conscription is reprehensible and to point out that Christians are strictly obligated to refuse conscription. Thereafter, this idea would have to be taken up immediately by the bishops and priests and disseminated in religion classes in schools, in meetings, in sermons, in personal relations, and in the press, and efforts made to make it a reality.

We are thoroughly convinced that success would completely vindicate such an action by Rome and that, with the sad experience of two world wars behind us, the time would be extraordinarily favorable for such a move to free the nations from the shameful chains of the slavery of universal conscription. Every nation on earth would greet such a message with jubilation.

F. Stratmann wrote, "That this right and duty [meaning conscientious objection] has hardly ever been exercised is a morally deplorable state of affairs, only to be excused by an inadequate training in judgment."[161]

This inadequacy, which Stratmann described as "morally deplorable," would be rectified by a papal message against conscription, which we have urgently requested in the name of all humanity. At the same time, such a message from Rome would also splendidly invalidate the accusation made by Professor Keller when he addressed the national assembly of the Catholic Peace League in Munich in September 1928: "The teaching about war (customary in the Catholic Church today) because of its ignorance of the world and its harmlessness is a testimony to the poverty of our Christian and academic moral effort."

Above all, the various peace organizations of the world would immediately and most enthusiastically take such a proclamation against conscription from Rome and pass it on effectively in their sphere of influence.

Therefore, our suggestions are not at all utopian. If our efforts to do away with wars and to work for world peace are called utopian, then all of Christianity and all of Christ's teachings have to be called utopian because, presumably, no one will ever observe his teachings without reservation. However, Christ's command remains: "Go, therefore, make disciples of all nations . . . and teach them to observe all the commands I gave you" (Matt 28:19–20).

Who would now dare to call these constant efforts and struggles to spread the gospel of Christ utopian? As we have proved, it is in keeping with Christ's gospel to forego self-defense and war and, consequently, to abolish conscription. Differences of race, language, nationality, and religion are not and should not be an obstacle to the abolishment of conscription, which, in the interest of humanity, is urgently necessary. As the largest of all Christian denominations, the Roman Catholic Church has to be at the forefront. Conscientious objection is a universally human and, therefore, a Christian and international obligation as Cardinal Benoit-Marie Langenieux, the archbishop of Reims, commented aptly in 1890: "Universal military service is godless in principle and destroys freedom of conscience."

Therefore, the comment that H. de Man made is particularly applicable to those who call themselves Christians but are afraid to participate in the struggle against conscription: "There is no better way to conquer fear than to forego causing fear oneself. As paradoxical as it may sound, there is no better lesson in the strategy of spiritual struggle, no better school to

161. Stratmann, "Neue Bekenntnisse," 29.

learn true superiority and the highest art of conquest, than Christ's Sermon on the Mount."[162]

If in this sermon Christ praises peacemakers and calls them "children of God," what would he call those who do not want to work for peace, who even justify killing under certain circumstances, who support war, and who call those "utopian" who understand the Sermon on the Mount literally and sincerely strive to be peacemakers?

The issue is not whether or not our work against war and for peace is successful but whether or not we fulfill our duty to work against war and for peace. No one can seriously contend that this sincere work is completely in vain, just as no one can deny that every Christian is obligated to work for peace, that is, to eliminate the causes of war.

7. The Spanish Civil War as a dreadful and, at the same time, an instructive example for what causes wars

FOLLOWING IS A SPEECH we gave in 1936 in Graz, while the bloody civil war was raging in Spain. We tried to point out the path other European nations should follow to save themselves from a similar fate.

Everywhere, communism and Bolshevism are being blamed for having caused the Spanish Civil War, but those who maintain this are either ill-advised or say it only to have something to say. Certainly, in Spain, which has always been a strict Catholic country, communistic and Bolshevik ideas have created a way of thinking that has made the horrors of this war somewhat comprehensible. The communism of Spain is not as Friedrich Marx taught, but as Mikhail Bakunin (1814–76) taught. This Russian, who strongly opposed the precepts of Marx, based his ideas on materialistic Darwinism and regarded anarchy as the highest developmental stage of the state. An atheist, Bakunin denied the sovereignty of God and taught that no human being should rule over another. He strove for a stateless society

162. De Man, "Sozialismus und Gewalt," 168.

with collective property and wanted to achieve his goals with violence and ruthless terror.

One has to ask how Catholic Spain became the victim of such criminal ideas.

Cardinal Gomo, primate of Spain, stated, "Today we are no longer the ideological leaders of our people, who regard us not only as suspect but as the declared enemy of their welfare . . . Catholic Spain is experiencing a Golgotha and must walk a bitter way of the cross."

Father Marina, SJ, dug below the surface when he wrote in the journal *Razon y Fe*,

> The moment has come when, if we look closely, we see the enormous moral and religious misery of our nation and, deeply shocked, we strike our breast because of the responsibility we undoubtedly bear for this collapse . . . We can see now that in Spain, as well as in other countries, the Catholic Church was too closely allied with the state. When the supporting pillars of the state collapse, fissures appear in the structure of the Church that had not been noticed before. In national churches the vigor of church organizations wanes because the strong support of the state seduces to comfort. To start with, the Spanish church has to adjust to the new order and to regain its strength. Above all, she has to have an attractive social program. If the Right could not maintain its success of 1933, it was because it failed in the social arena.

And Father Mäder-Basel, certainly a Catholic priest through and through, wrote in the journal *Schildwache* of September 12, 1936, "Always, whenever the social mortal sins reach a certain point, there is war, which means that blood flows in order to wash away the social guilt. There is only one way to prevent this social bloodletting: the social disorders have to be suppressed which, from time to time, lead to these horrible purification processes we call wars."

And a certain Dr. Cona wrote in 1933, "Religious truth (in Spain) has not penetrated the depths of conscience with sufficient clarity and power. Lacking is the formation of the Catholic conscience regarding our Christian obligations in the state, in politics, and in society."

It follows from the comments of these reliable witnesses that the failure in the social domain has made some Catholics receptive to the precepts of Bakunin's communism, which means they listen more to these communists than to Catholic bishops and priests. For this the authorities of the Catholic Church bear a heavy responsibility, as stated by Cardinal Gomo and Pater Marina.

We have to consider the details because the revolutionary atmosphere in Spain did not develop overnight but over a number of years, and also point out that in the Spanish Civil War the fight between the two opposing sides, the communistic government and the rebellious national army led by General Francisco Franco, is not a struggle of socialism against communism. The national army, supported by the aristocracy and the Church hierarchy, is fighting to regain the rights of the owners of large estates whose land was confiscated by the communistic government party. Prior to that Spain's land was completely in the hands of the nobility and the Church, while the masses were landless. No real peasant class existed. Farmers could lease land only out of third or fourth hand, and these intermediaries greatly increased the rents. Therefore, it is no wonder that the ordinary man viewed the nobles and priests only as landowners who exploited him. Besides that, industrial capitalism, with all its disadvantages, established itself in Spain in the last decades. In addition, the Spanish government has linked the fate of its money to the fate of gold, which has led to dreadful deflation and unemployment. All of this added fuel to the fire.

In 1929 the amount of currency issued was 4,433,000,000 *pesetas*, in 1933 it was 4,800,000,000 *pesetas*, and by 1936 it had risen to 5,424,000,000 *pesetas*. Of these, around two billion were hoarded and moved to foreign countries, so that a severe deflation lowered prices, especially for farm products, and increased unemployment. The public deficit in 1936 was around twenty-one billion gold *pesetas* so that, converted to Austrian currency, the government debt per person amounted to eight hundred *Schillinge*. No wonder that a country in such dire economic straits also declined culturally.

At the beginning of the twentieth century, twelve million of the eighteen and a half million inhabitants of Spain were illiterate. State and Church, which harmoniously cooperated and protected their mutual interests, that is, their property, cannot be absolved from their grave responsibility for all of these conditions. Unfortunately, all governments have failed to dismantle capitalism—the interest economy—in order to combat the economic misery, and Church authorities also stood idly by. Neither has the present leftist government—after the republic was declared and King Alfonso XIII fled—taken any effective measures to better economic conditions. Spain remains a capitalistic country, that is, a victim of the interest economy, exploited by it. While the present government has socialized the land of large estates and distributed it among the people, it is unable to prevent a shortage of money and an onset of deflation with its falling prices, so that those who received the socialized land still are perishing.

What caused the outbreak of the civil war? Who financed the revolt of the nationalist troops under Franco, with whom the aristocracy and the Church are siding?

Financing this nationalist revolt against the red government was the notorious banker Juan March, owner of the Banca March in Palma, Mallorca. A peasant boy, he rose through extensive smuggling and created his own smuggling organizations, which, during World War I, he transformed into a commercial organization. Once he arranged for all pigs on the Pityusic and Balearic Islands to be bought up on one day after having secured orders for them from the Allies during the war. Thus he could dictate the prices and became a millionaire. In addition, he sold shoes and other items, which brought him huge profits, so that at the end of the war his wealth was estimated at three hundred million *pesetas*. Then he bought up huge tracts of land and joined two large organizations of owners of landed estates, the aristocracy and the Church.

When, in 1923, Primo de Rivera became dictator of Spain, March became his secret finance minister. He bought several newspapers and established contact with the well-known Spanish Catholic leader Gil Robles, a fascist. He built a magnificent villa with fifty-two rooms near Palma, opened his bank there, and became presentable at court.

When King Alfonso had to flee abroad in 1931, and a republic succeeded the monarchy, March was thrown into prison for several years by a republican court, and his entire wealth confiscated. Only a few months later, however, he arrived in Paris by car with the director of the prison and several wardens, all of whom he had bought. Not quite a year later, March, the smuggler, was elected a member of the *Cortes*. He had bought the necessary votes and, protected by diplomatic immunity, returned to Spain. There he was able to regain all of his wealth—through bribery, of course.

In 1934, March and Gil Robles decided to support General Franco financially, enabling him to organize a military coup against the republic. A few days before the coup, March left Spain with his entire fortune. From the interest of his financial holdings he financed the war the National Front waged against the Popular Front. Thus the National Front, financed by capitalists from abroad, carried out the interests of the great landowners in order to rescue the fatherland—meaning the landowners—from communism.

Thus European nations—whose government bonds March had cleverly bought up, pocketing the interest—financed and maintained the horrors of the Spanish fratricide. The exploited nations had to supply the criminal smuggler March with the means to finance the Spanish Civil War, which he had helped instigate, first, as revenge against the communistic government for daring to imprison him and confiscate his fortune, and second, in order to maintain the old, exploitative capitalistic economy because it provided him with his huge income, for which he did not have to perform any work.

Who is to blame for the Spanish Civil War? Who burned churches, killed hundreds of priests and members of religious orders, and mercilessly destroyed all opponents? Blood flowed day and night in the streets of the contested cities. The unfortunate combatants on both sides who sacrificed their lives did not know that they were only tools of the "Golden International," that is, the interest economy.

Already during the Inquisition, the unfortunate Spanish people, with their religious fanaticism, literally waded in blood and demonstrated a mass sadism when the victims, decried as "heretics," were tortured or burned. The barbaric bull fights by which the people in this Catholic country still amuse themselves are a sign that the Spanish are easily intoxicated by blood.

What value does human life have? None! This is especially true when a nation like Spain has lost its faith and acts like a madman. For if Spain had practiced a Christianity of action, the interest economy, the main cause of social, economic, and political class antagonism, would have been abolished long ago, and that nation would have had peace, not war. For the question is, how do we create economic and political conditions that make life worthwhile for each citizen? As long as there are economic crises, peace is impossible.

Therefore, whoever wants to work seriously for peace above all has to help abolish income without work, extorted by land ownership and money guaranteed by gold. Profiteering with money and land must end, and also the stagnation in the demand for goods and the resultant unemployment, because as long as people are cheated out of the fruits of their labor by interest, they cannot have a dignified existence. It is no wonder that people resort to weapons in order to take revenge on their exploiters and seek to gain by force that which they have been deprived of.

Yet this is hopeless, as clearly demonstrated by Spain's example, because as long as the real culprits—capitalism and interest—are not destroyed, the masses will be condemned to misery. All the blood has been shed in vain, and it will continue to flow. Therefore, everything depends on exposing those responsible for the deplorable conditions and then effectively eliminating them.

In a lead article from September 17, 1936, the *Grazer Volksblatt* wrote, "Gil Robles, the former leader of Spain's Catholics, explained in the newspaper *YA* why the right front he led had lost the election and the road was paved for subversives who burned churches and murdered priests. He stated, "After the election of 1933 in which the parties on the right, in a spectacular victory, gained a majority in parliament, employers thought of nothing better to do than to quickly reduce wages, lengthen the workday, and fire unruly workers. Nothing was done to stop them, and now we have to suffer the consequences, which are that these employers literally pushed workers to join the Socialists and Communists.'"

The *Volksblatt* added this comment to Robles' statement:

> Robles' comments are certainly a sad admission of various omissions but also an authentic correction of statements that reached even our newspapers. Only recently a local paper in West Styria helped convey the impression that the Catholics under Robles had prevented and even dismantled needed reforms. According to a competent witness, the truth is that the liberal employers, because of self-interest, supported the right front and at times strengthened the Catholic front and thus by their arbitrary and unjust actions prevented economic reform and improvement of social conditions. This is a warning for democratic nations, including Austria, which the Holy Father articulated in Castel Gandolfo to Spanish refugees: "We need a society in which the principles of religion and the Catholic Church are able to spread unhindered and are applied in their entirety."

Thus one begins to realize that those who defend the capitalistic economy have communism and also the bloody horrors of the Spanish Civil War on their conscience. If this is correct, Catholic economists may not depict a "good capitalism" as being morally justified. But we have to reject the justification for interest, as did the infallible teaching authority of the Catholic Church at the Council of Vienna (1311–12) and at the Second Lateran Council (1139). That is why we believe that Catholics have to accord the principles of the "free economy" the importance they deserve, if no better solution can be found.

If Gil Robles and the rightist parties, which won a sensational parliamentary victory, had been familiar with the principles of "free money," "a free currency," and "free land," they could easily have brought about the downfall of the capitalist economy by reforming the currency, preventing wage decreases, eliminating unemployment, and providing the entire Spanish population with land, thereby preparing a deserving end to the large estates.

The landowner pockets the basic rent for his land and lives from the interest, which raises the rent as well as prices for agricultural products. Since Spain's owners of large estates, primarily the Church and the aristocracy, control practically all of the land, they oppress the farmers by the high rents they charge. The more rent a farmer has to pay, the more he has to reduce his standard of living. In this way, the Spanish people have become slaves to the great landowners. The unjust profiteering of those liberal entrepreneurs, whether or not they call themselves Catholic, can be stopped only if the principles of the "free economy" are instituted.

As long as on the Catholic side nothing is done to abolish the interest economy and as long as only "social politics" are pursued instead of thoroughly changing economic conditions, beginning with the creation of a just money economy, Catholics must share the blame that today's unjust economic conditions are forcing the proletariat into the hands of the communists.

We dare to say that as long as the Catholic Church believes that all that is needed is a "reconstruction of the social order," as Pope Pius XI states in his encyclical *Quadragesimo anno*, but leaves the interest economy alone, the world will continue to be ripe for communism and revolution, and the above demand of the pope cannot be realized.

It is the capitalistic economy that obstructs the unimpeded dissemination and complete application of the principles of religion and of the Catholic Church. Or, to put it another way, the capitalistic economy was able to come into existence only because the principles of religion and of the Catholic Church were not disseminated freely or ever applied completely.

If we as Catholics want to draw the only correct conclusion from this realization, we have to deal with the precepts of "free money," "a free currency," and "free land." We have to become familiar with them and study them, at least, instead of rejecting them from the start (as is frequently the case in Catholic circles) because of ignorance. This does not concern Spain alone but all of Europe because whatever is happening in Spain today can and will take place elsewhere. Leaders of state and Church have the greatest responsibility for what happens in the future.

May Spain's burning churches, all the bloodshed and the horrors committed there move us to search within our own ranks for who is to blame. It is only by action—not just by praying, complaining, pitying, accusing, and, least of all, by the force of weapons—that we can establish the kingdom of God and his justice, which Christ demanded us to seek and establish without fail, promising that everything else will be added. Only when we use Christian means do we create those social and economic foundations that make it possible for every person, by ethical work, to secure the prosperity that, according to St. Thomas Aquinas, he needs to lead a virtuous life.

Today we do not need "social politics," nor an attack on the consequences of these abysmal conditions, but a complete renunciation of the causes. We have to crush interest slavery at any price and create a new economy according to Christian demands of justice.

General Franco, the leader of the National Front, cannot and will never achieve the desired recovery of Spain, because he is fighting on behalf of and with the support of the great landowners and the capitalistic criminal Juan March. He is fighting, as he told the *Evening Standard*, to prevent the destruction of the fatherland through redistribution. He intentionally represents the interests of the great landowners, that is, he defends capitalism, just as the government he is fighting against carries out the interests of capital while calmly ignoring deflation.

What right do the capitalists have to say they are fighting communism and also working on behalf of the interests of people deprived of their rights, as long as they remain capitalists? After all, he who does not seriously combat capitalism has to share the blame for the existence of communism.

Whoever seriously desires peace and the people's welfare and with determination struggles against interest needs no weapons and does not have to kill anyone. Wherever we see weapons and violence used, we know that someone is tending the affairs of capitalism—for example, the great landowners of Spain—to protect their unjustly held property against those who want to take it for good reasons and only by ethical means because, according to Christian precepts, every citizen has a right to the land needed to live.

Therefore we, as serious opponents of capitalism and war, may side neither with the Popular Front nor with the National Front, both of which are defending the ownership of large estates. However, we are intentionally intervening in the Spanish situation by shouting out to both warring parties, "You are gravely wrong. You are transgressing against your people. We may not supply weapons to either party because whoever does so supports injustice. If you are truly concerned about promoting the people's welfare, you have to stop all hostilities against each other, join together and form a united front against your mutual enemy, the interest economy. We believe that your weapons should be "free money," a "free currency," and "free land."

Then peace will come to Spain and will remain there—and what is true for Spain is true for all countries and peoples of the world.

We will never get rid of communism by shooting or gassing all communists. Likewise, the communists will never succeed by simply confiscating land or even by killing the owners and destroying cultural treasures. Communism—excluding Christian communism—advocates violence and therefore will be finished the day each person can again work unhindered, receive just compensation, and acquire as much personal property as he needs for a dignified existence for himself and his family. In other words, if there no longer are capitalists and proletarians, exploiters and exploited—if income without work, meaning interest, has vanished—communism will have lost its power to attract. Baron Vogelsang said that interest remains the pivot of the social question. This is strikingly demonstrated by the atrocious events of the Spanish Civil War. The class struggle has to be fought with ethical means, without the use of force, until the poor proletariat is victorious.

There is no time to lose because all nations are armed to the teeth, and communism, which the capitalistic economy has enabled to grow, is knocking on homes in city and in countryside. Millions of people who no longer have anything to lose but their naked life are flocking to its banner. They prefer an end with terror to terror without end. The heavens are blood red, and soon Europe will perish in a bloodbath. Let the gruesome Spanish fratricide be our final, grave warning of how things will develop if the interest economy is permitted to prevail. You nations, you responsible men in Church and state, fulfill your obligations!

The victory of one or the other party in Spain will not result in a just distribution of goods. The thirty million *pesetas* the Civil War has cost as of today have made impossible, because of mutual hatred and bloodshed, the cooperation necessary to solve the question of a just distribution of goods.

Therefore, a new economy has to be created according to Christian justice. The concepts "free money," "a free currency," and "free land" show a way to social and economic peace in every nation and, consequently, to true peace among all countries.

This concludes the speech we gave in Graz in 1936.

Subsequent events have proved that, unfortunately, our comments and predictions were accurate. The year 1945, with the unspeakably sad and at the same time dreadful demise of the Nazi German Reich, is a graphic illustration and lesson such as the world has never experienced before. May the so-called winners of this terrible struggle take to heart this lesson and consider our remarks so that peace will finally reign among all peoples on Earth.

PART III

"Peace be with you"

(Luke 24:36)

From Parts I and II it is evident that this writer is a firm opponent of war and absolutely condemns every war, without exception—from the standpoints of reason and Christianity—as an unfortunate error of a will that is either incorrectly informed or ill-advised.

Wars are the product of sick minds, on one hand, and of cunning scoundrels, on the other. While condemning war unreservedly, we support peace by fighting against the causes leading to war and by making every effort to create social and economic conditions and institutions based on justice and love of neighbor that enable each individual to live in peace and to maintain the conditions that guarantee peace.

Ultimately, the issue of war and peace is not an economic one, not a national one, and not a political one, but purely and simply a religious one. For as war arises from a disregard of moral laws based on reason and revelation, peace is realized by the unconditional observance of God's commandments, which is, ultimately, the result of living a Christian life of action. How could war occur among human beings who give to others, who let others have what belongs to them, that is, who practice justice, are united in the bond of Christian love, and observe the revealed commandments of love?

Therefore, war and peace are the result of inner disposition. Peace results from the order created by unreservedly obeying the laws based on natural law and reason and the Christian moral commandments. However, whenever the good order God created and desired is violated, strife and trouble result, harmony is disturbed, violence is employed, and, ultimately, war breaks out.

Therefore, peace is the result of each person's reforming and renewing his life according to natural law, reason, and Christianity. It is the condition realized by transforming the life of pleasure, economics, politics, national and international relations to agree with Christ's teaching. He does not want to transform human beings and guide them toward peace by means of politics but to make politics Christian by means of spiritually transformed people leading a Christian life. Thus he seeks to guarantee peace without weapons, without armies, and without violence. And, as contradictory as it may sound, a church whose servants and spiritual leaders are totally apolitical will truly be pacifistic.

The words of the Apostle Paul, to "bring everything together under Christ" (Eph 1:10), should guide the life of nations. They are the means to create a new order of society and economy and a proper method of settling international relations through benevolent understanding; that is, they are the way to make and guarantee peace. "Under Christ" means to include Jesus in the daily life of each individual and to conform all communal life to the teaching and example of Christ, who sacrificed and carried the cross and gave himself for the salvation of all people without distinction.

It is high time that the nations that already know Jesus—about 820 million people on Earth are nominally Christians—call to mind their Christianity, if the world, because of the distorted image it has of "armed peace," is not to suffocate in blood and poison gas vapor and all of humanity to be annihilated by the dreadful atomic bomb.

Everything we have written above proves that Christianity is incompatible with war, with self-defense, with armaments, military training, conscription, violence, and being a soldier. For the essence of Christianity is expressed in one word: love. Every war is the exact opposite and a serious violation of the command to love, while the fruit of love is peace. Peace does not just happen, is not inborn, but has to be relentlessly worked for by obeying Christ's command: "Set your heart on his kingdom first, and his saving justice, and all these other things"—whatever human beings need for a dignified existence, and this, first of all, is peace—"will be given you as well" (Matt 6:33).

1. "I hear the good news, but I lack faith": An untenable contradiction among Christians

THE VIENNA *NEUE FREIE Presse* of May 4, 1937, reported that the Ligue nationale des prêtres anciens combattants[1] was planning to hold that year's meeting in Vienna, at the invitation of Chancellor Kurt Schuschnigg. These annual assemblies, which issued a general peace proclamation, were not only open to Jewish and Protestant veterans' unions, but considerable effort was made to encourage all of them to participate. The reason for holding this large international peace conference in the Austrian capital was to expand this religion-based peace movement into central Europe. Cardinal Theodor Innitzer of Vienna honored this meeting with his support. The program included the honoring of heroes; a field mass, celebrated by the Austrian prelate in charge of military chaplains, Bishop Ferdinand Pawlikowski; and a candle procession across St. Stefan Square and the Ring to the votive church. About two hundred thousand people were expected.

The true friends of peace had joyfully received this good news and were willing to work for the success of this significant international peace conference. The friends of peace, especially, out of religious conviction had every reason to rejoice, but only if the Christian concept of peace were presented purely and unreservedly, as well as the demands ensuing for each individual Christian and every nation.

Undoubtedly, this conference sought to give the Christian peace movement a new incentive, as did the activities of the worldwide *Rassemblement universel pour la paix* (RUP),[2] led by Lord Robert Cecil. The Vienna *Morgenpost* of April 16, 1937, reported about this newly formed organization on the occasion of the visit to Vienna of A. D. Tricard-Graveson, a Catholic French government minister, who served as Lord Cecil's deputy.

> The RUP is a result of the Congress of Brussels of 1936 at which five thousand delegates represented two billion members of organizations working for peace. Cooperating are trade unions, peace organizations, associations, churches, and women's organizations. Politics and religious questions are excluded. Everyone who is serious about peace is welcome. Here peace is not just something dreamed of or yearned for but something to be organized and worked for. Many prominent church leaders have

1. League of French Priests Who Served on the Front.
2. Universal peace assembly.

> been recruited for the RUP. Tricard-Graveson himself was able to persuade the bishop of Clermont-Ferrant to become active. The archbishops of York and Canterbury belong to the English section of the RUP, and Cardinal Jean Verdier of Paris is one of the great sympathizers of the movement. Nonsectarian as well as Catholic trade unions of France are part of it and also the Catholic *Jeune Republique*—a total of six million people. In England there are eight million and in the U.S. fourteen million persons affiliated. Forty-three countries are associated with the national committee.
>
> The assembly is working with the League of Nations, seeking to support it at the grassroots level with its large membership, and also to reform and improve it. It considers most important that peace be secured by automatic, obligatory arbitration. It works for the sanctity of agreements and for the revision of hard or intolerable treaty stipulations, for a limitation and decrease of armaments, for the mutual aid of nations in case of threats, for restraining profits from armaments, and for collective security.
>
> The RUP is not for immediate, total disarmament because as long as there are violators and enemies of peace, every country and also the League of Nations needs a large defense force . . . Of course, every group within the movement supports its demands for peace differently.
>
> The Catholic left, to which Tricard-Graveson belongs, does not tire to take its motivation from the words of Christ, "whoever wields the sword, dies by the sword" and "peace to all men of good will."

Everyone reading this report must have been greatly influenced by it because peace is the most fervent yearning of humanity. Peace is the cry of those who are deeply disturbed by the insanity of amassing armaments and who have no hope that there ever will be peace. And yet statesmen, especially, and also their nations are convinced that one has to arm in order to ensure peace.

"If you want peace, prepare for war" is the slogan that controls our political, domestic, and international life. It is total war with which all of humanity is threatened. Even many friends of peace are of the opinion that nations have to be heavily armed in order to keep the peace under the circumstances. Even members of the Catholic hierarchy share the view of the RUP that armaments are necessary at present.

Likewise, in E. Müller-Sturmheim's excellent and convincing pamphlet *Armaments as Salvation*, we are told that weapons are necessary today. He writes, "As already mentioned, having no armaments whatsoever is unthinkable under today's international conditions. . . . Unfortunately, today a nation's importance, influence, and ability to keep agreements depend on the amount of its weapons."[3] And again: "Archimedes was slain by a Roman soldier. The mind succumbed to brutal force. As of today, we have not progressed. This condition justifies armaments as a protective measure."[4]

All of the world's statesmen, at various occasions, day after day, solemnly declare their desire for peace—we assume that each of them believes it—but they do not trust others and regard them as violators of peace. Therefore, the nations arm, believing that this will prevent war and guarantee peace.

Whoever is still not convinced, after having carefully read the earlier cited Gospel excerpts regarding the love of enemies, that every use of a weapon and every defense with violence contradicts the essence of Christianity, will not be persuaded by the entire gospel. Self-defense, war, armaments, and military training are incompatible with Christ's teaching—this we learn from the Holy Scriptures. The only weapons for Christians are nonviolence, all-forgiving love, and gracious patience, which never harm the enemy but rather suffer the greatest injustice.

We have to ask, how can violence be compatible with these unambiguous commands of Christ, which everyone can readily understand upon first hearing them? Who dares to contend in face of these instructions, which are to be taken literally, that armaments and war are compatible with Christianity? We can only derive one truth from these commands: Christianity cannot be compatible with armaments and war, for to be armed for war means to be ready at all times to meet the attacker with violence, to harm the enemy, and, if need be, to kill him.

Is this the love Christ demands of us? How can the inhabitants of a nation that arms itself and wages war say that they are obeying the great commandment to love one's enemy? How can they say "love the enemy," "do good to the enemy," "do not render evil for evil," and "overcome evil with good" while they stab the foe with a bayonet, throw hand grenades at him in order to tear him to pieces, drop tons of bombs from airplanes onto men, women, and children below—when they mercilessly fire cannons and machine guns into the ranks of the enemy and drive their tanks over human bodies? Such people call themselves Christians? Are they who find this acceptable and defend it acting like Christ? Human beings capable of such deeds maintain that they seriously desire peace and say, "War never again!" Indeed!

3. Müller-Sturmheim, *Rüstungen als Rettung*, 17.

4. Ibid., 19.

Arming and training for war, supporting self-defense, being a soldier, and waging war are not compatible with Christ. Whoever wants to live according to Jesus' teaching may not touch a murder weapon, has no need for a rifle or revolver, cannons or poison gas.

Yet we are witnessing that Christian clergy and laymen defend the right of self-defense as a Christian obligation, maintain that armaments are justified, and represent the so-called just defensive war as morally permissible. They declare that it is just to kill the enemy in self-defense and, especially, in war. Soldiers are obligated by oath to defend their country with murder weapons when ordered by their superiors. We read in the Catechism of the Roman Catholic Church, published with the approval of the Austrian bishops and of the ministry of education, and used as a textbook for primary and secondary schools,

> Who sins against the life of his neighbor?
>
> He sins against the life of his neighbor who unjustly kills, wounds or beats him. . . . To kill a human being is only permitted in just self-defense:
>
> 1. To anyone, if it is not possible to protect his life against the unjust aggressor;
> 2. To the lawful authority to punish serious crimes;
> 3. To soldiers in defense of their fatherland.

On the other hand, it is taught that the great commandment of love, including love of the enemy, is strictly binding on all people without distinction, that it applies without exception to enemies of all kinds and is to be practiced without restriction in one's attitudes and actions.

However, those who violate Christ's commandments—"you shall not kill"; "you shall love your neighbor as yourself"; "love your enemies"; "do not render evil for evil"; "let yourself not be overcome by evil, but overcome evil with good"; "if someone hits you on one cheek, offer him the other, and if someone takes your coat, offer him your cloak as well"—and as soldiers pick up the sword and kill their enemies are celebrated as heroes and are decorated. Killing, shedding blood, laying waste, burning, and destroying are glorified as "heroic." But conscientious objectors who take Christ's teaching literally and refuse to kill any human being are called betrayers of the fatherland and shot.

Who is right? Are they true Christians who arm and train to kill and then, if they deem it necessary, destroy their enemies, or are they true Christians who refuse to kill the enemy but instead try to do good to him?

On whose side is Christ? On the side of the archbishops of Bologna and Tarent, who gave their gold rings and pectoral crosses to support Benito

Mussolini, who had attacked a poor nation, Abyssinia, with tanks and aerial bombs and alleged that he was doing this in order to bring that country the blessings of Christian culture? Or is Jesus on the side of the young man without a professed religion, Göschler of Kärnten, who on March 5, 1937, cited the commandment "You shall not kill," refused military service, and was sentenced to three months of prison? After completing his term, he once more refused to serve in the military and was sent to prison for another five to ten years. Is Christ on the side of all the conscientious objectors who were shot because of their refusal, or is he on the side of the officials who ordered the death sentence and defended their actions as morally justified?

Is Christ on the side of the Vatican newspaper *L'Osservatore Romano*, which in February 1937, in the name of Christianity, called upon the nations to take part in an armed intervention against the Republican troops in Spain? Is Christ on the side of the archbishop of Santiago de Compostela, who tried to prove that General Franco's war was a just, religious war of defense and asked the people of his diocese to pray for the victory of Franco's weapons?[5] Or is Jesus on the side of those who condemn as unchristian the actions of the Republican forces as well as those of Franco's forces and reject any intervention with weapons? Is Christ on the side of the mayor of Vienna, Richard Schmitz, who declared on March 26, 1935, "Regardless of how much someone loves peace, he still knows that his family, his fatherland, and everything he cherishes are only secure as long as his desire for peace is guarded by the will to defend these. There is no such thing as absolute pacifism. No nation can forego to train its men in the use of weapons and to kindle and nourish love of the fatherland in the family, so that in the hour of trial the inner strength needed is there to defend the homeland"?

Or is Jesus on the side of Cardinal Theodor Innitzer, whom Hermann Hoffmann cites in his book *Die Kirche und der Friede*:

> Neither Christ's comment about buying a sword nor the one about two swords should be interpreted that He favors war. The first one is to be understood in terms of spiritual willingness and the disciples' misunderstanding His words. Soon thereafter we hear Jesus' command to Peter: "Put your sword back, for all who draw the sword will die by the sword" (Matt 26:52). And following His resurrection he greeted the disciples with "Peace be with you" (John 20:19). Therefore, we can agree completely with the Protestant theologian Adolf von Harnack, who commented, "Nothing more needs to be said to determine that the

5. *Grazer Volksblatt*, January 30, 1937.

> Gospel excludes all violence and in no way is warlike or tolerates anything that is."[6]

Is Christ on the side of the high Catholic prelate who said at a review of officers in Vienna, "Military leadership makes this principle an obligation—the heart beats for God, the fists on the enemy"?[7] Or is Jesus right when he says "love your enemies" and "do not resist evil"?

Is Christ on the side of those countries that have instituted universal military service in order to guarantee peace, or is he on the side of Pope Benedict XV, who addressed the warring nations in his peace proposal of August 1917, "It appears to the Holy See that the only really effective and, with a little good will, realizable method is to abolish conscription in the civilized states by an international agreement"?

Is Christ on the side of Cardinal Benoît-Marie Langénieux, the archbishop of Reims, who in an 1890 pastoral letter described conscription as "godless in principle and destructive of the freedom of conscience"? And is he on the side of Bishop Kaller of Frauenburg, in Austria, who wrote in 1933, "Conscription, consciously or unconsciously, cultivates the spirit of war and under present conditions raises the danger of war. Theoretically, there may be a just war, but, actually, the requirements for such a war will never be met. Therefore, we have to reject conscription"?

Is Christ on the side of those who advocate pre-military training of our youth and teach them the techniques of killing on command? Or is Christ on the side of those who say with him, "Let the little children alone, and do not stop them from coming to me; for it is to such as these that the kingdom of heaven belongs" (Matt 19:14), who try to keep from the hearts of children all hate, bitterness, and party politics, and who therefore reject the pre-military training of youth as a crime perpetrated against them?

We could continue without end to ask questions such as these. Wherever we look, we see nothing but contradictions that are simply unbearable for an honest person striving for truth and that weigh heavily on Christian consciences.

A church that tolerates such contradictions betrays itself and gives up all claims to the name "Christian." Being Christian, that is, being faithful to Jesus' teaching, can only be either-or. Either Jesus and his gospel are right—and then we have to reject armaments, war, self-defense, military obligation and training, and serving as a soldier as unchristian—or armaments, war, self-defense, and military obligation are morally permissible and even necessary from the Christian viewpoint. If the latter is the case, we do not

6. Hoffmann, *Die Kirche und der Friede*, 5–6.

7. *Grazer Volksblatt*, September 6, 1936.

know what to do about Christ's command to love the enemy without fail and without limit. Then we have to despair of Christ and be confounded by the gospel.

The true disciple of Christ must renounce all violence and oppose war, regardless of the consequences. A true Christian fulfills the teachings of his divine master, who says, "I give you a new commandment: love one another; you must love one another just as I have loved you. It is by your love for one another, that everyone will recognize you as my disciples" (John 13:34–35). Or can anyone imagine Christ throwing hand grenades or mowing down enemies with a submachine gun?

Not even the noblest goals can justify self-defense, war, military training, or armaments. These contradict the commandment to love one's neighbor and, especially, the explicit commandment to love one's enemy—unless someone can prove to us that Christ permitted defending oneself when attacked, or even made it a duty in certain situations.

It follows from our arguments that in the face of attack, only the complete renunciation of violence agrees with the essence of Christianity, that is, with the love that Christ demanded of us, namely, love of the enemy. This renunciation does not turn one into a coward. On the contrary, it requires heroic courage to stand up to a world bristling with weapons and to suffer insult and death rather than do evil to others by means of violence. However, if a disciple of Christ has to give his life for his conviction and to endure violence, it is no defeat but rather a glorious victory, an eloquent witness for the moral power of Christendom, which is called to renew the face of the earth by means of justice and love. Whoever does this is truly a hero because he has true love. To be a Christian means to stand up for one's faith and, if necessary, to be a martyr.

That the world, condemned by Christ, justifies armaments and war and by these means hopes to achieve peace should not surprise us. That many of those who call themselves Christians defend the world with weapons in the hope that they will bring peace is an intolerable contradiction. We say to all who call themselves Christians and who pretend they are for peace but still defend killing in certain cases: "Before you do anything on behalf of peace, insist on a clarification of all the immense contradictions that have existed for hundreds of years among the Christian friends of peace. Let Christ alone decide without reservation what constitutes true peace. Let him show you the road to peace. We hear your message of peace; but as long as the glaring contradictions we have described are not clarified, we do not trust the accuracy of the war ideology generally held among Christians alleging to serve peace."

2. Christ, the Prince of Peace

SINCE CHRIST IS THE Prince of Peace, he cannot approve of war. He did not speak about organized killing and destruction or of revenge but desired that all relationships be ordered by means of justice and love.

Jesus' gospel is truly "the gospel of peace," as Paul wrote to the Ephesians (Eph 6:15). Christ's coming to earth was announced by the heartfelt song of the angels on the plains of Bethlehem: "Glory to God in the highest heaven, and on earth peace for those he favors" (Luke 2:14). And among Christ's last words before he died were "Peace I bequeath to you, my own peace I give you . . ." (John 14:27). The first words that Christ spoke to his apostles after rising were "Peace be with you!" (Luke 24:36). The seventy-two disciples selected by Christ were sent out with this instruction: "Whatever house you enter, let your first words be, 'Peace to this house!'" (Luke 10:5). As Jesus, during his festive entrance, was nearing Jerusalem and saw the city lying below him, he wept over it and said, "If you too had only recognized on this day the way to peace. But in fact it is hidden from your eyes" (Luke 19:42). Moreover, Christ sent his disciples out defenseless, like sheep among wolves.

The entire world talks about peace, but what it means is this: "If you want peace, prepare for war!" It is a peace backed up by huge numbers of bayonets, cannons, machine guns, air squadrons, bombs, pocket battleships, and million-member armies. On the contrary, Christ's gospel is nothing but "If you want peace, prepare for peace," and it reveals the way to love and reconciliation, the way to dismantle hate, and the way to overcome all who disturb the peace. For whoever puts first the commandment to love one's enemies and makes it fundamental in his life, whoever lets himself be crucified for his worst enemies in a holy spirit of reconciliation, whoever prays for his enemies—it is he whom all these supporters of the necessity of war and defenders of militarism, defensive wars, and military training of youth can never claim for themselves.

Jesus is the great, true, and genuine pacifist. His entire philosophy of life is about maintaining peace and about the benevolent, nonviolent, and bloodless settlement of all differences, even if one has to give up one's advantages and even one's life. Christ is not a pacifist because he is afraid or cowardly but, on the contrary, because he is not afraid of violence from anyone. He is a pacifist because he has the courage to confront the world and its violence with truth and to stand up for justice and love of neighbor, even by giving his life. This is true Christian heroism, which is incomparably greater than cutting down one's opponent with machine guns and bombs. Christ's death on the cross constitutes the victory of heroic pacifism over violence; and with his death, Christ pronounced a crushing judgment over militarism. He conquered violence with nonviolence, as we know from Easter Sunday, which followed Good Friday.

He is no supporter of war who lays down the eight Beatitudes as a way of life: "Blessed are the gentle . . ." and "Blessed are the peacemakers . . ." (Matt 5:4, 9); who teaches his followers to pray, "Our Father in heaven . . . forgive us our debts, as we have forgiven those who are in debt to us . . ." (Matt 6:9, 12); and who demands of his followers, "If anyone hits you on the right cheek, offer him the other as well . . ." (Matt 5:39). Whoever prays and acts like this cannot possibly believe in war as a natural law but strives to remove the terrible idea of war from human hearts, to fill them instead with ideas of peace and the prevention of war.

Whoever has understood Jesus and his teaching understands that in his Sermon on the Mount he commands, "Love your enemies and pray for those who persecute you; so that you may be children of your Father in heaven, for he causes his sun to rise on the bad as well as the good" (Matt 5:44–45). Therefore, the Apostle Paul preached to the entire world in Christ's name, "Never pay back evil with evil . . . Do not be mastered by evil, but master evil with good" (Rom 12:17, 21).

Jesus teaches love, forgiveness, nonviolence, not hate, revenge, or violence. Nowhere does he defend or advise war. He never spoke in support of organized mass murder but sought to remove all causes leading to war. All of the commandments Christ asks his disciples to obey are aimed to conquer the spirit of the world, a world centered on the sensual body, the lustful eye, and pride in possessions, all of which are opposed to Christ's Spirit. The world knows only politics of power and force. True work for peace in Christ's Spirit is to keep human hearts from being contaminated by the spirit of this world. Therefore, the Apostle John wrote in the name of Christ: "Do not love the world or what is in the world. If anyone does love the world, the love of the Father finds no place in him, because everything there is in the world—disordered bodily desires, disordered desires of the eyes, pride in possessions—is not from the Father but is from the world, and the world with all its disordered desires is passing away. But whoever does the will of God remains for ever" (1 John 2:15–17).

Lies and violence characterize the spirit of our times. The objective of the world, which God condemned, is to satisfy people's addiction to pleasure and power at the cost of others. Let us not be deceived: the politics of all of our so-called civilized states, even of the League of Nations, is godless, unchristian, and is therefore centered on war, not on peace.

These politics of war can be changed only if we try to persuade as many people as possible to conform to the spirit of Jesus. The peace politics of our nations will only be successful if the majority of people, guided by Christ, by deeds of justice and love, struggle against those who disturb the peace. For peace is tranquility in the good order, which results from unconditionally following God's commandments and is the essential prerequisite for every citizen being able to achieve a dignified life by his labor.

Yet when the majority of people who perform honest labor, as is the case in our so-called civilized states, are condemned to an undignified existence; when a large number are unemployed and homeless; when they are housed in miserable dwellings; when they are hungry and cold; when the capitalistic economy, bent on profit only, constantly cheats the working classes out of the fruits of their labor; when governments protect the interest economy and support speculation and profiteering with land; when the addiction to pleasure ruins the nation physically, economically, and morally; when lies are called an indispensable method of politics; when family life is destroyed; when people are taught to hate and take revenge; when youth is indoctrinated with the military sprit; when, by regulating prostitution, governments make fornication into a public, officially permitted institution; when in international relations only the right of the stronger prevails, and violence takes priority over law; when people adhere to the principle that whatever benefits the state is moral—we ask whether these are foundations on which peace can flourish. Never!

Rather, the foundation for peace consists of what will cause a merciful last judgment, as described in Matt 25:31–46: to give food to the hungry, drink to the thirsty, to welcome the stranger, to clothe the naked, to visit the sick, and to set prisoners free. In one word: We are obligated in conscience to eliminate all causes that make it impossible for so many people to lead a dignified existence and that are the basis for the disturbance of peace, for revolution and for turmoil.

People who do not comprehend the above questions, who believe in capitalism, who are addicted to alcohol and nicotine, who lead an immoral life, who do not do everything possible to save people who have been harmed and keep those who have not been harmed from falling, may often be enthusiastic about peace and peace gatherings, but they are not true apostles of peace. True Christian pacifism is only characterized by leading a life according to Matt 25:31–46, that is, by struggling against everything that harms people. This struggle may not be restricted by religion, political party, or race, and it must be international, even if it begins with and benefits primarily one's own nation. Christ is the merciful Samaritan for all people; he does not ask for a baptismal certificate or consider race, political party, or language when one needs help. For "Jesus went about doing good" (Acts 10:38). Justice and love of neighbor are the pillars of Christ's teaching. Therefore, his greeting was always "Peace be with you."

3. Peace Education

In March 1936, we gave a lecture about peace education to a Catholic social welfare group in Graz. What we said then still applies today. If we are to have peace someday, people will at last have to be educated for peace.

During World War II people constantly talked about "war morale." This morale, however, with which one indoctrinated even young people not yet able to make sound judgments, is nothing but training in the use of violence, in killing and destroying, and instruction in how to lie and hate, be unjust and cruel. We all have experienced this war morale with terror and do not want to live through the consequences of it a third time. Or should humanity become even more cruel, inhumane, and brutal than it already is?

Therefore, not war morale but peace morale! What constitutes peace education we discussed in detail in that lecture, which, because of its importance, we cite here verbatim:

"Peace is tranquility in good order. If we are to have peace, the life of each individual and of society has to be morally ordered, because what is not morally right can never be economically and politically right, nor right in any other way. Order has to reign in the heart of each individual, in social and political life, and in international relations, which means ordering all human relations according to reason, natural law, and Christian morality.

"Therefore, peace is the result of observing the moral order, which comes from abiding by the commandments of Christ's Sermon on the Mount which is the spirit contained in the 'Our Father.' If all people would lead unconditional Christian lives, no one would strike another on the cheek, there would be no hate, no injustice, no revenge, but only justice and love. No one would endanger the life of or seek the property of others. Instead, economic conditions would be such that everyone could create a decent existence by honest work. In one word: There would be peace. If one had real love, what need would one have for weapons or defense? For 'God is love, and whoever remains in love remains in God and God in him' (1 John 4:16). God is a God of good order and peace. Or does peace exist where day and night murder and destruction are schemed and preparations for war made?

"Christ is the Prince of Peace, not the commander of armies. His coming into the world was celebrated not with cannon salutes, not with fanfares and bugles, but with choirs of angels who sang, 'Glory to God in the highest heaven, and on earth peace for those he favors' (Luke 2:14). And the angel of the Lord announced to the shepherds, 'Look, I bring you news of great joy, a joy to be shared by the whole people. Today in the town of David a Savior has been born to you; he is Christ the Lord' (Luke 2:10–11).

"Savior! Christ the Lord! Now we know that we are not fools because we believe in peace and condemn war and, therefore, do not touch any murder weapons. For Christ, the Lord and Savior, forbids war. He proclaims peace and guides us on the way to peace. Christ wants to heal, not to rip wounds open, for he says, 'The spirit of the Lord is on me, for he has anointed me to bring good news to the afflicted. He has sent me to proclaim liberty to captives, sight to the blind, to let the oppressed go free, to proclaim a year of favor from the Lord' (Luke 4:18).

"Jesus also said, 'Come to me, all you who labor and are overburdened, and I will give you rest' (Matt 11:28); 'Remain in my love' (John 15:9); 'I have given you an example so that you may copy what I have done to you' (John 13:15).

"Christ gives light and life, not death and corruption, for he says, 'I am the Way; I am Truth and Life' (John 14:6) and 'I have come into the world as light, to prevent anyone who believes in me from staying in the dark any more' (John 12:46). And one of Christ's apostles said, 'This is the revelation of God's love for us, that God sent his only Son into the world that we might have life through him' (1 John 4:9).

"Love is the essence of Christ, not hate, for Christ is God, and this God of love says, 'This is my commandment: love one another as I have loved you. No one can have greater love than to lay down his life for his friends' (John 15:12–13). This relates to what his apostle says, 'This is the proof of love, that he laid down his life for us, and we too ought to lay down our lives for our brothers. If anyone is well-off in earthly possessions and sees his brother in need but closes his heart to him, how can the love of God be remaining in him?' (1 John 3:16–17). One look at the bloodstained cross on Golgotha tells us everything. Christ is justice, not injustice. Mercy and goodness are his companions, not brutal force, for it is written about him in the Psalms, 'Love and truth will meet; justice and peace will kiss. Truth will spring from the earth; justice will look down from heaven' (Ps 85:11–12).[8] Jesus says, 'Shoulder my yoke and learn from me, for I am gentle and humble in heart, and you will find rest for your souls' (Matt 11:29). And of this kindly Christ it was said, 'He will not break the crushed reed, or snuff the faltering wick, until he has made judgment victorious' (Matt 12:20). And this Christ should be a supporter of war or military training? No. This Christ said, 'I have given you an example so that you may copy what I have done to you' (John 13:15).

"Jesus does not want to dominate but to serve with love, for he says, 'The Son of man came not to be served but to serve' (Matt 20:28) and 'If anyone wants to be first, he must make himself last of all and servant of all' (Mark 9:35).

"Forgiveness and remission shine from his divine eyes, not unforgiveness and revenge. How often Christ says, 'Son, daughter, your sins are forgiven.' 'Do not judge, and you will not be judged; because the judgments you give are the judgments you will get, and the standard you use will be the standard used for you' (Matt 7:1–2).

"And in Christ's name, the Apostle Paul enjoined, 'Never try to get revenge; leave that, my friends, to the Retribution. As scripture says: Vengeance is mine—I will pay them back, the Lord promises' (Rom 12:19); and 'Be generous to one another, sympathetic, forgiving each other as readily as God forgave you in Christ' (Eph 4:32). How can human beings who want to be true disciples of Christ point rifles and throw bombs at one another and gas each other? How can people who embody the attitude of Jesus take part in organized mass murder at the command of their superiors, who themselves are only too often fallible and ruled by passions? Let us remember what Christ said, 'Remain in my love' (John 15:9) and 'I have given you an example so that you may copy what I have done to you' (John 13:15).

"The name of Christ is 'Prince of Peace' not 'commander in chief.' He does not rely on the sword; his weapons are justice and love. Jesus says to Peter as he is defending him with a sword, 'Put your sword back, for all who draw the sword will die by the sword' (Matt 26:52). Nowhere does Christ teach, 'If you desire peace, prepare for war.' Had he been an advocate of military training, conscription, or war, Jesus would have taught this, at least by way of suggestion. However, Christ's greeting was always 'Peace be with you,' not 'Be prepared to fight in war.' Christ proclaims, 'Blessed are the peacemakers: they shall be recognized as children of God' (Matt 5:9).

"Therefore, we have to make every effort to bring about peace by our actions. Wars do not have to be. They are not natural occurrences, and we are not fools because we believe in peace and strive to achieve it. Therefore,

8. Translation from the New American Bible.

it is up to us, up to the free decision of each single person, to the extent that it depends on him, whether there is peace or war.

"With Christ, with him alone, and only by obeying all of his commandments, can there be peace. Whether or not others obey Christ should not concern us. Instead, if we want to be true disciples, we have to keep Jesus' words unconditionally and to cultivate a disposition toward peace.

"Love and justice! When these two basic demands of the kingdom of Christ guide the life of each individual, of families, of states and of nations, there will be peace, and peace will remain. The Apostle Paul said, 'The fruit of the Spirit is love, joy, peace . . .' (Gal 5:22). Love and justice are spiritual, omnipotent, and irresistible powers. We only have to call to mind a few of Christ's commands about love for neighbor and enemy, and we will understand that peace has to be realized by fulfilling his demands without reservation, which all Christians are obligated to do.

"Whoever hears these words has to admit that Christianity and war, Christianity and military training are incompatible. To people who obey Christ's teaching literally, his words apply: 'If you make my word your home you will indeed be my disciples; you will come to know the truth, and the truth shall set you free' (John 8:31–32).

"Peace is not only possible, but it is the explicit command of Christ. There should be no wars. Therefore, he is no fool who believes and works for it, in the spirit of justice and love, and rejects and forbids every form of violence and military training as being incompatible with Christianity.

"From a Christian standpoint, the two peace treaties of St. Germain and Versailles cannot be condemned enough as examples of a criminal peace, attained by force. Peace will never be achieved by translating into reality the principle 'If you want peace, prepare for war.' Christ says clearly, 'Peace I bequeath to you, my own peace I give you, a peace which the world cannot give, this is my gift to you' (John 14:27). Therefore, only he can talk about an 'armed peace' who does not believe that Christ's commands are right and will triumph.

"A forced peace built on planned murder and destruction, on robbery and subjugation, produces only hate among the conquered people and calls forth the desire for revenge by those on whom such a peace has been forced. One merely needs to be the stronger in order to achieve this peace of pretense. Therefore, we have the relentless arms race. But where the peace of Christ reigns there can be no war, not even if the stronger attacks a disciple of Christ in order to subdue him, because whoever follows his example does not return violence for violence.

"The follower of Christ also does not aspire to worldly power because he has taken Christ's words to heart: 'You have only one Master, and you are all brothers . . . Nor must you allow yourselves to be called teachers, for you have only one Teacher, the Christ . . . The greatest among you must be your servant' (Matt 23:9–11). And also: 'You call me Master and Lord, and rightly; so I am. If I, then, the Lord and Master, have washed your feet, you must wash each other's feet. I have given you an example so that you may copy what I have done to you' (John 13:13–15). Furthermore: 'The greatest among you must behave as if he were the youngest, the leader as if he were the one who serves' (Luke 22:26).

"It depends entirely on the conviction of the individual whether he is a child of peace or is paving the way for war. Christ confirms this: 'What goes into the mouth does not make anyone unclean; it is what comes out of the mouth that makes someone unclean . . . Whatever comes out of the mouth comes from the heart, and it is this that makes someone unclean. For from the heart come evil intentions: murder, adultery, fornication, theft, perjury, slander' (Matt 15:11, 18–20).

"Man is not born with his convictions. They are learned and acquired. Ultimately, peace is a matter of education. Therefore, parents and teachers are obligated to present their convictions to young children. They should not depict war as heroic because murder and destruction are not heroic, nor should our young people be trained to be enthusiastic about war, but rather about the peace Christ desires. Desperate human beings, however, both clergy and laymen—as if they were possessed—make every effort to defend war and military training.

"The only right thing is to answer this question again and again: How do we educate human beings for peace? The primary question is not how do we prevent wars, but how do we create a conviction in people that leads to peace?

"But how can Christ live in the hearts of people who, in many cases, do not even know the gospel? It is a tremendous detriment and shame that most Catholics do not customarily read the Bible. We would like to know how many Catholics have ever even picked up a Bible. It is only when people know the Holy Scriptures well, namely, Christ's gospel, that the conviction develops in their hearts that leads to peace. Education means, first of all, to teach the necessary knowledge and the right principles by which to live and act. The word of Christ is always and everywhere the determining factor for the knowledge and will of Christians.

"Therefore, we Catholics have to be retaught, as soon as possible. We have to read the Holy Scriptures every day in order to form and sharpen our conscience according to Christ's teaching. Performing certain rituals is also part of our church life, but this alone does not give us life; no, 'It is the spirit that gives life, the flesh has nothing to offer. The words I have spoken to you are spirit and they are life' (John 6:63). Therefore, we have to learn first the words of Christ, and these we do not learn from the *Codex juris canonici*, nor from moral treatises and dogmas, but from the Bible and the preaching of the word of God.

"Therefore, if we regard it as our Christian duty to earnestly strive for peace and to awaken a true sentiment for it in the light of the gospel in human hearts, then we cannot do so without, at the same time, opposing and abolishing the causes that repeatedly lead to war.

"Everything depends on guiding people to be always aware of the command of Christ to be just, charitable, and helpful toward everyone. Since 'obedience to God comes before obedience to men' (Acts 5:29), the faithful disciple of Christ, as a true peacemaker, will always and everywhere refuse to serve in war, whatever the consequences. In today's world it takes an unshakable faith and the courage of a martyr to stand up for the peace of Christ in his kingdom. It takes heroic courage to rebel against the antiquated, deeply ingrained ways of thinking that have been blindly passed on from generation to generation for thousands of years, but this courage can only result from an inner moral conviction.

"Therefore, let no one say that Christianity has failed; it has never failed and can never fail, because its essence is summed up in love. Rather, those who call themselves Christians and do not live according to Christianity's demands, that is, those who lack true love, have always failed and will continue to fail.

"'Let us be concerned for each other, to stir a response in love and good works' (Heb 10:24). These words are the key to achieving peace. If individuals and nations, in their relationships, live up to this command, there will be everlasting peace. If I call myself a Christian and do not want to be a hypocrite or a betrayer of Christianity, then I have to fulfill all demands of the Christian moral law without reservation. The education for peace culminates in one sentence: 'Let us be true Christians!'"

4. "The dream of eternal peace"

THE ISSUE OF WAR and peace can be presented best in the light of the facts. We have already mentioned the peace congress of the *Ligue nationale des prêtres anciens combattants*[9] and used newspaper reports about it to point out the many flagrant contradictions among Christians who, on one hand, are working for peace but who, on the other hand, approve of war and everything connected with it, or at least find war compatible with the Christian commandment of love of neighbor and enemy. Pointing out these contradictions, which are intolerable for a Christian, we requested that the congress resolve them before taking any further steps toward peace. Following this meeting we composed some remarks that explained why Christians as well as Catholics seem unable to free themselves from the traditional teachings about war, despite attempts being made to correct these. Below we will cite these remarks, titled "The Dream of Eternal Peace." It was Austrian Chancellor Kurt Schuschnigg who coined this expression. It points to the fact that most Christians do not believe in eternal peace, or, more correctly, consider a lasting peace impossible, but believe that there will always be wars, and therefore one's country always has to be armed.

Following is our "Dream of Eternal Peace":

"From August 26 to 29, 1937, the congress of *La ligues nationale des prêtres anciens combattants* (PAC) met in Vienna with much ceremony and with the participation of church and state. The newspapers reported its proceedings and speeches more or less thoroughly, and based on these reports we would like to present our opinion.

"As a Catholic priest who desires to stand firmly on Christ's teaching, we have found it very strange and in bad taste—to refrain from using other words—that priests dressed in their robes and with their old regimental banners were marching like soldiers. As though we became priests to be soldiers! However, ultimately, it is only fair that whoever supports war should personally have to face the cannons.

"If anyone at all, the Catholic priests (in France, where in World War I they had to bear arms) would have had to refuse to serve in war, being faithful to Christ's teaching about loving one's enemy, which commands us not to return evil for evil, not to do evil to a neighbor, not to resist him who does evil, not to take revenge, but to feed the enemy if he is hungry, and if hit on one cheek, to offer the other as well—that is, to love the enemy and to be mindful of Christ's admonition that 'whoever wields the sword will die by the sword.' Or do the French priests and all Christians who defend

9. National League of Priests Who Served at the Front.

armaments and military obligations believe that it is a sign of the love of one's enemy when soldiers kill one another in war?

"And as for the speeches given at this congress by priests and laymen, most of them very distinguished persons! These speeches call for a comment. We would like to point out only a few of the major contradictions of Christ's gospel, which were painful to our ears, since as Christians we are convinced that peace can exist and remain only when Christ's commandments are unconditionally translated into action.

"Cardinal Theodor Innitzer of Vienna commented about the congress, 'The fighters at the front, who in faithful duty to the fatherland did not shrink from any sacrifice, not even death, want to announce before the entire world where alone true peace can be found, namely, in following Christ. This congress was called in the spirit of Christ and Church.'[10]

"French Cardinal Achille Liénart of Lille said, 'When we leave here, we have to be determined to help awaken the Christian idea of the peace of Christ in the world—the only true peace—and to establish this peace by letting Christ rule in us and around us.'[11]

"There is no doubt that Christ desires peace and that he says no word anywhere about war, armaments, and self-defense. It is also certain that his word and example condemn the pagan principle 'If you want peace, prepare for war.'

"At the reception for the participants at the Hofburg, on August 27, Chancellor Schuschnigg said, 'We are not chasing utopias. As long as there are people in the world, it won't be possible to overcome dissension completely. In our era and our experience there is very little reason to believe that the vision of eternal peace is possible, but that is not most important. Most important is that in the coexistence of nations and states, politics do not center on fighting for the sake of fighting.'[12]

"Mayor Richard Schmitz of Vienna commented at an August 26 ceremony on the Heldenplatz, 'The Christian peace is not a peace of weaklings and cowards but a peace that men would like who are aware of their defiance, courage, fidelity, love, and ability to sacrifice for the fatherland. Aware of this, we soldiers desire peace and call to one another, 'Let us stand together for the just, for the Christian peace.'[13]

"Cardinal Liénart said in the opening address, 'As spiritual power, the Church avoids—whatever is said to the contrary—to deal with secular

10. *Neue Freie Presse*, Vienna, August 27, 1937.

11. *Grazer Volksblatt*, August 27, 1937.

12. *Neue Freie Presse*, August 28, 1937.

13. *Neue Freie Presse*, August 26, 1937.

matters. She leaves public affairs and even the waging of war to the heads of states. . . . Our opinion has to strengthen the statesmen in their efforts to remove matters of conflict. In this difficult task they need to have the support of all of us, just as commanders in war count on us to obey when ordered to assault.'[14]

"The Austrian military vicar, Prince Bishop Ferdinand Pawlowski, stated at a field mass held at the congress, 'The Church does not refuse war service, but she always exhorts people to draw closer to each other and to work for peace.'[15]

"Dr. Pilz, Austria's minister of justice, stated in his address on August 26, in front of the memorial for heroes, 'We bow respectfully before the dead and have renewed the vow to stand by our fatherland, as they did, and to struggle for true world peace so that the world will no longer be threatened by a similar disaster.'[16]

"Most remarkable are some of the comments Abbé Bergey, president of the PAC, made at the closing of the congress, on August 29, 1937:

> Among all Christians, priests and their superiors are clearly called to comprehend and spread the eternal truth—namely, the truth about peace, love, and brotherliness. They whose hands, hearts, and words were consecrated eternally for the holy task of filling the human mind with that spirit of peace, and the human soul and heart with that harmony, must lead the way and prepare the laying down of arms . . . We do not believe that superior strength in war alone can settle international conflicts. We do not believe that the triumph of a nation or group of nations, having the most soldiers, tanks, airplanes, machine guns, poison gas, and pocket battleships, necessarily is also the triumph of eternal justice and absolute justice.

"Abbé Bergey's speech contains much about which we can rejoice and many truths we can take to heart, but neither he nor any of the secular or religious speakers said a single word about the great commandment to love the enemy. Without being unconditionally obedient to it there can be no peace of Christ.

"No wonder all of the speakers, contrary to their constant demands of 'peace in the kingdom of Christ,' have become totally fixed on the slogan 'If you want peace, prepare for war,' and, accordingly, depicted armaments and the just defensive war as being sometimes morally permissible from

14. *Grazer Volksblatt*, August 27, 1937.

15. *Neue Freie Presse*, August 27, 1937.

16. Ibid.

the Christian point of view. It did not occur to a single speaker, including members of the clergy—priests, bishops, or cardinals—to make even a single reference to the gospel's command to love the enemy. This alone is a serious shortcoming, because how can one bring about the peace of Christ in the kingdom of Christ without obeying literally his command to love the enemy?

"These precepts of the gospel should be familiar to all who speak at peace conventions—the speakers of this congress are all Catholic Christians. And if these precepts are familiar to them, every one of them should readily be able to determine that the statements cited here are in obvious contradiction to Christ's demands.

"Before the French veteran priests hold another peace congress somewhere, intending to work for the peace of Christ in Christ's kingdom, these contradictions must first be cleared up and removed. For either Christ is right—and then we have to work for peace on the basis of total nonviolence by 'seeking first his kingdom and its righteousness' (because then, as Christ promised, 'everything will be added on')—or the veteran priests' congress and its speakers are right, in which case they have to prove that all of Christ's commands about loving one's enemy are not to be understood and obeyed literally. They will have to demonstrate that the peace that Christ desires and leaves his followers is an 'armed peace' and that weapons are needed to settle international conflicts. If this can be proved, we will admit that the idea of an eternal peace is merely a beautiful, unrealizable dream, as Austria's Chancellor Schuschnigg maintained. Yet as long as Christianity has the power to renew the face of the earth, we believe we can realize the peace of Christ in his kingdom. This belief gives us the courage to stake everything, and therefore, first of all, to renounce force by means of weapons.

"Whether and when eternal peace will be achieved—we do not doubt it can be in light of the prophecies of Micah and Isaiah—does not matter at all. But simply because a condition of eternal peace cannot be reached at this time, it does not follow that the nations have to be armed. Whoever is for peace, especially if he bases his desire on Christ's teaching, has to renounce all armaments because the peace of Christ is based on nonviolence, justice, and love of neighbor, including love of the enemy. This peace we should and can strive to bring about every moment of our lives.

"We agree completely with Abbé Bergey that 'the Church has the right and obligation, even if its members should become martyrs, to proclaim above the heads of all Caesars the eternal truths, which have to be the foundation of all human politics . . . In our tormented times, in which even the most pernicious ideas are allowed to be heard, the Catholic teaching, in whatever country it is at home, may not remain silent.'

"Yes, Abbé Bergey was entirely right when he pointed out this truth at the Vienna congress. Therefore, we Catholics have the right and the duty to ask that the Church's highest authority tell us finally whether or not there was a contradiction, as we maintain, in the entire presentation of the congress and in the various statements of its speakers. For only the truth will make us free. However, it seems to us that many responsible men in state and Church, who constantly emphasize their Christianity, lack the will for martyrdom, as it is more comfortable to live with a moderated Christianity."

With such an attitude, even among Christians, it is not surprising that today the right of the stronger, of force, counts as justice and is triumphant. What happened in Abyssinia, Japan, South Tyrol, Palestine, and, finally, in World War II, shows how bad things can get for human beings when Christ's commands are ignored and one expects peace from the work of weapons. An armed peace is not peace but a preparation for the next war.

5. Oswald Spengler and the possibility of world peace

In 1936 Oswald Spengler, in a telegram, gave this answer to an inquiry by an American whether peace will ever be possible:

> Only someone who is knowledgeable about history can answer the question whether peace will ever be possible. To be familiar with history means to know people as they were and as they always will be. It is a vast difference, which most people will never understand, whether one looks at the history of the future as it will be or as one would like it to be. Peace is a desire, war a reality, and human history has never concerned itself with human wishes and ideals. Life is a struggle among plants, animals, and human beings, between the various classes of society, between nations and states, whether it is played out economically, socially, politically, or militarily. It is a power struggle to get one's will, advantage, or opinion of what is useful or just; and when other means fail, one will always resort to the final method, violence. One can describe an individual who uses violence as criminal,

> a class as revolutionary or traitorous, and a nation as bloodthirsty. But this does not change the fact of the matter. Today's world communism calls its wars "uprisings"; colonial empires call their wars "pacification of foreign peoples"; and if the world were a single state, one would call wars "uprisings." The only difference is in words. It is a dangerous fact that today only the white nations talk about world peace, not the more numerous, colonial nations. As long as some individual intellectuals and idealists do so—as they have always done—it is futile. However, when entire nations become pacifistic, it is a symptom of senility. Strong and stalwart races they are not. It is a renunciation of the future because the pacifistic ideal is a final state that contradicts the facts of life. As long as there is human progress, there will be wars. However, if the white nations were to become so tired of war that under no circumstances could their governments make people participate, then the world would become the victim of the colored races, just as the Roman Empire fell to the Germans. Pacifism means to let the born non-pacifists have authority, who also include men of wisdom, adventurers, conquerors, and born masters, who are sought after as soon as they are successful. If today in Asia large uprisings against white people were to take place, many whites would join because they are tired of a peaceful life. Pacifism will remain an ideal. War is a reality. And when the white nations are determined to no longer wage war, the colored races will do so and become the rulers of the world.[17]

If it had not been Oswald Spengler who gave this answer, we could keep silent and ignore it in the belief that it is only one of many viewpoints. Spengler's answer, however, should not be silently passed over because many people accept his words as gospel truth, as they also trustfully accept his writings about the decline of the West.

Spengler is entirely correct when he declares that world peace will remain nothing but a desire of humanity. To determine that, one does not need to send a questionnaire around the world, because everyone who knows human beings—be he a historian, a moral philosopher, or a politician—takes people as they are and is convinced that there probably always will be war; that is, conflicts will be settled by means of violence. For war and peace are born in the hearts of individual human beings—I am speaking here as a Christian moral philosopher—however, people, burdened by the consequences of original sin, are inclined toward evil, starting when

17. Spengler, *Reden und Aufsätze*.

they are young. Wherever human beings transgress the laws of nature and God's commandments, the order established by God is disturbed, and an atmosphere is created in which conflicts are settled by means of violence, that is, by war.

It is false and totally illogical to say that since there have been wars in the past, there will always be wars in the future. Whoever says this assumes that waging war is part of human nature. Such a view is understandable if one teaches with the followers of Darwin that a human being is nothing but the result of breeding in the animal kingdom. Given this assumption, Spengler is right. Human beings are more than that, however. Because of their reason and freedom they are God's image, and therefore unconditionally subject to moral law.

Where man's freedom is taken into account and also our conviction that there is a personal God and that Christ, as God's Son, appeared among us and commanded us to obey his teaching, we may no longer talk about war as a law of nature. War and peace are ultimately the result of the decision of man's free will. Therefore, the question whether world peace is possible has to be examined not only by the historian but also by the teacher of ethics. Because human beings are free, they do not have to wage war. They can either misuse their moral freedom and wage war, or they can act morally free and do whatever serves peace.

The question is whether all human beings can be persuaded to always make decisions with their free will so that the result is peace. Here it is irrelevant whether people are of the white race or belong to the colored races because all human beings, without distinction, are subject to moral law, and the commandments of this law include "You shall not kill!" and "You shall not steal!" and "You shall not lie!"

Just as Spengler may not maintain that there will always be wars and that world peace is therefore impossible, we may not insist that there will never be wars again and that world peace will be a reality. However, we may (and must) say that if human beings obeyed natural law in all decisions made with their free will and unreservedly adhered to God's commandments, world peace would be forever guaranteed. Conflicts and struggles—these are certainly not yet always wars because there are also conflicts over differences of opinion—would then be resolved by reasonable agreements and just mediations without the use of violence.

It follows from Spengler's comments that the efforts of pacifism are unnecessary and even detrimental. However, we have to conclude that future wars can be prevented and that we should do everything possible to prevent them, among the white race as well as among the colored races. Pacifism—and we do not mean "salon pacifism," which merely coins beautiful phrases like "war never again" but does nothing to change conditions and even less to bring about a change of people's attitudes—but a pacifism that employs the works of justice and love of neighbor and is not at all a symptom of senility, as Spengler maintains, but is the only right approach by reasoning and free people who are subject to the unchangeable moral law, not to mention those who are Christians. Christianity and war are incompatible. A Christian is obligated to love his enemies, not to resist violently if attacked, to give his cloak to the person who has taken his coat, and not to resist evil but to overcome evil with good—in short, to allow Christ's fundamental commandment, "You shall love your neighbor as yourself," to guide his entire life in every situation.

Two worlds are facing each other: the animal-pagan assessment of human beings and the Christian, moral evaluation. Representing the former, Spengler uses only the purely instinctual (animal) controlled aspects as criteria for man's behavior. Christians, instead, also take into account the spiritual-moral, supernatural powers. Human beings are free, and their attitude toward peace and war is determined by which of these opposing views they adopt.

Humanity has to choose between Christ and Spengler. If people follow Spengler, they must expect there to be wars; but if they follow Christ, it is possible to prevent wars. There is no pacifism with Spengler, but there certainly is with Christ.

We believe that choosing between Spengler and Christ should not be difficult for anyone. Above "whatever is" there is "whatever should be." Whatever should be is also a reality, a fact one has to take into account.

It is worth every sacrifice and worthy of human beings alone to strive for this ideal condition. Whatever depends on the decision of man's free will should be in harmony with natural law and with the unchangeable moral law as God desires.

Both war and peace are in our hands. Humanity will have war if it wants war and peace if it desires peace. Yet which one it wants to have is another question.

6. A word to all women of the world

If men, wrongly advised and blinded by senseless sayings, defend war ever so vigorously, the true woman, the high-minded wife, is instinctively the strongest opponent of war, in fact, has to be an opponent. If men shout, "If you want peace, prepare for war," the idealistic woman has to call out even louder, "If you want peace, prepare for peace." The sword does not belong in a woman's hands but only the palm branch of peace.

Women have to demand peace—in their own interest, that of their husbands, and especially that of their children. Girls, married women, and mothers have to demand peace for themselves, for their families, and for the entire nation. To work for peace, to make peace and to keep it—these are part of the nature of the uncorrupted woman. The true woman with motherly feelings has to hate war and, therefore, the soldier's uniform and everything connected to it. Only the prostitute who wants to earn money at the cost of her body and the woman who feels only like a "little woman"[18] throw themselves at men in uniform. The true woman sees in the man in uniform someone trained to kill and destroy whenever the state orders. However, the "little woman" sees in the man in uniform—especially if it glitters with decorations earned for being specially skilled in murder and destruction—only the "little man"[19] she wants.

Men often are too cold and indifferent when told that in World War I, for four full years, there were six to seven thousand deaths every day, including on both sides. And as for the women? Is it not compassion that characterizes a high-minded woman? Just think about it! Who were the seventy-five million men who fought in that war? Girls and women on both sides, these were your sons, your husbands, your brothers whose suffering was beyond words. Eleven million did not return to their families in World War I. In World War II it was fifty million. Many of their bones are lying beneath foreign soil. Certainly, there were women and mothers who were proud that their sons, fathers, and husbands went to war. Yes, some of them used the words "in proud sorrow" when announcing in newspapers that their son or their husband had lost his life in war. Yet, we have to say that the war was insane and an illusion. All those men who died sacrificed their lives in vain because it was not about homeland, fatherland, and nation; as we have noted often, behind all our modern wars hovers cold, calculating

18. The German word is *Weibchen.*

19. The German word is *Männchen.*

capitalism—which walks over blood and corpses—and the criminal megalomania of so-called leaders.

Girls! Women! You have to shout, with one voice, "Never again war!"

Or did your mothers give life to your sons so that they can be drilled to commit mass murder on the battlefields? Girls! Women! Tell us, is the purpose of mother love and care only that your sons, in the full strength of their youth, are consecrated to death for the greed and addiction to power of a few men? Do you give life so that this life, in the prime of youth, should be snatched away by death?

This cry has to sound around the world in unison: "Never again war! We women demand peace!"

You have given birth to your sons so that they might love and not hate, build and not destroy—not bring misery and a curse upon the world but work cooperatively to enable every person to have a dignified existence. You have not given birth to your sons for war, for employing violence, but so that they might participate in the important international work of peace. The enemy of the German is not the Frenchman, the Englishman, the Russian, the Italian, nor the citizen of any other nation; and the German is not the enemy of other nations. We all are and should be brothers and sisters of a loving Father who is in heaven, who lets the sun rise on the good and the bad, and rain fall on the just and unjust, and who teaches all, whatever their nationality, to pray, "Our Father . . ." And mothers, these your sons whose hands you fold, teaching them to pray the "Our Father" on their knees, these your sons—on the cold command of international capitalism—are to be forced by a few power- and profit-hungry men to be always prepared to murder on command and to sacrifice their life.

Girls! Women! Mothers! Don't you know what our God commands? "You shall not, you may not kill" commands Christ the Lord, who predicted that all who wield the sword will die by the sword. International capital and international leaders, however, command, "Your sons must kill and sacrifice their lives if we wish and order it." And even the churches administer the oath by which your sons swear to the heavens that they will blindly kill on command.

Girls! Women! Mothers! Don't you know that you must obey God more than human beings? Therefore, shout so that all men in the world can hear it, shout so that it resounds throughout the earth, "Never again war! The women of the world demand peace."

Shout so that all men on Earth hear: "The horrendous amount of money you men spend for armaments, without asking us women, should instead be used to eradicate poverty. We do not need gunpowder and bullets, but bread; not cannons and machine guns, but plows and scythes; not barracks, but family homes; not warships and warplanes, but the opportunity to work. We do not need poison gas bombs and hand grenades but everything necessary to lead a dignified life with our loved ones."

Shout louder and louder, "You world leaders, you responsible men in all countries, first of all, fulfill your primary and most sacred duty—taking care of the poor and those whose existence is endangered. And if you seriously want to do this, all available time, labor, and resources will be needed for the works of social welfare. Thus there will be no more time, workers, or money to produce all the advanced instruments used for organized slaughter of human beings and for destruction. We no longer permit that our nation's sons have to swear an oath in churches to commit mass murder on command, but all of us want only to seek the kingdom of God and his righteousness. Then, as Jesus promised, everything else will be added on.

"We women have to tell you men that no modern war between civilized states may claim to be a 'just defensive war,' because which of today's states or governments can claim that it never gave any cause to the entanglements of war?"

Therefore, regardless of what men who flirt with violence and military preparedness may say, you women must shout: "Never again war! We women demand peace."

The expression "total war" should be sufficient for you to shout with conviction into the faces of all who support war everywhere and who agitate for it with the spoken word and in books and in the press: "There is no right of self-defense in total war—assuming that this right even exists—because total war is about destruction, and against this we women and mothers have to rise up from our innermost being. For a woman does not give birth to her children so that they are killed but that they live."

Of course, there are women who are in favor of war and want to place the entire women's world into the service of war—as, for example, the Nazi Reich Women's Leader, Gertrud Scholtz-Klink. The lead article of the *Grazer Tagespost* of May 22, 1944, cited an excerpt from the speech she gave on that Mother's Day, which had the theme "Mothers, you are the support of the fatherland." Frau Scholtz-Klink—we do not know whether she has sons who were forced to risk their lives at the front—dared to say to the German mothers,

> Mothers are giving life twice. Once when as young women they give birth, and today when they continue to sacrifice life, doing both for their fatherland. They are giving their sons for a newly created Europe, just as they once bore their own pains for Germany. However, what they are sacrificing today is incomparably

> harder than the labor pains they once suffered because at the end of that pain there was a life they could hold, while today the mother is left empty-handed and has to console herself that there is something great behind those empty hands, the supra-personal life of her nation. This is the most difficult sacrifice a mother can make, and it does not start when she is notified that he to whom she gave life was killed by the enemy. Actually, her sacrifice began the moment she first saw him in his soldier's uniform. It was then that she consciously gave him up to his nation . . . But from then on she always subconsciously worried about her son and felt that at any moment he would be demanded of her forever. Thus, the moment she is notified that the sacrifice she made over and over has become irreversible is only the conclusion of an inner willingness, present from the beginning, out of which develop the bravest and strongest pillars of our nation.

Then Frau Scholtz-Klink turned to the mothers who had borne children or were continuing to do so during the war:

> As different as are the terror of bombs and the bearing of children, as urgent is it, especially with the increasing severity of the war, to call for children and willing mothers to look beyond themselves. The longer the war becomes and the more the enemy lets us know his determination to destroy, the more fanatic must be our determination to live and persevere. And since even in times of peace—when the Führer honored me by decorating me with a "Mother's Cross"[20]—we talked about the woman as the mother of the nation, the harshness of the war teaches us that—being aware, fully responsible, and looking to the future—we alone are faced with the decision which no one can take from us. The ultimate meaning of this war and the heroic struggle of our men and brothers is to guarantee the existence of our nation for eternity. . . . There is no other way for a nation to guarantee its eternal existence than the engagement of its mothers and soldiers with their own blood.

So much for Mrs. Scholtz-Klink and the many others everywhere who share her views.

German mothers: Permit me to tell you something. First of all, it is our observation that you do not seem to have sensed the highly unreasonable demand and grave insult Frau Scholtz-Klink directed against you in her heartless Mother's Day speech. For if you had been fully conscious of these, you, who desire to be good mothers, should have risen up united and

20. *Mutterkreuz*

protested loudly. Sadly, this did not happen. Please let me explain to you this unreasonable demand Frau Scholtz-Klink made of you German women and mothers and how exactly you were insulted.

Frau Scholtz-Klink, who spoke to you about your duty from the viewpoint of National Socialism, claimed nothing less than that you have no other function than to give many children to the German nation—no, not the German nation (we were then living in a totalitarian state) but to its *Führer*, who arbitrarily controlled life and death and all possessions of the German people, and to the Nazi party. These children would grow up and be used as cannon fodder by those ruling our nation, whenever they wished to wage war.

Frau Scholtz-Klink, who because of her National Socialist outlook regards German girls and mothers only as breeding machines to serve the war, expects that you agree and will be always ready to let your sons be slaughtered on the battlefields like millions of others. Especially during a war should you bring many children into the world so that subsequent generations can again fight wars. Frau Scholtz-Klink audaciously maintains, "The ultimate meaning of this war and the heroic struggle of our men and brothers is to guarantee the existence of our nation for eternity." And "there is no other way for a nation to secure its eternal existence than the commitment of its mothers and soldiers with their own blood."

In other words: You women must diligently bear children—it does not matter who fathers them—for there must be children so that the National Socialists in power in Germany at the time can always wage wars and so guarantee the existence of our nation for "eternity." This means that the "eternity" of our nation should be guaranteed by constant warfare, that is, by the continual sacrifice of millions of your sons! For, according to the view held by Frau Scholtz-Klink, the eternal existence of a nation demands nothing but continually to bear children and to sacrifice the sons on the battlefields.

We conscientious objectors now ask the German women and mothers: According to Frau Scholtz-Klink's exacting demand, do you really want to bring children into the world so that your sons can bleed to death in horrible pain on the battlefield, while those children who are still too young for the front are destroyed by bombs? Do you really believe that this guarantees the continued existence of our nation?

It is true that it is a noble calling to give life to children, one that cannot be valued highly enough. We know that every nation whose families do not have an average of four or five children unfailingly dies out. However, if every ten years, as has been the case in the last decades, of these four or five children one or two—and usually the healthiest and most prolific—are sacrificed to the monster that is war, how should the existence of a nation be guaranteed in the long run? In face of these facts, does your bearing children even make sense?

Therefore, we have to say that either Scholtz-Klink is right—but then it is indeed senseless and most unfortunate to bring children into the world so that one after another can bleed to death on the battlefield—or she is not right, and then you German women and mothers, without fail, have to become passionate opponents of war and work to achieve the kind of social, economic, and political conditions that enable you and your children to live happily in peace. Every woman and every mother who is for war is endangering the happiness of her children and risking the existence of her nation.

Mothers, you uphold the fatherland—not the kind the grim Nazi Reich Women's Leader, Gertrud Scholtz-Klink, has in mind, but the fatherland envisioned by every healthy, reasonable, and especially, every truly Christian person, namely, a fatherland that does not heartlessly, relentlessly sacrifice millions of its children to war, but one where families can lead a dignified and happy existence in peace and can rejoice over their life. True women and mothers gladly dispense with being decorated with the "Mother Cross" by one or another insane and criminal "Führer." Even without such a decoration they will joyfully give children to the fatherland, but only when the men in power finally cease to prepare for and wage war. For to preserve life in order to let it be destroyed constantly by the arbitrary decisions of a few ambitious or mentally inferior but all the more brutal men is contrary to all healthy emotions, especially those of women and mothers. Therefore, a nation of sound mind that is serious about the continuation of its existence will reject with indignation all those women and mothers who share the opinions of Gertrud Scholtz-Klink.

If men, influenced by antiquated, calcified ways of thinking passed on through the generations, do not want to realize this, the women will have to shout even louder and more forcefully, "Never again war! We women demand peace!" Christian women, especially, must do so because, as the British Brigadier General Crozier stated, "In war, a Christian country ceases to be Christian. Christ's message of peace has nothing to do with war. War is a compromise with the devil."

You girls and women will become apostles and champions of peace, not because your mouth cries out, "Never again war! We women demand peace!" but only because you actually perform the works of peace. First of all you have to oppose and destroy the enemies of the social, economic, and political order within yourselves; if you do this, we will have peace. Every woman should unrelentingly insist on this in her family and thereby continually promote peace and work for it.

Therefore, you girls and women, if you are serious about demanding peace, you have to take a stand against the enemies of the social order. You must oppose alcohol, the vice of tobacco, sexual immorality in all its forms, luxury, antisocial fashion, religious and civic hypocrisy, injustice, exploitation, hate, and the pursuit of power.

If you could only succeed in getting rid of alcohol and tobacco in the German Reich, the German people would save about 7.5 billion *Reichsmark* annually. What could be done for the people with this money! How many homes could be built! How many families could be established because people would not have to prevent the birth of children or to abort them! And if all the billions spent each year in the world for armaments and war—and, furthermore, the money spent for immoral entertainment, for luxury, for fashion—were devoted to social welfare and the prevention of poverty, high unemployment, hate, and envy would soon be banished and the international atmosphere thereby decontaminated. The German people are burdened annually with 4.5 billion *Reichsmark* for armaments and war expenditures, including reparations.

Therefore, if you women honestly and sincerely want peace, then prepare for peace. Work for the right of every person to have a dignified existence—and do not talk so much about it but go to work without delay. Start with yourself and then, by work and example, win over others to a simple, natural, and sensible lifestyle in which the vegetarian way of life plays an important role. Who could do this better than women?

Therefore, women of all nations, women of all beliefs, women of all political parties, I beseech you by your maternal nature to unite into a single great world organization with the cry of "Never again war! We women demand peace!"

This means, first of all, that you speak up in your own country on behalf of the poor, the victims, and those deprived of their rights. Then tear down the walls of the senseless national hatreds, abolish the terrible class war, and everywhere take each other's hands to create a great world organization of women with this motto on its banners: "A dignified existence for every single member of every nation." Struggle relentlessly, first of all, against the seeking of pleasure, capitalism, communism, and everything that causes disorder.

This is the way to peace and understanding among nations. It means to prepare for peace. As mothers, it is in your hands to instill a true attitude of peace in your children, in your sons. As housewives, it is in your hands to create a sensible, natural lifestyle for your families and thereby contribute to the social and economic betterment of the nations.

As companions of your husbands, you should use the ability and energy God gave you to influence your men concerning your demand "Never again war!" This is how you can be true apostles of peace. You should discover in yourselves the eternally feminine that attracts us men, as the poet says. In your hearts must flare up the fire of that true and genuine love that enables you to create a pleasant and loving home for your husband and children, because the question of war and peace is ultimately decided in the bosom of the family. Men have no right to decide this question without you. War concerns you as a woman as much as it does the man—and you as a mother even more than the man.

If all women and girls seriously opposed war and championed this idea to their men, persistently and unyieldingly, in their words and by example—as did the high-minded Frau Bertha von Suttner, who coined the expression "Never again war"—then the problem of war would soon be solved and their demand for peace realized. And if, in particular, women and girls of all nations, conscious of the honor and dignity of women, avoided associating with soldiers—instead of celebrating them as heroes and literally throwing themselves at them—then the world of men would put an end to this stupid militarism.

Unfortunately, a significant number of our German women and girls conducted themselves dishonorably and behaved in an undignified manner in relation to the Allied soldiers who occupied our Austria after World War II. This should make one ashamed to be a German. An American officer of the occupation troops said, "It took us six years to conquer you, but only six months to make your girls and young women accommodating." Therefore, those women and girls who kept their honor and dignity deserve to be thanked even more.

There will be wars as long as the women of the world do not earnestly desire and strive for peace. What we have to say now sounds harsh. The two world wars prove that the women of the countries that waged war did not fulfill their responsibilities to their families and their nation.[21]

21. The *Neue Steirische Zeitung* (Graz), on November 21, 1945, reported that American women are supporting conscription and are even calling for the establishment of a female army corps and women's navy reserve in peacetime. The report stated, "Representatives of three women's organizations declared to a Congressional committee for military affairs that the majority of women desire general military training for their sons. These three organizations are the Federation of Women's Organizations, the National Organization of Women Lawyers, and the Citizens' Committee for National Military Training. Erneste Barlow, vice-president of the Citizens' Committee, said that women support military training first for the defense of the nation, and secondly, for the benefits it has for its young people. The American Association of University Women is urgently calling for the permanent establishment of a female army corps and

Finally, I am taking you women to the battlefields in the east, the west, the north, and the south. All of Europe is one huge cemetery, and every year on All Souls' Day, over mountains and valleys, bells ring out the sorrowful *memento mori*: "remember that you will die." Then silent sorrow again arises in the land, and many tears are shed in faithful memory of the beloved dead who took each other's lives out there in such a gruesome manner, year after year, with the assistance of technology and when ordered by a few men. And now comes winter and spreads its white shroud over the millions of graves of the fallen, who opposed each other as enemies without having known one another while alive. A poet expressed these ideas in the following stanzas:

> The snow is spreading
> Over blood and sorrow.
> No hate or curse can penetrate the shroud.
> Now friend and foe, alike in death,
> Lie here united.
>
> Brothers, "Fratricide!"
> Continues to echo far and wide.
> The sorrow-filled bells
> Give out a shivering sound
> And heaven shudders
> At what it sees here on Earth.

I feel as though I heard the millions who fell on the battlefields call out from their graves with one voice, "Do not follow your inclination to retaliation, vengeance, or hate, but to mercy and love!" At the graves of the fallen soldiers—in good faith they performed their dreadful duty, which in reality they should not have done because the right to kill does not exist, and therefore neither does the duty to kill—you women and girls should vow, "Never again war! We women demand peace. We shall not rest until there is peace." This is the deeply felt conviction of the American journalist Dorothy

---

a women's navy reserve in peacetime."

Author's note: If American women had experienced the horrors of World War II, they would undoubtedly condemn universal military service. After the killing and destruction of that war, whoever supports conscription because of "the benefits it has for its young people" and even calls for a women's army corps is either morally impaired or a sadist. Or do American women consider war a sporting event at which they want to compete with men? The seven thousand girls and women of Salzburg who, forgetting their honor and dignity as women, became involved with American soldiers and are expecting children should make American women think again about a female military corps.

Thompson, who directed the following appeal to the United Nations Security Council in the name of all mothers:

> Gentlemen of the United Nations Security Council, I would like to share my opinion and ask you sincerely to listen to me. You asked us to give you our sons in order to save the world. We gave you our sons. Some of them are dead, some are blind, some walk without feet, and others work without hands. And each one of them was more precious to us than the whole world. When our sons left, we prayed. This prayer was silent, but its ripples spread all over the world. They rose from the air raid shelters of London and Coventry, Plymouth and Bristol, just as from the darkness of Vienna and Berlin. They echoed in the rubble of Kiev, just as in LeHavre and Chungking. We believed you, gentlemen; we believed in a beautiful future. Our sons died so that this good world could exist. Yet now, once again, there is talk about war and disputes over the most frightening weapon of war ever invented.
>
> Gentlemen, everywhere on this earth people are living and are connected with one another. These families of all nations, regions, and spheres, regardless of whether their skin is white, brown, or yellow, are praying for peace. But your peace, gentlemen, seems to us more terrible than was the war.
>
> Talk to us about law, freedom, equality of rights, love of neighbor, and grace, and translate these great concepts into practicality. While you are talking and devising plans, millions of mothers and children are close to death by starvation. These are the children of allies and of enemies. However, we mothers do not know any children who are enemies.
>
> Gentlemen, some of you are Christians—your mothers taught you the Holy Scriptures. They taught you to pray: "Make me into a good boy," and not, "Make me into a world leader." To be good is the only source of all power that heals and helps and is the enemy of all violence that destroys.
>
> We mothers constitute half of the human race. We were put into this world to think about what it means to be truly human, to practice it, to teach it, and to protect it. This is the world given to us by nature and by God. We are the largest International of the world. We speak the same language, from Chungking to Moscow and from Berlin to New York.
>
> Gentlemen, I am warning you. Put away your cannons! Then we will show you that the healing powers of the world are not in earth and fire, not in cold reason, but in the everlasting power of the indestructible force of love.

7. The League of Nations and the World Court of Arbitration

In the collection *Catholic Voices against War*,[22] the theologian Don Sturzo counters the view held by many Catholic moral theologians and teachers of ethics that under certain circumstances a war is not preventable but is necessary—namely, the case of a "just defensive war."

Sturzo denied this and pointed to the then existing League of Nations, which was dedicated to resolving conflicts by arbitration. He was right because to all nations with goodwill was available the power of arbitration of the League of Nations—which at this time no longer exists but has already been revived in a new form in the United Nations Organization—as a means of achieving a bloodless, nonviolent resolution to conflict so that a settlement with weapons is unnecessary, which means that nations can no longer use war as the last resort (*ultima ratio*) of settling conflicts.

Therefore, today all wars are unjust—this also agrees with Catholic teaching—because the "necessity" to wage war, required by Catholic supporters of war, no longer exists. For this reason alone a "just defensive war" can no longer exist today—and therefore conscientious objection has become an international duty.

Besides that, settling conflicts with lethal weapons is never an appropriate means of deciding what is just or unjust. For, in light of the incredible refinement and advances in armaments technology, every sensible person must admit that, apart from everything else, the prerequisites demanded by those who support a "just defensive war" are no longer applicable—for example, that the good to be gained by the war must undeniably surpass the damages and horrors it would cause. Let us think only about the atom bomb.

Modern war—which, alarmingly, has grown into total war, with the only goal being to forestall the enemy by completely destroying him first—surpasses all boundaries of self-defense. In total war, the attacker and the attacked vie with each other to produce superior weapons, each trying to get ahead of the enemy, that is, to surpass him in the thoroughness and speed of killing and destruction.

However, if there actually is a victor because he was able to endure longer, had more and better weapons and more soldiers, this still does not prove that the victorious nation—or nations—has justice on its side, while the conquered one does not.

22. *Katholische Stimmen gegen den Krieg.*

The wounds and damages inflicted by both sides in a total war are unspeakably, immeasurably extensive, and most of them can never be redressed. Both the victor and the vanquished emerge from total war weakened, and the subsequent "peacetime" is only a time of truce; both are using it to prepare for the next war by devising even more extensive and superior armaments with which to outdo the opponent, intending to wage the next total war even more totally. It is a vicious circle!

So, why do nations fight if war proves nothing but that the side that has superior weapons and is more violent and cunning destroys the less violent, inferiorly armed and less cunning? We already know this, without a war.

However, because conflicts—which do not always result in war—continually break out between nations (just as between individuals), everything depends on settling these justly by means of rational negotiations. For mutual violence in the form of war is in no way suitable to determine which state or states have justice on their side. Only reflective reason is capable of deciding that, after evaluating the situation and all circumstances, provided the willingness exists to adhere to the most rigorous demands of justice.

Reason guides the negotiations on the path of rational reflection. Of course, whoever holds the view "*sic volo, sic jubeo, stat pro ratione voluntas*" (thus I will, thus I order; my will stands, not reason) proves that he is not capable of rational reflection and negotiation. If a government holds this view and if the citizens submit to such an approach, they have to put up with war, the consequence of such a method. Unfortunately, since World War II the peace negotiators of the victorious nations have been operating for three years under the above motto, even if it has been a mere "veto." Therefore peace is no closer today than before.

However, all who condemn war and want to prevent it, having had enough of militarism, will joyfully welcome with us the fact that humanity has already attempted to create institutions to resolve warlike entanglements peacefully, by arbitration—in the League of Nations in Geneva, in the World Court at The Hague, and, finally, in the United Nations Organization. Even though the League of Nations was far from what it should have been, its concept can and should be improved. It is our hope that the United Nations Organization will be the appropriate institution to settle conflicts between states peacefully. However, this will only be the case if God's Ten Commandments form the basis for its negotiations.

One would think that the governments of all nations would have joyfully welcomed the League of Nations or similar organizations working cooperatively and would have tried to develop these into useful instruments of peace. Yet several states that joined the League of Nations have already withdrawn from it. In the Nazi Reich, which also seceded—almost with a curse—a certain Ottheinrich Schoetensack commented, "The weapons of the Tripartite Powers will see to it that the experiment of the League of Nations, which has been a complete failure and served only the aspirations to hegemony of a few powers, will never be resurrected in any form."[23]

The Tripartite Powers (Germany, Italy, and Japan) were actually afraid of an association of nations because they realized that an ideal league was possible. Instead of the ill-fated League in Geneva, the nations of the world can and should continue to make a sincere effort to establish an ideal institution to guarantee peace on the basis of mutual understanding without weapons.

From the start, however, the Tripartite Powers did not want to give up the use of lethal weapons and went so far as to view the attempt to create a model association of nations with powers of arbitration as a reason to get involved in war. In view of the Fascist, National Socialist, and Japanese ideologies, the rejection of the League by Italy, Germany, and Japan was quite logical, because their ideologies would have had to be repudiated the day these states sincerely approved of the League of Nations.

All of the other nations of the world have to change ideologically and ethically if they want to be sincere members of the United Nations, since this organization can only be effective in settling conflicts nonviolently if its member states renounce every kind of lethal weapon—that is, if they earnestly disarm and end the thrice-cursed militarism, that is, if they try honestly to battle against all causes that could lead to a violent settlement of conflicts.

Yet, since the United Nations does not renounce the use of weapons but rather espouses an "armed peace," we cannot consider this organization an appropriate means to establish true peace but are convinced that it will lamentably fail, according to Christ's words: "He who wields the sword will perish by the sword."

Therefore, everything depends on persuading all nations of the world to unite in an alliance—it is not important what it is called—in order to achieve in international affairs the victory of justice, with ethical means and without the use of weapons. Every member state has to pledge at the start to turn immediately to this alliance when conflicts arise between nations and to earnestly submit to the decision of the court of arbitration. This presupposes that the member states outlaw war and, consequently, abolish conscription and armaments. It goes without saying that only the most capable and ethically high-minded men should be chosen to serve on the court of arbitration, men who are able to decide what is just and what is unjust, who

23. *Tagespost*, Graz, December 17, 1943.

are incorruptible, and who are willing to reach the best decision according to their conscience.

Nations that refuse to cooperate to establish and develop such an alliance with binding arbitration powers would by their refusal only demonstrate that they do not want to give up waging war. The more states of the world unite, the more difficult it would be for those still resorting to war to make their influence felt and to disturb the international peace because these resisting, armed states would soon experience the effects of the sanctions with which the association of nations can and must enforce compliance with the judgments of its court of arbitration.

However, these sanctions should never consist in a military attack by the association of nations—as, unfortunately, some supporters of the idea of such an organization advocate and the United Nations is planning to translate into reality. A league of nations that, despite its powers of arbitration, maintains an army and believes in an "armed peace" capitulates because it does what it seeks to prevent: fight a war. The devil can never be driven out by Beelzebub. An alliance of nations can only be beneficial and will only enjoy the confidence of all nations if it completely foregoes violence with lethal weapons and, instead of brutal force, allows the superiority of the mind to govern by means of negotiations, based on justice and the love of neighbor, and sincerely strives, with the cooperation of all member nations, to oppose the causes leading to war.

The sanctions this organization would establish should only be those coercive measures that do not contradict the guidelines of the noncooperation and nonresistance movement we outlined earlier. Here we are thinking primarily of all measures that make armaments and war impossible for any state that resists. For example, no food, raw materials, means of transportation, or credits would be allowed to enter such a state—that is, everything that directly or indirectly serves armaments or war; also, all contacts with its population would be broken off. By being economically and socially ostracized, nations wanting to wage war have to be encircled and isolated from relations with all other member states until they realize that they are wrong and are ready to sincerely join the association of nations.

Above all, the task of this alliance would be not only to settle existing conflicts justly but also to prevent them in the first place. To accomplish this, the organization should strive to establish a systematically regulated world economy in which the production, distribution (trade), and consumption of everything needed for a dignified existence for all people would be achieved according to individual and social justice. Here the alliance would have to observe without fail the principles held by opponents of war if it wanted to be effective in its lofty mission of promoting and maintaining peace and preventing wars and other conflicts.

Yet this international organization should be not only the economic center—that is, the heart of the world economy—but also an agent for the exchange of culture, thus enabling the nations and peoples of the world to come closer to one another. The result of this work would be a world federation of nations.

Above all, the alliance of nations should work unceasingly to enlighten the peoples of the world in the spirit that desires peace and opposes war. We believe that this educational work should be its first and most urgent task, and it is especially called to do this work because it would have the means and energy of all nations. The ideas presented in this book should be disseminated at all times—by the written and oral word, especially by radio—to peoples of all regions and languages. If today meetings, newspapers, radio, and film are used everywhere with tremendous success, should it not be possible and imperative to use all means of communication to make people happy?

Another task for the organization would be to establish a common language that would be most valuable for fostering peaceful relations among nations.

However, as long as the most powerful countries believe that they can force their will on the smaller ones, a true alliance is impossible because in such an organization all nations should be equal, as demanded by natural law.

Such an alliance would literally bless all peoples of the world. The nations and races that were tormented and trampled upon during the Second World War, especially, would be revived and would thank God if all states were finally relieved of the unbearable burden of militarism, and if everything that heretofore has been sacrificed to the monster war were to be used for peaceful development and mutual understanding. It would be almost too beautiful if this were to come true, but it is not utopian. It could be realized immediately if the nations and their governments seriously wished it, and would be the start and basis for the realization of the new age that Micah and Isaiah prophesied.

It is not mere empty talk that we, the world's opponents of war and friends of peace, are always ready to work, as far as is in our power, so that this ideal association of nations will soon be established.

8. Democracy as the best form of government for true politics of peace

From the Christian perspective every form of government, whether monarchy, republic, or oligarchy, is recognized and legitimate as long as the purpose of the state is realized, namely, to attain the general welfare with ethical means. It actually does not depend on the form of government whether the citizens keep peace with one another and with their neighbors. Peace can and should be guaranteed by every form of government guided by natural law.

However, looking at it objectively, the democratic form of government seems to us the most appropriate to secure and guarantee peace—but, of course, only if the democracy is what it should be according to natural and moral law and Christian teaching. We dare to declare this even though democracies are outlawed by fascism, National Socialism, and every other dictatorial system and completely condemned or made impossible by autocratic actions.

Unfortunately, all democracies today are also materialistic, armed to the hilt, and make use of brute force, just as the dictatorial autocratic states; and capitalism, which has been and always will be the main harbinger of war, as we explained earlier, rules over all the world. Today's democracies are not true democracies as they should be according to natural law and Christian requirements. Ultimately, it depends on the people who call themselves democratic whether they truly are or only appear to be democratic. However, we believe that the democratic system of government is much more suited to achieve and guarantee peace than the structures of government of so-called authoritarian states.

The following explanation should show why we consider democracy a protector of peace. Not that by favoring democracy we are condemning or characterizing as inferior monarchy or any other type of government, but the democratic constitution and form of government offers better prerequisites and greater possibilities for effective peace politics than nondemocratic systems.

In a democracy the people themselves, every single citizen, hold joint power with their freely elected representatives, while in states with a dictatorial-autocratic form of government all of the authority is held by a single individual or a small group of people so that the will—or, more accurately, the arbitrary action—of an individual or a few persons can decide for peace or for war; the entire population is unconditionally at the their mercy with their life and their possessions. For years we experienced the terrors of such a rule by unrestrained dictators and know what it means to be robbed of every personal freedom.

If, however, the entire population is granted the right to decide for war or peace, an abuse of authority is not as easy. In a democracy, every citizen shares in the responsibility for the general welfare, and in exercising his right to govern, every citizen also decides about his own welfare or woe. If an election is held in a democracy, the prevailing views and opinions have first to be weighed in careful deliberation before a final decision is reached. An individual human being who alone has the power to make a decision can err much more easily, especially if—and this already has been the case—he is mentally impaired, possessed by megalomania, or lacks the necessary preparation to govern. Such a man, because of his arbitrariness or mistakes, is more likely to cause more irreparable damage than if millions of people with shared responsibility were to reach a decision in joint deliberation.

A monarch, a dictator—whether he is called a Führer or something else—who alone makes decisions is usually much quicker in reaching them because he is totally unimpeded and not bound by time-consuming deliberations. Thus he is at an advantage where quick action is required, whereas democracy slows down the decision-making process because so many people are involved, which can be disadvantageous. What is lost in speed is made up in thoroughness, however, especially in significant matters that affect the entire population, such as decisions about war and peace.

Since we are only concerned here with showing the relationship of democracy to war and peace, or, in one word, to militarism, the following basic considerations in favor of democracy carry considerable weight. Democracy demands a thorough civic education of all citizens, of men and women, because every person, by contributing to the general welfare, always has to deliberate and vote about how the matter affects him. Through such an education the entire adult population achieves an ever greater civic maturity and sense of responsibility for all public issues that either benefit or harm the individual citizen. True democratic actions require a democratic conviction that is in agreement with God's Ten Commandments. If each citizen is included in the decision whether the nation should arm and wage war, each person has to consider well whether he should and will freely and gladly sacrifice his life and hard-earned possessions for his country.

As a result of having responsibly reflected, the individual citizen will very likely leave no stone unturned to prevent a war from breaking out since his own life and property are at stake. However, it is much easier for one person or a small group ruling without restriction to decide for war, because they are able to stay safe at home and do not have to risk their lives. Also, as shareholders of the armaments industry they expect extraordinarily high profits from the war. The dictator, the monarch, or the Führer need to institute universal military service in order to force his "subjects," his "Volk," to commit the mass murder he decided upon and organized.

Since in a democracy personal freedom, free speech, and political rights are jealously guarded and defended, and since without these a democracy would be impossible, it would be very strange if the citizens of a truly democratic state suddenly, unanimously, and voluntarily sacrificed their personal freedom and relinquished their right to make decisions about the matter of conscription. This would be an incomprehensible self-enslavement at the cost of personal freedom. If, however, the citizens in a democracy make a rash decision that they later regret, they always have the right to rescind it in a new election.

For example, if the issue is whether the nation should arm and wage war, every citizen is able to consider carefully whether he should vote for or against militarization or war. He is able to decide which powers he will grant to his elected representatives and which ones he will reserve to himself. He will not willingly assume burdens he cannot or does not wish to carry, unless they are sacrifices that, in view of the general welfare, are required by natural law.

How much a citizen in a democratic state is to be envied, compared with the subjects in a dictatorial-autocratic state where each person, robbed of every freedom, is blind and uncritical and at the mercy of the arbitrariness of his "Führer." Every citizen in a democratic nation is a master, a ruler, while in an authoritarian state he is a miserable slave, a human being who is condemned to servile submission and silence, who has nothing whatsoever to say but has to do only what the Führer commands. However, woe to him who resists or wants to think differently than the Führer! The concentration camps, the prisons, the dungeons, the executions without respite, the expropriations, and the violent encroachments into all areas of life cry out loudly throughout the world what freedom means in authoritarian states.

In the face of such undeniable facts, one should suppose that every thinking person would without hesitation decide for democracy and would help, with ethical means—with the weapons of nonviolence that we described earlier—so that the authoritarian states, or more correctly, the slave states, would be eliminated. This is possible because those who govern are elected by the people and can only remain in office with the latter's consent. Unfortunately, this saying often proves to be true: "Only the most stupid cattle choose their own butcher."

For example, did not the German population in Austria, in frenzied jubilation, elect its Führer, in the person of Adolf Hitler, and freely and enthusiastically deliver itself up to him, for better or for worse? This proved to be ruinous. A true democrat does not do this. Unfortunately, most people do not have this democratic spirit but instead are servile, and of their own free will choose slavery under a Führer, whatever his name.

Instead of proudly making their own decisions, especially regarding war and peace, these unfortunate people leave such an important decision, which profoundly affects each one of them, to a Führer, a single individual, and probably even thank him for robbing them of their own will. They are at his mercy, for better or for worse. Even in today's democracies, dictatorship is more or less present. There is no true, ideal democracy in the world today. Willingly, without protesting, the "subjects" plod on, with their body, life, and belongings, as commanded from above. There is no help for such people and such nations. They should not even be pitied, and they should not complain about the fate they chose themselves or get upset when someone points out that "only the stupidest cattle choose their own butcher."

Yet no human being has sunk so low that he cannot get up with the help of others. Therefore, with the right kind of enlightenment, it is possible, in the course of time, to impart democratic thinking to those nations that have become apathetic and are groaning under the heavy yoke of authoritarian rule, in order to prepare them for the launching of democracy.

However, there is a huge difference between true and false democracy. All the present so-called democracies are that in name, I admit, but actually they are more or less cleverly disguised authoritarian states. The representatives have succeeded in seizing authority at the cost of the freedom of the citizens who elected them. They have been able to do so because, unfortunately, the people lack the sufficient, all-important education in the democratic form of government.

Therefore, the citizens of all nations have to be thoroughly taught their rights and duties. For to be a true democrat means to deliberately advance the public welfare with ethical means, that is, to assist in developing social, economic, domestic, and international relations according to the demands of natural law and, therefore, of Christianity. It means to assist in opposing the internal and external enemies of the general welfare; it means to regulate production and consumption according to individual and social justice; it means to provide work at a fair wage with the value of labor and compensation being equal and thus to destroy capitalism; it means to share in the responsibility for the common welfare and thereby also to abolish communism.

In a true democracy, organized and functioning according to natural law, there are unexpected possibilities for the individual to work effectively against war and on behalf of peace, that is, to eliminate violence and to educate the citizens by means of the written and spoken word.

Since the right of free expression is the most inalienable treasure of a true democracy, it will be relatively easy to champion, effectively and boldly, all of the suggestions we have made in this book about how to overcome militarism and about the unreserved observance of the commandment "You shall not kill," and to make these an object of a constant public exchange of ideas.

Whoever would try this in an autocratic state, however, could be killed, so huge is the chasm between an autocratic and a truly democrat state. In the former, the state exists for the sake of the state and its government, despite every high-sounding assurance and all talk about freedom, while in the latter the state exists for the sake of its citizens; in the former a man is slave and servant, a blind instrument in the hands of autocratic leaders, but in the latter he is a free and self-confident citizen, a jointly responsible and active promoter and guardian of the general welfare.

We are deeply convinced that in a truly democratic state a "Stalingrad" would be impossible, but it would be possible in an autocratic state, and also in a democracy controlled by capitalism and communism. It is simply unthinkable that the truly politically enlightened citizens of a genuine democratic nation could be as heartless and brutal as, for example, an Adolf Hitler, who caused the death of 250,000 soldiers in Stalingrad, besides the millions of human beings who were murdered by the Gestapo and the SS (*Schutzstaffel*) troops he sanctioned. This man, who ordered all Jews in the German Reich to be slaughtered in the most cold-blooded manner and caused every opponent to be eliminated, who raged insanely among Poles, Frenchmen, Yugoslavs, and other peoples, from whose hands dripped the blood of murdered millions, who hurled the torch of war across the world and made eighty-five million Germans subservient to his ambitions—to retrospectively call this man an insane criminal does not save the German people and the nations allied with her from the accusation of complicity in these abominable deeds. The German people, including those in Austria, freely elected Hitler as their leader, endured him for twelve years without opposition, often even applauded him, and remained silent about all his crimes or even approved them. A truly democratic Germany would have been spared all of this.

If, however, in the interest of justice, we accuse the German people—to whom we also belong—of complicity, we cannot fail to note that many other peoples were complicit in the horrible deeds and bloodshed caused by their governments during and after the last war.

Because every human institution can be misused even in a democracy, the danger of a demagogue rising to power exists. The demagogue finds an effective adversary only in a true democrat, just as the various political parties in a democracy monitor each other and can (and should) see to it that the interests of political parties are not placed above those of the state.

Yet there has never been a true, completely democratic state. However, by means of continuous civic education it will be possible to pave the way among nations to democratic principles. In the existing democracies, we the opponents of war would do well to let men and women who are true democrats represent our interests. Unfortunately, the authoritarian states are, to a greater or lesser extent, closed to us, but will become accessible to the degree the democratic spirit awakens.[24]

9. Peace as the result of observing the cosmic order

ON ONE HAND, PEACE is consequence, on the other, cause. Peace is consequence inasmuch as it is the result of human actions that are in accordance with natural law and ethics. For only if human beings observe natural and ethical laws in everything they do is the order and harmony established and desired by God the Creator kept, which constitutes peace. Peace is cause in that as a permanent condition in a society it is the prerequisite that, as an image of God, each human being is able to lead a dignified existence, is happy and content, and can enjoy the fruits of his labor in peace.

If true peace is to reign on earth, the cosmic order created and desired by God has to be maintained everywhere. Every disturbance of this order causes disorder and strife, which devastatingly affect all aspects of people's lives the greater and more lasting they are. For the story of creation describes in a way a child can understand how out of the existing chaos, God, step by step, fashioned the wonderful cosmos, consisting of the most varied species, which, in order to live and function, are all dependent upon each other and systematically incorporated into the harmoniously regulated system of natural law. For human beings, who are gifted with freedom, moral law is added to natural law in order to guide them on how to preserve the entire

24. Even in our "free" and "democratic" Republic of Austria the police prohibited the Austrian Peace Society (*Friedensgesellschaft*) from holding a public debate about a proposed law to reinstitute conscription.

cosmic order. "God saw all he had made, and indeed it was very good" (Gen 1:31). These words conclude the story of creation. They proclaim that the cosmos created by God is a unified whole in which there is complete peace and the most splendid harmony.

As the Bible's first chapters tell us, God connected man's happiness with the observance of the natural law and moral law in the operation of the cosmos. Therefore, peace is the result, the consequence, and the effect of the cosmic order observed by human beings.

The Bible tells us further that man violated this order in paradise by acting against God's will. By this disobedience, the first sin, in the cradle of humanity, the cosmic order was seriously violated, so that peace and harmony were thoroughly disturbed. From then on, disease, misery, sterility, failure, death, murder, war, and destruction have been the constant companions of human beings, because they incessantly disturb the cosmos by ever more sins and violations of the law of nature and the moral law.

People began to exploit the creation, sparing neither human beings, animals, and plants nor inanimate nature. Human beings have tried to make everything subservient to their many passions and disordered inclinations instead of keeping the commandment God gave them in paradise: "Be fruitful, multiply, fill the earth and subdue it. Be masters of the fish of the sea, the birds of heaven and all the living creatures that move on earth . . . Look, to you I give all the seed-bearing plants everywhere on the surface of the earth, and all the trees with seed-bearing fruit; this will be your food. And to all the wild animals, all the birds of heaven and all living creatures that creep along the ground, I give all the foliage of plants as their food" (Gen 1:28–30).

God placed man in paradise, in the garden of bliss, to cultivate and take care of it, and then commanded, "You are free to eat of all the trees in the garden. But of the tree of the knowledge of good and evil you are not to eat; for the day you eat of that, you are doomed to die" (Gen 2:16–17).

As the Holy Scriptures tell us, the first human beings ate from the forbidden tree. As soon as this sin was committed, as human beings carried out their own will in opposition to that of God, they disturbed the cosmic order and disconnected themselves from the harmonious totality of the cosmos. Almost immediately, punishment followed. God said to Adam, "Because you listened to the voice of your wife and ate from the tree of which I had forbidden you to eat, accursed be the soil because of you! Painfully will you get your food from it as long as you live. It will yield you brambles and thistles, as you eat the produce of the land. By the sweat of your face will you earn your food, until you return to the ground, as you were taken from it. For dust you are, and to dust you shall return" (Gen 3:17–19). And so

"Yahweh God expelled him from the garden of Eden, to till the soil from which he had been taken" (Gen 3:23).

Because human beings disturbed the cosmic order, the entire universe retaliates, so to speak. We have to point out that part of that order is that human beings were at the beginning told by God to nourish themselves with fruit—and, after the fall, with vegetables also—but not with animals so that man would not have to kill these in order to live. To be sure, initially, God gave human beings the most ideal and most natural nourishment, namely, fruit and, secondly, vegetables. Therefore, all our explanations concerning the great commandment "You shall not kill"—you shall not destroy life against God's sacred will—would be incomplete, as would our discussion of peace, if we did not inquire whether the commandment "You shall not kill" applied only to the life of human beings or also to the life of animals, and to a certain extent to plant life, and in a sense to the entire cosmos.

It is true that God designated human beings as rulers of all creation, but they may only claim for themselves such rights of intervention in the cosmos that do not violate the order established by God because moral law—based on natural law and reason—make it man's duty to observe the cosmic order. Man is created in the image of God, and should govern and function in God's creation only as the Creator desires. According to God's direction, the things of this world should help human beings create a dignified existence here on earth, and by obeying the moral law human beings can attain their eternal destiny.

We know from experience that people relate in one way or another to all things in the cosmos and are dependent on them. However, the moral order, perceived with their reason, and God's will, as revealed by Christ, show them how they should relate to all of creation.

Human beings, animals, and plants comprise the living creation, while everything else constitutes the inanimate creation. Man is placed into and is dependent on the three kingdoms of nature, which interact with one another. The plants take their nourishment from the soil and the air and, with the action of sunlight, change the inanimate materials into organic matter, which nourish animals and human beings.

The highest purpose of each created being is to glorify God. Since everything that has been created is the realization of God's eternal ideas, his wisdom, power, and goodness are reflected in all things. Man perceives God while observing nature, and this realization should move the reasoning human being to appreciate God freely and gladly, to honor and obey him—in a word, to be religious, which means to be connected with God.

As are human beings, animals are created by God to be happy because the latter also have perceptions, aims, consciousness, and memory and can feel pain and happiness. God desires the happiness of human beings and animals, which is also nature's design, and it is touching how God also provides for the animals, for the smallest as well for the largest. As Scripture tells us, God hears the cries of the hungry young crow; no sparrow falls from a roof without the will of the Heavenly Father; and he commands that the mouth of the threshing oxen not be tied shut.

However, God has created the animals for another purpose, namely, to serve man, to help him realize a dignified existence on earth. The use of animals by human beings should be governed by love, the kind of love that God has for every animal. Man may use but not misuse animals. Every abuse of an animal, that is, every unwarranted use that is detrimental to its pursuit of happiness, is ethically reprehensible, disrupts the cosmic order, and contradicts the Christian concept of the relationship between human beings and animals. Instead, man should, as much as he can, enable each animal to have as painless and happy an existence as possible.

Therefore, compassion for animals and their protection is not merely a matter of feelings but a sign of a noble heart aligned with the true, eternal, fatherly love that God has for them. This love cares about their well-being. The statement "the upright has compassion on his animals," which already appears in the Old Testament (Prov 12:10), is given even more importance in the New Testament, the testament of love. St. Francis of Assisi, who preached to the animals and called them brothers and sisters, who bought a lamb to keep it from being slaughtered, and who pointed out his cruelties to a wolf and admonished him to mend his ways, is a wonderful example of Christian goodwill for the silent, often helpless creatures that are often abused by humans. This ideal is given to us not only to admire but to imitate.

Certainly, some people will object that animals living in nature, left to themselves, have to bear all sorts of suffering, but this is not our fault, and most of the time we cannot change it. But if we get to the root of this matter, ultimately people are responsible for all this suffering of the animals because death, suffering, and pain entered the world as a consequence of human sin. As Scripture tells us, all of creation is groaning under the consequences of sin and is impatiently waiting for deliverance. Human beings may not subject animals that are rendering service to them to excessive pain. All torture of animals is ethically reprehensible and a sin, according to the Christian perception. Even if the purpose for inflicting pain on an animal be ever so good, it is nonetheless torture. Therefore, we have to condemn unreservedly all vivisection, even though the vivisectionists assure us a hundred times that it is necessary "in the interest of science" or "in the interest of suffering humanity." Vivisection is sadism bordering on insanity and a disgrace to our so-called culture. It is the product of a perverted inclination to do research that has become pathological, and in the majority of cases is a crime. Only morally impaired persons or criminal scoundrels could conduct this most brutal torture, to which every year millions of animals are subjected. Every form of torture of animals is indicative that a person is inferior and savage.

Those animals that human beings use to serve them should be regarded as friends and companions, as brothers and sisters, and should be treated according to their nature. This alone is ethical, is Christian. Everywhere and always, the respect of the sacredness and inviolability of life should lead man to treat reverently all living beings, including plants, because no human being can restore destroyed life. It is downright cowardly and mean if a human being claims that his mental and technical superiority gives him the right of the stronger to torture or even to kill a weak, defenseless animal.

Yet in the case of one life against the other, certainly, the life of a human beings is to be valued above that of an animal, and if an animal has to be killed, it should be done as quickly and painlessly as possible.

If someone should maintain that human beings have to eat meat and, therefore, kill animals, we would like to point out again the instructions of God to human beings concerning what to eat. He prescribed as the ideal nourishment a vegetarian diet and not one of bloody meat. The person who is a vegetarian lives doubly right, as he is expanding the commandment "You shall not kill" to include the animals.

Therefore, we may say that the vegetarian way of life—that is, doing without meat in order to preserve the life of animals and to spare them the excruciating pain of being slaughtered—is definitely a noble and ideal way that, we believe, is more consistent with the commandment to love than is a meat diet.

Whoever foregoes the eating of meat because of his compassion for animals and his respect for life—that is, for ethical reasons, apart from the great advantage of the vegetarian way of life for health and the economy—displays a nobler view of the value of the life of animals than he who orders "lampreys roasted alive" as a Baltic firm advertised. While we do not know how profitable this business was, we do know that people ordering these lampreys and the newspapers advertising them share in the responsibility that these animals were raised only to be slaughtered and subjected to gruesome pain.

In any case, the vegetarian way of life is one of the best and most effective means to comprehensively protect animals and is also very advantageous for the economy. For example, if one hectare of soil, of an average quality, is planted with fruits and vegetables, seven people can live splendidly on the harvest for a year. If grain is planted on this land, one can feed three people a year. If one operates a dairy farm, only one person can live from the products gained from each hectare. And if this area is used to raise hogs for slaughter, the meat produced will feed only one person for seventy days. Therefore, it takes five times as much land for a diet of meat than one of plant products. Also, meat protein is ten to fifteen times as expensive as plant protein.

If human beings decided to live on a vegetarian diet, the issue of protecting animals would largely be solved because it is included in the commandment to love, as only he who has true love will practice the kind of compassion toward animals that Holy Scripture commands: "The upright has compassion on his animals" (Prov 12:10). Only when true love is practiced without exception is there peace, the peace that existed in paradise between God and man, among human beings, and between humans and animals.

As for the life of plants, they have no feelings and therefore cannot experience pain. They are the lowest form of life and, according to God's design, support the life of animals and human beings. Without plants, neither animal nor human life would be possible. Because of this dependence on plants, man, as instructed by God, has to cultivate the soil, which often requires hard work.

From experience and study has come the realization that the life of plants intended for human beings is by innumerable threads connected with that of all other plants on Earth, but also with the life of animals, as well as with the soil and climate and even with the heavenly bodies. For example, it is known that the entire plant kingdom is affected by and strongly affects precipitation. Wherever man uproots vast stretches of forest, the climactic conditions, precipitation, and, therefore, the condition of the soil are adversely affected. The topsoil is flushed away and the soil loses its fertility.

The result of these experiences and studies is that man may not despoil nature. He may not senselessly destroy and exploit but should exercise his God-given right to rule over nature according to the cosmic laws, because every instance of disregarding them disrupts the entire cosmic order and will avenge itself on those who sin against this order.

Throughout history, the human addiction to profit and pleasure has caused immense and often irreparable damage to the plant and animal kingdoms as well as to inorganic matter. How many plant and animal lives have been destroyed senselessly and needlessly? How many plant and animal species has man wiped out? By deforestation man has turned vast stretches of land into deserts. Young and old, senselessly and barbarically, often destroy flowers and blossoms, so that some alpine plants have become nearly extinct. Boys catch and spear insects and butterflies; little girls run across meadows and pull up flowers only to throw them away as quickly; blasé city residents roll thoughtlessly in the lush grass of country meadows and break off branches, thus littering and defacing nature. All of these actions disrupt the cosmic order and peace that God desires in nature. And how greatly does war-waging mankind abuse all of nature's kingdoms! Human beings, animals, plants, and raw materials are all used to serve murder and destruction. Above all, the capitalistic economy subordinates the entire cosmos to the vulgar, immoral pursuit of profit at all costs, without concern whether God's cosmic order is violated by capitalistic machinations.

Everywhere there is incessant, ruthless exploitation, destruction of life, disruption of the cosmic order, and encroachment upon God's harmony in the universe; and so nowhere is there peace in the entire cosmos. The reason is that man largely uses as a criterion for his behavior toward living things and inorganic matter only his stomach, his addiction to pleasure and profit, his desire for power, and the violence of his hands. Instead, in his conduct toward the world around him, he should observe the law of nature operative in the cosmos, that is, live according to moral law. For only he acts morally who does everything according to nature's law, because whatever is according to nature also is moral. Whoever does not live in harmony with nature cannot be moral. Therefore, you must act in accord with nature in everything because then and only then will you be a true peace activist.

The protection of human beings, the protection of animals, the protection of plants, and the protection of nature should never be separated because these are mutually dependent, so that is impossible for one to exist without the protection of the others. These four kinds of protection, rooted in God and derived from him, are our obligation, lead again to God, and create the kind of perfect order in which alone peace can flourish.

Let us act in harmony with nature in everything. If we do this, we will become peacemakers and thus "blessed children of God." Everything a person does that is unreservedly directed toward the protection of human beings, animals, plants, and nature will become for him an inexhaustible source of joy and happiness, a fountain of true peace.

10. *The Anatomy of Peace*

Emery Reves wrote the book *The Anatomy of Peace*.[25] First, let us note that the title selected for this work, frankly and most unfortunately, is

25. Reves, *Die Anatomie des Friedens.*

misleading. Judging from its content, we would instead title it "To World Peace by Organizing a World Government," or, perhaps even better, "By the Relinquishment of Sovereignty by Today's Nation-States to a Federation of the World's Nations."

Reves wants to prove that the claim to sovereignty of the approximately eighty nation-states is the sole cause of wars, as the industrialization and mechanization of the global economy move peoples and nations so close together that the economies of the individual states cause conflicts of interest, and therefore wars.

From this Reves concludes that the sovereignty of each nation-state has to be surrendered to a higher institution ruled by law, a federation of states with a common government, elected by all nations, and, of course, without prejudice toward the individual nationalities, as far as they are justified by natural law. Here we refer to our *Sociology*,[26] in which we dealt thoroughly with this question.

Human nature makes the joining of families into states necessary because of the inability of individual human beings and families, separately, to attain their earthly well-being and of individuals to develop to their unlimited capacities. Neither nationality nor religion is the basis for forming states, although it cannot be denied that belonging to a certain nationality or religion facilitates the development of states.

The state never exists for itself but is only a means of establishing the general welfare. The state should exist for the people, not the people for the state. To fulfill the state's purpose, people joined into a state receive their leadership from the executive branch of the government, which has to carry out its duties justly and prudently—by protecting justice, by passing equitable laws and seeing that they are obeyed, and by creating all the necessary and beneficial institutions and support structures needed for each citizen, by his own actions and by safeguarding his own rights, to create a dignified existence for himself. The state is responsible for the general welfare, which serves the personal welfare of the citizens without discrimination.

The person or persons who hold the governing power are elected, directly or indirectly, by the people. Likewise, the people joining into a state freely determine its form of government and constitution and may alter these, if necessary. The natural law does not prescribe that the various forms of government are everlasting or unchangeable. Rather, forms of government and constitutions are positive human dynamics, not static institutions. History proves that states come and go.

26. Ude, *Soziologie*, 46–97.

As soon as the external or internal circumstances require a change of government, natural law demands that this alteration be made. This occurs if a government or constitution endangers the welfare of its citizens, the well-being of other states, or both. Natural law demands that each nation has to be considerate toward all other states. Every state has to refrain from doing anything that would damage the general welfare of other states or make its attainment impossible, because all states of the world, whether small or large, have equal rights. Natural law does not permit master states or slave states. All are obligated by natural law to focus on the single goal of not endangering the general welfare in any way, but creating and maintaining it.

However, the present eighty sovereign national states are a constant danger to peace, as Reves points out convincingly in his book. Since all states are drawing closer because of industrialization and mechanization, the sovereignty claimed by each one continually gives rise to wars. Therefore, it is wrong to contend that the sovereignty of a nation-state has to be maintained under all conditions, that it is an absolutely static concept. On the contrary, sovereignty is something highly relative. It means something like supremacy—to have authority in a certain power sphere—which is exercised internally, independently of an outside, higher authority. Yet sovereignty is not an end in it itself but only a means to an end. It serves the general welfare of the state in question and is limited within and by the state, which is responsible for ensuring that the exercise of its sovereignty in no way encroaches upon or makes impossible the general welfare of other states.

The claims of unlimited sovereignty, meaning that each government is permitted to do anything that benefits its nation, and the friction caused by conflicting economic interests as a result of industrialization and mechanization are ultimately resolved only by raw force, that is, by wars. History proves this irrefutably. However, if there were a sovereign body above the nation-states that would look after and settle their individual interests, that is, a body with the authority to provide for the welfare of all people on earth, it would eliminate the necessity to solve the problems of the individual states by means of violence.

It follows that the entire development of the world is pressing to organize a large, unified economic structure and to settle differences by means of law instead of violence. For only in this way will it be possible for all people, without distinction, by honest work to procure whatever is necessary to lead a dignified existence in every respect. For God gave the world with all its treasures at no cost for the use of all human beings. Yet the manner in which mankind as a whole acts in this world—which was given only once and has its limits—in order to guarantee all people a dignified existence, is up to the freedom of human beings. And the proper use of freedom presupposes the right understanding of the demands of natural law.

If, therefore, the institution of the nation-state is an obstacle[27] to complying with the primary demands of natural law—if, in their conceit about sovereignty, the states simply disregard these demands—then it is high time to get rid of the institution of the nation-state. States should consider that they have not only rights but also serious duties—first of all, the obligation to realize that they exist for the benefit of people, not people for the benefit of states.

At one time the nation-states had their duties only temporarily, and as long as that was the case it was suitable. Today, however, the development of technology strictly demands that all states of the world create new social institutions that meet the changed economic conditions, which includes uniting into a world federation with judicial power. This federation's government, elected by all nations, would have the duty to ensure the individual and social nature of work and property so that peace among working people is not disturbed by either individualism or collectivism, so that in the entire world there would be neither exploiters nor exploited, neither expropriators nor expropriated; it would then be possible, by honest work, for everyone to acquire the private property needed for him and his loved ones to lead a dignified existence. This work and our *Sociology* explain how to do this.

After this brief explanation of the state and its duties, sovereignty, national states, and a world federation, we are discovering that the concepts we have discussed over the past decades by the oral and written word largely agree with the ideas Reves expresses in *The Anatomy of Peace*. Since World War I we have championed a world economy structured on civil law, natural law, and Christianity, in conjunction with a ministry of world peace.

We are advocating that all people, without distinction, create a single, large family founded on truth, justice, and love of neighbor because all human beings are dependent on one another and because everything concerns everybody. We can prove that cooperating and promoting peace among the world's peoples and states in a true democratic manner is only possible if society, the economy, and national and international life are governed by the principles and basic demands we advocate. First there must be created an inner conviction and attitude, which alone will enable mankind to establish corresponding institutions that will guarantee the peaceful cooperation of all of the world's peoples.

27. Ude: Reves definitively calls it an obstacle, which we challenge.

Also, I am deeply convinced that the world government suggested by Reves, which will include all states and will certainly be a means to serve the peace, can and will only become a reality if everything that disturbs peace has been eliminated—that is, if society, the economy, and national and international life are based on and ruled by the demands of the Ten Commandments.

For peace is tranquility in good order, an order of all social, economic, national, and international relationships according to the demands of natural law and Christianity. Reves will certainly agree when we say that true peace, that is, properly regulated social, economic, and national, and international relations, can only exist where God's Ten Commandments, the Magna Carta of freedom and peace, are obeyed completely and unconditionally; in these commandments, God's sovereignty speaks to us, and this, if recognized and acknowledged by individual human beings and states, is the only unfailing guarantee of peace.

Reves will most likely also agree when we say that the world's social problems are by no means solved by simply integrating the sovereignty claimed by nation-states for themselves into a world federation with the power to make laws. For if and as long as the individualistic economy exists and the working people are cheated out of a portion of the fruits of their labor, that is, if societies are divided into a relatively small, excessively rich class of exploiters and a very large class of the exploited and propertyless (in other words, if the great commandment "You shall not steal" is violated); if and as long as collectivism expropriates and takes from the workers the right to private property; if and as long as individualism and collectivism sin against the personal rights granted by natural law, that is, by God the Creator of nature, thus making it impossible for an immense number of people to obtain a dignified existence; if and as long as all over the world the problems of currency and land are not regulated according to individual and social justice; if and as long as in any and all economies the problem of the distribution of goods is not solved; if and as long as the individual and social aspects of work and property are not observed and the entire legislation of the world federation we proposed is not instituted consistently in the entire world, then there can be no peace, nor can a "united states of the world" be realized.

In other words, only by constructing the world anew, not merely by rebuilding it, can we solve the unspeakably sad social and economic national and international chaos stemming from the struggle for power among nations as a result of World War II and other causes. What is needed is not to rebuild the world but to construct it anew.

Therefore, the primary challenge we pose to human beings for bringing about peace by preventing wars is *metanoia*. Convert! Transform yourselves from the bottom of your hearts! Let go of your erroneous views, respect the law of nature of the cosmos and the precepts of the eternal, unchangeable moral law. We must understand that whatever is according to nature is also always moral, and whatever is moral is also always according to nature.

While we constantly refer to the great commandment "You shall not kill," demand that it be observed in the name of Christianity, and grant this commandment an absolute validity, we disagree to a certain extent with Reves and the existing nation-states. Without going into detail, we simply refer to what we have said in this work, as well as to our book *The Economic Ideal of the State Budget*[28] and to our pamphlets *The Right to Work*,[29] *The Right to Property*,[30] *The Right to Personal Freedom*,[31] *Natural Rights, Christianity, and Democracy*,[32] and *Solving the Social Question through Christ*.[33]

All of these writings make clear that only a freedom that is uncompromisingly bound by morals is a true freedom. Therefore, the belief of the sovereign nation-states that they have to maintain their sovereignty is a serious abuse of freedom. Today's industrialization and mechanization seriously abuse freedom. While the misuse of technology serves the profit economy at any price, the mission of an ethical economy should be to establish an economy of need, which seeks to provide a dignified existence for every person who labors diligently.

Laws and justice—we mean the positive man-made laws to which Reves always refers—have to observe all the demands of natural law. This means that in order for laws to be legally binding, they cannot be contrary to a single requirement of natural law, if they wish to achieve their purpose of preventing wars and guaranteeing peace.

Therefore, a world government must face many questions and tasks, all of which have to be solved before the kind of good order that we call peace can be achieved. Without getting ahead of ourselves—we are in the process of writing a book entitled *Panbiologie*—we can say that the prevention of wars and the securing of peace is a pan-biological problem that touches all areas of life by trying to make the entire life of human beings serve their highest goal: to live up to being created in the image and likeness of God by

28. *Das Wirtschaftsideal des Volks- und Staatshaushalts.*

29. *Das Recht auf Arbeit.*

30. *Das Recht auf Eigentum.*

31. *Das Recht auf persönliche Freiheit.*

32. *Naturrecht, Christentum und Demokratie.*

33. *Die Lösung der sozialen Frage durch Christus.*

serving so that the world order God created and desires will be established and maintained. Man is responsible to all of humanity for each free action because by natural law and Christianity he is connected with God, and bound by the demands of the Ten Commandments and the Sermon on the Mount to observe the order established by God.

Reves can be assured that we will support him in his attempt to establish a world government in the form of a federation of all nations by continuing to work in this spirit for world peace because, championing the unchanging natural law and Christianity, we realize that it is right to do so. Therefore, above all, we have to strive to make the ideas of this book the common property of all of humanity.

Conclusion

We conclude this work with the wish that the ideas presented here will influence our readers according to this motto: "We know in order to be willing." Right knowledge is the prerequisite for right willingness.

Much would be gained if human beings, at least leading personalities, realized that the problem of war and peace can only be solved if we set to work to resolve social problems by always consulting the demands of justice and love, that is, by considering the laws of the entire cosmic order. The social problem is the sum of all misery, suffering, and disorder, which arise from sinful and weak people living together, and is linked to the question, how do we effectively put an end to all of this misery? In the pamphlet *Solving the Social Question through Christ*,[1] citing these words of Scripture, "to bring everything together under Christ" (Eph 1:10), we showed how social problems can be solved and peace thereby established. If people would realize and think about this, it would no longer be very difficult to persuade them to heal the damage to society by their care and assistance, according to Matt 25:31–46, and thereby work continuously against war and for peace.

Once someone has gained the necessary knowledge, he has a great responsibility, first, for his attitude toward his community, and then for his attitude toward the cosmos as a whole into which every human being and each animal is placed. "We know in order to be willing!"

Every heartbeat of every living being proclaims to each person who is aware of the significant connections within and the harmonious unity of the cosmos the great commandment of nature and God: "Life is holy. You should not, you may not kill!"

> The delicate flower breathes: "You shall not kill!"
> The flower you break off while dallying.
> The animal that you slay in your malicious play
> In its agony of dying looks at you beseechingly,

1. *Die Lösung der sozialen Frage durch Christus.*

Its glazed eye pleading, "You shall not kill!"
When all around the fields are reddened with blood,
With human blood shed by "friend" and "foe,"
Is it not as though from this red flood are arising,
In blazing script, these words, visible far and wide:
"You shall not kill!"

—*Zlatnik*

May Christ—the Way, the Truth, and the Life—accompany this book, and may God's Holy Spirit make people's hearts receptive for the thoughts expressed herein. Therefore, we ask: Father in heaven: "Send out your breath, and life begins; you renew the face of the earth" (Ps 104:30).

We are fully aware that our views will not be popular with many people, including Christians, because for some their religion stops where the pleasures they have grown fond of and the satisfaction of their passions are endangered. Yet all of our comments always close with this one statement: without a thorough reform of the life and the attitudes of every individual there can never be peace.

Therefore, minds will be divided on the views we have expressed. As for people whose "god is the stomach" and whose "minds are set on earthly things," as St. Paul comments in Phil 3:19, they will reject us and our explanations. However, to whoever can say, with St. Paul, "Our homeland is in heaven" (Phil 3:20), Christ's words in Matt 25:34–46 are of prime importance, for there he says that at the Last Judgment the decision about eternal happiness or eternal damnation will depend on whether or not we have practiced the works of mercy. Therefore, we will close this work with a brief reflection on these words, which we consider most important and crucial:

> Then the King will say to those on his right hand, "Come, you whom my Father has blessed, take as your heritage the kingdom prepared for you since the foundation of the world. For I was hungry and you gave me food, I was thirsty and you gave me drink, I was a stranger and you made me welcome, lacking clothes and you clothed me, sick and you visited me, in prison and you came to see me. . . . In truth I tell you, in so far as you did this to one of the least of these brothers of mine, you did it to me. Then he will say to those on his left hand, "Go away from me, with your curse upon you, to the eternal fire prepared for the devil and his angels. For I was hungry and you never gave me food, I was thirsty and you never gave me anything to drink, I was a stranger and you never made me welcome,

> lacking clothes and you never clothed me, sick and in prison and you never visited me. . . . In truth I tell you, in so far as you neglected to do this to one of the least of these, you neglected to do it to me." And they will go away to eternal punishment, and the upright to eternal life.

In light of these serious words of Christ, the social question looms before us in all of its dreadfulness and dimensions. Facing us is all material and moral misery, all the affliction and poverty of humanity, which is suffering physically and spiritually; and, as though the misery of each individual is not enough, humanity tears itself to pieces and destroys itself in bloody wars. According to God's holy will, human rights should not be violated or human dignity disrespected, but every person should be granted a dignified existence. Whoever violates human rights and disrespects human dignity sins against others and shares in the guilt for the existence of poverty and misery, which time and again cause wars.

A serious responsibility of our conscience is Christ's demand that the world's hunger, misery, illness, poverty, crime, homelessness, and oppression are to be eliminated as much as possible, which means that the social question can be solved by resolving social, economic, political, national, and international relations in the spirit of justice and love.

Christ's teaching is the renewal of the human community by renewing the personal life of the individual person. Although Christ did not establish a political program, he pointed out the principles by which all social problems could be solved satisfactorily, as we explained in detail in our writings *Solving the Social Question through Christ* and *The Ideal Citizen and His Economic Ethics.*

The Apostle Paul calls the work of solving the social question "to bring everything together under Christ" (Eph 1:10). Our *Sociology* is a guide to how to properly create and develop the kind of society and economy in which peace is guaranteed.

We ask, why are so many people hungry? Why do some become criminals and languish in prison? Why do so many die young? Why does all the horror of war exist? To pose these questions is to seek the causes for all this misery.

Therefore, it is not enough to occasionally give a piece of bread to a hungry person, some worn clothing to someone who is naked, or to provide shelter for a homeless man or woman. It goes without saying that we Christians should do everything in our power to decrease misery and poverty and to demonstrate love of neighbor wherever we see a need and are able to help, without asking the needy person for his baptismal certificate or inquiring about his race or his politics.

First of all, it is our duty to help the poorest of the poor, that is, everyone who would perish physically or spiritually if not helped. Concern and care should first be given to people who are sinking into the morass of the large cities and whose physical and moral misery all of society, without exception, is responsible for. The morass of our cities is a constant source of contagion and danger to all of human society.

But even more important than relief is prevention, that is, the elimination of everything that causes a physical and spiritual breakdown and continually demands new victims from the ranks of the healthy. Therefore, all of us human beings, without exception, have to strike our breast and admit our profound guilt because of our addiction to pleasure, our uncontrolled passions, our failed economy, our greed, our self-seeking, materialistic way of thinking and acting, our untruthfulness and injustice, our lack of love, our hate and indifference, our religious and civic hypocrisy—all of which causes millions and millions of human beings, and even entire nations, to fall into physical, economic, spiritual, and moral misery and perish.

We name only these vices: alcoholism; addiction to tobacco, fashion, and luxury; unhealthy diets; prostitution; capitalistic exploitation; lack of housing and substandard housing; profiteering from and speculating with land; lust for power and megalomania; class and race hatred; forcible expropriation; birth control; setting a bad example; leading others astray; vindictiveness; a lack of compassion; injustice, and greatly exaggerated nationalism. We do not have to prove in detail that every one of us is more or less responsible for the extensive, manifold misery that surrounds us in cities and rural areas and that these conditions are partly responsible for war.

Let us consider all the misery resulting from addiction to alcohol and tobacco, from capitalism and government-regulated prostitution—which ultimately can only exist with the approval of the entire population—and we will not ask for further evidence of our complicity.

We share more or less in the responsibility, to the extent that each of us does or does not take part in the struggle against the various causes of the social plight. Every single human being, all institutions—family, state, and church—and all nations are more or less responsible for the existing social problems.

Whoever is addicted to pleasure in its various forms; whoever participates in capitalistic exploitation; whoever produces, sells, buys, or uses antisocial, harmful, unnecessary, or useless goods; whoever does not lead an irreproachable life; whoever regards government-regulated prostitution and the production and use of birth control devices as justified; whoever, in any way, sets a bad example; whoever lives in enmity; whoever is guilty of speculating with and profiting from land; and whoever lies is complicit in the social misery resulting from all of the above. But those who do nothing to effectively combat these adverse conditions also sin gravely against Matt 25:31–46 and have no right to call themselves opponents of war and friends of peace. On the contrary, they are supporters of war and enemies of peace.

Therefore, the question of war and peace can only be solved properly and effectively in relationship to all social problems, according to Christ's words: "Set your hearts on his kingdom first, and on God's saving justice, and all these other things will be given you as well" (Matt 6:33). This command is obligatory for the individual as well as for institutions; family, state, and church should unite into a kingdom of Christ in which justice and love reign. In Christ's kingdom there exists mutual consideration based on individual and social justice, inspired by love, which accords everyone what is his. In his kingdom everyone strives for a natural, sensible style of life and respects the order and laws God established in the cosmos.

This brief summary points out again that the problem of war and peace is a question of education, that ultimately it is a religious-moral question, that peace can only reign where one's entire life, with all its connections to the cosmos, is seeking the kingdom of God and his righteousness and is completely and unconditionally incorporated into the cosmic order established and desired by God.

Whoever respects this natural and supernatural order and acts accordingly is a peacemaker, and therefore a relentless opponent of war, because he obeys the great commandment "You shall not kill!" without exceptions—without exceptions!

As to the question of war or peace, given that this formulation of the problem is accurate, there exists no so-called neutrality for him who acknowledges natural law and Christianity as the only criteria by which to judge every action or failure to act. For neutrality means indifference, not to join or commit oneself to anything, to stand by irresponsibly, not to get involved in anything.

It should never be a matter of indifference whether one supports war or peace. Everything in this book proves irrefutably that everyone who is serious about natural law and Christianity may work only on behalf of peace and has to reject any participation in war, even "armed peace."

Unfortunately, people in responsible positions all over the world support "armed peace," believing that in the light of today's realities, being armed is the lesser evil and a necessary protection against attacks from other nations. Those holding this viewpoint explain that today every state, whether large or small, has to be armed and that, in this respect, neutrality does not exist.

But we have the courage to declare to the entire world: Whoever wants to be a true believer in the unchangeable law of nature, and, above all, in Christianity, has to reject every kind of militarization and must do everything to work for peace in the manner we have outlined.

Therefore, we may not be merely neutral about armaments and proposals for an "armed peace" but must rigorously oppose this attitude by confronting an "armed peace" based on violence with the completely non-violent peace of Christ's kingdom and by summoning all our strength so that it can be realized.

Should one call our approach utopian, we will respond: It is not we human beings who determine how we have to behave. Our guiding principle is not the miserable view of utilitarianism at the cost of God's commandments but solely the demands of natural law and Christ's commands. God has to be obeyed more than human beings. Therefore, regarding the great commandment "You shall not kill," there should be no compromises, even if we have to give up all of our possessions and even our lives while observing this commandment without exception. Thus only those with the courage of their convictions and the spirit of martyrs can be true peacemakers.

Therefore, not "war or peace." Only peace! The only right idea is peace without compromise!

Bibliography

Cathrein, Victor. *Moralphilosophie.* 2 vols. Freiburg im Breisgau: Herder, 1890.

Demulier, Henri. "Kirche und Krieg." In *Katholische Stimmen gegen den Krieg: Eine internationale Sammelschrift*, 8–17. Berlin-Wilmersdorf: Hans Winter, 1928.

Eher, Franz, ed. *Hitler's Speeches on the Party Day of Freedom.* Munich: Zentralverlag der N.S.D.A.P., 1935.

Ewald, Oskar. In *Gewalt und Gewaltlosigkeit: Handbuch des activen Pazifismus*, edited by Franz Kobler. Zürich: Rotapfel-Verlag, 1928.

Fassbender, Martin. *Des deutschen Volkes Wille zum Leben.* Freiburg im Breisgau: Herder, 1917.

Finger, Ernest. *Der Krieg und die Bekämpfung der Geschlechtskrankheiten.* Wien-Leipzig. Anzengruberverlag, 1917.

Friedrich, Ernst. *Krieg dem Kriege!* Berlin: Verlag Freie Jugend, 1924.

Galen, Clemens August, Graf von. *Das Recht auf Leben: Predigt.* Salzburg: Friedens-Verlag, 1946.

Hoffmann, Hermann. *Die Kirche und der Friede: Von der Friedenskirche zur Friedenswelt.* Vienna: Reinhold, 1933.

Kathechismus der katholischen Religion. Approved by the bishops of Austria, November 25, 1930, and accepted for use in schools by the Ministry of Education. Graz and Vienna: Ulrich Moser, 1931.

Keller, Franz. *Der Menschheitskämpfer*, November 1933, 10.

Kobler, Franz, ed. *Gewalt und Gewaltlosigkeit: Handbuch des activen Pazifismus.* Zurich: Rotapfel-Verlag, 1928.

Lehmann-Rußbüldt, Otto. *Die blutige Internationale der Rüstungsindustrie.* Berlin: Fackelreiterverlag, 1933.

Man, Hendrik de. "Sozialismus und Gewalt." In *Gewalt und Gewaltlosigkeit: Handbuch des activen Pazifismus*, edited by Franz Kobler. Zürich: Rotapfel-Verlag, 1928.

Müller-Sturmheim, Emil. *Rüstungen als Rettung.* Vienna: Österreichische Völkerbundliga, 1937.

Nietzsche, Friedrich. *Der Antichrist.* Leipzig: Alfred Kröner, n.d.

Ozaki, Yukio. *Japan at the Crossroad.*

Ragaz, Leonhard. "Jesus Christus und die Gewaltlosigkeit." In *Gewalt und Gewaltlosigkeit: Handbuch des activen Pazifismus*, edited by Franz Kobler, 63–. Zürich: Rotapfel-Verlag, 1928.

Remarque, Erich Maria. *Im Westen nichts Neues.* Berlin: Propyläen-Verlag, 1929.

Reves, Emery. *Die Anatomie des Friedens.* Vienna: Europa Verlag, 1947.

Rosenberg, Alfred. *An die Dunkelmänner unserer Zeit.* Munich: Hoheneichen, 1935.

Schwarz, Leopold. *Stehe Fest im Glauben.* Munich: Verlag für katholisches Schrifttum Josef Schinner, 1938. (Printed with permission of the Archdiocese of München-Freising.)

Sörensen, Wulf. *Die Stimme der Ahnen.* Berlin: Nordland-verlag, 1937.

Spengler, Oswald. *Reden und Aufsätze.* 2nd ed. Munich: Beck, 1938.

Stratmann, P. Franziskus. "Neue Bekenntnisse zur Kriegsdienstverweigerung." In *Katholische Stimmen gegen den Krieg: Eine internationale Sammelschrift*, 25–31. Berlin-Wilmersdorf: Hans Winter, 1928.

Sturzo, Luigi. In *Katholische Stimmen gegen den Krieg: Eine internationale Sammelschrift*, 6–7. Berlin-Wilmersdorf: Hans Winter, 1928.

Ude, Johannes. *Ethik.* Freiburg im Breisgau: Herder, 1912.

———. *Das Geld, sein Einfluss auf Gesellschaft, Wirtschaft und Kultur.* Gams, St. Gallen, Switzerland: Internationer Befreiungsbund, 1935.

———. *Soziologie: Leitfaden der vernünftigen Gesellschafts- und Wirtschaftslehre.* Gams, St. Gallen, Switzerland: Internationaler Befreiungsbund, 1931.

Ziegler, Matthes. *Was sagen die Weltkirchen zu diesem Krieg?* Berlin, Kommissionsverlag: O. Stollberg, 1941.

Zischka, Anton. *Der Kampf um die Weltmacht Öl.* Leipzig: W. Goldmann, 1934.

Zweifel, . *Die Prostitutionsfrage in der Schweiz.* Zurich: Albert Müller, 1913.

Zweig, Stefan. *Die Augen des ewigen Bruders: Eine Legende.* Leipzig: Insel-Verlag, 1933.

www.ingramcontent.com/pod-product-compliance
Lightning Source LLC
Chambersburg PA
CBHW032343280326
41935CB00008B/437